Dyes and their Intermediates

E. N. Abrahart

**CHEMICAL PUBLISHING
NEW YORK**

© E. N. Abrahart 1977

First published 1968
by Pergamon Press Ltd.

Second edition 1977
published by Edward Arnold (Publishers) Ltd.,
25 Hill Street, London W1X 8LL

ISBN: 0 7131 2580 2

First American edition, 1977
Chemical Publishing Co., Inc.
155 W. 19 St., New York, N.Y. 10011

PRINTED IN THE UNITED STATES OF AMERICA

Preface to the First Edition

The author has attempted, in this book, to give a bird's-eye view of the dye-making industry, which view, it is hoped, will prove useful to students of chemistry and to others as an introduction to the field and as a stimulus to further reading and study. The treatment throughout is based on synthesis and the order in which the various groups of dyes are introduced follows that of volume 4 of the Colour Index. Allusion has been made, wherever possible, to the technology of dyeing and printing in order to present dyes in their proper environment. For elegant and ingenious as many dye syntheses are and fascinating the molecular structures of their products, the true function of a dye or pigment is to impart colour to a substrate.

Separate chapters are devoted to pigments and reactive dyes since various chromophoric systems are involved, whereas earlier chapters or sections of chapters deal with one chromophoric system at a time; an exception is a mixed anthraquinone-azo dye described in Chapter 7.

Apart from a few dyes of historical interest, all those colorants for which a Colour Index number is quoted are believed to be in use at the present time. Examples of dyes taken from the patent literature have been chosen to illustrate modern trends. Such a choice cannot but be fallible and it should accordingly be remembered that most of the dyes described in patent specifications are born to blush unseen.

In the final chapter, a brief account is given of the large-scale manufacture of dyes and their intermediates to illustrate, among other aspects, the aims of the dye-maker in serving user industries.

Many colleagues and friends have helped, some albeit unwittingly, in the preparation of this book. The author's thanks are especially accorded to Dr. S. Coffey, Dr. R. L. M. Allen and Dr. R. R. Davies of Imperial Chemical Industries Limited, Dyestuffs Division, to Mr. J. Barker, Dr. H. R. Bolliger, Mr. G. H. Bullock, Dr. M. C. Clark, Mr. J. H. F. Hilton, Dr. I. G. Laing and Mr. J. Lockett of the Clayton Aniline Company Limited, to Mr. J. C. Brown, Mr. T. Green, Mr. B. Kramrisch, Mr. E. Tomlinson and Mr. D. M. Varley of CIBA Clayton Limited, to Prof. H. Suschitzky (University of Salford), to Mr. H. Blackshaw (Dyestuffs Controller, Board of Trade) and to Mr. G. Spencer.

Grateful acknowledgement is made to the Clayton Aniline Company Limited for library facilities, to its Engineering Division for the preparation of flow-sheets used in Figs. 16.2, 16.3 and 16.4, to Imperial Chemical Industries Limited, Dyestuffs Division, for that used in Fig. 16.1, and to Mr. J. F. Proctor for preparing the chromatogram for Fig. 16.5.

Finally the author wishes to record his indebtedness to the General Editors, Mr. J. Davidson Pratt and Dr. T. F. West, for their help and encouragement.

E.N.A

1968

Preface to the Second Edition

Since the appearance of the first edition in 1968, there have been many important advances in the chemistry of dyes and of the dyeing process. Accordingly it has been necessary to make extensive amendments and additions to the sections on Direct dyes, Basic (cationic) dyes, Azo-metal complexes, Reactive dyes and Pigments. The material on Disperse dyes has been brought up to date and collected together to form a new chapter. By this means it has been possible to lay appropriate emphasis on the influence of chemical structure on fastness and dyeing properties, for instance in relation to thermofixation, solvent-dyeing and transfer-printing. In order to make room for new matter certain sections which dealt in a general way with aromaticity and reaction mechanisms have either been curtailed or omitted entirely.

In preparing the second edition however, the author's aim remains unchanged in attempting to give a broad view of the synthetic dye-making industry which will be of help to students preparing for the Associateship examination of the Society of Dyers and Colourists or a degree in colour chemistry, or simply to those who would like to know more about a fascinating branch of chemistry and its technical applications.

The author wishes to thank Dr. R. L. M. Allen and Mr. B. Kramrisch for their useful suggestions, Mr. G. H. Bullock, Mr. J. F. Proctor and the Clayton Aniline Company Limited for help in preparing the chromatogram for the illustration on page 240, and Dr. J. P. Roberts of Edward Arnold (Publishers) Ltd for his help and advice.

1976   E.N.A.

Contents

Abbreviations of Names of Firms

AAP	Koppers Company Incorporated.
ACY	American Cyanamid Company.
AH	Arnold Hofmann Incorporated.
Acna	Aziende Colori Nazionali Affini.
BASF	Badische Anilin- und Soda-Fabrik A.G.
CCC	American Cyanamid Company.
CFM	Cassella Farbwerke Mainkur A.G.
CGY	CIBA-Geigy Limited.
CIBA	CIBA Limited.
DH	Durand & Huguenin S.A., Basle.
DUP	E.I. du Pont de Nemours and Company Inc.
FBy	Farbenfabriken Bayer A.G.
FDN	N.V. Franken-Donders, Tilburg, Holland.
FH	Farbwerke Hoechst A.G.
Fran	Compagnie Française des Matières Colorantes S.A.
G	General Dyestuff Corporation.
General Aniline	General Aniline and Film Corporation.
Gy	J. R. Geigy, A.G.
HWL	Hickson and Welch Limited.
IC	Interchemical Corporation.
ICI	Imperial Chemical Industries Limited.
LBH	L. B. Holliday and Company Limited.
NAC	National Aniline Division, Allied Chemical and Dye Corporation.
S	Sandoz A.G.
YCL	Yorkshire Chemicals Limited (formerly YDC).
YDC	Yorkshire Dyeware and Chemical Company Limited.

Other Abbreviations

A.A.T.C.C.	American Association of Textile Chemists and Colorists.
B.P.	British Patent.
Belgian P.	Belgian Patent.
Chem. Soc.	The Chemical Society.
C.I.	Colour Index
E.C.E.	Europäisch-Continentale Echtheits-Convention.
F.P.	French Patent.
I.S.O.	International Organization for Standardization.
J.C.S.	*Journal of the Chemical Society.*
J.S.D.C.	*Journal of the Society of Dyers and Colourists.*
R.I.C.	The Royal Institute of Chemistry.
S.C.I.	The Society of Chemical Industry.
S.D.C.	The Society of Dyers and Colourists.
T.I.	The Textile Institute.
U.S.P.	United States Patent.

Glossary of Technical Terms

After-chroming. The process of treating a textile, immediately after dyeing, with a solution of a chromium compound usually a dichromate.

After-treatment. Any process which follows dyeing proper.

Bleeding. (a) The staining of adjacent white material or the coloration of surrounding liquor by the diffusion of dye during wet treatment of dyed or printed fabrics. (b) The coloration of a solvent or vehicle in contact with a pigment.

Blowing. See **Decatizing**.

Conditioning. The process by which a pigment is transformed from one physical modification to another of significantly different properties.

Cutting. The process of diluting a dry, concentrated dye by grinding and mixing with substances such as salt, sodium sulphate, dextrine. See **Standardization**.

Decatizing. The process of subjecting woollen cloth, usually stretched over a perforated metal cylinder, to the action of steam in order to set the woven structure in a regular manner; the process is also known as 'blowing'.

Dyeing. Apart from its participial meaning it is also used as a noun meaning a specimen of dyed material, a dyed hank (of wool, cotton, or other fibre).

Exhaustion. The process, during dyeing, of transfer of dye from dyebath to fibre.

Hydrophilic. Describes the propensity of a fibre to absorb water and is characteristic of wool, cotton and regenerated fibres.

Hydrophobic. Describes the reluctance of a fibre to take up water and is characteristic of man-made fibres, e.g. polyamides, polyesters. Part of the wool fibre, i.e. the outer layer or cuticle, is hydrophobic; the core is hydrophilic.

Kier-boiling. A scouring treatment of cotton goods by heating them with aqueous alkali under pressure in iron or steel vessels (kiers).

Levelness. The quality, in dyed yarn or fabric, of having the same depth of shade everywhere.

Mass-coloration. The incorporation, by mechanical means, of pigments with a mass of plastic material, e.g. rubber, polymers, to produce an even coloration.

Mercerizing. The process of treating cotton with aqueous sodium hydroxide, at room temperature, followed by washing, whereby the properties of the fibres are modified.

Migration. The transfer of dye from heavily dyed parts of the substrate to lighter dyed parts during the dyeing process.

Milling. Processes designed to bring about the felting of wool by treating it, to the accompaniment of mechanical beating, with soap or aqueous alkali (alkaline milling) or with dilute sulphuric acid (acid milling).

Mordant. A substance applied to textiles to permit dyeing with dyes for which the fibre would otherwise have little or no substantivity.

Padding. The process of passing cloth, in full width, through a solution or suspension and then between rollers to impregnate the cloth and to squeeze out surplus liquor.

Phototropism. The term, when used in connection with dye technology, refers to the reversible fading, induced by light, of certain dyes in association with substrates.

Skitteriness. The variation in depth of colour between one fibre and another in a dyeing, usually a wool dyeing.

Slubbing. Wool prepared for spinning by having been given a slight twist.

Spin-dyeing. The incorporation of pigment with a polymer solution (e.g. viscose dope) or molten polymer (e.g. polyamide) prior to extrusion through minute orifices (spinnerets) to produce a coloured fibre.

Standardization. The dilution of concentrated dry dye with suitable solids (see **Cutting**) or high-strength pastes with water or other liquids, to standard strengths acceptable to the user.

Stripping. The removal of unwanted dye from a fibre by chemical means.

Substrate. The material to which a colorant is applied by one of the various processes of dyeing, printing, surface coating (e.g. spraying) and so on. Examples of substrates are vegetable, animal and synthetic fibres, the textiles derived from them, anodized aluminium, leather, paper, hair, rubber, solvents.

Tendering. The deterioration in mechanical strength which develops in cotton goods dyed with certain dyes, especially sulphur dyes (blacks).

Tippy. An adjective describing the variations in depth of shade in a wool dyeing caused by differences in the fibre itself, i.e. between the lower or root portion and the outer end or tip.

Topping. The expedient of adding a small proportion of a bright dye to a dull dye to improve its shade.

Wet-treatments. A general term applied to those aqueous processes to which dyed textiles are subjected in the course of manufacture and in use. It is a term often used with reference to the fastness properties of individual dyes.

1
Introductory

The synthetic dyes industry was founded in 1857 by W. H. Perkin in setting up a factory, at Greenford Green near London, for the manufacture of Mauveine from coal tar benzene. The previous year he had obtained in the laboratory, by the action of potassium dichromate and sulphuric acid on crude aniline, a coloured substance which he recognized as having the properties of a dye. That is to say the substance, in hot aqueous solution, had a certain substantivity for silk fibres and dyed them purple. Such dyeings were greatly superior, in brightness of shade and fastness, to those obtainable from the natural dyes of similar shade then in use. Mauveine hence became accepted by dyers, especially as a relatively simple process for dyeing cotton by first treating it with tannic acid was soon developed by Perkin and others. More synthetic dyes followed as organic chemistry itself grew rapidly in the research schools of Europe and as the discoveries proliferated in the laboratories of the dye manufacturers who had quickly followed Perkin in establishing dye-making factories.

Nowadays there are very few natural dyes in use in significant quantities; an exception is logwood (C.I. Natural Black No. 1, 75290). Almost all dyes are now derived synthetically, i.e. by known chemical steps, from raw materials—principally the hydrocarbons, benzene, toluene, naphthalene and anthracene—obtained from coal tar produced by distillation of coal out of contact with air, and also, to an increasing extent, from certain operations in the petroleum industry. These hydrocarbons, known as aromatic hydrocarbons, provide the molecular framework for the final dye molecule, such aromatic nuclei or other conjugated systems being essential to the structures of substances having the property of colour.

Colour

The visible region of the spectrum consists of electro-magnetic radiation of wavelengths covering the range 400 nm to about 800 nm

$$1 \text{ nm} = \text{one nanometer} = 10^{-7} \text{ cm}$$

$$1 \text{ nm} = 10 \text{ angstrom units} = 10 \text{ Å}$$

$$1 \text{ Å} = 10^{-8} \text{ cm}$$

Radiation below 400 nm is invisible and lies in the ultraviolet region, that above 800 nm is also invisible and lies in the infrared.

Ultraviolet u.v.		Blue	Green	Yellow	Red	Infrared i.r.
Invisible			Visible			Invisible
	400 nm				800 nm	

White light, i.e. radiation more or less evenly spread over the range 400–800 nm, may be split into the colours of the spectrum by means of a prism or diffraction grating, the spectral colours being violet, indigo, blue, green, yellow, orange and red.

When a coloured surface is illuminated by a beam of white light certain wavelengths are absorbed and the reflected light, being deficient in the absorbed wavelengths, induces the sensation of colour on striking the retina of a normal eye. Thus an orange surface will absorb radiation chiefly from the region 400–550 nm and also, to a smaller extent, from the region 550–650 nm. The reflected light will thus be enhanced as regards the yellow/red region, 600 nm and beyond, and so an orange hue will be seen. If this orange surface is now illuminated solely by green light, i.e. of wavelengths corresponding to those absorbed, the surface will appear to be black. It follows, therefore, if the incident light is deficient in certain wavelengths then an apparent change of hue will occur compared with that seen under 'normal' white light. It is a matter of common experience that the same coloured object changes greatly in appearance according to whether it is viewed in daylight, under a mercury vapour lamp, in sodium light or other artificial illumination.

Black surfaces absorb light of wavelengths covering the whole visible range, white surfaces reflect light more or less evenly over the entire visible region. Grey surfaces are the result of general absorption of part of the incident white light.

Table 1.1 The relation between colour absorbed and colour seen

Wavelength nm	Colour absorbed	Colour seen
400–435	Violet	Yellow–green
435–480	Blue	Yellow
480–490	Green–blue	Orange
490–500	Blue–green	Red
500–560	Green	Purple
560–580	Yellow–green	Violet
580–595	Yellow	Blue
595–605	Orange	Green–blue
605–750	Red	Blue–green

All coloured substances, dyes and pigments, have the power of absorbing radiation selectively from the visible region, such absorption being characteristic of the molecular species concerned. Table 1.1, after Mohler, shows the relation between absorbed radiation and colour seen for a set of specially chosen substances each having a single narrow absorption band. If light of the wavelengths corresponding to the colour seen is added to the radiation absorbed, white light results. Pairs of seen and adsorbed colours are said to be complementary.

Absorption Spectra

The actual absorption characteristics of a dye or a pigment are much more complex than is implied in the above table. Intensity of absorption is measured in the absorption spectrophotometer, measurements in the case of dye being made over the visible range. In the spectrophotometer white light is passed through a prism or diffraction grating to give a spectrum. By suitable rotation of the prism (or grating) an emergent beam of specific wavelength (or a very small interval of wavelengths) can be obtained and by such means the whole visible range may be traversed. Light of known wavelength produced in this manner is divided, by a suitable optical device, into two beams, one of which passes through a transparent cell containing a solution of the dye in known concentration. The second passes through an identical cell containing solvent only. The emergent beams are caused to fall on photoelectric cells which compare intensity of incident light I_0 (i.e. which has passed through solvent only) to the intensity I of the beam emerging from the dye solution. Modern instruments are usually automatic and record, on squared paper, intensity of absorption against wavelength, measurements being made at very small intervals over the visible range. The curve obtained is unique and characteristic of the dye being studied and is known as the *signature* of the dye.

The relation between absorption and wavelength is given by a combination of Lambert's and Beer's Laws.

Lambert's Law expresses the relation between incident and absorbed radiation at a given wavelength by the equation

$$I = I_0 \, e^{-kd}$$

where

I_0 = intensity of incident light
I = intensity of transmitted light
k = absorption constant
d = thickness in centimetres

$$E = \log \frac{I_o}{I} = 0.4343kd$$

E is known as the *optical density* or 'extinction'.

The above applies to a transparent coloured substance of thickness d cm. For solutions of coloured substances in a solvent, the absorption of which is negligible, a factor is introduced for the concentration of solute:

Lambert–Beer Law

$$E = \log \frac{I_0}{I} = \epsilon ct$$

where

ϵ = the molecular extinction coefficient
c = concentration of solute in moles per litre
t = thickness of the solution in centimetres

It should be noted that while Lambert's Law is universal, Beer's Law (which states that the light absorbed is proportional to the number of molecules of the absorbing substance through which the light passes) does not hold where there is interaction between dye molecules (association) and among dye and solvent molecules.

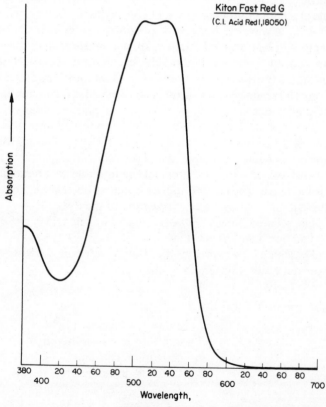

Fig. 1.1   Absorption curve for monoazo dye.

Fig. 1.1 shows absorption in the green, rather less intense absorption in the blue region, the resulting hue being red. Absorption spectrophotometry is of great importance in the dye industry for purposes of identification and assessment.

Relatively minor differences in molecular structure between one absorbing substance and another may bring about a shift in absorption wavelength, λ_{max}, or a change in intensity or both. A shift of λ_{max} to a region of longer wavelength is termed a *bathochromic effect*, the colour seen being 'deeper', a term denoting a change of hue in passing from the red region through green to the blue end. A shift of absorption to shorter wavelengths is known as a *hypsochromic effect*.

The absorption of radiation by molecules

Molecules contain at least two atoms and these are capable of certain limited motions relative to each other. The internal energy of a molecule (excluding translational energy) may be written:

$$\text{total energy} = E = E_{\text{rotation}} + E_{\text{vibration}} + E_{\text{electron}}$$

Molecular rotation is responsible for the absorption of radiation in the far infrared. A combination of molecular rotation and vibration causes absorption in the near infrared. Absorption in the visible and ultraviolet regions, with which dyes and related substances are concerned, is electronic in origin. In general colourless organic substances absorb radiation in the ultraviolet, relatively high energies being required to raise the molecule from the ground state E_0 to the excited state E_1.

According to quantum theory, which lays down that energy transformations on an atomic or molecular scale occur discontinuously in discrete packets or quanta,

$$\Delta E = E_1 - E_0 = h\nu = \frac{hc}{\lambda}$$

where

$\nu = $ frequency
$\lambda = $ wavelength of absorbed radiation
$h = $ Planck's constant

In saturated aliphatic compounds the electrons concerned with bond formation are tightly bound and ΔE is thus large.

In the simplest unsaturated molecule, ethylene $CH_2{=}CH_2$, ΔE is about 710 kJ/mole and absorption occurs in the u.v. at *ca.* 175 nm. As more and more unsaturated linkages occur in the molecule so λ_{max} (principal absorption peak) is displaced towards longer wavelengths. Thus in C.I. Natural Yellow 27

(Lycopene), the chief colouring matter of the marigold, there are thirteen double bonds and the substance absorbs strongly in the blue region.

For any substance to be coloured its molecule must contain mobile electrons which can be raised from ground to excited states at values of ΔE which lie between 297 and 148.5 kJ/mole. From the relation $\Delta E = h\nu$ it will be seen that the higher the frequency (and the shorter the wavelength) the less the energy needed for excitation.

	400 nm	800 nm
ΔE	297 kJ/mole	148.4 kJ/mole

Structural factors determine whether or not a molecule will absorb in the visible and they also decide where such absorption will occur.

Theory of O. N. Witt (1876). Witt regarded the dye molecule as a combination of an unsaturated kernel with certain groups called chromophores, such a combination being called a 'chromogen', and one or more characteristic substituent groups called auxochromes, the function of which was to intensify colour and to improve the substantivity of the dye for the substrate (fibre, yarn, cloth, plastic or in fact any material which is to be coloured).

Examples of *chromophores* are:

—N=N—	azo group
—NO	nitroso group
—NO$_2$	nitro group
$\diagdown$ C= $\diagup$	characteristic of the triarylmethane system
$\diagdown$ C=O $\diagup$	anthraquinone dyes and others

and of *auxochromes*:

—NH$_2$,—NHMe,—NMe$_2$	as such or as cations, e.g. =$^+$NMe$_2$Cl
—SO$_3$H,—OH,—COOH	often as anions, e.g. $\vert$O$^-$,—SO$_3^-$

In the relatively simple substance azobenzene 'benzenoid unsaturation' is present as is the azo chromophore. No auxochrome is present, however, and although coloured the substance is useless as a dye, having no aptitude for imparting colour to a substrate.

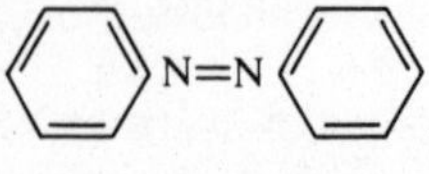

Fig. 1.2

On the other hand the substance which contains the dimethylamino group —NMe$_2$ as auxochrome, is strongly coloured and is used as a dye.

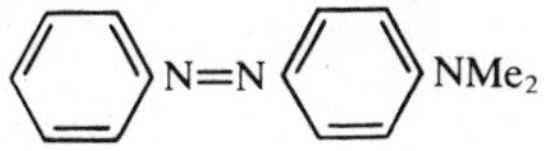

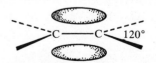

Fig. 1.3   C.I. Solvent Yellow 2, 11020.

Although the Witt theory has served for a long time as a rough working hypothesis its theoretical implications have remained obscure until comparatively recently. One of the fundamental concerns of chemistry is to explain how and why atoms are joined together to form molecules, how their linkages are disrupted and new ones formed under the conditions of chemical change. The most significant contribution to knowledge in this field has come from the wave-mechanical treatment of atoms, leading to the motion of atomic orbitals and molecular orbitals. In particular our ideas concerning unsaturation have undergone clarification with regard to the absorption of energy by the transition of electrons from ground to excited states, a matter of special interest in dye chemistry. A mathematical treatment is outside the scope of this book, but a few of the conceptions that have emerged from this approach to molecular structure and reactivity will be briefly dealt with in a non-mathematical way.

Unsaturation and benzenoid character

In the ethylene molecule CH$_2$=CH$_2$, there is the relatively simple situation in which two carbon atoms and four hydrogen atoms become linked together in a certain way. Each hydrogen atom contributes a single electron contained in its atomic orbital. Each carbon atom has four electrons, three of which become concerned in the formation of covalencies (σ or sigma bonds) which are coplanar and at 120° to each other. The two carbon atoms each have atomic orbitals, occupied by single electrons, called $2p$ atomic orbitals. The overlap of these gives rise to a π bond, shown here as sausage-shaped orbitals above and below the plane of the molecule, responsible for the reactivity of the ethylene molecule, the π electrons being mobile and requiring a lower energy of excitation than the firmly held electrons in the σ bonds. Thus ethylene absorbs radiation in the ultraviolet ($\lambda_{max} = 171$ nm). The ethylene molecule may on this view be represented diagramatically thus:

Fig. 1.4

and in the ready addition of a molecule of bromine to ethylene, for example, the current view is that the π bond, being a negatively charged cloud, can interact with a bromine molecule.

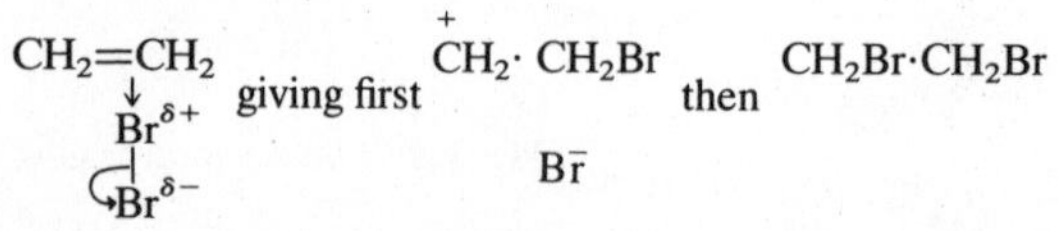

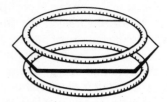

Fig. 1.5

In the case of benzene, where there is a cyclic conjugated system of alternate single and double bonds, overlap of p orbitals gives rise to a cyclic π orbital above and below the plane of the benzene ring, Fig. 1.6. This negative ring

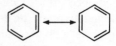

Fig. 1.6

confers the characteristic stability on the benzene molecule itself, on substituted benzenes and on benzenoid compounds generally. As a result of the delocalization of the six π electrons, benzene shows a great reluctance to add on halogen molecules and can only be persuaded to do so under energetic conditions, the products being no longer benzenoid in character. In benzene itself all six carbon atoms are identical, each C—C bond being 1.39 Å compared with 1.33 Å (ethylene) and 1.54 Å (ethane). The structure of benzene thus cannot accurately be represented in terms of covalent bonds since its properties indicate a structure that lies between the contributing forms. This view is that of the resonance theory, sometimes called mesomerism, and the actual structure is called a resonance hybrid of the contributing classical structures A and B,

Fig. 1.7

represented as

Fig. 1.8

the dotted line representing the 'ring-current' or cyclic π orbital referred to above.

As a consequence of resonance, ground and excited states become possible as represented in Fig. 1.9. In this case $\Delta E = 481$ kJ and the excitation of a π electron into this energy level causes characteristic absorption in the u.v. at

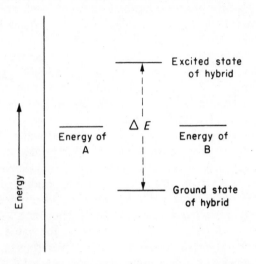

Fig. 1.9

260 nm. In the progression benzene–naphthalene–anthracene, ΔE becomes less and hence absorption shifts towards longer wavelengths as the molecule becomes longer, i.e. as the space in which the π electron is free to move increases. Most coloured organic substances are resonance hybrids of two or more classical structures and a simple example is the blue cation produced when Michler's Hydrol is dissolved in glacial acetic acid. The cation is a resonance hybrid of the two structures:

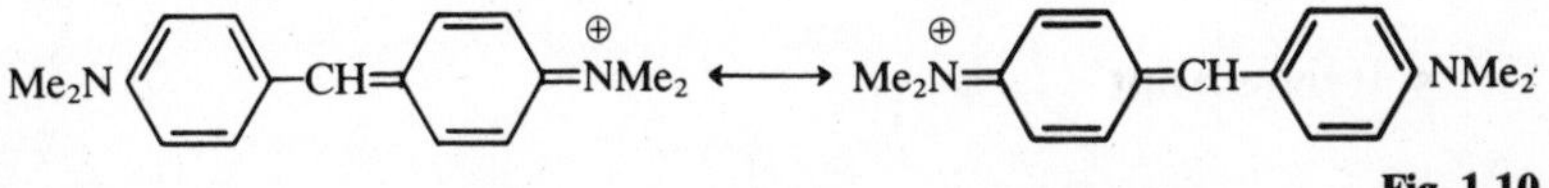

Fig. 1.10

The contributing forms are of identical energy, each is coplanar, i.e. the atoms lie in one plane, and the two structures differ only in distribution of electrons. If hydrochloric acid, or other strong acid, is added to the blue solution in acetic acid the blue colour disappears, the protonated ion:

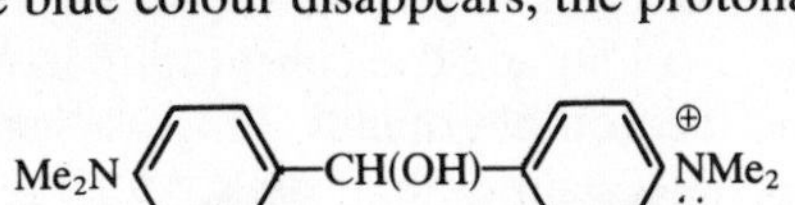

Fig. 1.11

being produced. Coplanarity has disappeared with hydroxylation of the central C atom and resonance, apart from that in the two benzene rings, has also been suppressed. The presence of the two dimethylamino groups in the blue cation is clearly responsible for the extension of resonance, π electron delocalization having being brought about over the whole length of the molecule, ΔE is small, and absorption occurs in the longer wavelengths, the colour seen being blue.

Quantitative studies of electron transitions which cause absorption in the u.v. and visible regions have followed three main lines, *viz.* the valence-bond, free electron and molecular orbital methods. The mathematical models and their treatment are highly complex and are outside the scope of this textbook. Some of the more important literature sources are given in the bibliography. The molecular orbital approach to organic chemistry is however so well established in student courses that it seems reasonable to include some generalizations here, relating to absorption and colour.

The energy of an outer (valency) electron determines the particular atomic orbital that it occupies and the overlap of two such orbitals, provided that the electrons have opposite spins, results in a molecular orbital (covalency or σ bond). Excitation may cause an electronic transition to an anti-bonding orbital, denoted by $\sigma \rightarrow \sigma^*$, and ΔE being large λ will be small and absorption will occur in the far u.v. Similarly π electrons may undergo the transition $\pi \rightarrow \pi^*$, ΔE being less in this case, with corresponding increase in the value of λ. Non-bonding orbitals designated n, are derived from inner electrons or from lone pair electrons associated with O, N or S atoms in groups such as OH, NH_2, NHR, NR_2 and SH. The $n \rightarrow \pi^*$ are low energy transitions and the value of λ is higher, the absorption being in the near u.v. or visible region. The relation between the various energy levels is shown diagrammatically in Fig. 1.12.

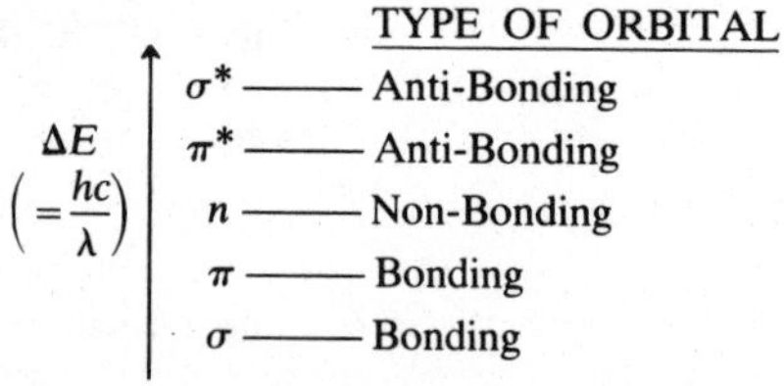

Fig. 1.12

The addition of a proton to a lone pair causes an absorption band in the longer wavelengths to disappear, demonstrating the role of lone pair electrons in excitation processes. Dye molecules are highly complex and, as pointed out by Allen,[17] there are the same number of π levels as there are conjugated atoms. It should not be inferred from the foregoing that more than a few of the qualitative and quantitative aspects of colour and dye constitution have so far been satisfactorily accounted for on theoretical grounds. Progress has chiefly been made in the cyanine series and in certain cationic dyes. Many problems remain with other types, notably with azo and vat dyes.

Phototropy. Deliberate inhibition of coplanarity, by preventing resonance, produces a colourless substance even when the molecule contains a chromophore associated with an aromatic system. Such a case is the monoazo dye, prepared by Brode in 1952 in *cis*- and *trans*-forms:

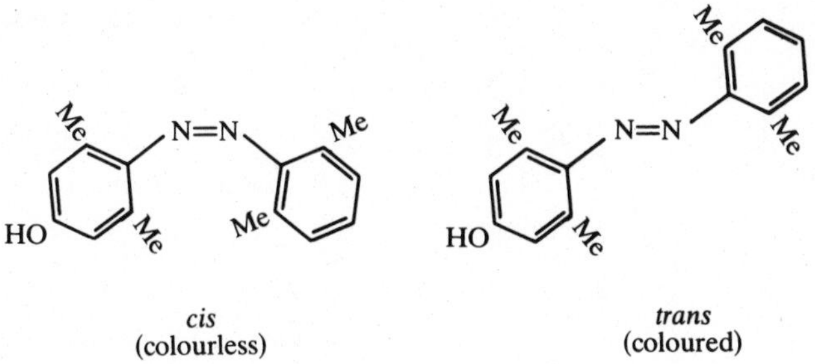

cis
(colourless)

trans
(coloured)   Fig. 1.13

cis

Coplanarity is prevented
by *ortho*-Me groups
(steric hindrance).

trans

The molecule is
coplanar and resonance
can take place.

It is noteworthy that the *cis*-form changes to a coloured *trans*-form on standing. Certain cases of transient fading in azo dyes brought about by light (phototropy) are known to involve *trans*→*cis* conversion, reversal and restoration of colour occurring on storing in the dark.

Axis of polarizability. Oscillations of delocalized π electrons may occur in more than one direction in a dye molecule. For absorption to occur the direction of oscillation (axis of polarizability) must be at right angles to the electric vector of the incident light. This vector is at right angles to the direction of propagation of the light. Where there is a centre of symmetry in the molecule as in C.I. Basic Violet 3, 42555, Fig. 1.14, in the cation of which all three benzene rings

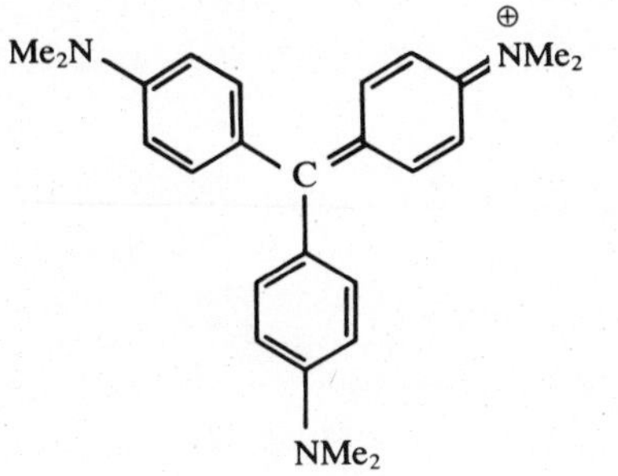

Fig. 1.14

participate in resonance via their dimethylamino groups, polarizability is equal in all directions in the plane of the molecule and there is only one principal absorption peak (λ_{max} 590 nm). In the unsymmetrical Malachite Green (C.I.

Basic Green 4), Fig. 1.15, on the other hand, there are two axes of polarizability differing in degree, lying at right angles, and thus two absorption peaks occur (λ_{max} 423 nm and 625 nm).

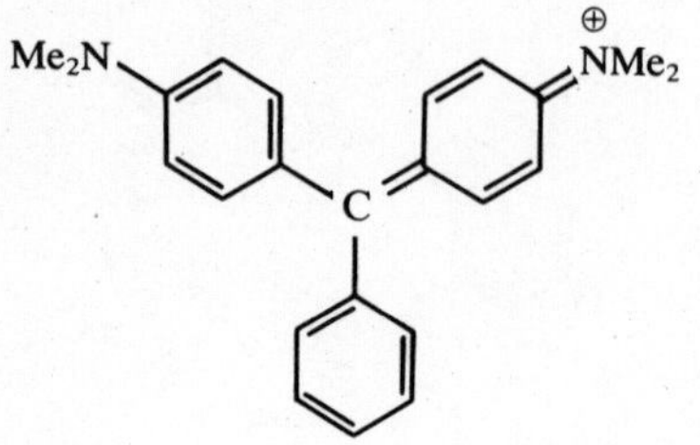

Fig. 1.15

2
Classification of Dyes

Dyes and pigments may be classified according to their structure or, alternatively, according to the methods by which they are applied to the substrate, i.e. in dyeing and printing textiles, leather and fur dyeing, in paper manufacture, in the mass coloration of plastics and as paints and surface coatings. Neither system of classification is satisfactory by itself; the same chromophoric system may be present in dyes differing widely in usage and application, the presence or absence of solubilizing groups, proton-accepting groups, long-chain alkyl groups, etc., being among the factors determining dyeing characteristics and suitabilty for a particular technical purpose.

Classification according to constitution

Part II of the third edition of the Colour Index groups colouring matters on the basis of their chemical structures or rather upon their chromophoric system or systems. Table 2.1 gives a typical example from each of these groups.

Table 2.1 Dyes classified according to constitution

Class	Example	Structure
Nitroso	C.I. Mordant Green 4 10005	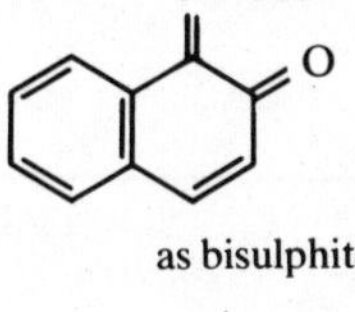 $N \cdot OH$ as bisulphite compound
Nitro	C.I. Pigment Yellow 11 10325	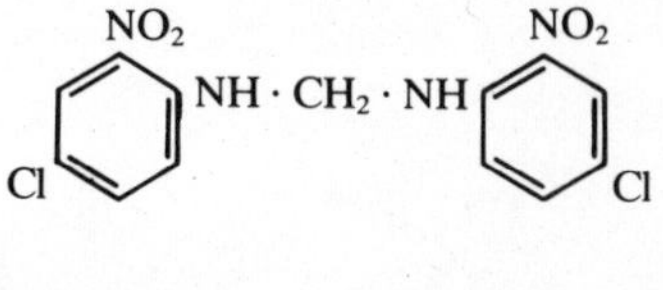

The nitro group is often found in dyes having a different chromophoric system; in the example given here, and in all the other members of this group, no other chromophore is present.

Table 2.1   *(Contd.)*

Class	Example	Structure

Azo
Monoazo — C.I. Disperse Red 1 11110

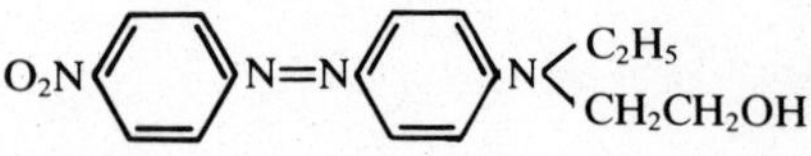

$$O_2N\text{—}\bigcirc\text{—}N{=}N\text{—}\bigcirc\text{—}N\begin{matrix}C_2H_5\\CH_2CH_2OH\end{matrix}$$

Disazo — C.I. Acid Blue 87 20415

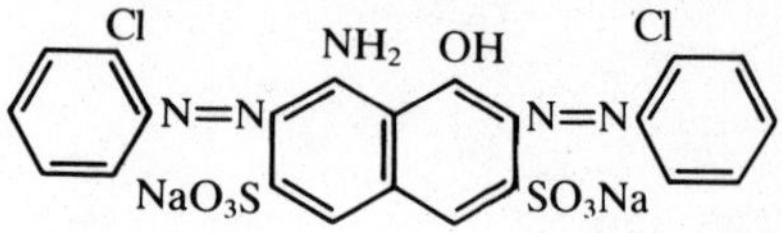

Trisazo See p. 105–107

Polyazo
(tetrakisazo,
  etc.) See p. 107

Azoic — C.I. Azoic Diazo Component 19 37065

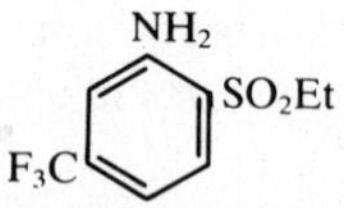

(as stabilized diazo component)

C.I. Azoic Coupling Component 2 37505

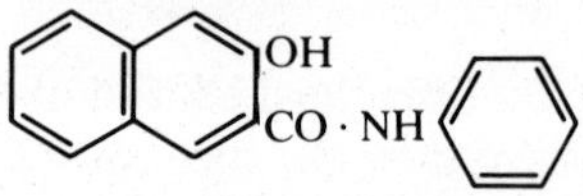

Note that combination of diazo and coupling component, generally carried out on the substrate, gives rise to dyes of the type.

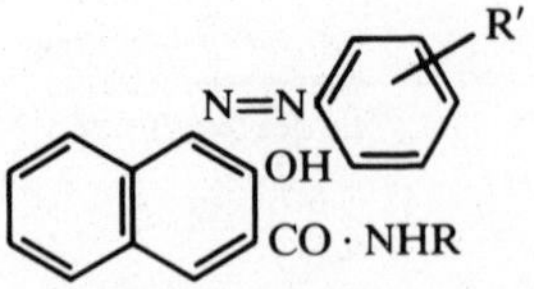

Stilbene — C.I. Direct Orange 71 40205

condensation product of

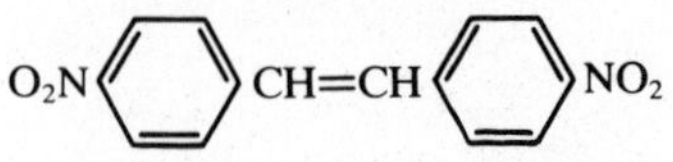

$$O_2N\text{—}\bigcirc\text{—}CH{=}CH\text{—}\bigcirc\text{—}NO_2$$

and

$$NaO_2C\text{—}\bigcirc\text{—}N{=}N\text{—}\bigcirc\text{—}NH_2$$

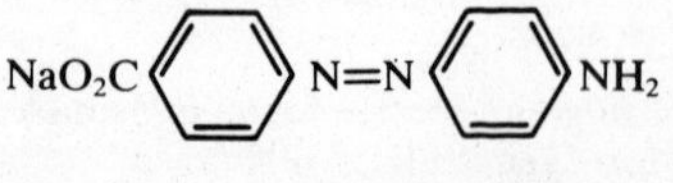

Table 2.1 *(Contd.)*

Class	Example	Structure

The product contains both azo —N=N— and azoxy —N=N— (with O) groups as chromophores, dyes obtained by tetrazotization of diaminostilbene derivatives and subsequent couplings are classed as Disazo dyes.

Diphenylmethane (Ketone/imine)	C.I. Basic Yellow 2 41000 (Auramine)	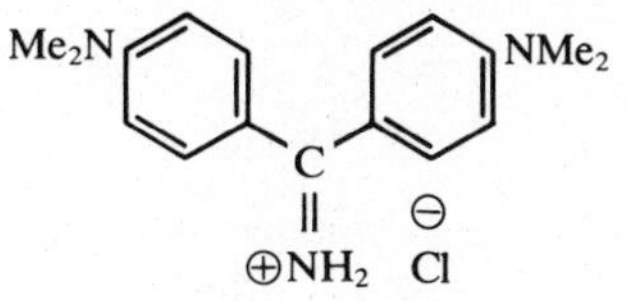 Auramine O
Triarylmethane	C.I. Acid Green 16 44025 (Naphthalene Green V)	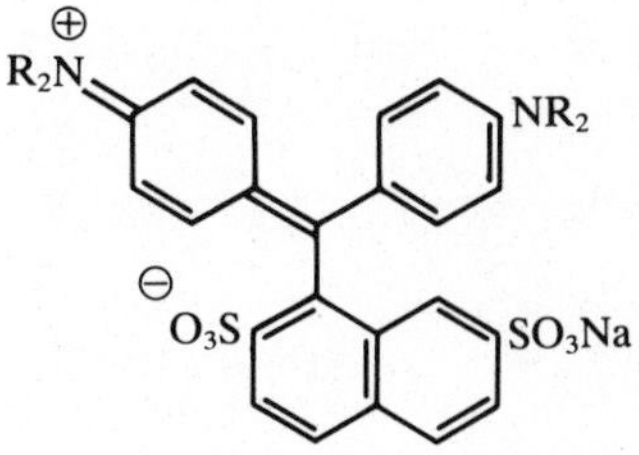
Xanthene	C.I. Basic Violet 10 45170 Rhodamine B	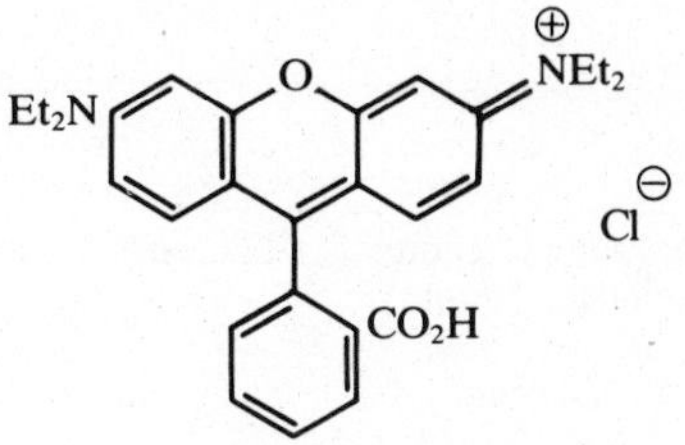
Acridine	C.I. Basic Orange 14 Solvent Orange 15 (Acridine Orange) 46005	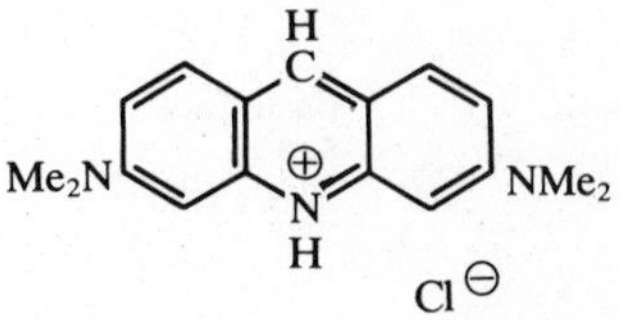
Quinoline	C.I. Solvent Yellow 33 47000 (Quinoline Yellow, Spirit Soluble)	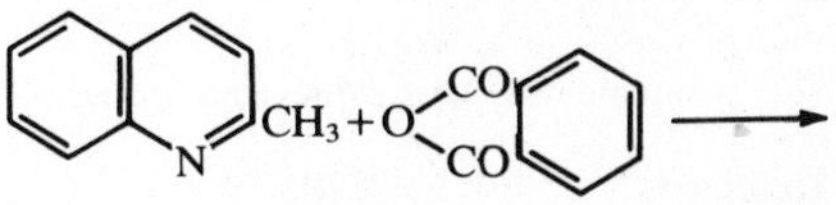 (main product) and

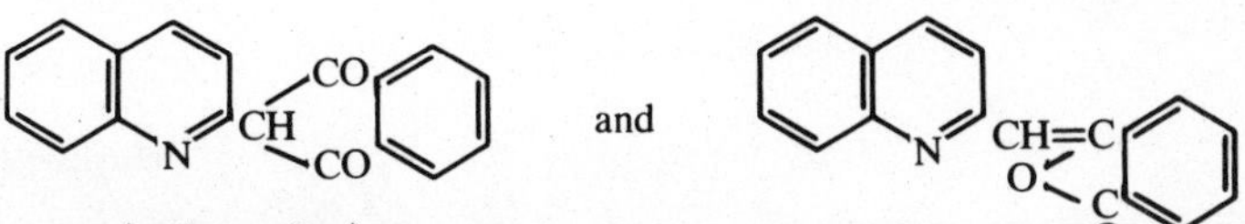

Table 2.1 *(Contd.)*

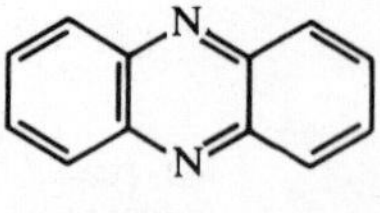

Class	Example	Structure
Methine	C.I. Basic Red 12 48070	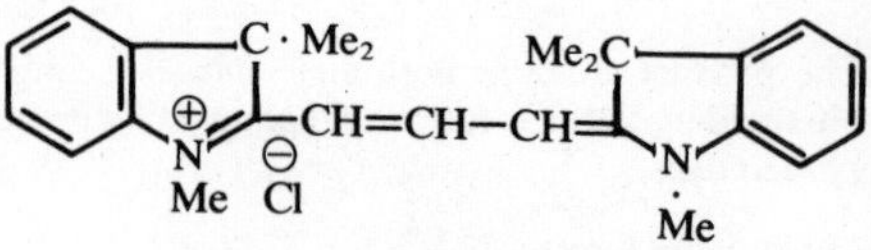
Thiazole	C.I. Basic Yellow 1 Pigment Yellow 18 (=phosphotungsto- molybdic acid lake) 49005 (Basic Yellow T)	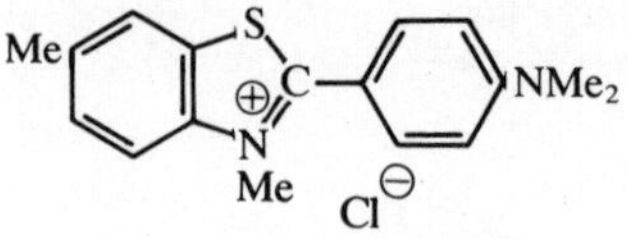
Indamine	C.I. Solvent Blue 22 49705	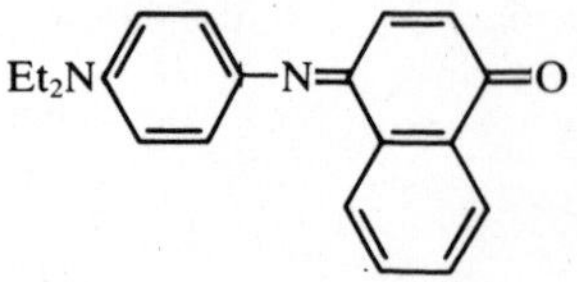
Azine	C.I. Basic Red 5 50040	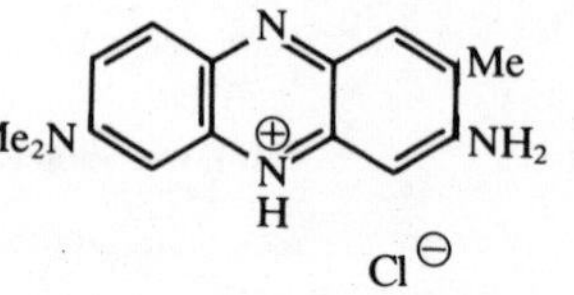

The example quoted is a 'Eurhodine'; there are ten subdivisions in the azine class, the common chromogen being

Oxazine	C.I. Basic Blue 6 51175 (Meldola's Blue)	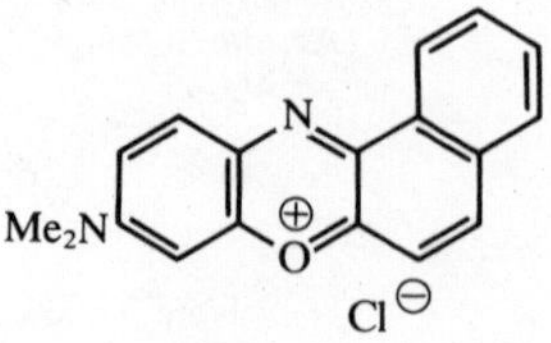

This group includes Dioxazines and Oxazines.

Thiazine	C.I. Basic Blue 9 C.I. Solvent Blue 8 52015 (Methylene Blue)	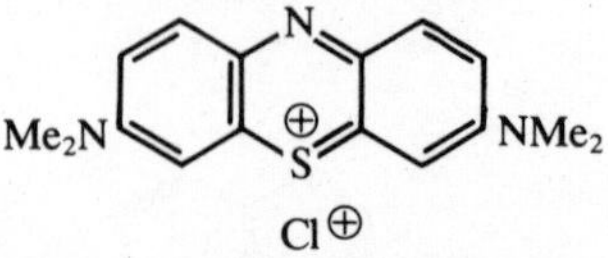

Methylene Blue

as zinc double chloride

Table 2.1   *(Contd.)*

Class	Example	Structure
Sulphur	These dyes are obtained by heating certain organic compounds with sulphur or alkali polysulphides, the products being largely of unknown constitution. It is not possible, therefore, to assign a precise chromophoric system to this class. C.I. Sulphur Black 3 53180 (Vidal Black)	
Lactone (amino-ketone and hydroxy-ketone dyes)	C.I. Vat Yellow 5 56005	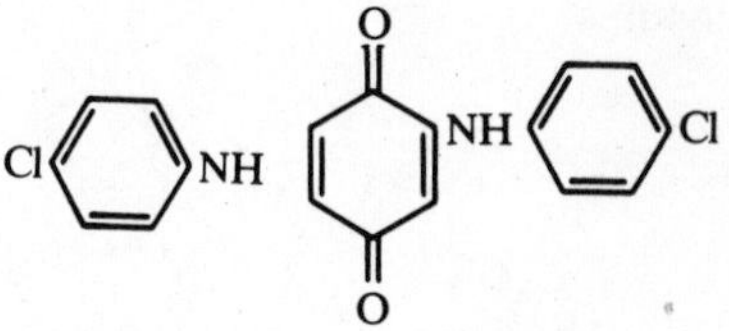
Anthra-quinone	C.I. Solvent Violet 13 60725	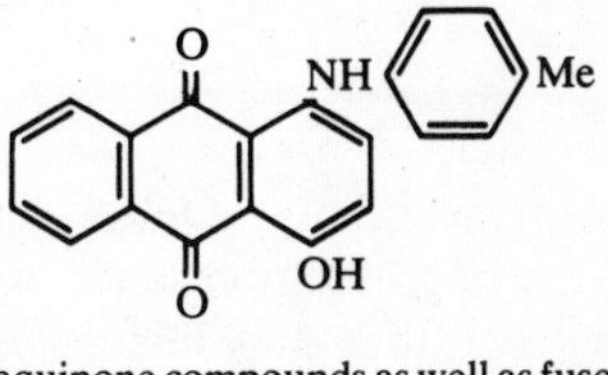

This very large group contains variously substituted anthraquinone compounds as well as fused ring structures formally related to anthraquinone.

Indigoid	C.I. Vat Blue 1 73000 Indigo (Synthetic)	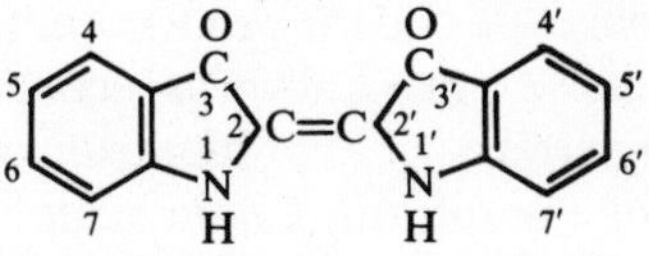

The group includes thioindigoid dyes in which NH is replaced by S.

Phthalocyanine	C.I. Pigment Blue 16 74100 Copper Phthalocyanine	See Pigments, Chapter 15

The remaining groups in the Colour Index Classification are 'Natural', 'Oxidation Bases' and 'Inorganic Pigments'. There is little point in giving examples of these, but reference to them will be made in subsequent pages.

Dye applications

So far as the user and manufacturer of dyes are concerned the function of a dye is to give rise to a particular hue in association with a substrate. Natural and synthetic fibres form the most important substrates in dyeing and printing, though fur, leather, plastics and polymers (i.e. mass coloration) must be included as substrates also. Before the chemistry of dyeing and printing processes is discussed, the more important natural and synthetic fibres will be dealt with briefly.

Natural fibres

Cellulosic. Cotton consists of almost pure cellulose, the most abundant of all organic polymers, natural or otherwise; cellulose is a linear polymer of glucose molecules:

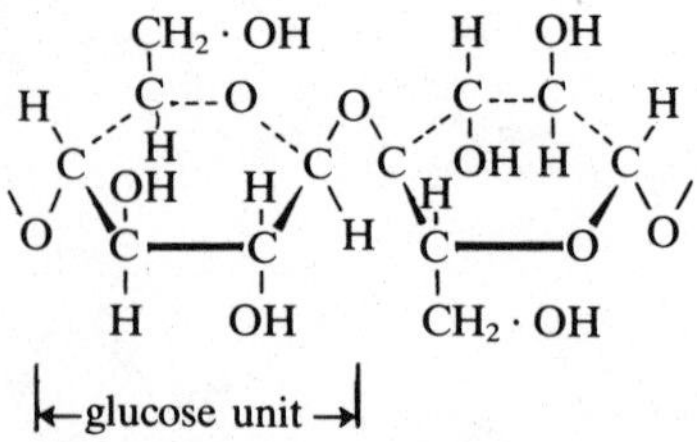

|←glucose unit →| **Fig. 2.1**

The presence of —OH groups, the size and configuration of the glucose units, are of great importance in the physics and chemistry of cotton dyeing. It will be seen that each hexose unit has three —OH groups and these can be acetylated, cellulose triacetate (CT) being the fully acetylated product. By controlled alkaline hydrolysis, some of the acetyl groups can be removed from the triacetate and the product containing an average of about 2.3 acetyl groups per hexose unit is known as secondary acetate (CA). These products, which are widely used as fibres, differ from cellulose in being soluble in certain solvents, (CT in chloroform; CA in acetone) whereas cellulose is not. Moreover, the Direct Dyes used in cotton dyeing have little or no substantivity for either the triacetate or secondary acetate. (See Chapter 14, Disperse Dyes.)

Protein. Wool is a protein fibre and is a polymer of great complexity having as its structural units about twenty different α aminoacids. Wool can be represented diagrammatically as:

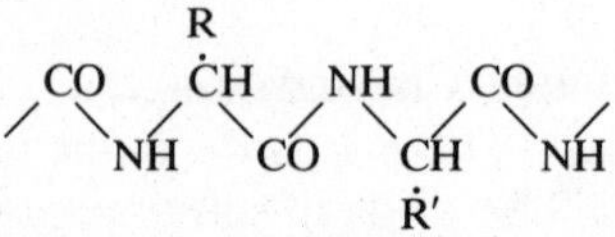

                                                                    Fig. 2.2

being composed of units

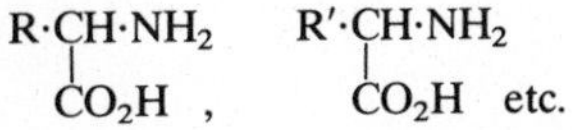

$$\begin{matrix} R\cdot\underset{|}{C}H\cdot NH_2 & R'\cdot\underset{|}{C}H\cdot NH_2 \\ CO_2H \; , & CO_2H \;\; \text{etc.} \end{matrix}$$

Fig. 2.3

Where R, R' contain free amino ($-NH_2$) groups or free carboxyl ($-CO_2H$) groups not concerned in forming the amide links in the protein molecule, they provide basic and acidic centres important in wool dyeing. It should be noted that silk, fur and leather are protein substrates.

Synthetic fibres

The three chief kinds are:

Polyamide. A typical example is:

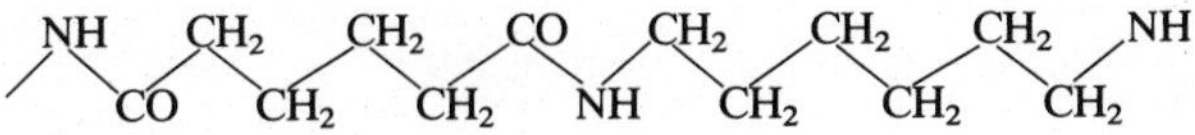

Nylon 6.6†

Fig. 2.4

obtained by condensation of adipic acid and hexamethylene diamine.

Polyester. The best example is:

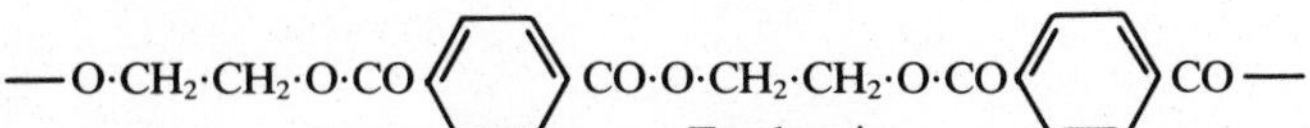

Terylene†
(terephthalic acid/ethyleneglycol polymer)

Fig. 2.5

Polyacrylonitrile. This type is obtained by the polymerization of acrylonitrile, $CH_2=CH\cdot CN$,

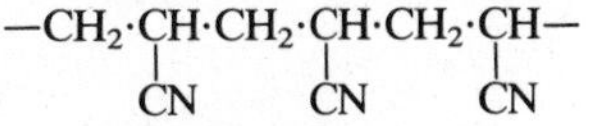

$$-CH_2\cdot\underset{\underset{CN}{|}}{C}H\cdot CH_2\cdot\underset{\underset{CN}{|}}{C}H\cdot CH_2\cdot\underset{\underset{CN}{|}}{C}H-$$

Orlon 42

Fig. 2.6

† *Nylon* and *Orlon* are the registered trade marks of E. I. du Pont de Nemours and Company Inc. *Terylene* is the registered trade mark of ICI Ltd.

in which, however, acidic centres (sulphonic acid groups) may be present resulting from the addition of polymerization inhibitors:

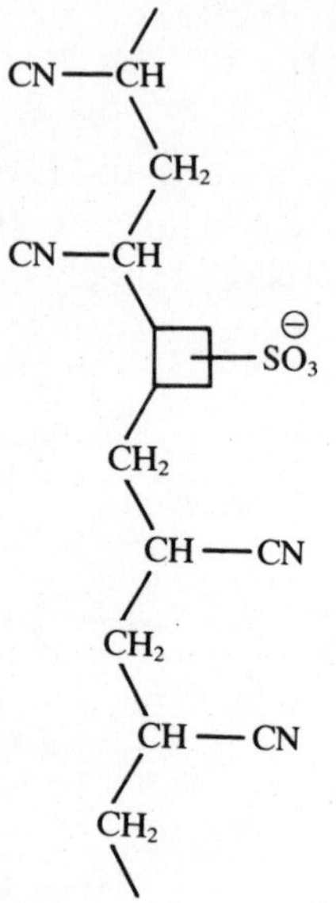

Fig. 2.7

The presence of these negative groups enables the fibre to be dyed with cationic dyes. Modified acrylic fibres are now produced by the co-polymerization of acrylonitrile with other molecules in order to achieve improved dyeing and other properties. Among other commercial brands are Acrilan†, Creslan†, Dynel† and Courtelle†.

Dyeing

Dyeing is in general carried out in aqueous solution. The process of attachment of the dye molecule to the fibre is one of adsorption. As such, the application of physical chemistry, especially the thermodynamic approach, has been the most useful in studying the dyeing process. For further information the student should consult more detailed works (see Bibliography).

There are four kinds of forces by which dye molecules are bound to the fibre:

1. Ionic forces.
2. Hydrogen bonds.

---

† *Acrilan* is the registered trade mark of Chemstrand Corporation, Decatur, Ala, U.S.A. *Creslan* is the registered trade mark of American Cyanamid Co. *Dynel* is the registered trade mark of Union Carbide Corporation. *Courtelle* is the registered trade mark of Courtaulds Ltd.

3. van der Waals' forces.
4. Covalent linkages.

Ionic forces, as the name implies, are the mutual interactions between positive centres in a fibre and negative centres in a dye molecule and between negative fibre sites and positive centres in a dye molecule. The dyeing of wool provides a simple example.

A 'free' amino group and a 'free' carboxyl group in wool may be represented thus:

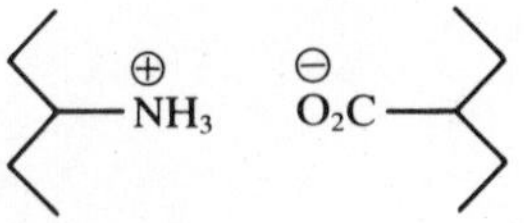

$$\rangle\!\!-NH_3^{\oplus} \quad {}^{\ominus}O_2C-\!\!\langle$$

Fig. 2.8

Most wool dyes are the sodium (or other metals) salts of sulphonic acids, dyeing being carried out in the presence of acid, often dilute sulphuric acid. The action of the acid, designated HX, is:

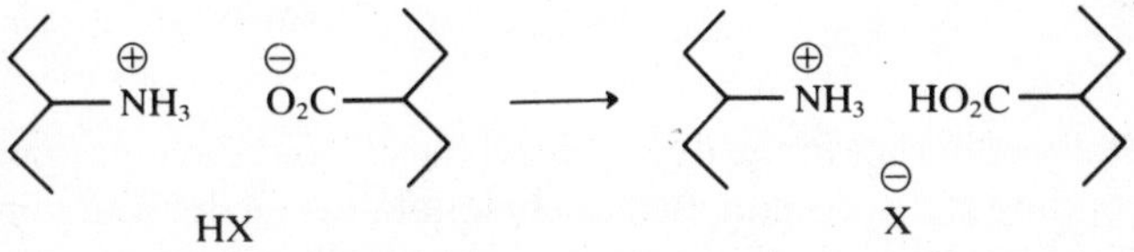

$$\rangle\!\!-NH_3^{\oplus} \quad {}^{\ominus}O_2C-\!\!\langle \quad \longrightarrow \quad \rangle\!\!-NH_3^{\oplus} \quad HO_2C-\!\!\langle$$

HX $X^{\ominus}$

Fig. 2.9

and that of the dye, designated NaD, is:

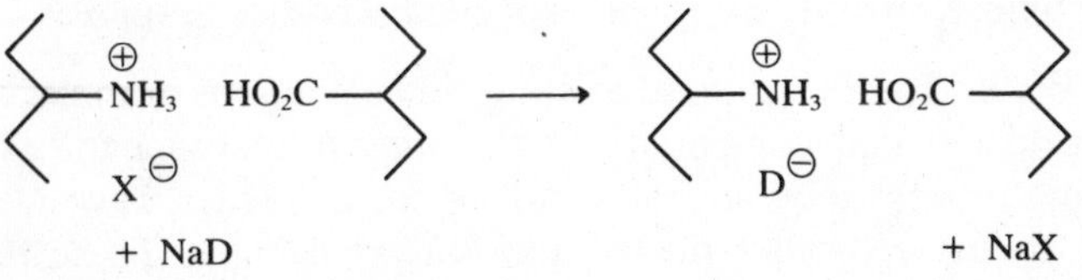

$$\rangle\!\!-NH_3^{\oplus} \quad HO_2C-\!\!\langle \quad \longrightarrow \quad \rangle\!\!-NH_3^{\oplus} \quad HO_2C-\!\!\langle$$

$X^{\ominus}$ $D^{\ominus}$

+ NaD   + NaX

Fig. 2.10

Hydrogen bonds result from the acceptance by a covalently bound hydrogen atom of a 'lone pair' of electrons from an electron donor atom. The association of water molecules is to be explained by hydrogen bonding, represented below by dotted lines:

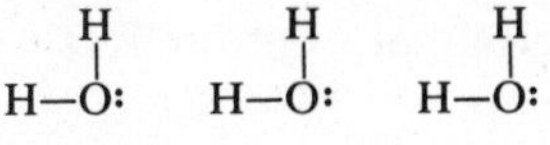

$$\begin{array}{ccc} H & H & H \\ | & | & | \\ H-\ddot{O}\!: & H-\ddot{O}\!: & H-\ddot{O}\!: \end{array}$$

Fig. 2.11

individual molecules lining up and giving rise to:

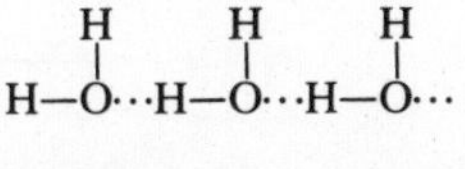

$$\begin{array}{ccc} H & H & H \\ | & | & | \\ H-\dot{O}\cdots H-\dot{O}\cdots H-\dot{O}\cdots \end{array}$$

Fig. 2.12

Such bonds are weak, second-order bonds sometimes referred to as polar van der Waals' forces. They are of importance in the theoretical study of dyeing processes, i.e. in explaining certain aspects of substantivity.

Examples of electron *donor* groups are:

$$-N=\underset{\cdot\cdot}{N}- \qquad -NH_2 \qquad -\underset{\cdot\cdot}{N}H\cdot R \qquad -\underset{\cdot\cdot}{N}\cdot R_2$$

azo   amino   alkylamino etc.   dialkylamino etc.

$$H-\underset{\cdot\cdot}{O}- \qquad R-\underset{\cdot\cdot}{O}-$$

hydroxy   alkoxy etc.

R = alkyl, aryl, or aralkyl

Fig. 2.13

and of *acceptor* groups (i.e. their hydrogen atoms):

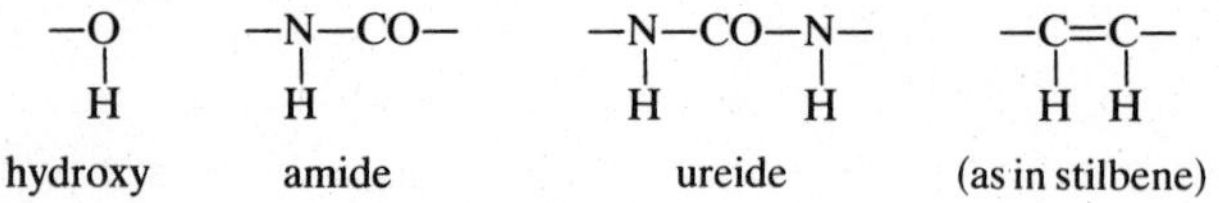

$$\underset{H}{\overset{-O}{|}} \qquad \underset{H}{\overset{-N-CO-}{|}} \qquad \underset{H}{\overset{-N-CO-}{|}}\underset{H}{\overset{N-}{|}} \qquad \underset{H\ \ H}{\overset{-C=C-}{|\ \ \ |}}$$

hydroxy   amide   ureide   (as in stilbene)

Fig. 2.14

It is generally held that in the dyeing of wool, silk and the man-made fibres, hydrogen bonding is involved in the attachment between dye and fibre. This is not thought probable with cellulose, since the attachment through hydrogen bonding of water molecules of the amorphous areas of the fibre is such that the dye molecule is not able to displace these water molecules. The substantivity of a dye for cellulose must therefore be explained on other grounds.

Van der Waals' forces are those existing between atoms or molecules of all substances and are small compared with the other interatomic forces present. In the dyeing process they are the result of second-order wave mechanical interaction of the π orbitals of dye and fibre molecules. These forces are especially effective when the dye molecule is linear, i.e. long and flat, and can thus approach close enough to the fibre molecule or molecular unit (cotton substantivity), and when dye and fibre both contain alkyl or aryl groups as is the case with certain wool dyes and with the majority of polyester dyes.

Covalent linkages are actual chemical bonds between dye and substrate molecules. They are brought about by chemical reaction between a 'reactive' dye molecule and, for example, a hydroxyl group of a cotton fibre.

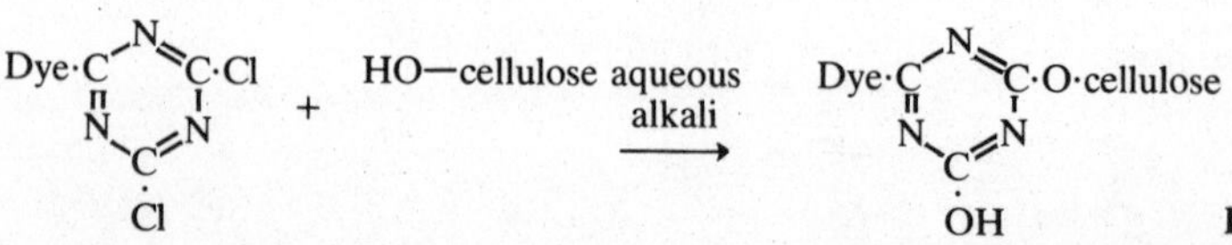

Fig. 2.15

Fastness properties

General. It has been estimated that there are in excess of 2000 individual dyes available today to dyers and other consumers. There are various reasons for this diversity. Dyes of fundamentally different constitution are required according to whether the fibre to be coloured is wool, cotton, cellulose acetate, polyester, polyamide, polyacrylonitrile and so forth. Other kinds of colorants are needed for the mass coloration of plastics and polymers. Again different dyes are called for according to the processing treatment which the dyed or printed substrate must undergo before it becomes a finished article. The finished article may be exposed to a number of agencies: sunlight, washing with soap or 'detergent', dry cleaning, water, perspiration, and so on. The ability or otherwise of a dye, in association with a given substrate, to withstand the various agencies in processing or in use is called its fastness properties. The various kinds of fastness have been given quantitative expression by carefully standardized comparative tests. In 1934 the Fastness Tests Committee of the Society of Dyers and Colourists published methods for the determination of light, perspiration and washing fastness. By 1948, methods for thirty-three agencies subdivided into four fibre groups had been laid down. A fair degree of international agreement as to standards of fastness has been achieved, the principal active bodies in this work being The American Association of Textile Chemists and Colorists (A.A.T.C.C.), Europäisch-Continentale Echtheits-Convention (E.C.E.) and The Society of Dyers and Colourists, Bradford, England (S.D.C.).

Through the International organization for Standardization (I.S.O.) efforts have been made to set up a unified system using the best procedures from the U.K., the Continent and the United States.

For complete information on fastness tests the student is referred to the Bibliography. The following is intended as an outline only of some of the principal fastness properties with which the dye manufacturer is concerned.

Colour fastness. By colour fastness is meant the resistance of the hue of textiles to the different agencies to which they may be exposed during manufacture and subsequent use. The standard methods may be used not only for determining the colour fastness of textiles but also for determining the colour fastness of dyes. When so used, the dye is applied to the textile in specified depths of shade by stated procedures and the textile is then tested by the prescribed methods.

Light fastness. Light fastness is assessed on a scale of eight, 1 representing the least fastness and 8 the best. (Fastness to all other agencies is assessed on a scale of 5.)

A specimen of the dyed or printed textile is exposed to daylight under standard conditions, including protection from rain, along with eight dyed wool standards. Thus if the test specimen has faded more than the wool standard of fastness rating 6 and less than that of rating 4 and, in other words, its behaviour towards light is similar to the standard of rating 5, then the light fastness is assessed at 5.

It will be seen from Table 2.2 that the standard wool dyes are all blue dyes. This at first sight may appear strange when one considers that dyes of every hue, applied on different substrates, have to be tested for light fastness. This range of standard blue dyes has been adopted since a scale of eight is thereby possible in which each unit in the scale represents an approximately twofold increase in the time of exposure to light which is needed to produce a detectable change in colour. The *change* in colour is assessed by eye by reference to five pairs of grey dyed cloths, each pair representing a visual difference and contrast. By this means the degree of fading of any hue can be assessed, via the standard grey scale, in relation to the official standards. The process of fading in daylight is generally slow and tests may take months to complete. Laboratory instruments have been designed and are in use in which intense artificial light is employed to accelerate the fading process. Such instruments are for the most part used comparatively.

The method of testing dyes as to behaviour towards each of the various agencies is as follows:

a specimen of dyed textile in intimate contact with an undyed specimen of the same or a different textile is subjected, on the laboratory scale, to conditions simulating those met with in processing or use. In all cases the change in colour of the dyed specimen and, where appropriate, the staining of the undyed cloths, are assessed visually using the standard grey scale. In certain cases, e.g. bleach fastness, gas fading, there is no need to have undyed cloths present, only the change in colour being relevant.

Table 2.2 List of standard wool dyes

Light fastness rating	Dye	C.I. designation	C.I. number	Chemical class
1	Acilan Brilliant Blue FFR	C.I. Acid Blue 104	42735	Triarylmethane
2	Acilan Brilliant Blue FFB	C.I. Acid Blue 109	42740	Triarylmethane
3	Coomassie Brilliant Blue R	C.I. Acid Blue 83	42660	Triarylmethane
4	Supramin Blue EG	C.I. Acid Blue 121	50310	Azine
5	Solway Blue RN	C.I. Acid Blue 47	62085	Anthraquinonoid
6	Alizarine Light Blue 4GL	C.I. Acid Blue 23	61125	Anthraquinonoid
7	Soledon Blue 4BC Pdr.	C.I. Solubilized Vat Blue 5	73066	Indigoid
8	Indigosol Blue AGG	C.I. Solubilized Vat Blue 8	73801	Indigoid

The fastness scale is in each case 1–5 in ascending order of fastness, and it is possible to describe both degree of alteration in colour or the degree of staining as follows:

Alteration in shade
Corresponding to fastness 5 = Shade unaltered.
Corresponding to fastness 4 = Very slight alteration or loss in depth.
Corresponding to fastness 3 = Appreciable alteration or loss in depth.
Corresponding to fastness 2 = Distinct alteration or loss in depth.
Corresponding to fastness 1 = Shade much altered or great loss in depth.

Degree of staining
Corresponding to fastness 5 = No staining of adjacent white.
Corresponding to fastness 4 = Very slight staining of adjacent white.
Corresponding to fastness 3 = Appreciable staining of adjacent white.
Corresponding to fastness 2 = Deep staining of adjacent white.
Corresponding to fastness 1 = Adjacent white dyed deeply.

Fastness tests

A few of the more important tests are given below under two headings, viz. Processing Conditions and Conditions in Use.

Processing Conditions

Water. I.S.O. Recommendation R105, part 22. British Standard 2681:1956. The test is designed to determine the resistance of the colour of a dyed or printed textile to immersion in water. Dyed and undyed specimens are immersed in water, drained and placed in a Perspirometer, or equivalent apparatus, in which dyed and undyed pieces are held in contact under compression between sheets of glass. The pieces are dried separately. The change in colour of the dyed cloth and the staining of the undyed cloths are assessed by means of the standard grey scale.

Bleaching with hypochlorite. British Standard 2666:1956. A dyed specimen is treated with hypochlorite solution, washed, treated with hydrogen peroxide solution, washed, dried and the alteration in colour assessed in the standard manner.

The test reproduces normal commercial bleaching conditions and is applicable chiefly to natural and regenerated cellulose.

Milling (acid). British Standard 2686:1956. A dyed specimen of wool is made into a small bag in which are placed an undyed cloth and two porcelain balls.

The assembly is rotated in a wash wheel in contact with dilute sulphuric acid. Alteration in colour and degree of staining in washed and dried test pieces are assessed.

Milling is a severe mechanical washing process applied to wool in manufacture.

Milling (alkaline). As in the last except that the dilute sulphuric acid is replaced by alkaline soap solution.

Sublimation. A dyed specimen, in contact with an undyed piece, is subjected to dry heat. Alteration in colour and degree of staining are assessed.

The test is mainly applied to dyed hydrophobic fibres, polyamide, polyester and polyacrylonitrile. Fastness to dry-heat pleating and setting is determined in a similar manner, a molten metal alloy bath being employed.

Conditions in use

Washing fastness

Hand washing. Dyed and undyed specimens in contact are agitated in a soap solution, rinsed and dried. Change in colour of the dyed specimen and degree of staining of the undyed specimen are assessed in the normal way. Two other tests, carries out under the conditions of technical washing, have been devised. In both tests the soap solution contains washing soda and in one case the test is carried out at the boil.

Rubbing. Dyed and undyed specimens are tested in special machines of which an example is the Crockmeter developed by the Calico Printer's Association.

Rubbing fastness is the resistance of dyed textiles to rubbing off and staining other materials; tests are carried out under both wet and dry conditions.

Perspiration. Dyed and undyed specimens in contact are immersed in a solution of histidine (α-amino-β-iminazole-propionic acid). After draining, the specimens are placed in contact under compression in a Perspirometer or similar apparatus. See Fastness to Water. The change in colour of the dyed specimen and the degree of staining of the undyed specimen are assessed.

Burnt gas fumes. A dyed specimen is exposed to oxides of nitrogen until a control specimen, exposed simultaneously, has changed colour to a predetermined extent. Alteration in colour is assessed.

This particular fastness refers to the resistance of dyed hydrophobic fibres, polyamide, polyester and especially cellulose acetate, to the action of oxides of nitrogen which may be produced, e.g. when air is passed over heated filaments or during the combustion of coal gas, oil and other fuels.

In addition to the above tests there are many others which test the behaviour of dyed textiles in various applications, e.g. against the action of sea-water, the process used in felting, degumming, mercurizing and others.

As new processes of textile manufacture and new synthetic fibres are invented, so tests must be devised to determine fitness or otherwise of the dyes available and for the appraisal of new dyes coming from the research laboratories.

Classification of dyes according to application

Sulphur dyes. Mainly used for cellulosic fibres, dyeings having moderate all-round fastness, the blacks, greens, some blues and browns having good light fastness. They are water-insoluble dyes, containing sulphur both as an integral part of the chromophore and in attached polysulphide chains. They are normally applied from a sodium sulphide bath, the dyes being reduced to a water-soluble form, reoxidation to shade occurring on the fibre by contact with the air.

Azoic dyes. The term describes a system of producing an insoluble azo dye *in situ*, i.e. on the fibre, one intermediate (coupling component) having affinity for cellulosic fibres being 'padded' onto the material, i.e. the cloth is passed in full width through a bath containing a solution of the component and is squeezed dry by being passed through rollers. The impregnated material is then brought into contact with a solution of the second intermediate (diazo component) whereupon the insoluble dye is formed. The major application is the dyeing and printing of cellulosic fibres especially cotton, giving shades of a high standard of fastness to light and wet processing. They give bright, intense hues particularly in the yellow, orange and red ranges. Azoic dyes made not *in situ* but in bulk, are of increasing importance as pigments.

Ingrain types. The term ingrain is applied to all types of dyes formed *in situ* on the substrate by the development or coupling of intermediate compounds which are not themselves true finished dyes. The group thus includes Azoic and Oxidation Dyes, but the C.I. limits the Ingrain section to those developed 'from growing knowledge of phthalocyanines'.

Direct dyes. Anionic dyes having substantivity for cellulosic fibres, normally applied from an aqueous dyebath containing an electrolyte and not requiring the use of mordant are termed direct dyes. In addition to those used as such, there are direct dyes designed for development on the fibre through diazotization and coupling with an added coupling component or through coupling with added diazotized *p*-nitraniline. Other direct dyes are designed specially for aftertreatment on the fibre with salts of metals especially copper salts or chromium salts. Still other dyes are intended for aftertreatment on the fibre with formaldehyde. Direct dyes are used on substrates other than textiles chiefly leather and paper.

Vat dyes. This large and important group comprises:

1. Indigoid and thioindigoid dyes.
2. Anthraquinonoid dyes.

They are applied from aqueous medium as leuco compounds (vats) obtained by alkaline reduction using sodium hydrosulphite (hydros), subsequent oxidation reforming the original insoluble dye on the substrate. Water-soluble *leuco esters* are valuable for producing pale shades, or for colouring materials that are difficult to penetrate. The original dye is regenerated by simultaneous hydrolysis and oxidation.

The major application is the dyeing and printing of cotton. Such are the outstanding fastness properties of this group that special methods for the dyeing and printing of substrates other than cotton, e.g. wool, silk and cellulose acetate, have been developed.

Acid dyes. Acid dyes find their main application in the textile field on wool, but are also used on silk, polyamide, acrylic and regenerated protein fibres, also paper and leather: they are normally applied from a dye liquor containing sulphuric, formic, or acetic acids; neutral and even slightly alkaline dye baths are occasionally used. Chemical types involved are azo, anthraquinone, triarylmethane, azine, xanthene, ketonimine, nitro and nitroso compounds. They include dyes giving very bright hues and have a wide range of fastness properties from very poor to very good.

Wool is dyed in all forms: loose wool, slubbing (slightly twisted wool prepared for spinning), yarn, knitted and woven fabrics, felts and garments. Dyes having good migration and levelling properties, which readily give even (i.e. level) dyeings, are used on yarns and fabrics. Those having good wet fastness, but inferior levelling properties are used on loose wool and slubbing, which may have to undergo the process known as milling (see Fastness). As a consequence of these different requirements acid dyes are subdivided into acid levelling dyes and acid milling dyes. Dyes of inferior levelling properties can now be applied successfully with the aid of certain commercial preparations.

Mordant dyes. In the C.I. the group covers 'dyes sold by their makers under such names as mordant dyes, chrome dyes, metachrome dyes, afterchrome dyes, chrome printing colours'. It does not include the basic dyes which are dyed on tannin-antimony mordanted cotton, a mordant being a substance, e.g. tannic acid, with which cloth (cotton) must be treated before being dyed, the dye otherwise having no affinity for the fibre. Certain types of acid dyes can form complexes with metals, in particular chromium, the lake formed on the fibre conferring better wet fastness than that of the acid dye itself.

Metal complex dyes. These dyes, though formally related to the chromium lakes formed *in situ* and referred to above, are produced as metal complexes of *o,o'*-dihydroxy-azo dyes in bulk for use by the dyer as acid dyes mainly for wool; they also find application on silk and polyamide fibres. The dyes are of two kinds:

1. Acid dyeing premetallized dyes (1 metal atom, usually chromium, combined with one molecule of azo dye) known as 1 : 1 dyes and introduced in 1919. The chief use is in wool dyeing, but the large amount of sulphuric acid needed in the dyebath is often a disadvantage. Methods for overcoming this drawback have been proposed recently, but there is little information so far concerning the nature of the additives used.
2. Neutral-dyeing premetallized dyes, introduced in 1951, are much the more important type. They are 1 : 2 complexes (1 metal atom, chromium or cobalt, combined with two molecules of azo dye) dyed from a neutral or slightly acid bath. They give dyeings of very high all-round fastness properties and they possess particularly good levelling properties.

Solvent dyes. As the name indicates these dyes, usually containing no sulpho or other water-solubilizing groups, are soluble in organic solvents the nature of which varies according to application. The range of solvents covers alcohols, esters, ethers, aliphatic and aromatic hydrocarbons, chlorinated hydrocarbons, oils, fats and waxes. Uses for the dye solutions include stains, varnishes, lacquers, printing inks, copying papers, typewriter ribbons and ball point pens. Solvent dyes are used for colouring candles, soaps, cosmetics, petrol and fuel oils, and for the mass coloration of synthetic polymers. Of recent years the possibility of using tetrachloroethylene (perchloroethylene) instead of water in suitable dyeing processes especially for the dyeing of polyester fibres, has been the subject of a number of patents. Examples of suitable dyes are given in Chapter 14.

Disperse dyes. The C.I. (1953) definition was 'a class of water-insoluble dyes originally introduced for dyeing cellulose acetate and usually applied from fine aqueous dispersion'. Recent work has shown that such dyes do, however, dissolve to a very slight extent in water and the degree of solubility influences the dyeing and levelling processes. They belong to three main classes, viz. nitroarylamine, azo and anthraquinone. Almost all contain amino- or substituted amino-groups, but do not contain solubilizing groups such as sulphonic groups. They are usually ground in a mill to fine particle sizes (1–4 μ) in a aqueous solution containing a dispersing agent. The latter normally stabilizes the dye suspension and acts as a restraining and retarding agent.

The principal uses are the dyeing of cellulose acetate, nylon, polyester and polyacrylonitrile fibres. The mechanism in each case is believed to be one of solution in the fibre, no specific electrically charged dye sites being needed for dyeing to take place.

Disperse dyes are also used for dyeing woolled sheepskins (i.e. skins to which the wool is still attached) and for the surface dyeing of plastics.

Pigments

In general pigments are inert, stable, coloured substances, insoluble in water, which are used for imparting colour by incorporation within an article during manufacture, e.g. mouldings from an evenly coloured mass of plastic material or by surface application in the form of paint. Colour is the result of absorption of light of certain wavelengths and the reflection of other wavelengths from individual particles of the pigment. The physical form of the pigment is *a priori* of great importance in affording maximum colouring power and reflectance.

The C.I. distinguishes among 'pigments', 'lakes' and 'dyes for lakes' for the purposes of classification. The lakes of acid dyes are precipitated from aqueous solution by (a) organic acids such as tannic acid, or (b) inorganic complex acids such as phosphotungstomolybdic acid. The metal salts of mordant dyes are also used as lakes. All the above lakes are technically pigments. These and the highly important synthetic organic pigments are dealt with in Chapter 15.

Solvent dyes, as the name implies, are those soluble in organic solvents. The range of solvents is a fairly wide one from the simpler aliphatic alcohols, esters, ketones, methylated glycols, aliphatic and aromatic hydrocompounds to oils, fats and waxes. The chief chromophoric systems employed are:

Azo including premetallized azo dyes	yellow, orange, brown and red/violet hues
Anthraquinone and triarylmethane	violets, blues and greens
Nigrosine and certain azo dyes	blacks

Among the many uses for solvent dyes are the manufacture of stains, varnishes, transparent lacquers, inks, copying papers, typewriter ribbons and for the coloration of candles, sealing waxes, polishes and surface finishes. They are also used for the mass coloration of moulding powders, synthetic polymer compositions and for colouring soap, cosmetics, petrol, fuel oils and the preparation of signalling smokes.

Reactive dyes have already received brief mention and are dealt with in more detail in Chapter 13.

The chief applications, in dyeing, of the various classes in relation to the more important fibres are shown in Table 2.3.

Table 2.3 Application class and suitability for natural and synthetic fibres

Class	Wool	Cotton	Cellulose derivatives	Polyamide PA	Polyester PE	Poly-acrylonitrile PAC
Basic	X	X	X	X	X	X
Direct		X				
Sulphur		X				
Azoic		X	X		X	
Ingrain						
Vat		X	X			
Acid levelling	X			X		Acid wool
Acid milling	X			X		
Mordant	X	(X)		X		
Metal complex	X			X		X
Disperse			X	X	X	X
Reactive	(X)	X				
Pigment				X	X	X

Pigments may be applied to any substrate by the use of adhesives.
    X—suitable.
    (X)—of secondary importance.

Textile printing

The creation of pattern in coloured fabrics has, from earliest times, been achieved by printing methods. There are three chief mechanical means of textile printing.

Block printing. Suitable blocks of wood are carved so as to leave raised the particular pattern carried by one of the colours in a given design. The block is 'furnished' with the colorant, i.e. dyestuff or pigment, in association with a thickener, e.g. a gum or starch solution or a thermosetting resin and other adjuvants, and an imprint made on the fabric. Blocks appropriately carved for the part of the design carried by each of the other colours are used in sequence (and also in accurate register) to complete the design.

Roller printing. Here, engraved copper rollers apply the printing paste to the fabric from the channels incised in the surface of each roller, one for each colour in the design being used. After receiving the imprint, the fabric passes through a dryer into a steamer for fixation and is thereafter rinsed, soaped, rinsed again and finally dried. A modern variation used especially in the printing of polyester fabric and made-up garments is the Transfer Printing Process. This process is referred to again in Chapter 14.

Screen printing. In this method screens are made by stretching silk fabric over a wood frame and the design (for a single colour) transferred to the screen, e.g. by photographic means using bichromate/gelatin. The part of the design corresponding to the raised parts of block or roller consists of soluble gelatin and is removed by washing with water, the insoluble gelatin (rendered insoluble by a photochemical process) remaining on the silk and rendering it impervious to the colour paste as required by the design. When such a screen is placed on a textile and colour paste gently 'squeezed' over the screen, the colour goes through only where the silk is uncoated. A second screen, prepared according to the designer's requirements for the next colour, is placed in careful register with the first imprint and the process carried out for the second colour and so on.

In addition to these mechanical methods of printing several different printing techniques often called styles are used by the textile printer.

Dyed style

The textile is first printed with a paste containing mordant but no dye. The printed fabric is then 'fixed' by steaming or ageing and the fabric is then dyed. Only those parts printed with the mordant retain colour and thus a pattern is obtained. The method is an ancient one, still used in the less sophisticated countries of the Far East, particularly in the printing of cotton fabrics with Alizarin.

Direct style

As its name indicates, the technique consists in printing the fabric with dye or dye-precursors in association with thickening and other agents present to hinder diffusion of the dye and thus to achieve a clear print. The chief classes of dye used are:

Direct dyes	cotton, cellulosic fibres.
Basic dyes	mordanted cotton, wool, silk, polyacrylonitrile.
Acid dyes	wool, silk, acetate rayon, nylon.
Mordant	cotton, linen, viscose rayon.
Vat and solubilized vat	cotton, linen, viscose rayon.
Azoic	cotton, linen, viscose rayon.

Reactive dyes	cellulosic fibres, viscose rayon, natural silk and wool. The printing paste contains reactive dye and sodium bicarbonate; on steaming, the conditions become sufficiently alkaline to cause combination with, for example, cellulose. Starch cannot be used as a thickener since the hydroxy groups would be affected by the reactive dye. Alginates or hydrocarbon emulsions are used instead. The use of reactive dyes in printing is a most important application.
Disperse dyes	acetate rayon, polyester and polyamide fibres.
Ingrain dyes	cotton and linen.
Pigments (oxidation colours)	cotton, limited use on acetate rayon, silk.
Pigments (resin bonded)	all classes of fibres. In this modern, important method the printing paste contains pigment, a thickening agent of the volatile solvent emulsion type and a thermo-setting resin. After printing, the fabric is dried and then 'baked', usually at 160–170 °C, when the resin undergoes polymerization firmly binding the pigment particles to the fibre. During the heat treatment the solvent emulsion thickener, being volatile, is driven off. This technique and a careful choice of resin are necessary to ensure an acceptable 'handle' or 'feel' to the goods.

Discharge style

In this method, a dyed fabric, called a 'ground', is printed with a paste containing a chemical able, during subsequent processing to bleach or destroy the dye in a specific pattern. The ground may of course have been printed in several colours before printing in the discharge style, a pattern of several colours including white being possible. The dyes used in this technique must obviously be chosen for their power of being discharged readily and irreversibly to give a white or near white. They include:

Azoic, direct and reactive azo dyes—cotton and cellulosic fibres. Here the azo dye is discharged by reduction with sodium sulphoxylate-formaldehyde $NaHSO_2$—CH_2O, which is oxidized in the process to formaldehyde bisulphite $NaHSO_3$—CH_2O, subsequently removed by washing. To increase the efficiency of the 'stripping' process, zinc sulphoxylate–formaldehyde is used. For the same purpose anthraquinone is added to the printing paste to faciliate proton transfer in the reduction.

Vat dyes—cellulosic fibres, acetate rayon (limited). Sodium hydrosulphite ('hydros') and potassium carbonate mixtures are used in the reductive discharge. In indigo printing, discharge may also be effected by oxidation using bichromate applied locally followed by hot acid treatment at full width.

Basic and mordant dyes are also employed in the discharge style of printing.

Resist style

In this method certain parts of the pattern are protected from applied dyes by printing with wax emulsions, silicones, etc., and also by printing with chemical 'resists', e.g. with oxidizing agents that prevent vat dyes from being fixed, or with reducing agents that inhibit the fixation of azoic dyes and of the leucoesters of vat dyes.

Criteria

The printer's requirements as regards dyes differ somewhat from those of the dyer. Dyes for printing must be of maximum solubility since in general the amount of water allowable in making up the printing paste is strictly limited. Inorganic diluents such as salt, sodium sulphate, though acceptable to the dyer, are ruled out by reason of the salting-out effect in a restricted amount of water. Again the printer, in contrast to the wool dyer, is less interested in the levelling properties of an acid dye than in its compatibility with the thickening agent and other additives of the printing paste. In both dyes and pigments the absence of extraneous matter, rust particles and the like, is essential to the production of satisfactory prints. In this the dye manufacturer has progressed considerably over the last twenty years in the use of stainless steel, rubber-lined and glass-lined equipment which go far to keep his products free from extraneous matter.

Good, all-round fastness is demanded of the dyes used in all printing techniques, especially in cotton and linen printing. Of particular importance are fastness to light, rubbing, washing and perspiration.

3
Intermediates

The manufacture of a dye from benzene, toluene, xylene, naphthalene, anthracene and other primary raw materials involves a number of prior synthetic stages and transformations such as nitration, reduction, halogenation, amination, sulphonation, diazotization, oxidation and others. The products, precursors of the dyes themselves, are collectively known as 'intermediates'.

Unit processes

The term 'unit process' is employed in the study of applied chemistry to describe a general reaction or synthetic step in organic chemical manufacture and is distinct from the term 'unit operation' which denotes a physical step, e.g. sublimation, distillation, filtration. The manufacture of a relatively simple intermediate, e.g. N,N-dibenzylaniline disulphonic acid involves a number of unit processes, namely the nitration of benzene, the reduction of nitrobenzene to give aniline, the aralkylation of aniline leading to N,N-dibenzylaniline the sulphonation of which gives, finally, the disulphonic acid.

In the following account of the common unit processes as many examples as possible are taken from current technical practice. It is with the object of stressing the general character of these processes that no artificial division into benzene and naphthalene (or other parent hydrocarbon) intermediates has been made.

Nitration

Aromatic nitration is the establishment of a $C-NO_2$ linkage, C being part of an aromatic system. Nitro compounds are useful sources of amines. The nitro group is a chromophore (see nitro dyes). The presence of one or more nitro groups in an aromatic system enhances the reactivity of suitably placed halogen atoms, influences the properties of appropriately positioned amino groups by reducing their basicity (see Chapter 4).

The most common method of nitration used in the dye-making industry is that employing 'mixed acid', i.e. a mixture of nitric and sulphuric acids, the composition of the mixture varying according to the substance to be nitrated. It is well established from physical evidence such as u.v. and Raman spectra that the attacking species in nitrations involving mixed acid is the nitronium ion NO_2^+ derived from

$$2HNO_3 \rightleftharpoons H_2\overset{+}{N}O_3 + \overset{-}{N}O_3 \quad \text{(fast)}$$
$$H_2\overset{+}{N}O_3 \rightleftharpoons NO_2^+ + H_2O \quad \text{(relatively slow)}$$

Benzene is mono nitrated with a mixture of nitric acid and sulphuric acid monohydrate, HNO_3, 29.3; H_2O, 10; H_2SO_4 60.7 parts per hundred by weight, the temperature not being allowed to exceed 50 °C. A moderate excess of nitric acid (10–20% theory) is customarily employed in technical nitrations and where feasible the nitro compound is separated from the 'spent' acid which is then re-cycled, i.e. re-used in the next batch. Nitrobenzene itself may be

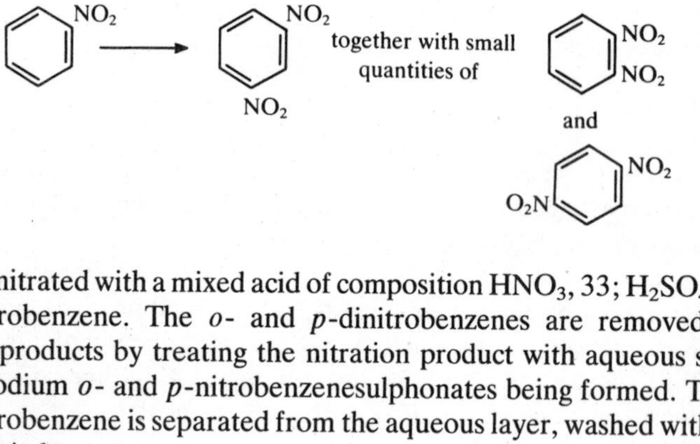

Fig. 3.1

further nitrated with a mixed acid of composition HNO_3, 33; H_2SO_4, 67, giving m-dinitrobenzene. The o- and p-dinitrobenzenes are removed as water-soluble products by treating the nitration product with aqueous sodium sulphite, sodium o- and p-nitrobenzenesulphonates being formed. The residual m-dinitrobenzene is separated from the aqueous layer, washed with water and finally dried.

Toluene. All three ni..otoluenes o-63%, p-33% and m-4% are produced by nitrating with the mixture HNO_3, 30; H_2O, 12.5; H_2SO_4, 57.5; the temperature being controlled within the limits of 30–35 °C. In most modern nitration plants it is so arranged that the addition of nitrating mixture is automatically stopped if the agitator is not in motion (e.g. through electrical fault, power failure or other cause). Serious accidents have been caused in the past by the uncontrolled addition of nitric acid to an unstirred reaction mixture, a violent explosion being caused when the agitator was set in motion again. The isomeric nitrotoluenes are separated by a combination of fractional distillation, and a process of crystallization known as 'sweating'. The following is a very brief description of the operations concerned. The mixed nitrotoluenes are first washed, treated with caustic soda solution to remove small quantities of nitrocresols formed during nitration, as the water-soluble sodium salts, steam distilled to remove unchanged toluene and finally dried by heating in an evacuated vessel. The nitrotoluene mixture is then distilled, using a large fractionating column, under a vacuum of approx. 15 mmHg and a kettle temperature of 160 °C. The first fraction consists mostly of nitrobenzene, the second fraction being technical grade o-nitrotoluene, setting point −9 °C. p-Nitrotoluene is now distilled off, still under vacuum, the column being by-passed (differential distillation via 'swan-neck'). The crude p-nitrotoluene is then slowly cooled in a controlled manner to 18 °C during 24 hr, the mother liquor being drained off from the crystalline p-isomer, setting point 53 °C. These mother liquors are redistilled to obtain further quantities of o- and p- and also the m-nitrotoluene present. So far as the dye industry is concerned p-nitrotoluene is the important isomer, being a source of p-toluidine and, ultimately, of diamino-stilbenedisulphonic acid, important as an intermediate for fluorescent brightening agents. Both o- and p-nitrotoluenes give mainly 2,4-dinitrotoluene on further nitration.

Naphthalene. High-grade technical naphthalene on nitration with mixed acid, corresponding to HNO_3, 28%; H_2O, 15%; H_2SO_4, 57% by weight, at a temperature of 35–50 °C gives a good yield of 1-nitronaphthalene, setting point 57 °C; this is the main source of 1-naphthylamine and its derivatives. Although present to the extent of 5% in the 1-nitronaphthalene prepared above, 2-nitronaphthalene cannot be manufactured satisfactorily by nitration; its derivatives are made by indirect means.

The further nitration of 1-nitronaphthalene gives a mixture of 1,5- and 1,8-dinitronaphthalenes, then 1,4,5,-trinitronaphthalene together with the 1,3,8 derivative and finally tetranitro derivatives.

Amines. The nitration of aromatic amines has its difficulties in that the amino group is very vulnerable to the oxidizing action of nitric acid. Accordingly it is customary to 'block' the amino group by acetylation, the formation of a p-toluene-sulphonyl derivative or by other means. Thus acetanilide gives the p-nitro derivative which may be hydrolysed to p-nitroaniline though it should be noted that the ammonolysis of 4-chloronitrobenzene is an alternative route of technical importance.

p-Toluidine. N–acetyl-p-toluidine can be smoothly nitrated, and the product hydrolysed to give 4-amino-3-nitrotoluene, a most important intermediate used as a diazo component in the preparation of pigments. It is usually known as m-nitro-p-toluidine (MNPT).

A particularly neat method of blocking two vulnerable groups is provided by the action of phosgene on 2-aminophenol to give the benzoxazole which can then be nitrated. On hydrolysis 2-amino-5-nitrophenol is obtained.

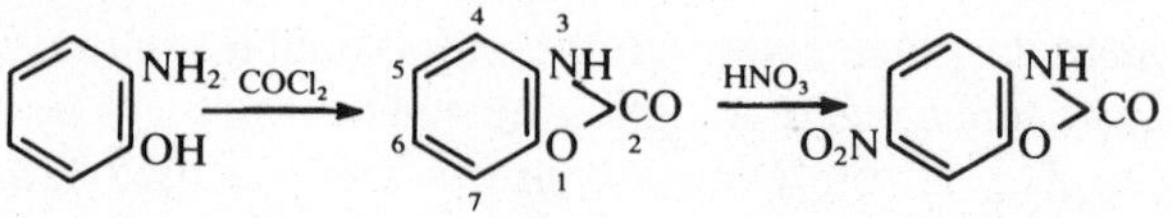

2-aminophenol   benzoxazole   6-nitrobenzoxazole   **Fig. 3.2**

o-Anisidine may be nitrated directly. The free base is added to a slight excess of 15% nitric acid to form the nitrate which separates as easily filtered crystals. The filter-cake is transferred to a centrifuge where most of the mother liquor is removed. The product containing not more than 4% by weight of mother liquor is added to stirred 95% sulphuric acid as 0–5 °C.

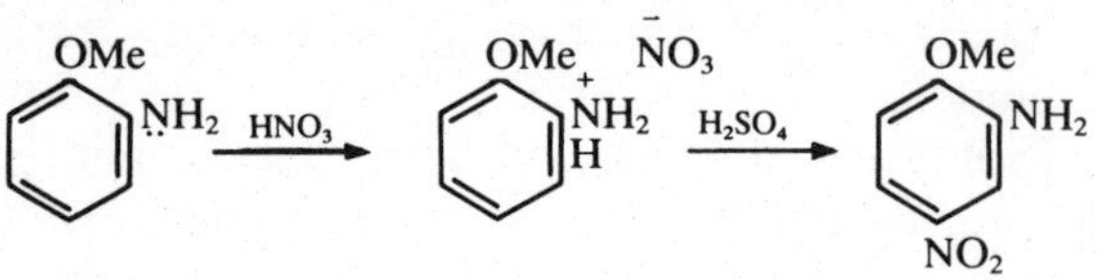

(1)   **Fig. 3.3**

The product 2-amino-1-methoxy-4-nitrobenzene (1), which is obtained in 82% yield, is used for azo dyes and as an azoic diazo component (see Table 3.4, p. 67).

When N-acetyl-*o*-anisidine is nitrated at 25 °C with mixed acid (30% sulphuric acid, 12% nitric acid by weight) and the product hydrolysed with dilute sulphuric acid two nitro compounds are formed,

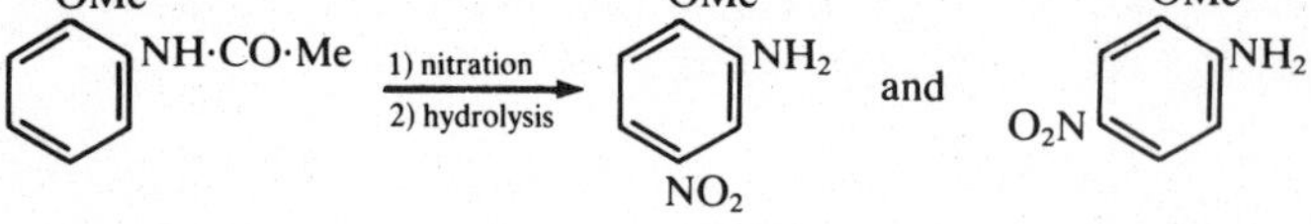

(1)   (2)   **Fig. 3.4**

The result of the competing *para*-directing effects of methoxy- and acetylamino-groups. The isomers are relatively easily separated, as follows.

2-Amino-1-methoxy-4-nitrobenzene (1) is more basic than 2-amino-1-methoxy-5-nitrobenzene (2) since in (2) the electron-withdrawing nitro group affects the *p*-amino group (see p. 74), but is relatively without influence on the *m*-amino group in (1). In consequence (1) remains in solution in the acid hydrolysis liquors from whence it is recovered as the sparingly soluble salt of naphthalene-1,5-disulphonic acid, which gives the free base with alkali. The isomer (2) separates during the acid hydrolysis and is purified by recrystallization from water. It is also used for azo dyes and as an azoic diazo component (see Table 3.4).

Chloro derivatives. The nitration of chlorobenzene, dichlorobenzenes and chlorotoluenes leads to substances of considerable value in dye chemistry in that nitro groups in positions 2- and 4- relative to chlorine have an activating effect. Further details of the nucleophilic reactions of 'hydrolysis' and 'ammonolysis' of chloronitro compounds will be dealt with later in this chapter. At this point only the orientation of the nitro compounds and their separation will be considered.

When chlorobenzene is nitrated with a mixed acid of composition HNO_3, 35; H_2O, 12; H_2SO_4, 53, a product consisting of a mixture of 35% o-chloronitrobenzene (setting point 32 °C) and 65% p-chloronitrobenzene (setting point 82 °C) is obtained. By somewhat tedious processes of vacuum fractional distillation and of crystallization the two isomers can be separated as reasonably high quality technical products and are available commercially. When either isomer or the mononitration mixture is further nitrated, 2,4-dinitrochlorobenzene, in which the chlorine atom is highly reactive, is obtained. This important intermediate has a number of uses among them the synthesis of certain nitro dyes (q.v.) used to disperse dyes. The nitration of

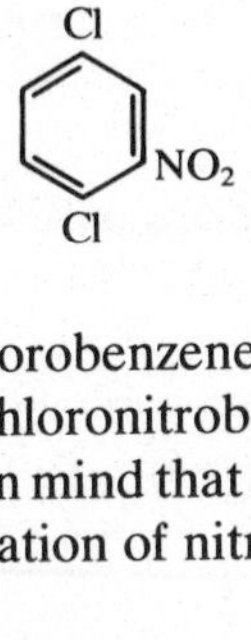

Fig. 3.5

p-dichlorobenzene leads to only one possible mono-nitro compound, viz. 2,5-dichloronitrobenzene which is a source of 2,5-dichloroaniline. It should be borne in mind that other important chloronitro compounds are obtained by the chlorination of nitro compounds (see Halogenation, below).

Halogenation

Chlorination

The replacement of nuclear hydrogen by chlorine in the benzene series is mostly done directly using gaseous chlorine. Chloro derivatives of naphthalene, on the other hand, are not manufactured this way but by some less direct route, e.g. by a Sandmeyer or Gattermann reaction.

The chlorination of benzene is accomplished by passing chlorine through well-stirred benzene containing ferric chloride or finely divided iron to act as a halogen carrier. The optimum temperature is 30 °C. Hydrogen chloride is liberated and, after being scrubbed with chlorobenzene to remove entrained organic material, is absorbed in towers, the aqueous acid being recovered for use elsewhere in the factory. The chlorobenzene is purified by fractional distillation, a process from which p-dichlorobenzene and the less valuable o-dichlorobenzene may also be recovered. The proportion of dichloro compounds to monochlorobenzene can be increased to 8% or more by prolonged chlorination; the ratio of o : p is 1 : 2.

The chlorination of toluene is carried out in a similar manner, using anhydrous ferric chloride as carrier, equal quantities of o- and p-chlorotoluenes being produced. These isomers, both liquids, differ in boiling point by 3 °C, and are therefore separable by fractional distillation. p-Nitrotoluene may be chlorinated at 55–60 °C as follows:

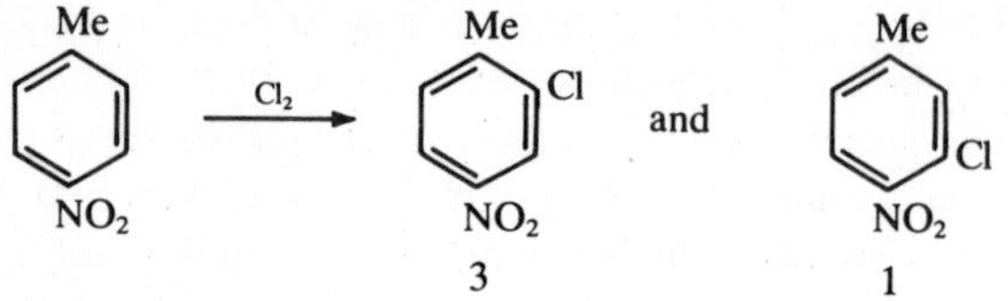

Fig. 3.6

Side chain chlorination of toluene and suitable derivatives is usually carried out at or near the boiling point in the absence of a carrier. By this means benzyl chloride, used in the manufacture of ethylbenzylaniline and of dibenzylaniline for triarylmethane colours, benzal chloride and benzotrichloride can be obtained.

Chlorinating agents other than gaseous or liquid chlorine are used industrially in special cases.

Hypochlorite. When acetanilide is acted on by sodium hypochlorite in the presence of mineral acid, p-chloroacetanilide is formed and, through hydrolysis, p-chloroaniline results.

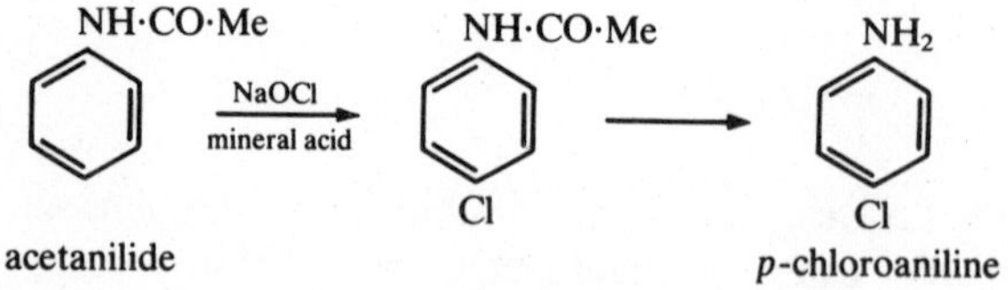

Fig. 3.7

Sulphuryl chloride. Nuclear chlorination can be brought about, e.g. with indanthrone to give dichloroindanthrone by the action of sulphuryl chloride in nitrobenzene. With the same reagent, aniline hydrochloride gives the 2,4,6-trichloroderivative. 2,4-Dichlorotoluene is formed when toluene is acted on by sulphuryl chloride in the presence of antimony trichloride.

Replacement of —SO_3H *by* —Cl. In the anthraquinone field use is made of the fact that the —SO_3H group may be replaced by —Cl through the action of hot concentrated hydrochloric acid and 10–15% aqueous sodium chlorate. Such a case is the preparation of 1,5-dichloroanthraquinone:

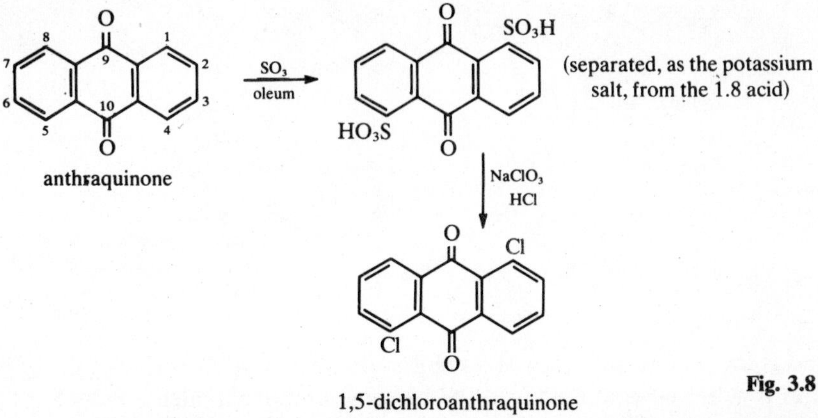

anthraquinone

(separated, as the potassium salt, from the 1.8 acid)

Fig. 3.8

1,5-dichloroanthraquinone

Replacement of —NH₂ *by* —Cl. This transformation is used rather rarely and then chiefly in the naphthalene field when a hydrochloric acid solution of the diazonium chloride is warmed with cuprous chloride (Sandmeyer) or with finely divided copper (Gattermann). In either case the overall result is

$$R \cdot \overset{+}{N_2} \overset{-}{Cl} \xrightarrow[Cu]{Cu_2Cl_2 \text{ or}} R \cdot Cl + N_2 \uparrow$$

Bromination

Bromination is usually carried out using liquid bromine and is most frequently employed in the anthraquinone series where the greater reactivity of a bromo compound compared with the corresponding chloro compound is advantageous. Two most important cases are 1-amino-4-bromo-2-methylanthraquinone (3) and 1-amino-4-bromoanthraquinone-2-sulphonic

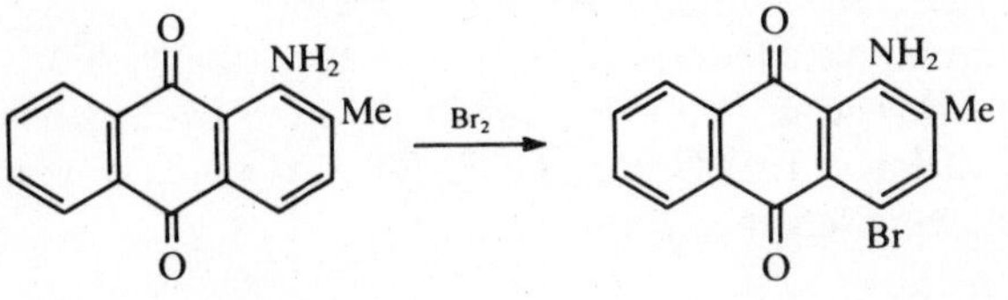

(3)

Fig. 3.9

acid, 'bromamine' acid (4). The intermediate (3) results from the action of bromine on an aqueous acid suspension of 1-amino-2-methylanthraquinone and is used in the manufacture of C.I. Acid Blue 23 (p. 122). Bromamine acid (4) is obtained by the following route:

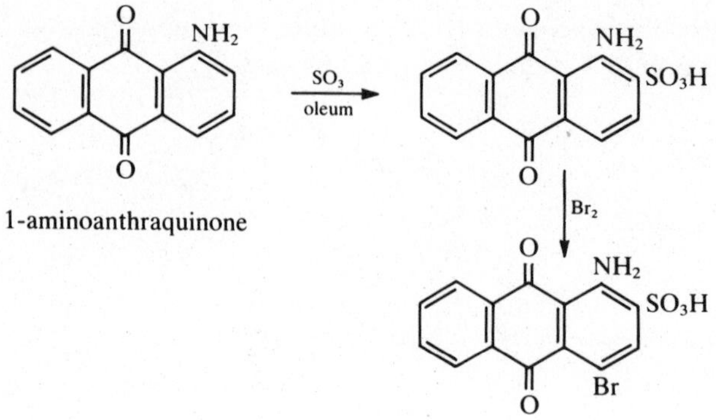

1-aminoanthraquinone

(4)   Fig. 3.10

and is the parent substance of a number of useful acid dyes (p. 121).

A few bromo compounds in the benzene and naphthalene series are produced from the diazonium compounds by Sandmeyer or Gattermann procedures.

In a few cases direct-bromination of dye molecules is carried out to deepen shade or to improve other properties, e.g. fluorescein is brominated to give the red dye Eosin (p. 165) and indigo is brominated to give 5,5′,7,7′-tetrabromoindigo (p. 144).

Fluorination

Hydrogen fluoride can be safely handled in steel plant and conveyed in steel pipes, providing that effective precautions against the entry of water are taken. As a result it is possible to introduce fluorine into the aromatic nucleus on the large scale by the addition of dry nitrite to a stirred, dry mixture of hydrogen fluoride and an amine hydrochloride.

$$R \cdot NH_2, HCl + HF + NaNO_2 \rightarrow NaCl + R \cdot F + N_2 + 2H_2O$$

Much more important in dye chemistry is the conversion of a trichloromethyl group to a trifluoromethyl group by the action of anhydrous hydrogen fluoride. Such a case is the synthesis of Fast Orange GGD Base (5) which is synthesized according to the following scheme:

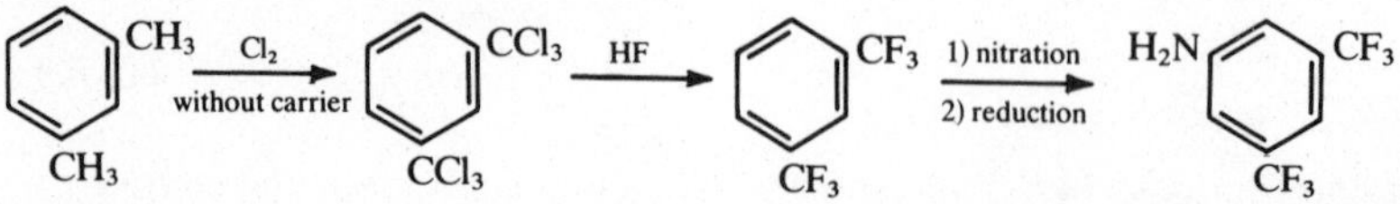

1-amino-3,5-bis-(trifluoromethyl)-benzene (Fast Orange GGD base)

(5)   Fig. 3.11

Sulphonation

The chief methods used in industry for introducing the sulpho group $-SO_3H$ into the aromatic nucleus are:

(a) By the direct action of concentrated sulphuric acid or of a solution of sulphur trioxide in sulphuric acid (oleum, usual strengths 20% and 65%, i.e. 20 and 65 parts by weight of free SO_3 in 100 parts respectively).

(b) By 'baking' aromatic amine sulphates.

Other, less frequently used methods are:

(c) The use of free SO_3 in an inert solvent such as nitrobenzene.

(d) The action of SO_3/pyridine addition complex.

(e) The action of chlorosulphonic acid.

(f) Nucleophilic attack by sulphite at positions occupied by active halogen, hydroxy groups, etc.

Most aromatic compounds can be sulphonated by the action of sulphuric acid or of oleum. Sulphonation is a reversible process and desulphonation, i.e. the replacement of a sulpho group by a hydrogen atom is an important process in the manufacture of compounds otherwise difficult or hazardous to synthesize, e.g. derivatives of the carcinogen, 2-naphthylamine (see later). Benzene itself can be monosulphonated by heating with sulphuric acid (100%, monohydrate) at 100 °C. If the solution is now cooled to 50 °C and run into 65% oleum, benzene-1,3-disulphonic acid is produced in good yield after 3 hr at 80 °C. The sulphonation mass is run into an ice–water mixture, neutralized with slaked lime or powdered limestone ('liming out') and the solution is filtered from calcium sulphate. To the filtrate is added sodium carbonate ('ashing out') until no more calcium carbonate is precipitated. After filtration the solution is evaporated to dryness and the disodium salt is used in resorcinol manufacture. The method of liming out and conversion to sodium salt is a general one and where possible the sodium salt is 'salted out' by the addition of sodium chloride, thus avoiding the need to evaporate.

Naphthalene. The sulphonation of naphthalene gives a mixture of 1- and 2-naphthalenesulphonic acids:

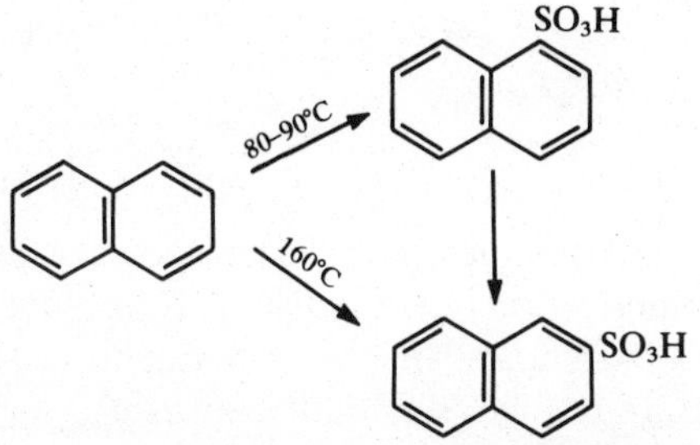

Fig. 3.12

At lower temperatures naphthalene-1-sulphonic acid predominates whereas at higher temperatures (up to 160 °C) the yield of the 2-acid approaches 85%. According to the I.G. Leverkusen process for naphthalene-2-sulphonic acid 96% sulphuric acid is added to molten naphthalene, initially at 110–125 °C, the temperature thereafter not being allowed to exceed 160 °C. Sodium sulphate solution is added, unchanged naphth•!ene is distilled off in steam and the sodium salt is isolated by the addition of sodium chloride. The sodium naphthalene-2-sulphonate is sufficiently pure to be used for the manufacture of 2-naphthol (below). It should be noted that 1-naphthol cannot be made satisfactorily from the naphthalene-1-sulphonic acid and is in fact made from 1-naphthylamine.

According to temperature and to concentration of SO_3, further sulphonation gives rise to di-, tri- and tetra-sulphonic acids, the orientation of which follows the Armstrong and Wynne rule which states that no two sulpho groups can occupy 'ortho' (1,2 or 2,3), 'para' (1,4) or 'peri' (1,8) positions. The important naphthalene-1,3,6-trisulphonic acid can be obtained directly from naphthalene and is used in the manufacture of Koch acid and H acid (see p. 232).

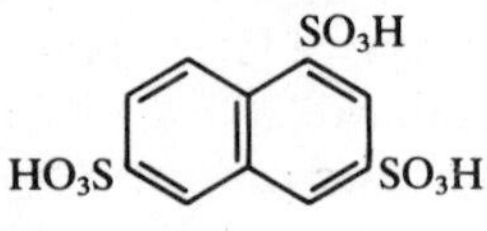

Fig. 3.13

2-Naphthol. The sulphonation of 2-naphthol gives rise to a variety of products according to temperature and proportion of sulphuric acid. If the sulphonation is carried out at −12 °C 2-hydroxynaphthalene-1-sulphonic acid (Oxy Tobias acid) is the product; at 20 °C 7-hydroxynaphthalene-1-sulphonic acid (Crocein acid) is the main product. The suggested mechanism is that the 2-sulphonic ester (6) undergoes rearrangement at low temperatures to give the 1-acid, migration occurring at higher temperatures as follows:

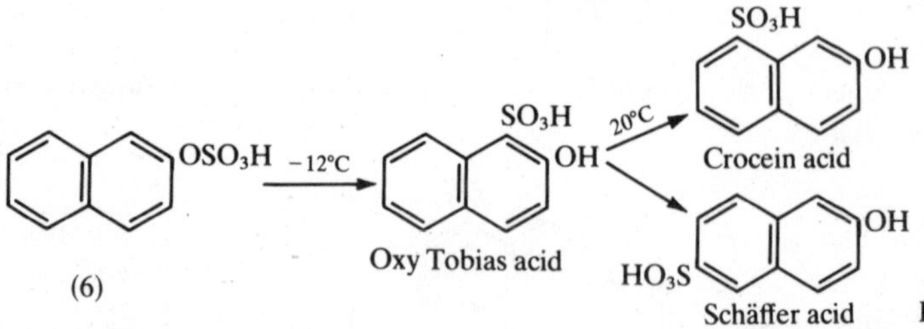

Fig. 3.14

Important disulphonic acids are also obtained from 2-naphthol (see Table 3.7, p. 69). An unusual method of sulphonation is that of Böniger, employed on the large scale for the manufacture of 1-amino-2-naphthol-4-sulphonic acid used in making C.I. Mordant Black 3. In Böniger's method 1-nitroso-2-naphthol is treated with sodium bisulphite at 18–20 °C. Sulphuric acid is added and the mixture is heated to 40–50 °C. The product crystallizes out and is filtered off. In its simplest form the reaction may be represented thus:

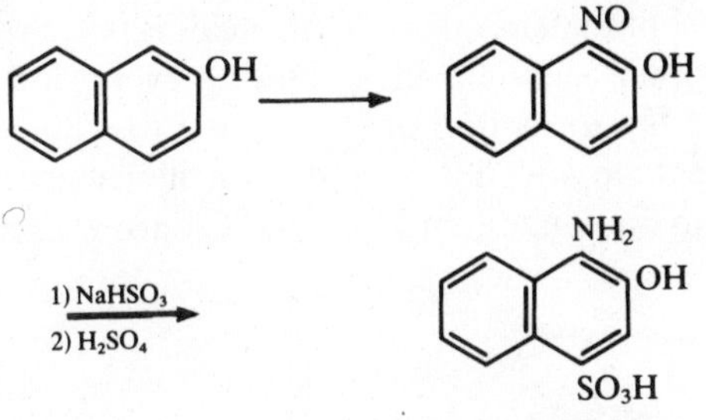

1-amino-2-naphthol-4-
sulphonic acid (7)

Fig. 3.15

The role of the sulphuric acid is doubtless to hydrolyse an intermediate, soluble bisulphite compound; the precise mechanism of the reaction is still obscure. It is worth noting that on diazotization (7) gives a particularly stable diazo-oxide (see p. 75), used for the manufacture of C.I. Mordant Black 3, and which may be nitrated to give the diazonium derivative of 1-amino-6-nitro-2-naphthol-4-sulphonic acid, a valuable intermediate for Chrome Black T (p. 94).

Anthraquinone. When an excess of anthraquinone is treated with oleum at 120–140 °C the product is mostly the 2-sulphonic acid and small quantities of the 2,6 and 2,7-disulphonic acids together with unchanged anthraquinone. After the hot, aqueous solution has been filtered from insoluble anthraquinone, sodium anthraquinone-2-sulphonate can be salted out, the disulphonic acids remaining in the filtrate. One recrystallization from water gives an almost pure product which is known in the dye industry as 'silver salt'.

The presence of mercuric salts in the sulphonation mixture influences orientation and causes the formation of anthraquinone-1-sulphonic acid; further sulphonation leads to a complex mixture of disulphonic acids chiefly 1,5 and 1,8 with lesser quantities of 1,6- and 1,7-isomers.

Sulphonation by baking. Amines may be converted into sulphonic acids by heating the dried sulphate in a vacuum when by rearrangement sulphonic groups enter the aromatic nucleus. Sulphanilic acid (8) is manufactured this

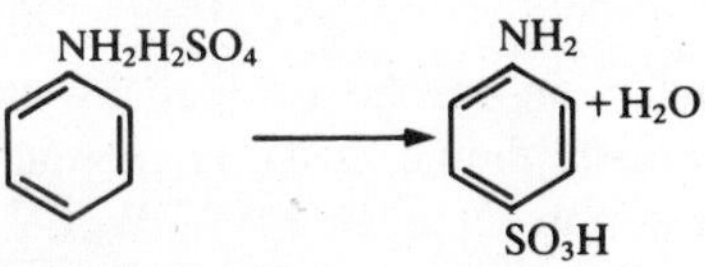

(8)

Fig. 3.16

way from aniline sulphate. The sulphonation mass is dissolved in caustic soda solution, chalk is added and the filtrate can then be used for diazotization in azo dye manufacture. Where necessary the sulphanilic acid can be isolated as a paste by acidifying the sodium salt solution.

Naphthionic acid, 1-aminonaphthalene-4-sulphonic acid, is prepared similarly by heating 1-naphthylamine sulphate in a rotating cylindrical baker, containing steel bars to avoid the formation of lumps, at 170–180 °C under vacuum. A former I.G. process employed a solvent, o-dichlorobenzene, the reaction being carried out at the boiling point 178–180 °C during 12 hr.

Desulphonation

The removal of a sulpho group and its replacement by a hydrogen atom is a useful device in synthesizing dye intermediates, and is also used in anthraquinone chemistry in dye manufacture proper. An interesting example in the benzene series is the desulphonation of 2-chloro-1-methylbenzene-4-sulphonic acid in super-heated steam at 150 °C to give pure o-chlorotoluene. The full synthesis is:

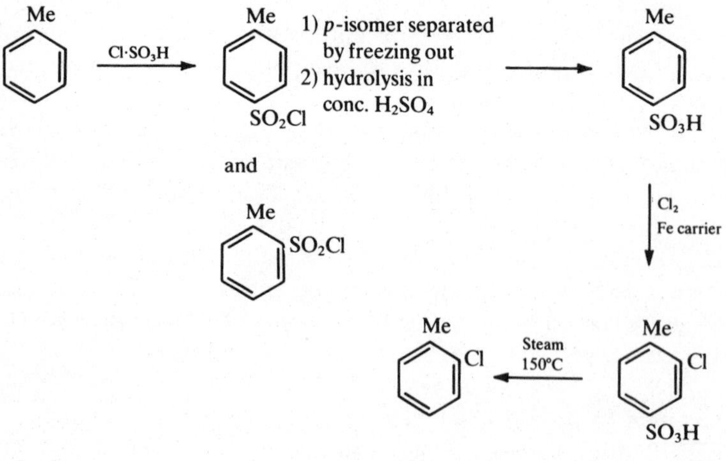

Fig. 3.17

The use of the carcinogen, 2-naphthylamine can be avoided by using the non-carcinogenic 2-aminonaphthalene-1-sulphonic acid (Tobias acid), followed by desulphonation, to give, for example, Naphthol AS-SW, C.I. 37565 (9):

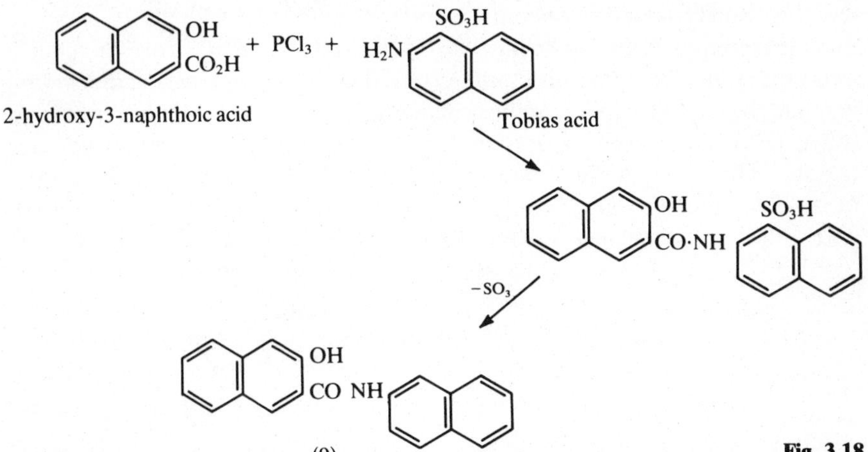

2-hydroxy-3-naphthoic acid

Tobias acid

(9)

Fig. 3.18

Any unchanged Tobias acid will be desulphonated to give 2-naphthylamine itself and this must be destroyed usually by extraction with solvent and diazotization, the products of the latter being harmless. The plant design must be such that the operators do not come into contact in any way with harmful products whether as solids, liquids, vapours or dusts.

Amination by reduction

The most widely used method of converting a nitro compound into an amine is the Béchamp method which uses iron (filings, 'pin-dust', borings, etc.) in water containing a small quantity of hydrochloric, formic or acetic acid. The reaction may be represented by the equation:

$$2R \cdot NO_2 + 5Fe + 4H_2O \rightarrow 2RNH_2 + Fe_3O_4 + 2Fe(OH)_3$$

In the case of the reduction of nitrobenzene to aniline low costs depend on the recovery of the 'black oxide' residues for use in inorganic pigment manufacture or as an absorbent for hydrogen sulphide, e.g. in the purification of coal gas. In the case of the simpler amines, aniline, o- and p-toluidines it is usual to separate the top layer of amine from the settled iron sludge by mechanical means, the amine being subsequently purified by distillation. The Béchamp method can also be used in reducing the nitro derivatives of sulphonic acids, a typical example being the manufacture of metanilic acid (11) and related substances. The starting point is nitrobenzene which is first sulphonated in oleum at 100–105 °C to give the m-sulphonic acid (10); the diluted mixture is neutralized with chalk and filtered from gypsum. At this stage the calcium salt can be converted with sodium carbonate into the sodium salt of *m*-nitrobenzenesulphonic acid which is widely used as a mild oxidizing agent in anthraquinone chemistry, in quinoline synthesis (Skraup), and as a levelling agent in the dyebath. In metanilic acid manufacture the solution of the calcium salt is reduced by the Béchamp method at the boil. The reduction liquor is made alkaline with caustic soda solution, filtered from iron sludge, the residue being discarded, the solution evaporated to 50% strength as sodium metanilate and either used as such as starting material in azo dye manufacture, or

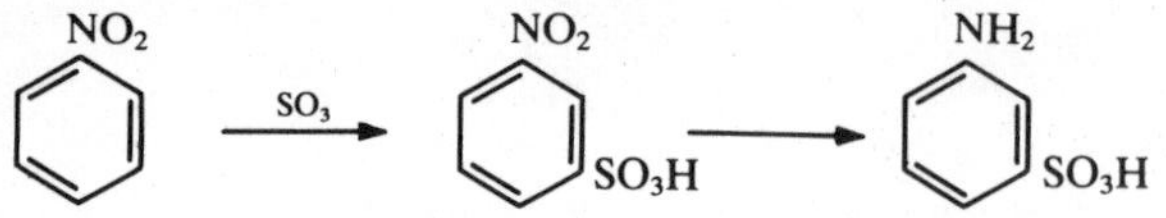

(10)   (11)   **Fig. 3.19**

precipitated as metanilic acid paste by acidification. The Béchamp method is also used in the naphthalene series, e.g. for the manufacture of 1-naphthylamine and of certain naphthylaminesulphonic acids.

Sulphide reductions

The reduction of nitro compounds can also be accomplished by the use of aqueous sodium sulphide (Na_2S), sodium hydrosulphide, (NaHS), or sodium polysulphide (Na_2S_x). Such reductions are usually easily carried out; the special advantage of the method is in bringing about partial reductions of dinitro compounds to nitroamino compounds. Perhaps the best known example is the reduction of *m*-dinitrobenzene to *m*-nitroaniline with aqueous NaHS at 95 °C. The reaction is facilitated by the addition of magnesium sulphate which, according to Fierz David,[9] ensures that the solution does not become more than weakly alkaline. Other examples are the reduction of picric to picramic acid:

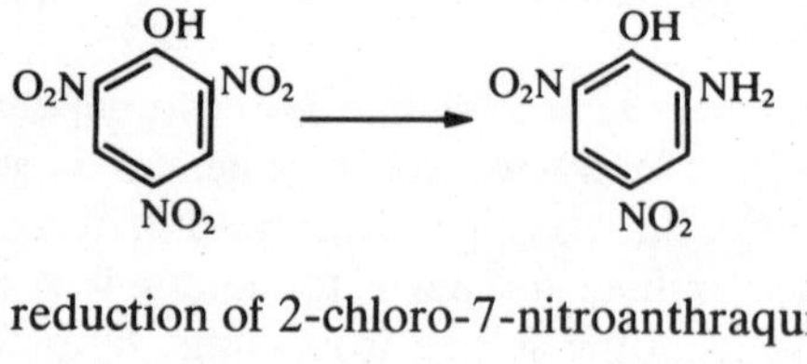

Fig. 3.20

and the reduction of 2-chloro-7-nitroanthraquinone, the chlorine atom being

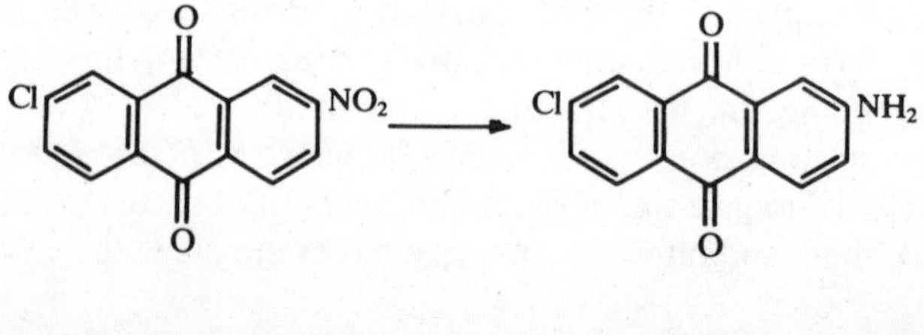

Fig. 3.21

unattacked. Nitroso compounds may also be reduced to amines by sulphide reduction, e.g.

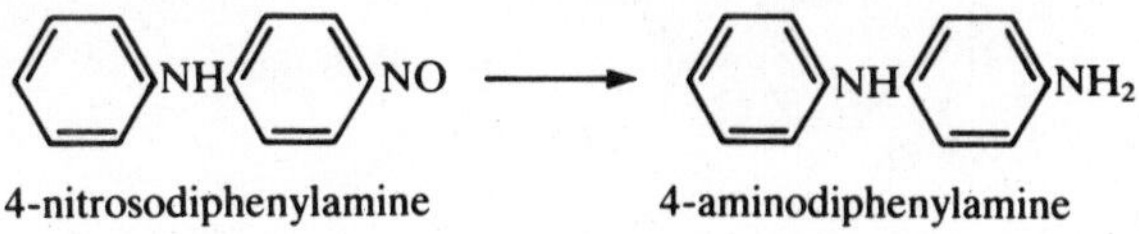

4-nitrosodiphenylamine   4-aminodiphenylamine   **Fig. 3.22**

p-Aminodimethylaniline can similarly be obtained from the p-nitroso compound and is used in the manufacture of Methylene Blue, C.I. Basic Blue 9.

Benzidine rearrangement

A process of fundamental importance in dye chemistry is the process of producing 4,4′-diaminobiphenyl derivatives by the alkaline reduction of the appropriate nitro compounds to the hydrazo compounds by the action of zinc and caustic soda solution. The hydrazo compound is then caused to undergo the benzidine rearrangement by treatment with 15% hydrochloric acid.

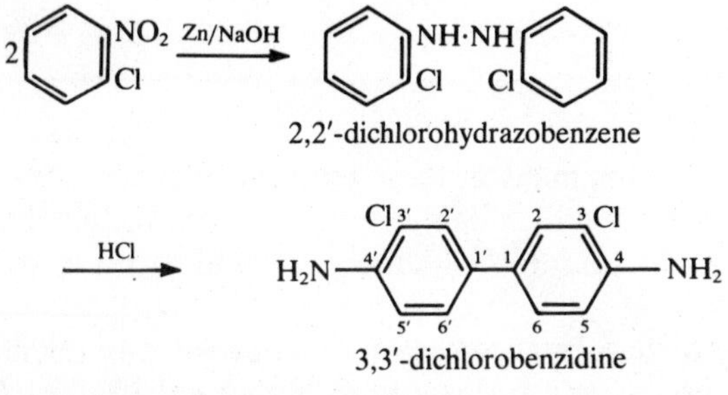

2,2′-dichlorohydrazobenzene

3,3′-dichlorobenzidine   **Fig. 3.23**

A great deal of work has been done on the mechanism of the rearrangement notably by Ingold and his school. While a theoretical treatment of the reaction is beyond the scope of this book the reader is referred to the definitive paper by Ingold and co-workers and to the account by Sykes.[45] The reaction is a general one and serves for the manufacture of a number of substituted benzidines that are used as tetrazo components in the manufacture of dyes and pigments. Some of the more important benzidine derivatives are given in Table 3.1.

On the plant scale the zinc dust is usually mixed with a little iron borings or pin dust to initiate the reduction to the hydrazo compound. This step may also be carried out using:

1. Iron powder and caustic soda solution, i.e. in the absence of zinc dust.
2. Electrolytic reduction in presence of alkali.
3. Formaldehyde or glucose, also under alkaline conditions.

Table 3.1 Nitro compounds and derived benzidine compounds

Parent nitro compound	Product	Name
o-Nitrotoluene	H_2N ⟨ring⟩–⟨ring⟩ NH_2 (Me, Me)	o-Tolidine
o-Chloronitrobenzene	H_2N ⟨ring⟩–⟨ring⟩ NH_2 (Cl, Cl)	3,3′-Dichlorobenzidine
2-Nitroanisole (o-methoxynitrobenzene)	H_2N ⟨ring⟩–⟨ring⟩ NH_2 (MeO, OMe)	o-Dianisidine
2,5-Dichloronitrobenzene	Cl, Cl H_2N ⟨ring⟩–⟨ring⟩ NH_2 (Cl, Cl)	2,5,2′,5′-Tetra chlorobenzidine
3-Nitrobenzenesulphonic acid	H_2N ⟨ring⟩–⟨ring⟩ NH_2 (SO_3H HO_3S)	2,2′-Benzidinedisulphonic acid

Solvent naphtha is employed in many of these rearrangements to dissolve the hydrazo compound, the solution then being separated from the alkaline layer and treated separately with cold 30% hydrochloric acid to bring about the rearrangement.

Benzidine is a highly toxic substance known to be a source of papilloma of the bladder[46] and its use in any form is now prohibited by law. Certain derivatives, designated 'controlled substances', such as o-tolidine and the other substances listed above may be manufactured provided that certain safeguards are rigidly observed. Modern plant is therefore designed to prevent all contact between this substance and the workers engaged in its manufacture since the most frequent and dangerous method of absorption is through the skin. Thus totally enclosed plant is employed throughout the process. That is to say the separation of liquids, transfer to other vessels, filtration and discharge of filters are all done by remote control.

Amination by ammonolysis

Aniline is no longer manufactured exclusively by reduction of nitrobenzene. In the Dow process monochlorobenzene is heated with 25% aqueous ammonia under pressure at 240 °C in the presence of catalytic quantities of copper oxide to give aniline, together with a small amount of phenol which can be removed by washing with caustic soda solution. With 2- and 4-chloronitrobenzene and especially 2,4-dinitrochlorobenzene the activated chlorine atom readily undergoes ammonolysis under pressure with aqueous ammonia and use is made of this fact in the manufacture of the appropriate amines.

Replacement of $-SO_3H$

When anthraquinone-1-sulphonic acid is heated with aqueous ammonia (24%), in the presence of sodium 3-nitrobenzenesulphonate as oxidizing agent, in an autoclave at 170-175 °C and a pressure of 24–27 atm a 95% yield of 1-aminoanthraquinone is obtained. 2-Aminoanthraquinone is obtained in similar yield when the 2-sulphonic acid is heated with ammonia and arsenic acid to 200 °C at a pressure of 40 atm.

Replacement of $-OH$

Halcon process. Phenol may be directly converted into aniline by treating with ammonia under a pressure of 15–16 atm, temperature ca. 385 °C, in the presence of a silica-alumina catalyst (Belgian P. 740 758, Halcon International Inc.).

Bucherer reaction. When a naphthol is heated under pressure at 100–150 °C with an aqueous solution of ammonium sulphite and excess aqueous ammonia, smooth replacement of the $-OH$ group by $-NH_2$ takes place. The reaction has only limited application in the benzene series, but is of outstanding importance in naphthalene chemistry. The Bucherer reaction is reversible and can in consequence be used for the replacement of aromatic amino groups by hydroxy groups, in the naphthalene series. The reaction may be represented as follows:

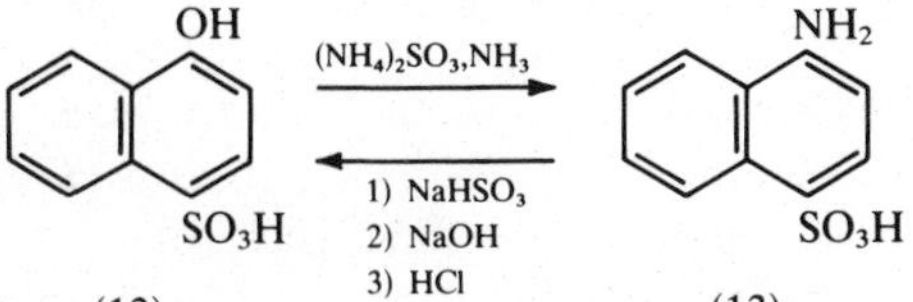

Fig. 3.24

in which 1-naphthol-4-sulphonic acid, Nevile and Winther's acid (12) is converted into 1-aminonaphthalene-4-sulphonic acid, naphthionic acid (13) and vice versa. On the industrial scale Nevile and Winther's acid is manufactured from naphthionic acid by the Bucherer reaction. Naphthionic acid is exclusively made by baking the sulphate of 1-naphthylamine (see p. 46).

According to Rieche and Seeboth (1960) the action of sodium bisulphite on (12) gives rise to 1-tetralone-3,4-disulphonic acid (14) which on treatment with ammonia gives the ketimine (15) the action of acid on which gives naphthionic acid. The various equilibria are summarized in the following scheme:

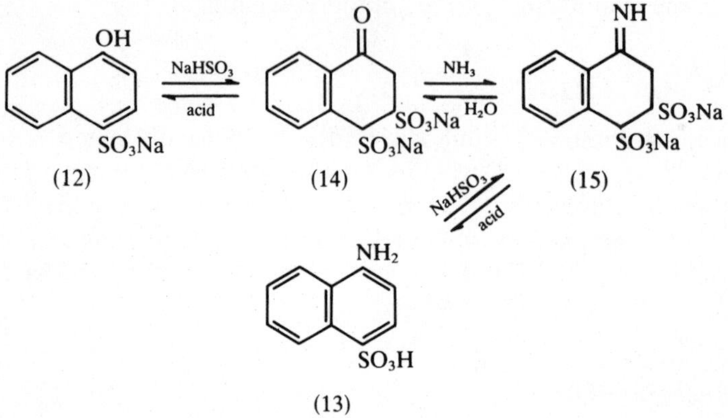

Fig. 3.25

The rate-determining step is considered to be the conversion of the tetralonesulphonic acid to the tetraloneimine-sulphonic acid or vice versa. Supporting evidence for the 'tetralone' intermediate has been obtained from infra red spectral data. 2-Naphthol similarly gives 2-tetralone-4-sulphonic acid (16) which is converted to the imine by ammonia and finally to 2-naphthylamine by acid.

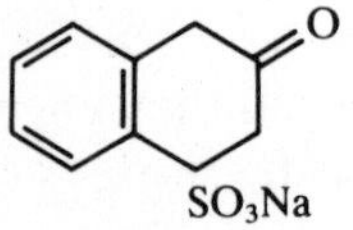

Fig. 3.26

2-Naphthylamine (β-naphthylamine) was manufactured for many years by the Bucherer reaction from 2-naphthol but, following its recognition as a dangerous carcinogen giving rise to papilloma of the bladder in those exposed to the compound,[46] its manufacture has been discontinued in Switzerland since 1938, in Great Britain since 1952. It is no longer manufactured in Germany and Italy and manufacture has largely been abandoned in the United States and Japan. Several useful intermediates were formerly obtained from 2-naphthylamine, but synthetic routes have now been devised which obviate the use of this compound. Two examples are Amino J acid (17) and Amino G acid (18), important azo dye intermediates, both formerly made directly from

2-naphthylamine by sulphonation and separation of isomers and now man-ufactured as follows: ·

Amino J acid. 2-Naphthol is sulphonated to give oxy Tobias acid (see p. 44) and converted into Tobias acid by the Bucherer reaction. The product is sulphonated to give 2-aminonaphthalene-1,5,7-trisulphonic acid (19) which on desulphonation gives 6-aminonaphthalene-1,3-disulphonic acid, Amino J acid (17).

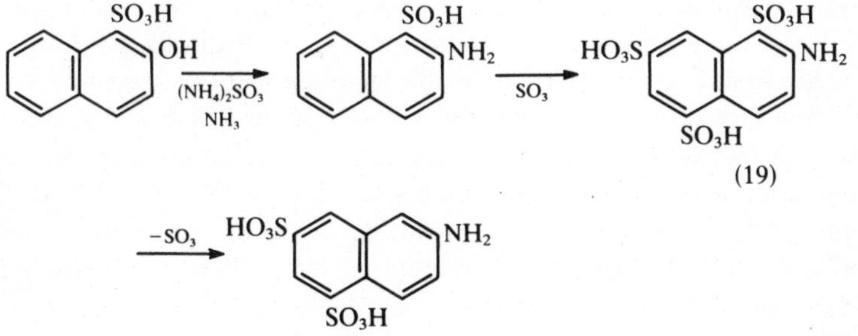

(19)

(17)   Fig. 3.27

Amino G acid. 2-Naphthol is sulphonated at a higher temperature to give 2-naphthol-6,8-disulphonic acid (20), which on amination by the Bucherer reaction leads to 7-aminonaphthalene-1,3-disulphonic acid, Amino G acid (18).

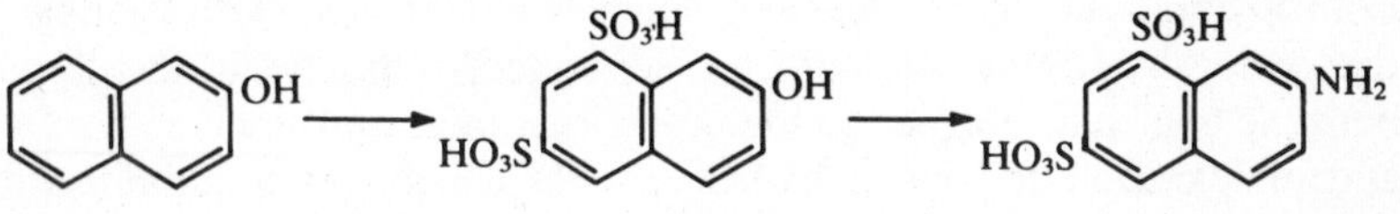

(20)   (18)

Fig. 3.28

2-Aminonaphthalene-1-sulphonic acid (Tobias acid) is manufactured by the following method. The reaction vessel, usually a cast-steel autoclave working pressure 15–20 atm, is charged with aqueous ammonia, sulphur dioxide gas is passed in to form ammonium sulphite, then more ammonia is added followed by 2-naphthol-1-sulphonic acid in the form of a wet filter-cake. The autoclave is then sealed off and the charge heated to 150 °C, the pressure reaching 8–10 atm. After 36 hr the charge is blown to a suspension of calcium carbonate and the evolved ammonia absorbed in water for use in the next batch. The hot charge is now filtered and the filtrate acidified with hydrochloric acid to precipitate the Tobias acid. The product is filtered, washed acid-free and dried on trays in a hot-air circulation stove at 70 °C. The yield is 95% of the theoretical. The product contains up to 0.5% of 2-naphthylamine and it is necessary to take the fullest precautions, face-masks and self-contained breathing apparatus, to prevent contact between operator and dust or solid product.

The introduction of hydroxy groups

Aromatic hydroxy compounds find wide application as coupling components in the manufacture of azo dyes. The simplest of such hydroxy compounds is phenol, which in addition to being employed in a large number of azo dyes is used in huge quantities in the plastics industry. Accordingly great efforts have been made to devise processes to synthesize phenol at the lowest possible cost. In the Dow process chlorobenzene is heated with excess aqueous caustic soda to 320–340 °C, the pressure reaching 240 atm. In the 'cumene' synthesis, which is a development from the petroleum chemical industry and is the chief source of phenol at the present time, the 'cracker' products benzene and propylene are caused to react in the presence of aluminium chloride to give cumene.

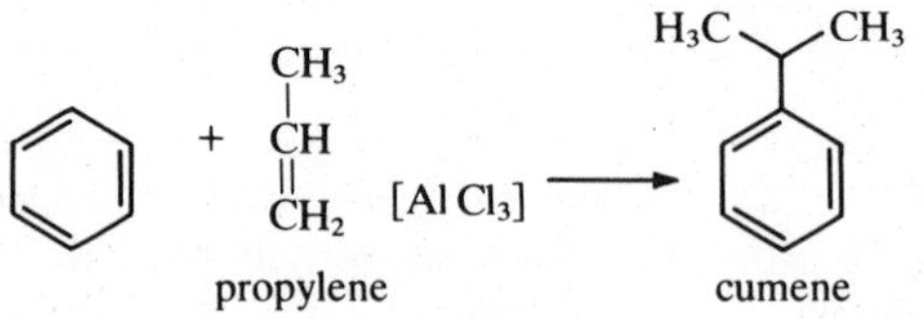

propylene   cumene   **Fig. 3.29**

An excess of benzene is employed to reduce the formation of di-isopropylbenzene, the presence of which would interfere with the next stage of the synthesis. High-grade cumene, separated by fractional distillation from benzene (which is returned to the process), is then emulsified with dilute alkali and air-oxidized to give a hydroperoxide which, on treatment with acid, decomposes into acetone and phenol. The mechanism of the reaction is thought to be as follows:[45]

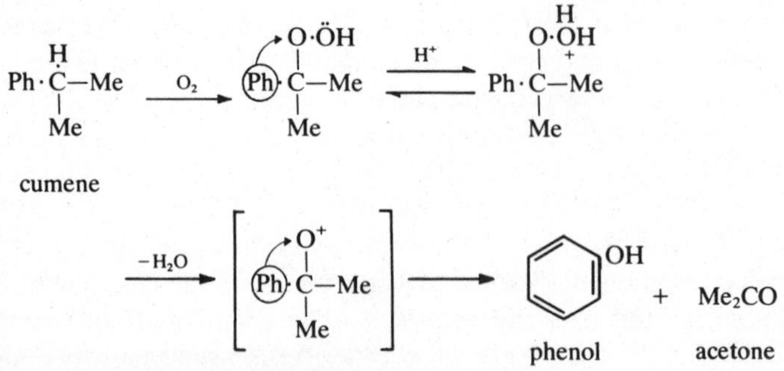

cumene

(Ph represents phenyl, C_6H_5-
Me represents methyl, CH_3-)   **Fig. 3.30**

Alkali fusion. What may be termed the classical method of introducing —OH groups into aromatic nuclei is by fusing the sodium salt of a sulphonic acid with potassium or sodium hydroxide or a mixture of the two. Thus sodium benzene-sulphonate gives sodium phenate from which phenol can be obtained by liberating with an acid:

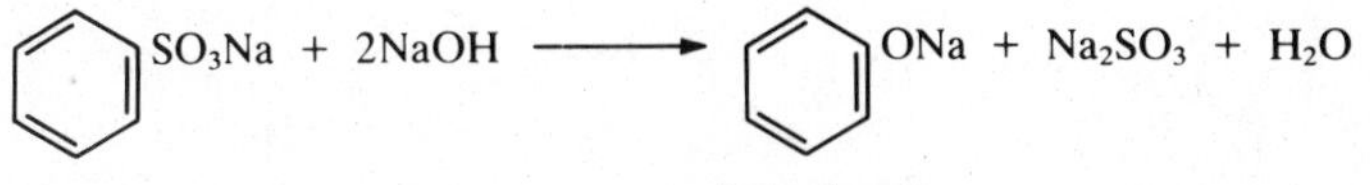

$$\text{C}_6\text{H}_5\text{SO}_3\text{Na} + 2\text{NaOH} \longrightarrow \text{C}_6\text{H}_5\text{ONa} + \text{Na}_2\text{SO}_3 + \text{H}_2\text{O}$$

sodium phenate   **Fig. 3.31**

and sodium naphthalene-2-sulphonate gives finally 2-naphthol. It should be noted that 1-naphthol is prepared by other means. The method is used extensively in the naphthalene series, an important example being the conversion of Koch acid into H acid by heating with 50% sodium hydroxide liquor to a

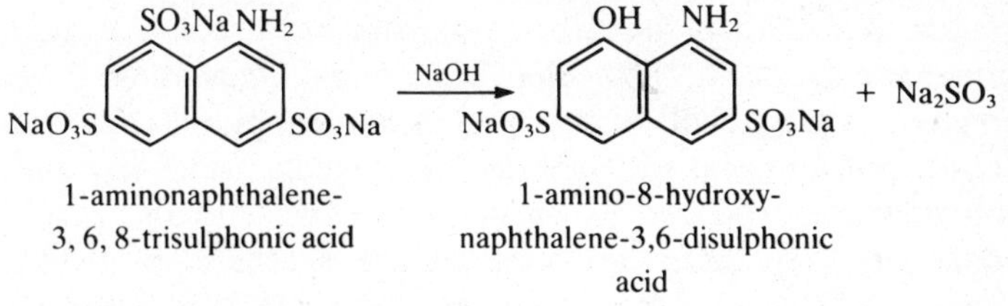

1-aminonaphthalene-
3, 6, 8-trisulphonic acid

1-amino-8-hydroxy-
naphthalene-3,6-disulphonic
acid

Koch acid   H acid   **Fig. 3.32**

temperature of 178 °C and a pressure of 5–6 atm. Substituted *m*-aminophenols are produced by this means, a typical route being

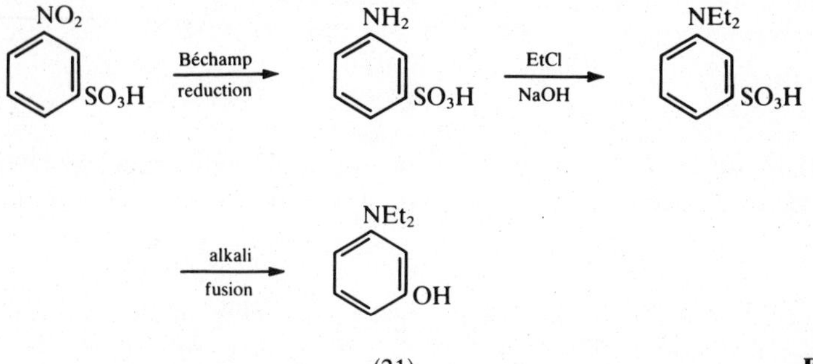

(21)   **Fig. 3.33**

m-Diethylaminophenol (21) is used in the manufacture of C.I. Acid Red 52 and of certain fluorescent brightening agents.

Hydrolysis of chloro compounds. Aromatic chloro compounds in which the chlorine atom is activated by *o*- or *p*-nitro groups are comparatively readily

56 INTERMEDIATES

hydrolysed by heating with caustic soda solution under pressure. *p*-Nitrophenol may be made in this manner from *p*-chloronitrobenzene, the

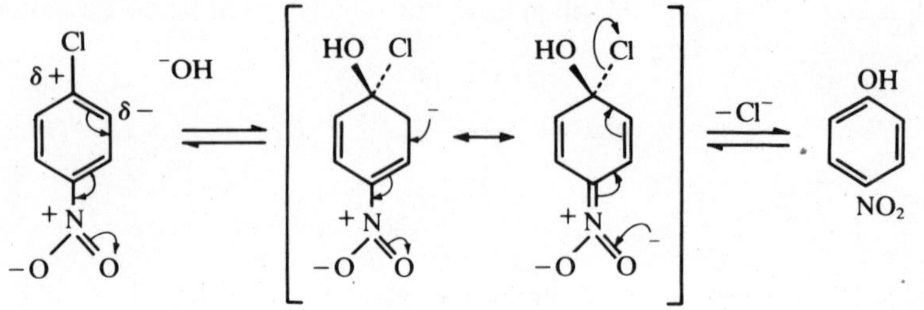

(22)   **Fig. 3.34**

reaction being one of nucleophilic attack by ⁻OH. The electron-withdrawing nitro group invites attack at the carbon atom attached to chlorine and stabilizes the intermediate species (22) by delocalization making possible the expulsion of Cl⁻ to give *p*-nitrophenol. A similar mechanism applies to the hydrolysis of *o*-chloronitrobenzene and of 1-chloro-2,4-dinitrobenzene. By such means *o*-nitrophenols are produced which can be reduced to the corresponding *o*-aminophenols. The latter are used in the synthesis of the important chromium and cobalt complexes of *o,o'*-dihydroxy azo dyes. Typical examples are the hydrolysis and reduction of *o*-chloronitrobenzene to give *o*-aminophenol (23):

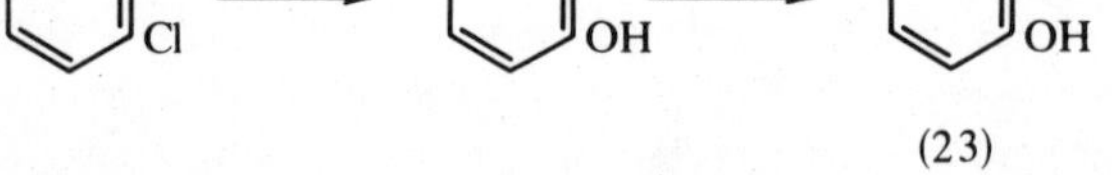

(23)   **Fig. 3.35**

and the hydrolysis and partial reduction of 2,4-dinitrochlorobenzene-6-sulphonic acid to the corresponding aminophenol (24):

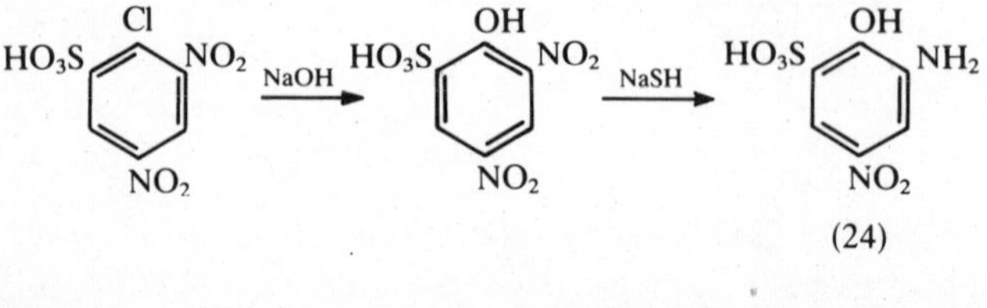

(24)   **Fig. 3.36**

Replacement of —NH₂ *by* —OH. 1-Naphthol (α-naphthol), is manufactured by hydrolysis of 1-naphthylamine under 10–15 atm pressure with 10% sulphuric acid, the product being distilled in vacuum to give a 95% yield of

1-naphthol. As previously noted the Bucherer reaction can be employed to produce hydroxy compounds from amino compounds, and a good example is Nevile and Winther's acid which is obtained in 80% yield from naphthionic acid (1-aminonaphthalene-4-sulphonic acid, p. 46) by heating with aqueous sodium bisulphite under reflux during 24 hr, then hydrolysing the product by the addition of caustic soda liquor and heating until no more ammonia is evolved. The solution gives a precipitate of 1-naphthol-4-sulphonic acid on acidifying with hydrochloric acid. The intermediate is valuable in azo chemistry as a coupling component.

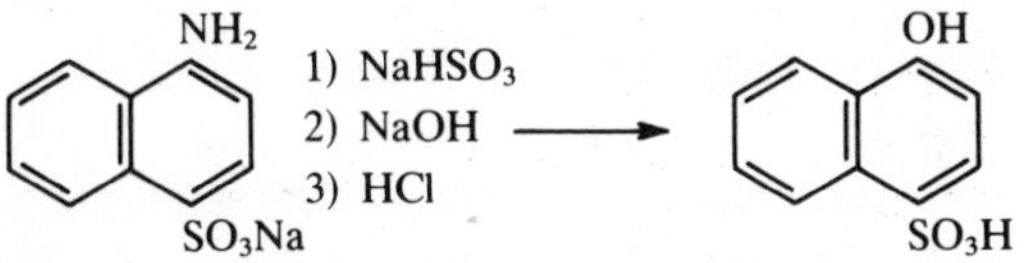

Fig. 3.37

Alkylation of amines

The replacement of hydrogen in amines by alkyl groups is a process of some importance in dye chemistry. Large quantities of mono- and di-alkylanilines are manufactured annually for use in the organic chemical industry. The usual alkylating agents are methanol, ethanol, methyl and ethyl chlorides, dimethyl and diethyl sulphates. N,N-Dimethylaniline is probably the most important of the alkylanilines and is made by heating high-grade aniline with an excess of methanol, in the presence of a small quantity of phosphorus trichloride, in chromium–molybdenum alloy steel autoclaves at temperatures lying between 270–280 °C and pressures of 70–110 atm. The process is interrupted after 7 hr to allow the water formed in the reaction to be distilled out. More methanol and a similar quantity of phosphorus trichloride to the original are charged and the autoclave is heated to 250–260 °C and 70–90 atm. After a further heating period the pressure is released and the small quantity of acid present is

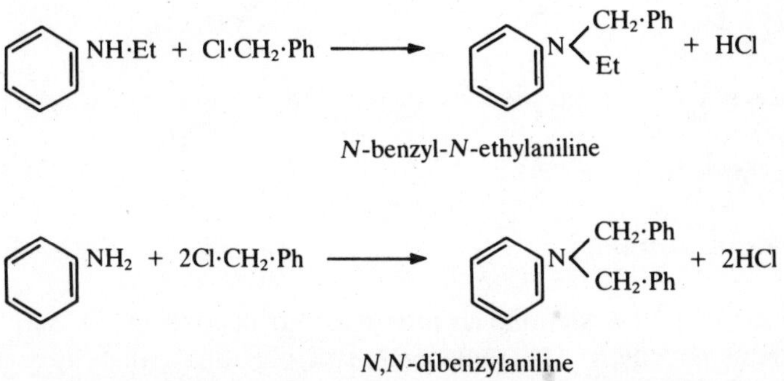

N-benzyl-N-ethylaniline

N,N-dibenzylaniline

Fig. 3.38

neutralized with caustic soda solution. The separated oil consists of 99.5–99.7% N,N-dimethylaniline and is further refined by either steam distillation or distillation in a vacuum. N-Methylaniline, N-ethylaniline and N,N-diethylaniline are manufactured by similar means, mono- and dialkylanilines being separated by fractional distillation. Two important aralkylanilines, N-benzyl-N-ethyl-aniline and N,N-dibenzylaniline are obtained by the action of benzyl chloride on N-ethylaniline and aniline respectively. The hydrochloric acid liberated is taken up *in situ* by sodium carbonate. It is not necessary to heat the reaction mixture under pressure and the reaction proceeds quite readily in boiling isopropyl alcohol.

Alkyl chlorides. Reference has already been made to the ethylation of metanilic acid using ethyl chloride (p. 55). N-Ethyl-1-naphthylamine is another case; 1-naphthylamine, ethyl chloride, calcium carbonate and a small proportion of water are heated together at 160–170 °C and 10 atm. The N-ethyl-1-naphthylamine is separated as the crystalline hydrochloride from which the product, an oil, is obtained by 'basifying' with alkali.

Other reagents. When ethyl ether and o-toluidine vapours are passed over heated alumina catalyst, N-ethyl-o-toluidine is formed in 91% yield according to the equation:

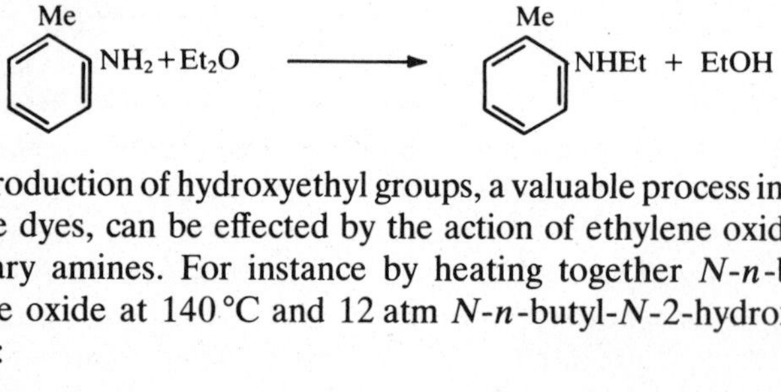

Fig. 3.39

The introduction of hydroxyethyl groups, a valuable process in the chemistry of disperse dyes, can be effected by the action of ethylene oxide on primary or secondary amines. For instance by heating together N-n-butylaniline and ethylene oxide at 140 °C and 12 atm N-n-butyl-N-2-hydroxyethylaniline is formed:

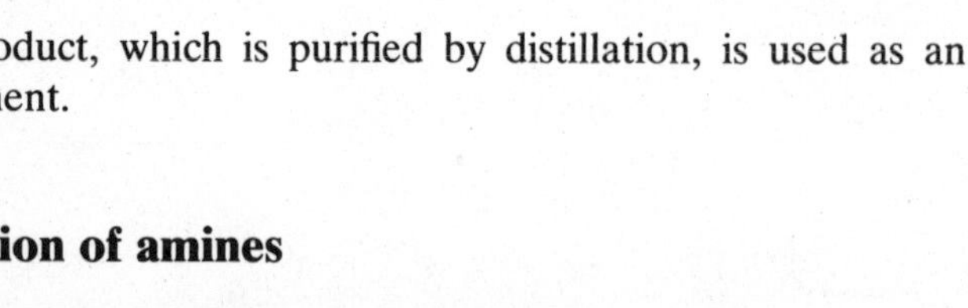

Fig. 3.40

The product, which is purified by distillation, is used as an azo coupling component.

Arylation of amines

The introduction of arylamino groups is often needed in the synthesis of intermediates and dyes. The replacement of phenolic groups is a common method, a typical example being the synthesis of 3-ethoxy-4'-methyldiphenylamine (25) used in making the triarylmethane dye C.I. Acid Violet 15, 43525 (p. 155) which is carried out as follows, starting from resorcinol:

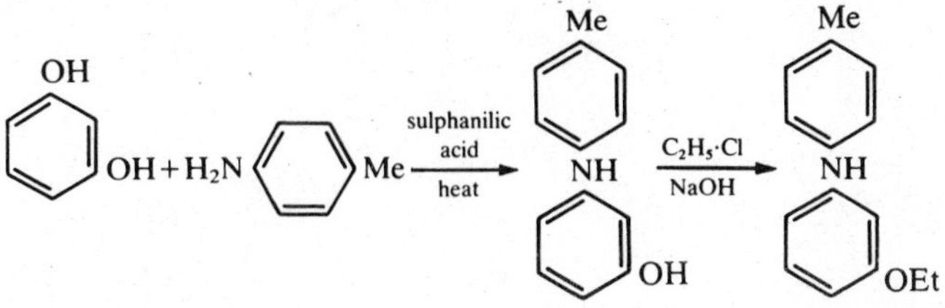

(25)   **Fig. 3.41**

A good example in the anthraquinone series is the synthesis of 1,4-di-*p*-tolylaminoanthraquinone (26) by the condensation of two molecules of *p*-toluidine with one of quinizarin (1,4-dihydroxyanthraquinone). In practice a

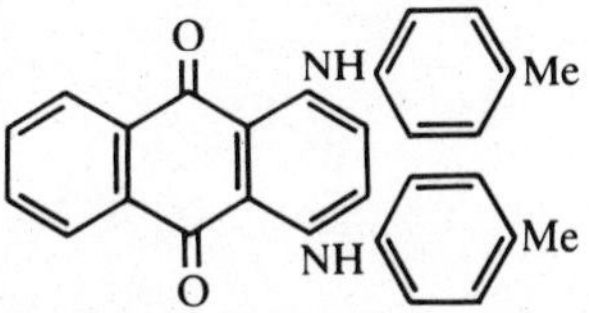

(26)

small quantity of zinc dust, which reduces part of the quinizarin to the leuco compound, is added to the heated mixture since leuco-quinizarin (27) condenses much more readily with *p*-toluidine than does quinizarin itself:

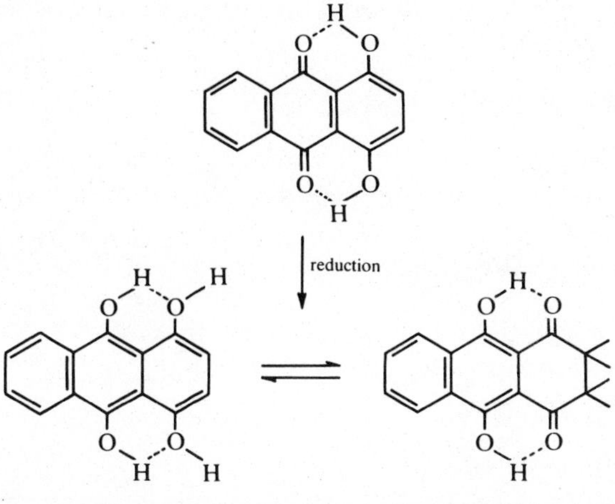

(27a)   (27b)

Fig. 3.42

(contd. overleaf)

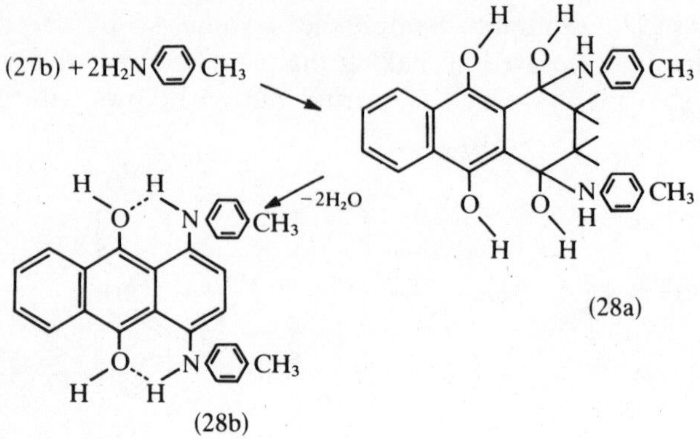

(28a)

(28b)

Once formed the leuco compound (28b) becomes oxidized by the excess of quinizarin present:

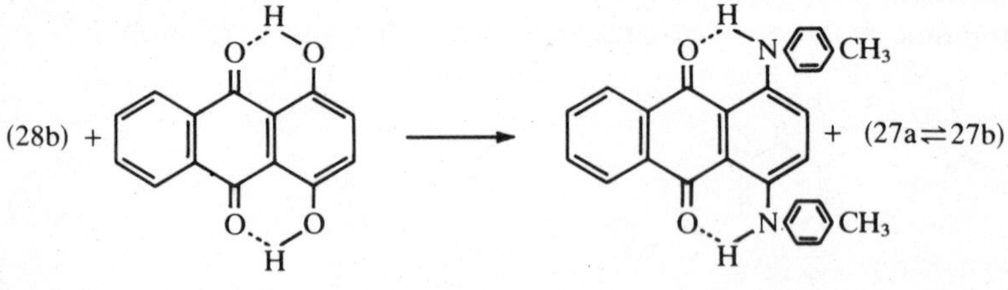

(29)   **Fig. 3.43**

and the process is repeated. The principle is applicable to the condensation of quinizarin with other primary amines, both aliphatic and aromatic. Improved yields are obtained by using a small proportion of separately prepared leuco-quinizarin as part of the quinizarin charge.

The replacement of bromine, by nucleophiles, is another widely used method of introducing arylamino groups:

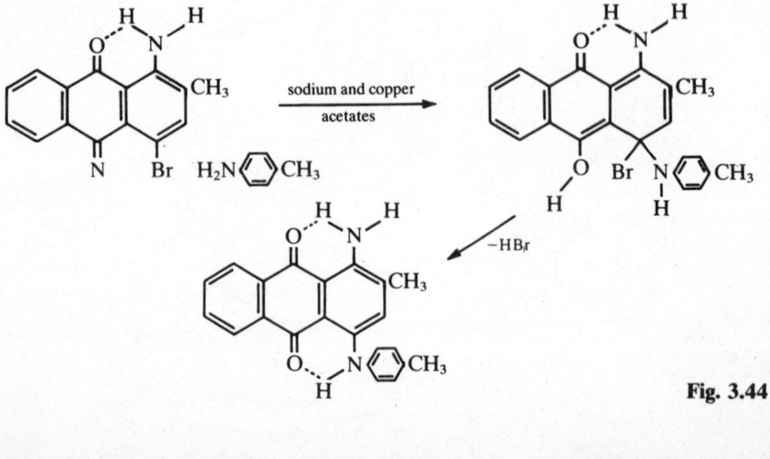

Fig. 3.44

Both (26) and (29) are bases which on sulphonation give important wool dyes (see Chapter 7).

N-Phenyl-1-naphthylamine is manufactured on the large scale by heating 1-naphthylamine, with an excess of aniline in the presence of sulphanilic acid as catalyst, to 195–215 °C. The product is widely used in rubber technology as an accelerator and is also used in the manufacture of Victoria Blue B (p. 153).

Oxidation

One of the classical processes in industrial organic chemistry is the oxidation of naphthalene to phthalic anhydride nowadays carried out as a continuous process using oxygen of the air and vanadium pentoxide as catalyst. In recent

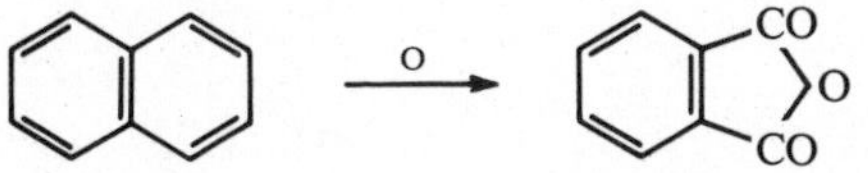

Fig. 3.45

years *o*-xylene, obtained by 'cracking' processes from crude petroleum oil, has been introduced as starting material. Phthalic anhydride is used in very large quantities in the plastics industry and plays a significant role in dye chemistry. It is used as such in the manufacture of Fluorescein, Rhodamines, Phthaleins and Quinoline Yellows and also serves as a starting point for the manufacture of certain benzene intermediates such as phthalimide, phthalodinitrile, anthranilic acid and others, and also of anthraquinone and its homologues. Anthraquinone can be obtained by the oxidation of anthracene with nitric acid.

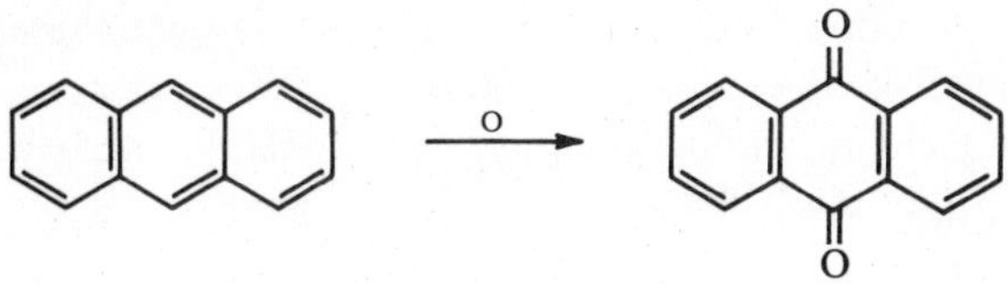

Fig. 3.46

The modern method of manufacturing anthraquinone is by air-oxidation of antracene using vanadium pentoxide as catalyst. The indirect method, it should be mentioned, is important in the synthesis of 2-methylanthraquinone (from phthalic anhydride and toluene).

Certain aspects of oxidation have already been mentioned, e.g. the oxidation of cumene (p.154), and others are dealt with in connection with triarylmethane dyes (p. 157), and stilbene derivatives (p. 178).

The oxidation of the methyl group in toluene derivatives to the aldehyde is an important stage in triarylmethane dye manufacture. *p*-Toluenesulphonyl chloride is first hydrolysed in concentrated sulphuric and then subjected, without isolation, to the oxidizing action of the manganic compound produced when a permanganate is added to a solution of manganous sulphate in

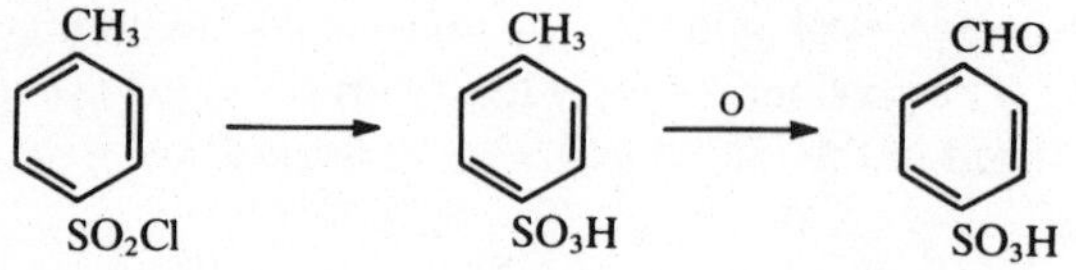

benzaldehyde-4-sulphonic acid   **Fig. 3.47**

concentrated sulphuric acid. Benzaldehyde-2,4-disulphonic acid is made in a similar manner from toluene-2,4-disulphonic acid.

Miscellaneous reactions

Kolbe-Schmitt reaction. The important hydroxycarboxylic acids salicylic acid and 2-hydroxy-3-naphthoic acid are manufactured by heating the sodium salt of phenol or of 2-naphthol under pressure in an atmosphere of carbon dioxide.

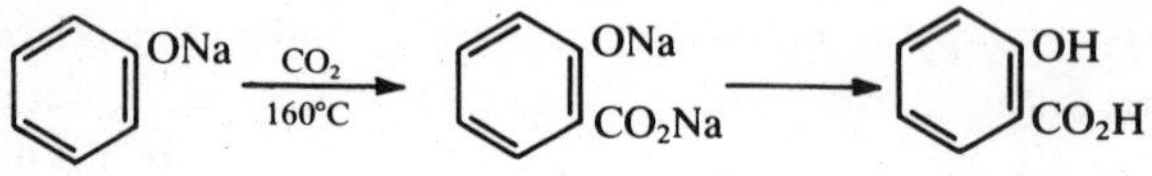

salicylic acid   **Fig. 3.48**

Salicylic acid is used as a coupling component in a very large number of azo dyes and is especially important in the manufacture of chrome dyes. By far the greatest usage, however, is in the medicinal field as the acetyl compound, aspirin. The important 2-hydroxy-3-naphthoic acid, see Azoic dyes (p. 116), is obtained in 72–76% yield by heating sodium-2-naphtholate in carbon dioxide at 260 °C and a pressure of 4–5 atm.

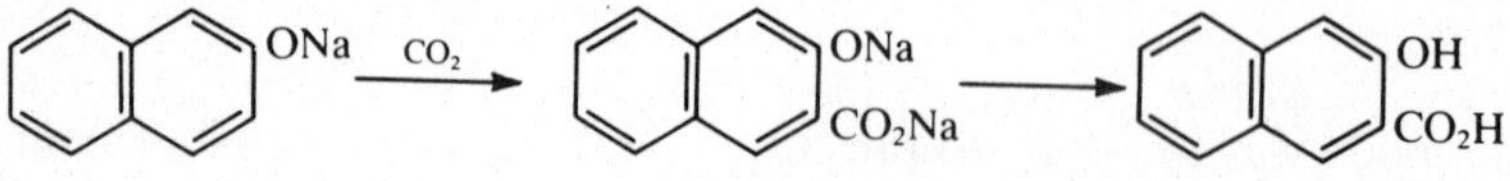

Fig. 3.49

About half the original charge of 2-naphthol is recovered unchanged and is re-used in the process.

Formylation. In addition to the oxidation of —CH$_3$ to —CHO already mentioned, there are three principal methods of obtaining aldehydes. Toluene derivatives may be chlorinated in nickel apparatus from which iron, which would act as a carrier for chlorine leading to nuclear substitution, is rigorously excluded, to give substitution in the methyl group. Hydrolysis of the benzal chloride with milk of lime or with moderately concentrated sulphuric acid gives the aldehyde (30). *o*-Chlorotoluene can be chlorinated with chlorine in the

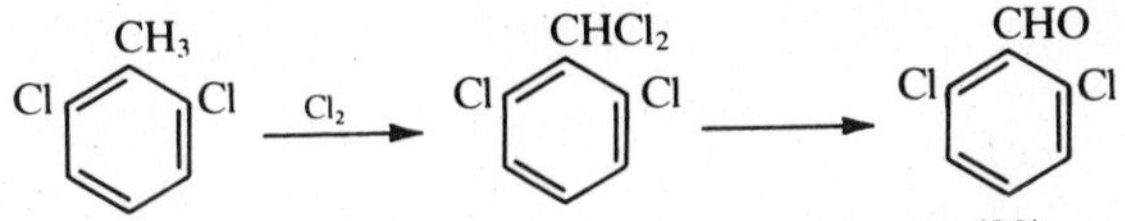

2,6-dichlorotoluene   2,6-dichlorobenzaldehyde   **Fig. 3.50**

presence of phosphorus trichloride at 120 °C to give *o*-chlorobenzal chloride, *o*-chlorobenzaldehyde being obtained on hydrolysis.

Tertiary amines may be formylated by the action of formaldehyde on a *p*-nitroso derivative followed by hydrolysis with hot dilute acid. The product

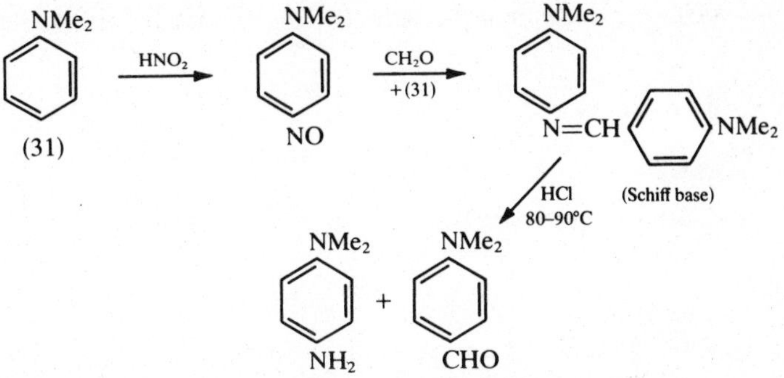

4-dimethylaminobenzaldehyde   **Fig. 3.51**

(33) is filtered off after the reaction mixture has been neutralized, the diamine (32) remains in the filtrate and is normally discarded. The aldehyde (33), which is used in the synthesis of certain valuable chrome colours, may also be obtained by condensing dimethylformamide with *N,N*-dimethylaniline by means of phosphorus trichloride and hydrolysing the product with dilute acid (Wilsmeier reaction).

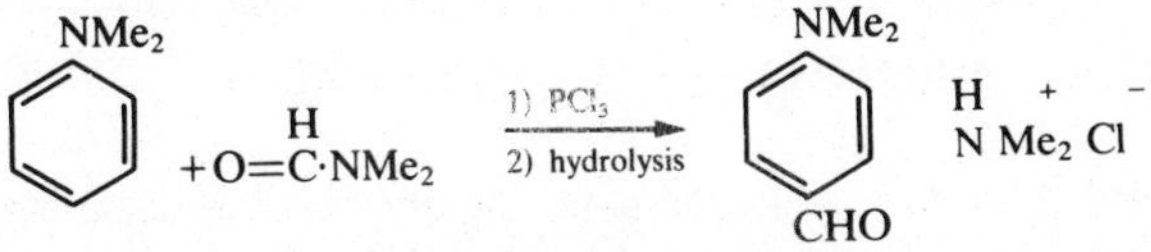

dimethylformamide   (33)   dimethylammonium chloride

Fig. 3.52

Hydrazines and pyrazolones

Pyrazolones of the type shown here in the enol, i.e. OH, form,

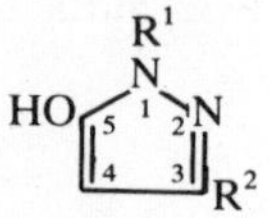

Fig. 3.53

in which R^1 = phenyl or substituted phenyl, R^2 = methyl-, carboxy-, carbethoxy-, etc., are of considerable importance in the manufacture of azo dyes and pigments. They are made by the condensation of a hydrazine with a β-keto ester and the synthesis is best illustrated by the case of 3-methyl-1-phenyl-5-pyrazolone, the commonest pyrazolone used in dye manufacture. A solution of diazotized aniline is run into neutral sodium sulphite solution when the disulphonate of phenyl hydrazone (34) is produced. On hydrolysis with dilute hydrochloric acid, phenylhydrazine hydrochloride is produced and is isolated as such, the base being liberated on treatment with caustic soda

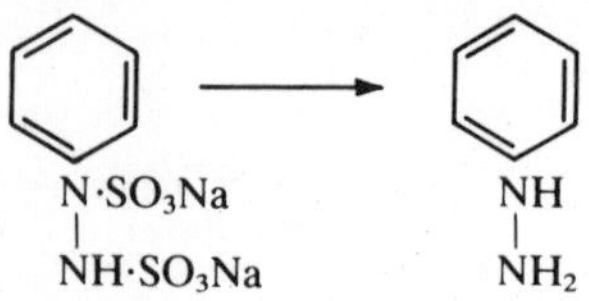

(34)

Fig. 3.54

solution. The base is condensed with ethyl acetoacetate giving the hydrazone (35) which, on boiling with alkali, undergoes ring-closure giving the pyrazolone (36) shown here in the keto, i.e. CO, form. Modern manufacturing processes

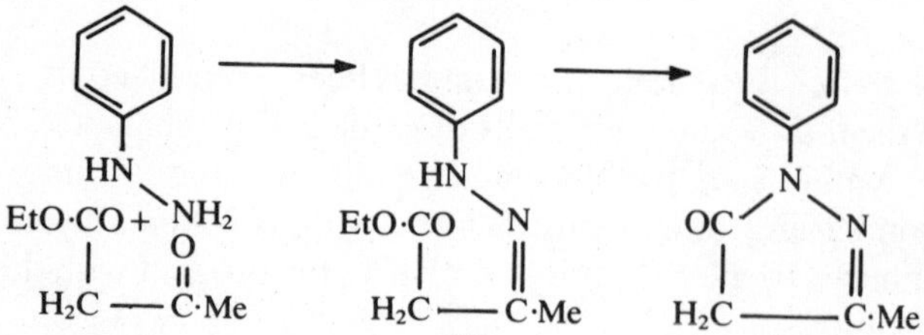

(35)   (36)   Fig. 3.55

for 3-methyl-1-phenyl-5-pyrazolone employ diketen instead of ethyl acetoacetate.

Pyrazolones in which the phenyl group is variously substituted e.g. by sulpho groups, chlorine, methyl and so on, may be produced by analogous means from the appropriate amine. Among the commonly used 3-methyl-5-pyrazolones are 3-methyl-1-*p*-tolyl-5-pyrazolone, 3-methyl-1-(4'-sulphophenyl)-5-pyra-zolone, 3-methyl-1-(2',5'-dichloro-4'-sulphophenyl)-5-pyrazolone. When 4-sulphophenylhydrazine is condensed with diethyl oxalacetate, 3-carboxy–1–(4'-sulphophenyl)-5-pyrazolone (37) is obtained.

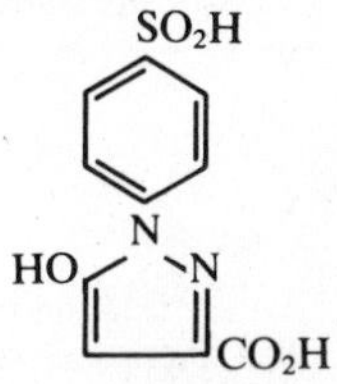

(37)

Fig. 3.56

Other intermediates

Elsewhere in the text, references are made to specialized intermediates, e.g. Fischer's Aldehyde (p. 176), bromobenzanthrone (p. 140), since these are best dealt with in the context of the colorants to which they give rise.

Table 3.2 Intermediates derived from benzene

Systematic name	Other name	M.p. or b.p. (if liquid at ordinary temp.) °C	Class(es) of derived dye(s)
Hydroxybenzene	Phenol	M.p. 42.5	Nitro, Azo, Triarylmeth-ane, Azine Hydroxy-ketone, Sulphur, Anthraquinone
1-Amino-3-chlorobenzene	*m*-Chloro-aniline	B.p. 236	Azo, Thiazine, Anthra-quinone
Aminobenzene	Aniline	B.p. 184.4	Most classes
4,4'-Diaminobiphenyl	Benzidine	M.p. 128	Azo
1-Amino-3-nitro-benzene	*m*-Nitroaniline	M.p. 114	Azo, Acridine, Sulphur
1,3-Dihydroxybenzene	Resorcinol	M.p. 119	Nitroso, Azo, Stilbene, Triarylmethane, Xan-thene, Oxazine, Oxidation bases
2-Aminobenzene-1,4-disulphonic acid	–	–	Azo
2-Aminophenol-4-sulphonic acid	–	–	Azo
2-Methoxyaniline-5-sulphonic acid	–	–	Azo
2-Amino-4,5-dichloro-benzenesulphonic acid	–	–	Azo

Table 3.2   (*Contd.*)

Systematic name	Other name	M.p. or b.p. (if liquid at ordinary temp.) °C	Class(es) of derived dye(s)
3-Amino-5-chloro-4-hydroxybenzene-sulphonic acid	–	–	Azo
2-Amino-4-chloro-phenol	–	M.p. 138	Azo, Oxidation bases
1,3-Diaminobenzene	*m*-Phenylene-diamine	M.p. 63–64	Azo, Acridine, Azine, Oxazine, Sulphur

Table 3.3   Intermediates derived from aniline

Systematic name	Other name	M.p. or b.p. °C	Class(es) of derived dye(s)
N-alkylanilines	*Sec.*-alkyl-anilines	–	Many classes; especially Triarylmethane
N-aralkylanilines	*Sec.*-aralkyl-anilines	–	–
N,N-dialkylanilines	*Tert.*-dialkyl-anilines		
N,N-alkylaralkyl-anilines	*Tert.*-alkylaralkyl-anilines	–	Many classes; especially Triarylmethane
N,N-diaralkyl-anilines	*Tert.*-diaralkyl-anilines		–
4-aminobenzene-sulphonic acid	Sulphanilic acid	–	Azo, Stilbene, Triaryl-methane, Azine
N-acetyl-1,4-diaminobenzene	Acetyl-*p*-phenylene-diamine, *p*-aminoacetanilide	M.p. 162	Azo, Anthraquinone, Oxidation bases —
4-Nitroaniline	*p*-Nitroaniline	M.p. 148	Azo, Azoic, Sulphur
1,4-Diaminobenzene	*p*-Phenylene-diamine	M.p. 142	Nitro, Azo (indirectly) Stilbene, Indamine, Azine, Sulphur, Anthraquinone, Oxidation bases
N-phenylaminoacetic acid	*N*-Phenylglycine	M.p. 126–7	Indigo
2-Methylquinoline	Quinaldine	B.p. 247	Quinoline

Table 3.4 Intermediates derived from 2-chloronitrobenzene

Systematic name	Other name	M.p. or b.p. °C	Class(es) of derived dye(s)
2-Nitroaniline	o-Nitroaniline	M.p. 71.5	Azo, Azoic, Anthraquinone
1,2-Diaminobenzene	o-Phenylene-diamine	M.p. 102–3	Triarylmethane, Anthraquinone,
2-Methoxyaniline	o-Anisidine	B.p. 218	Azo, Azoic, Azine
2-Chloro-5-nitroaniline	–	M.p. 124–5	Nitro, Azo
1-Chloro-2,4-diamino-benzene	4-Chloro-m-phenylene-diamine	M.p. 91	Azo, Oxidation bases
4,4'-Diamino-3,3'-dimethoxybiphenyl	o-Dianisidine	M.p. 137–8	Azo
2-Aminophenol	o-Aminophenol	M.p. 172	Azo, Sulphur, Oxidation bases
2,4-Diaminophenyl-methyl ether	4-Methoxy-m-phenylene-diamine	M.p. 67–68	Azo, Oxidation bases
1-Chloro-2,4-diamino-benzene-5-sulphonic acid	Chloro-m-phenyl-lene diamine-sulphonic acid	–	Azo
2-Amino-1-methoxy-4-nitrobenzene	4-Nitroanisidine (Fast Scarlet R Base) (MNOA) C.I. Azoic Diazo Component 13, 37130	– M.p. 117–18	– Azo, Azoic

Table 3.5 Intermediates derived from 4-chloronitrobenzene

Systematic name	Other name	M.p. or b.p. °C	Class(es) of derived dye(s)
4-Nitroaniline	p-Nitroaniline	M.p. 148	Azo, Azoic, Sulphur
1,4-Diaminobenzene	p-Phenylene-diamine	M.p. 142	See Table 3.3
4-Methoxyaniline	p-Anisidine	M.p. 57	Nitro, Azo, Anthraquinone
4-Phenoxyaniline-3-sulphonic acid	6-Phenoxymetanilic acid	–	Azo
2-Amino-5-nitro-benzenesulphonic acid	4-Nitroaniline-2-sulphonic acid	–	Azo
5-Amino-2-o-toluidino-benzenesulphonic acid	–	–	Azo
4-Chloroaniline	p-Chloroaniline	M.p. 70	Azo, Quinoline, Aminoketone, Anthraquinone
2-Amino-5-chloro-benzenesulphonic acid	4-Chloroaniline-2-sulphonic acid	–	Azo

Table 3.6 Intermediates derived from toluene

Systematic name	Other name	M.p. or b.p. °C	Class(es) of derived dye(s)
Benzaldehyde	–	B.p. 179	Triarylmethane, Xanthene, Acridine, Thiazole, Anthraquinone
2,6-Dichlorobenz-aldehyde	–	M.p. 71	Triarylmethane, Xanthene
Benzaldehyde-4-sulphonic acid	p-Sulphobenz-aldehyde	–	Triarylmethane
Benzaldehyde-2,4-disulphonic acid	–	–	Triarylmethane, Xanthene
2-Aminotoluene	o-Toluidine	B.p. 201	Azo, Triarylmethane, Xanthene, Azine Thiazine, Sulphur, Indigoid
2-Aminotoluene-5-sulphonic acid	4-Amino-m-toluene-sulphonic acid	–	Azo
4,4'-Diamino-3,3'-dimethylbiphenyl	o-Tolidine	M.p. 128	Azo
2-Amino-4-nitro-toluene	5-Nitro-o-toluidine	M.p. 109	Azo, Azoic
2,4-Diamino-toluene	m-Toluylene-diamine	M.p. 99	Azo, Acridine, Azine, Sulphur
4-Aminotoluene	p-Toluidine	M.p. 45	Azo, Triarylmethane, Xanthene, Acridine, Thiazole, Azine, Aminoketone, Anthraquinone
4-Aminotoluene-3-sulphonic acid	4-Amino-m-toluene sulphonic acid	–	Azo
4-Amino-3-nitro-toluene	m-Nitro-p-toluidine (MNPT)(Fast Red G Base)	M.p. 117	Azo, Azoic
4,4'-Diamino-stilbene-2,2'-disulphonic acid	–	–	Azo, Fluorescent Brightening Agents
5-Amino-2-chloro-toluene-4-sulphonic acid	2-Amino-5-chloro-p-toluene-sulphonic acid	–	Azo
5-Amino-2-chloro-toluene	6-Chloro-3-toluidine	M.p. 84	Azo
2-Amino-6-chloro-toluene-4-sulphonic acid	–	–	Azo

Table 3.7 Intermediates derived from naphthalene

Systematic name	Other name	M.p. or b.p. °C	Class(es) of derived dye(s)
1-Naphthylamine	α-Naphthylamine	M.p. 51	Azo, Azoic, Azine, Oxazine, Anthraquinone
1-Alkylaminonaphthalene or 1-arylaminonaphthalene	alkyl- or aryl-Naphthylamine	–	Triarylmethane, Azo
1-Aminonaphthalene-4-sulphonic acid	Naphthionic acid	–	Azo, Nitro, Triarylmethane
1-Naphthol-4-sulphonic acid	Nevile and Winther's acid	–	Nitroso, Azo
1-Naphthylamine-4,7-disulphonic acid	–	–	Azo
1-Naphthylamine-4,6-disulphonic acid	–	–	Azo
1-Naphthol	α-Naphthol	M.p. 94	Nitroso, Nitro, Azo, Stilbene, Indophenol, Indigoid, Oxidation bases
2-Naphthol	β-Naphthol	M.p. 123	Nitroso, Azo, Stilbene, Triarylmethane, Azine, Oxazine, Sulphur
5-(and 8-) Aminonaphthalene-2-sulphonic acid	1,6-1,7-Cleve's acid mixed and as separate compounds	–	Azo
8-Amino-1-naphthalene-sulphonic acid	Peri acid	–	Azo, Sulphur
5-Amino-1-naphthalene-sulphonic acid	Laurent's acid	–	Azo, Triarylmethane

Table 3.8 Intermediates derived from 2-Naphthol

Systematic name	Other name	M.p. or b.p. °C	Class(es) of derived dye(s)
2-Hydroxy-3-naphthoic acid	β-Oxynaphthoic acid, BON acid	M.p. 216	Azo
2-Hydroxy-3-naphthoarylamides	–	–	Azo, Azoic
1-Nitroso-2-naphthol	α-Nitroso-β-naphthol	M.p. 103	Azo, Aminoketone, Nitroso
1-Amino-2-naphthol	–	–	Azo
1-Amino-2-naphthol-4-sulphonic acid	–	–	Azo
1-Amino-6-nitro-2-naphthol-4-sulphonic acid	–	–	Azo
2-Naphthol-6-sulphonic acid	Schäffer's acid	–	Nitroso, Azo, Azine
2-Naphthol-3,6-disulphonic acid	R salt	–	Azo, Triarylmethane
2-Naphthylamine-3,6-disulphonic acid	Amino R salt	–	Azo
2-Amino-3-naphthol-6-sulphonic acid	–	–	Azo
2-Naphthylamine-6-sulphonic adid	Brönner's acid	–	Azo
2-Naphthol-8-sulphonic acid	Crocein acid	–	Nitro, Azo
2-Naphthol-6,8-disulphonic acid	G salt	–	Azo, Triarylmethane
4,6-Dihydroxy-naphthalene-2-sulphonic acid	–	–	Azo
7-Amino-1-naphthol-3-sulphonc acid	Gamma acid	–	Azo
7-Anilino-1-naphthol-3-sulphonic acid	Phenyl gamma acid	–	Azo
7-Aminonaphthalene-1,3-disulphonic acid	Amino G acid	–	Azo
2-Aminonaphthalene-1-sulphonic acid	Tobias acid	-	Azo
6-Aminonaphthalene-1,3-disulphonic acid	Amino J acid	–	Azo
6-Aminonaphthol-3-sulphonic acid	J acid	–	Azo
6-Anilinonaphthol-3-sulphonic acid	Phenyl J acid	–	Azo

Table 3.9 Intermediates derived from naphthalene-1,3,6-trisulphonic acid

Systematic name	Other name	Class(es) of derived dye(s)
1-Amino-8-naphthol-3,6-disulphonic acid	H acid	Azo, Hydroxyketone
1,8-Dihydroxynaphthalene-3,6-disulphonic acid	Chromotropic acid	Azo
1-Naphthol-3,6,8-trisulphonic acid	–	Azo, Hydroxyketone
1-Aminonaphthalene-3,6,8-trisulphonic acid	Koch acid	–

Table 3.10 Anthraquinone intermediates

Systematic name	Other name
1-Aminoanthraquinone	α-Aminoanthraquinone
2-Aminoanthraquinone	β-Aminoanthraquinone
1-Amino-4-bromoanthraquinone-2-sulphonic acid	Bromamine acid
1-Amino-4-bromo-2-methylanthraquinone	–
1-Amino-2,4-dibromoanthraquinone	–
1,2-dihydroxyanthraquinone	Alizarin
1,4-dihydroxyanthraquinone	Quinizarin
1,5-dihydroxyanthraquinone	Anthrarufin
1,8-dihydroxyanthraquinone	Chrysazin

The above compounds are of course intermediates for the anthraquinone series of dyes. In addition, 1-aminoanthraquinone is listed as C.I. Azoic Diazo Component 36, 37275, and is marketed not as the free base but as the stabilized diazo salt.

4
Azo Dyes—I

General

The azo dyes and pigments form the largest group of all the synthetic colorants and play a prominent part in almost every type of application. The chromophoric system consists essentially of the azo group, —N=N—, in association with one or more aromatic systems. There may be more than one azo group present in the dye molecule and thus one speaks of monoazo, disazo, trisazo, tetrakisazo and polyazo dyes according to whether there are one, two, three, four or more azo group present in the dye molecule. The range of hues covered by this group is very wide and includes yellows, a great number of reds and oranges, navy blues, violets and blacks. Greens are known but the range is comparatively limited.

Azo dyes are made almost exclusively by the *diazotization* of a primary aromatic amine to give a diazo or *diazonium salt*, a reaction of fundamental importance to the dye industry discovered by Griess in 1862. The diazo compound is then coupled with a second substance, usually a phenol, an enolizable ketone or an aromatic amine, an *azo* compound being formed. The participating molecules are known as *diazocomponent* and *coupling component* respectively.

It is the practice to describe azo dyes by the convention–

amine → coupling component E

diamine $\begin{array}{l} \rightarrow \text{coupling component E} \\ \rightarrow \text{coupling component E}' \end{array}$

and similarly for tris-, tetrakis- and polyazo dyes. In such cases the arrow indicates that the appropriate primary aromatic amine has been diazotized and coupled with a component, e.g. the dyestuff:

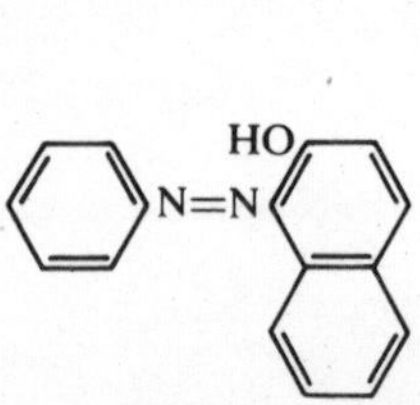

Fig. 4.1

is represented as aniline → 2-naphthol. This system is used in the Colour Index to describe all the azo dyes of declared constitution and has been adopted generally.

Diazotization

When a primary aromatic amine is acted on in aqueous acid medium by nitrous acid, a diazonium salt is formed and the amine is said to have been diazotized, a second nitrogen atom having been introduced into the molecule. This process may be envisaged as taking place as follows:

$$Ar \cdot NH_2 + HNO_2 \xrightarrow{(a)} Ar \cdot \overset{+}{N}H_2NO \rightarrow Ar \cdot NH \cdot NO$$

$$\rightarrow Ar \cdot N{=}N \cdot OH \rightarrow Ar \cdot \overset{+}{N}{\equiv}N \leftrightarrow Ar \cdot N{=}\overset{+}{N}$$

where Ar represents an aromatic hydrocarbon radical. Reaction (a) is the rate-determining step and is in effect a nitrosation of the amine. In support of this it has been shown that the diazotization of aniline and the nitrosation of N-methylaniline occur at similar rates and obey the same kinetic equation from pH 3 to somewhat higher acidities (Ridd and Kalatzis). The actual nitrosating species varies according to conditions and may be

$$\overset{+}{NO}, \quad NOCl, \quad \overset{H}{\underset{H}{\diagdown}}\overset{+}{O} \rightarrow NO \quad or \quad N_2O_3$$

the last arising from the equilibrium

$$2HNO_2 \rightleftharpoons N_2O_3 + H_2O$$

At low acidities it is probable that N_2O_3 is the effective agent, mechanisms in the case of aniline and N-methylaniline being as follows:

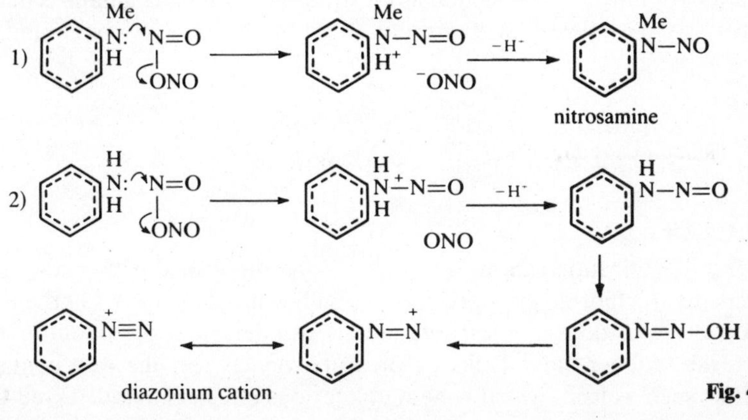

nitrosamine

diazonium cation

Fig. 4.2

Primary aliphatic amines do not form stable diazonium cations and on treatment with nitrous acid, breakdown occurs with the formation of various non-nitrogenous products, nitrogen gas being evolved. The relative stability of the aromatic diazonium cation on the other hand is the result of delocalization of the positive charge by the π electron system thus:

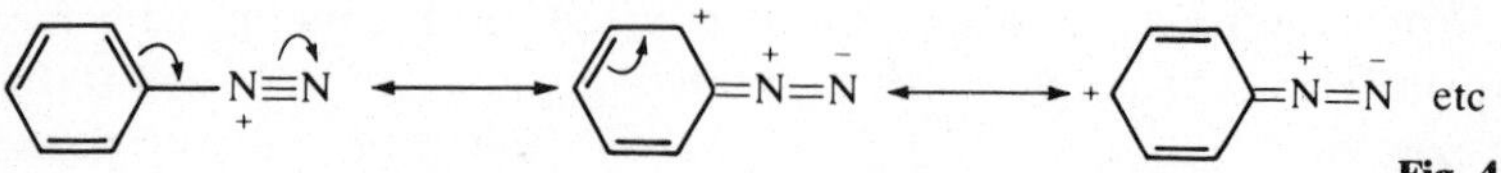

Fig. 4.3

Effects of substituents on diazotization

The readiness with which an aromatic amine may be diazotized depends on the nature and the position of substituents in the nucleus as affecting the basicity of the amine. Thus relative to aniline, *p*-nitroaniline and 2,4-dinitroaniline are much less basic by reason of the electron-withdrawing NO_2 groups and in fact require special methods for their diazotization. Weakly basic amines, e.g. 2,4-dinitroaniline, 1- and 2-aminoanthraquinones, are diazotized by adding the solid amine to nitrosylsulphuric acid.

Diazotization may also give rise to difficulties through low solubility in aqueous acid, the presence of easily replaceable groups such as $-SO_3H$, $-NO_2$, or the presence of easily oxidizable groups such as $-OH$, $-CHO$. Accordingly, a number of methods have been devised to overcome these difficulties.

Direct method

Here the amine is dissolved in $2\frac{1}{2}$–3 equivalents of acid, usually hydrochloric acid, ice is added to lower the temperature to 0–5 °C and the theoretical quantity of nitrite is now added as an aqueous solution. If aniline is diazotized with only 1 mole of acid present, then a diazoamino compound results (*N*-coupling):

$$Ph\cdot NH_2 + NaNO_2 + HCl \rightarrow PhN_2^+Cl^- + NaCl$$
$$\text{unreacted } Ph\cdot NH_2 + Ph\,N_2^+ \rightarrow Ph\cdot N{=}N\cdot NH\cdot Ph$$
$$\text{diazoaminobenzene}$$

Direct diazotization can in some cases be accomplished with a suspension of amine hydrochloride provided it is in a sufficiently fine form. On the technical scale diazotizations are carried out in wooden vats or, in more modern factories, rubber-lined tanks or pressure vessels. In this way contact with metals such as iron, which have a deleterious effect, is avoided (see Chapter

16). Amines like *p*-nitroaniline require a considerable excess of acid (6–7 equivalents) for their diazotization. Beyond a strength of 20% HCl the addition of nitrite causes considerable oxidation to occur, chlorine being produced. Concentrated sulphuric acid can be used as reaction medium, the nitrosating agent being nitrosylsulphuric acid; on the technical scale enamelled vessels are employed for this purpose. Diazotization can also be carried out in glacial acetic acid using amyl nitrite.

Unsubstituted 1-naphthylamine and 2-naphthylamine are readily diazotized by the direct method, the respective diazonium salts being very soluble in water. Diazotization is carried out at slightly higher temperatures (10–12 °C) than for benzene derivatives.

The various naphthylaminomonosulphonic acids are sparingly soluble in water but may be diazotized directly by first precipitating finely divided free acid by adding a solution of the sodium salt to well-stirred aqueous acid followed by addition of nitrite.

In the *inverse* method, often called *reversed diazotization*, sodium nitrite is added to an aqueous solution of the sodium naphthylamine sulphonate and the mixture run into a well-stirred mixture of ice and dilute acid.

In the case of naphthionic acid (1-aminonaphthalene-1-sulphonic acid) a 'zwitterion' or internal salt is formed. The insoluble diazo salt may be kept for a

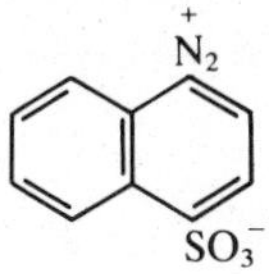

Fig. 4.4

short period as a wet filter cake. Many diazonium compounds are dangerously explosive when dry.

Naphthylamine di- and tri-sulphonic acids are readily soluble in water and may be directly diazotized.

Aminophenols and aminonaphthols. 2-Amino- and 4-aminophenols, 1:2, 2:1, and 4:1 aminonaphthols are readily oxidized by nitrous acid to the corresponding quinones. Sulphonic acids derived from such 1:2 aminohydroxy compounds are of great importance as diazo components in the manufacture of metal azo complex dyes (Chapter 6) and special procedures have been devised. The method commonly used is that of diazotization in the presence of copper sulphate and in the absence of mineral acid. The classical example is the diazotization of the important intermediate 1-amino-2-naphthol-4-sulphonic acid. To a 25% solution of the free acid in water at 20 °C is added copper sulphate solution. Sodium nitrite 30% solution is added with vigorous stirring, the temperature rising to 35 °C. The diazo-oxide may be used as such in solution or may be isolated as sodium salt by the addition of sodium chloride or

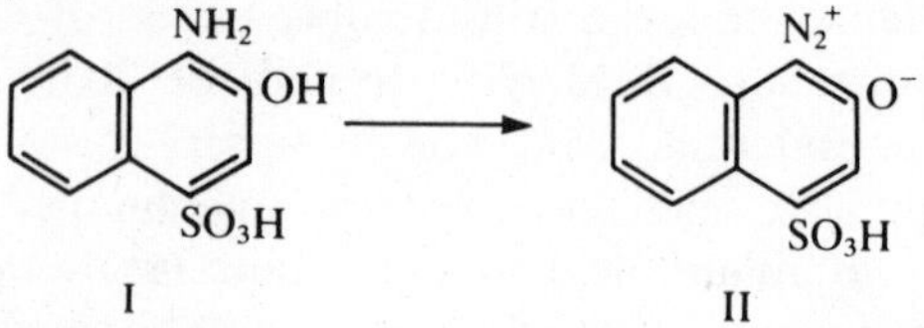

Fig. 4.5

as the free sulphonic acid by the addition of acid. The diazo-oxides are very much more stable than diazonium salts in general and the compound just mentioned is so stable that it may be nitrated or halogenated. Such stability is ascribed to resonance thus:

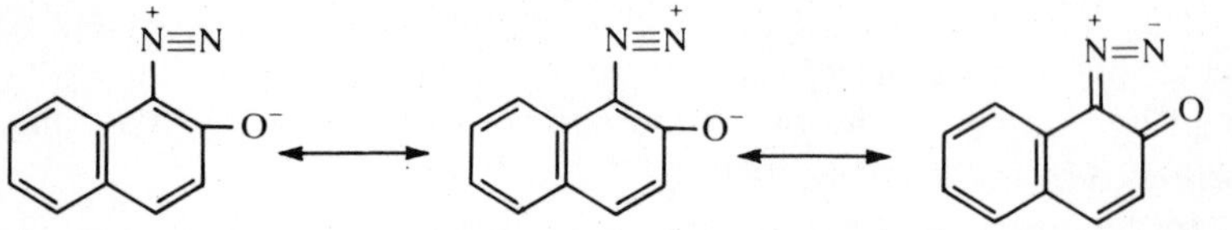

Fig. 4.6

The diazo-oxides undergo coupling reactions and in fact all the other reactions characteristic of diazonium compounds. 1,4-Aminophenols similarly form

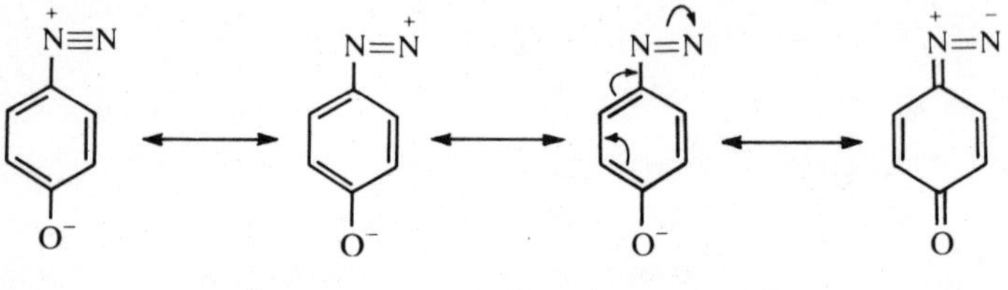

Fig. 4.7

diazo-oxides. 1,3-Aminophenols do not form diazo-oxides.

Diamines. Attempts to prepare a diazo or tetrazo derivative of *o*-phenylenediamine result in ring closure with formation of benztriazole which

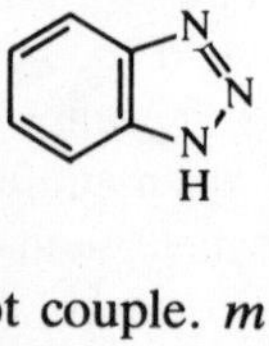

Fig. 4.8

does not couple. *m*-Phenylenediamine can be diazotized, but strongly acid conditions are essential if coupling with unchanged *m*-phenylenediamine is to be avoided.

p-Phenylenediamine is easily diazotized, less easily tetrazotized, the tetrazo-compound being very unstable.

Benzidine derivatives such as dichlorobenzidines, tolidines and dianisidines can be smoothly tetrazotized, the products being stable in solution and may be kept and even transported over substantial periods. Tetrazobenzidine can be made to couple twice, i.e. with formation of a disazo compound, with the same or different coupling components. The second coupling proceeds less readily than the first, a consequence of the electron-supplying properties of the azo group formed in the first coupling, the effect being to reduce the positive charge on the second diazo group and thus to weaken its electrophilic character. In the

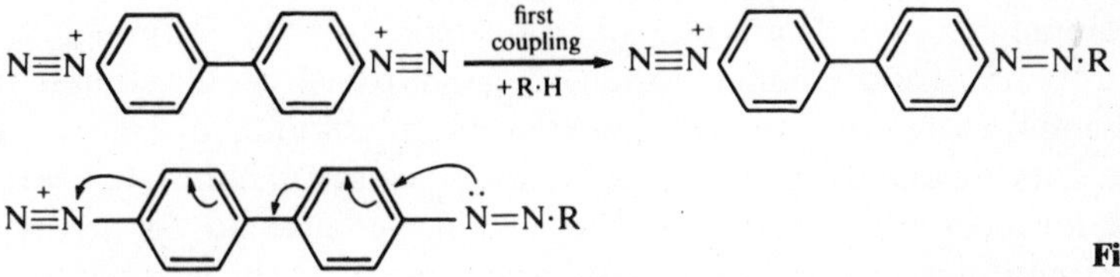

Fig. 4.9

case of a mixed disazo dye in which one coupling component is an amine or diamine, the first coupling is done under slightly acid conditions when the tetrazo is most energetic. The second is done under alkaline conditions to promote coupling: the second component is usually the more reactive of the two. A typical example is the direct cotton dye:

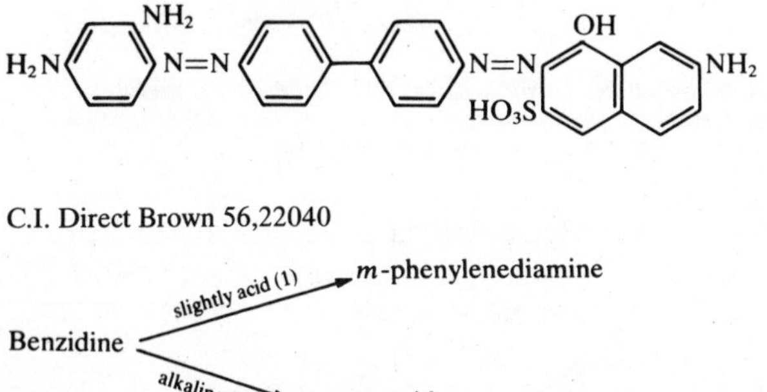

C.I. Direct Brown 56,22040

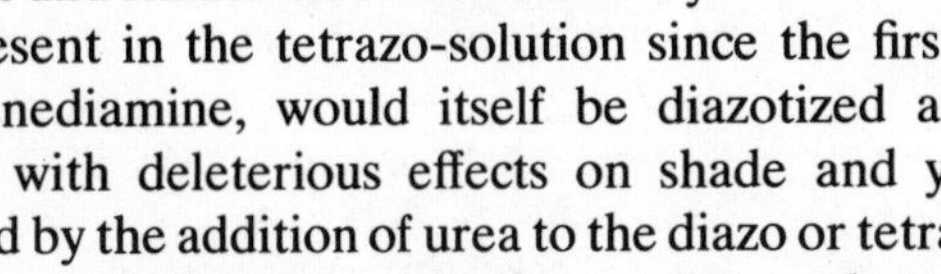

Fig. 4.10

In this and similar cases it is necessary to ensure that there is no free nitrous acid present in the tetrazo-solution since the first coupling component, *m*-phenylenediamine, would itself be diazotized and by-products would be formed with deleterious effects on shade and yield. Nitrous acid can be removed by the addition of urea to the diazo or tetrazo solution, when nitrogen and carbon dioxide are evolved according to the equation:

Sulphamic acid and its ammonium salt are used nowadays in preference to urea as these compounds react faster with nitrous acid:

$$HONO + H_2N \cdot SO_3H \rightarrow N_2 \uparrow + H_2SO_4 + H_2O$$

Stabilized diazo compounds

With the exceptions of diazo-oxides and the inner salts noted above, diazonium compounds are in general unstable in solution though some, e.g. p-nitrobenzenediazonium chloride, 2,4-dinitrobenzenediazonium chloride, are notably more stable than benzenediazonium chloride. In the dry state many diazo salts are explosive and as such cannot be used in industry. There is great need, however, of stable, easy to handle, diazo compounds for use by the dyer and printer in the various important processes where the colorant is produced by coupling on the fibre rather than prepared beforehand by the dye manufacturer. *iso-Diazotates or nitrosamines* are produced when diazo solutions are poured into warm dilute caustic soda, a stable sodium compound being precipitated. The compounds produced in transforming the diazo compound to a stable sodium salt are considered to be:

Ar·N‖NaO·N	Ar·N‖N·ONa	Ar·N·NO Na
syn- or normal diazotate (colourless, unstable, couples easily)	*anti*- or iso-diazotate (unstable, colourless, couples with difficulty)	'nitrosamine' (yellow, stable)

Fig. 4.11

The 'nitrosamines' are converted into the reactive *syn*-diazotate or diazonium compound by treatment with acids. The 'nitrosamines' are much used, together with coupling components, in printing pastes.

Diazoamino compounds

Certain diazonium salts may be converted to diazoamino compounds from which the original diazo salt can be regenerated by treatment with acid.

triazene   Fig. 4.12

Sarcosine $CH_3 \cdot NH \cdot CH_2 \cdot COOH$ and other aliphatic amino-acids are employed but not in cases where Ar is substituted by electron-withdrawing groups, since the triazene produced is not then easily decomposed by acid. The triazenes are of importance as Rapidogen Dyes (IG) and are used, together with coupling components, in printing pastes.

Colour salts

These are of great value to the dyer in using Azoic colours. In suitable cases, e.g. p-nitrobenzenediazonium chloride, the diazo salt can be 'salted' out, filtered off, mixed with anhydrous sodium sulphate or similar diluent whereby part of the moisture present is taken up as water of crystallization. The mixture is finally dried, with great caution, at 50 °C or below; similar care is needed in grinding the dried solid to the requisite fineness.

Methods of more general application are:

(a) Isolation as aryl sulphonate.

Certain naphthalenesulphonic acids, notably naphthalene-1,5-disulphonic acid, when added in solution to a diazo-salt solution bring about the precipitation of the diazo-arylsulphonate:

$$R{\cdot}\overset{+}{N_2}\overset{-}{Cl} + HSO_3R' \rightarrow R{\cdot}N{=}N{\cdot}O{\cdot}SO_2R' + HCl$$

On redissolving the arylsulphonate in water, the equilibrium is established:

$$R{\cdot}N{=}N{\cdot}O{\cdot}SO_2R' \rightarrow R{\cdot}N_2^+ + R'SO_3^-$$

and coupling can proceed until the conversion reaction from left to right is complete. The isolated arylsulphonate is diluted with an inorganic diluent, dried and ground.

(b) Isolation as zinc chloride double compound $(RN_2^+)_2$, $Zn\bar{C}l_4$

(c) Isolation as the fluoborate, $RN_2^+\bar{B}F_4$

This method is equally suitable for making stabilized tetrazo salts.

Among the inorganic diluents used are the anhydrous sulphates of sodium, aluminium and magnesium. The solids are in all cases dried at 40–50 °C and ground.

Diazo coupling

General

Diazo coupling can be regarded as an electrophilic substitution by a diazonium cation. It follows therefore that the positions where coupling will occur are those at which there is increased electron density, generally at carbon atoms in aromatic systems or heterocyclic systems aromatic in character, and, in some cases, at activated carbon atoms occurring in an aliphatic chain as in acetoacetanilide.

In benzenediazonium chloride, the diazonium cation can be represented as the resonance hybrid:

$$Ph \cdot N^+ \equiv N \leftrightarrow Ph \cdot N = N^+$$

Compared with $^+NO_2$ or SO_3 the diazonium cation is a weak electrophile and powerful electron-donating groups such as —OH, —NH$_2$, —NHR, —NR$_2$ must be present in the aromatic system of the coupling component for coupling to take place. Thus an azo compound results when diazotized aniline is added to a solution of phenol in caustic soda, the phenoxide anion being the reactive species:

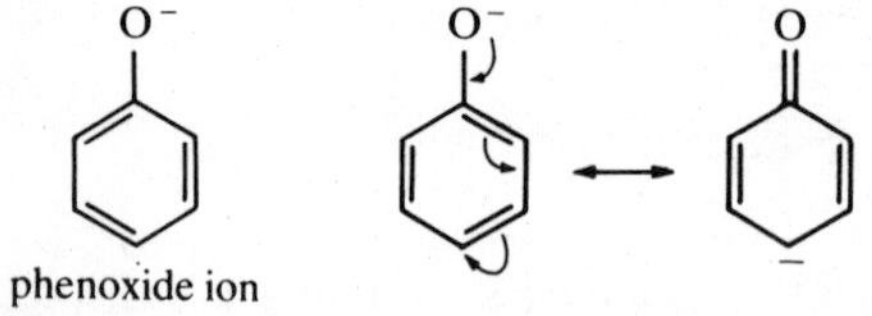

phenoxide ion

Fig. 4.13

Attack at the *p*-carbon atom is favoured and the mechanism may be represented:

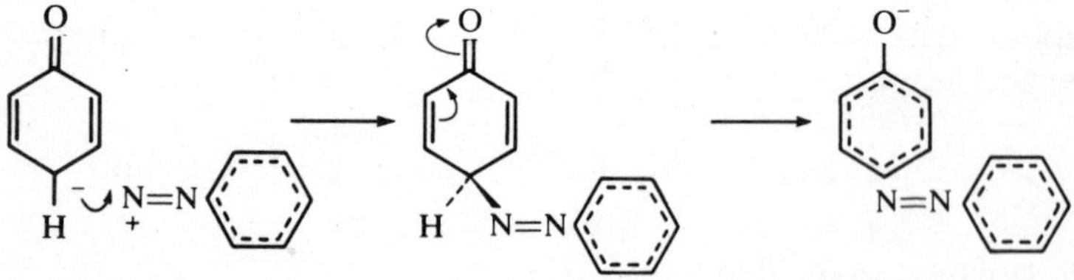

Fig. 4.14

With tertiary aromatic amines a similar situation arises:

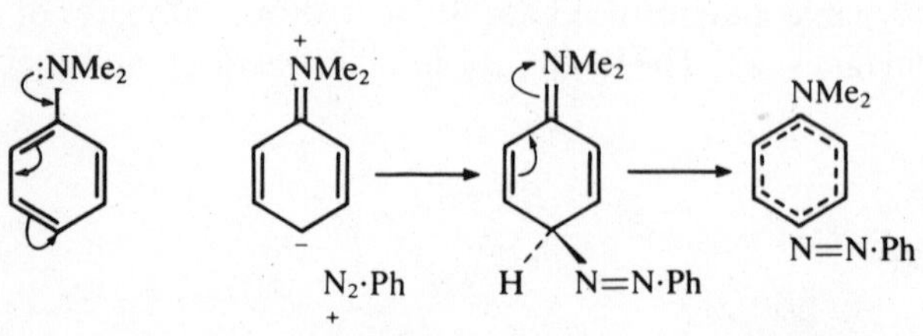

Fig. 4.15

Couplings with amines are usually carried out in slightly acid solution, the reactive species being the free amine molecule.

Where electron-withdrawing groups, in particular —NO$_2$, are in o- or p-position to the diazotized amino group, the diazonium cation has increased 'coupling energy', i.e. it is more electrophilic in character by reason of the increased positive charge on the diazo group thus:

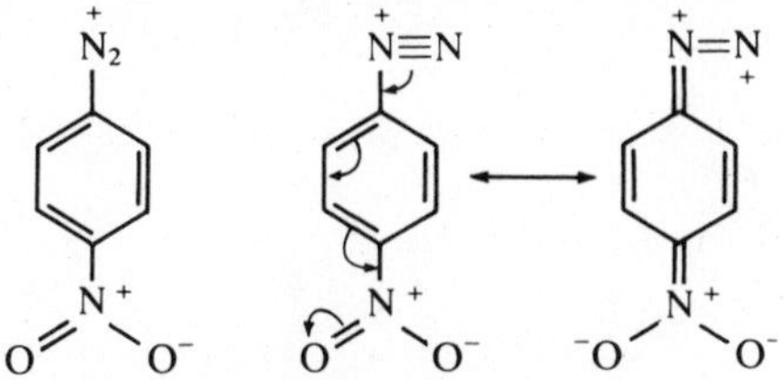

Fig. 4.16

This effect is increased in the 2,4-dinitrobenzenediazonium cation and still more in 2,4,6-trinitrobenzenediazonium cation: these cations will in fact couple with anisole, the —OMe group of which is far too weakly electron-donating to permit coupling to take place with the less reactive diazo components.

Coupling components

Benzene derivatives

Amines. Primary aromatic amines are useful as coupling components not only in their own right but also as a means of introducing another azo link by diazotization and coupling with another component. Some important examples are:

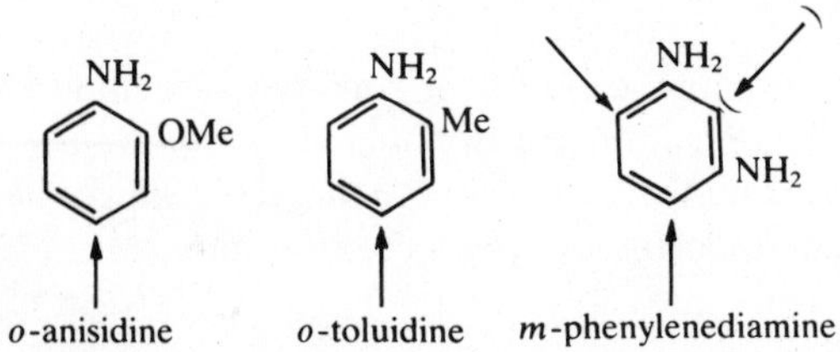

o-anisidine   o-toluidine   m-phenylenediamine   Fig. 4.17

The arrows indicate the usual coupling position. Coupling is usually carried out under acid conditions, an energetic diazo component being employed. Where less energetic diazo components are to be coupled with the amine, the amino group can be protected by first forming the methanesulphonic acid by allowing the amine to react with formaldehyde and bisulphite. The resulting compounds, e.g.

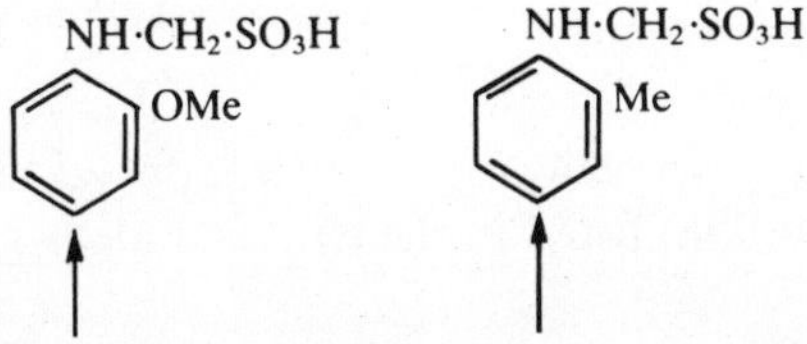

Fig. 4.18

can be coupled under alkaline conditions, the methanesulphonic acid group being subsequently removed by hydrolysis.

Examples of secondary and tertiary amines used as coupling components are:

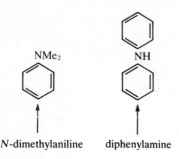

N-dimethylaniline   diphenylamine

Fig. 4.19

Hydroxy derivatives

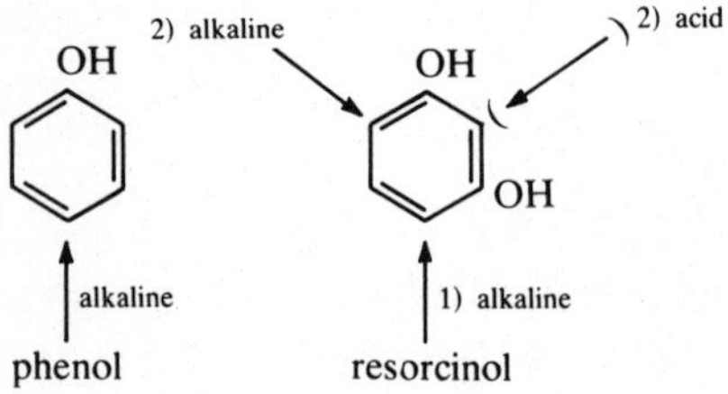

OH
2) alkaline

OH
2) acid

OH

alkaline   1) alkaline

phenol   resorcinol

Fig. 4.20

Phenol is an important coupling component and couples under alkaline conditions principally in the 4-position. Resorcinol is also important. Coupling occurs first in the 4-position and then according to the pH at which the second coupling is done, viz. pH 5–8, position 2; pH > 8, position 6.

Salicylic acid.

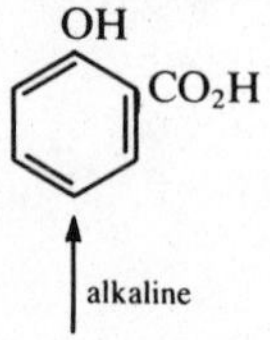

OH
CO_2H

alkaline

Fig. 4.21

is a widely used coupling component, especially for chromable dyes, and occurs in 179 azo dyes (of known constitution) listed in the Colour Index, 72 being disazo and 75 trisazo dyes.

Naphthalene derivatives

Naphthols.

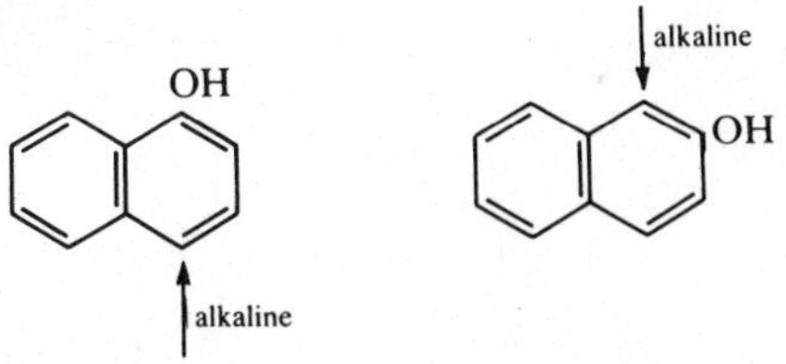

1-naphthol   2-naphthol   **Fig. 4.22**

Of these, 2-naphthol is the more important. Its derivative 2-hydroxy-3-naphthoic acid is a component used in development colours and gives rise to the widely used 2-hydroxy-3-naphtharylamides (see Pigments, Azoic Colours). 1-Naphthol will couple, under strongly alkaline conditions, in the 2-position especially with diazo-oxides (see p. 75).

Naphthylamines. Coupling is carried out under acid conditions in both cases:

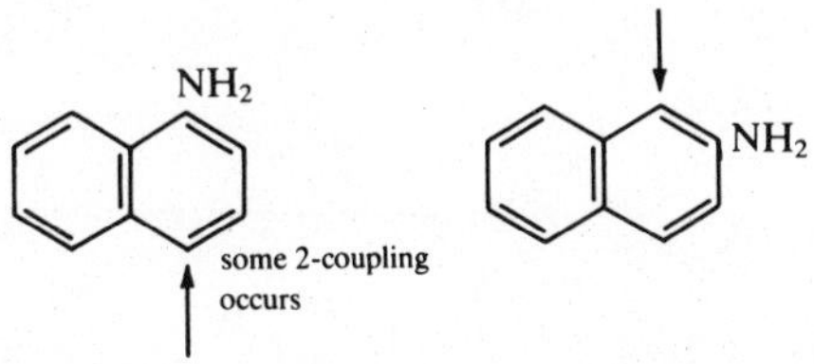

1-naphthylamine   2-naphthylamine   **Fig. 4.23**

2-Naphthylamine, a known powerful carcinogen, is no longer manufactured. 1-Naphthylamine is used as a diazo or a coupling component, or as both, and has to be handled by special methods to prevent contact with workers, since a small proportion of 2-naphthylamine is usually present (see Intermediates). Sulphonic acid derivatives of the naphthylamines, especially those containing more than one $-SO_3H$ group are not carcinogenic and are widely employed in azo dye manufacture.

    Examples of those naphthalene derivatives most extensively used as coupling components are given below:

Naphtholmonosulphonic acids.

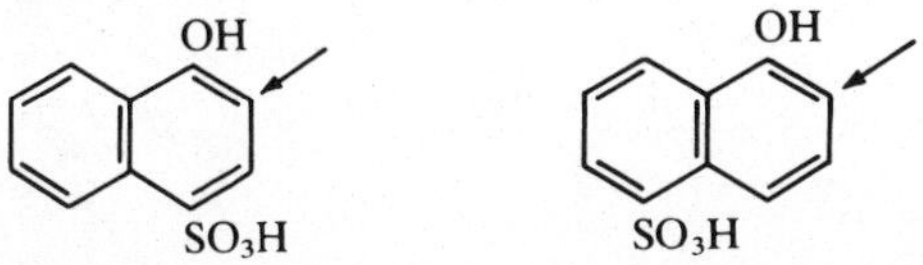

Nevile and Winther's acid   1-naphthol-5-sulphonic acid   **Fig. 4.24**

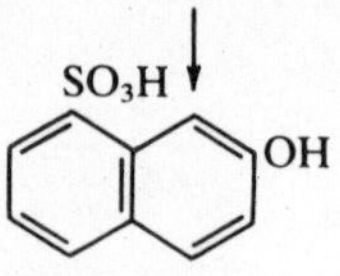

Crocein acid 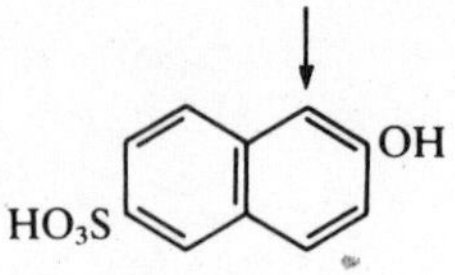   Schäffer's acid   Fig. 4.25

Naphtholdisulphonic acids.

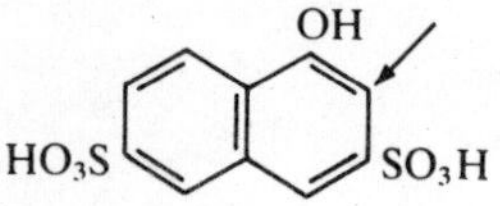

1-naphthol-3,6-disulphonic acid 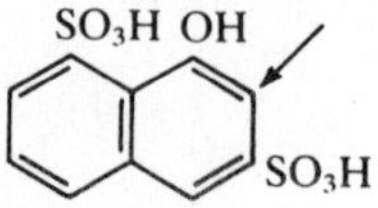   Epsilon acid   Fig. 4.26

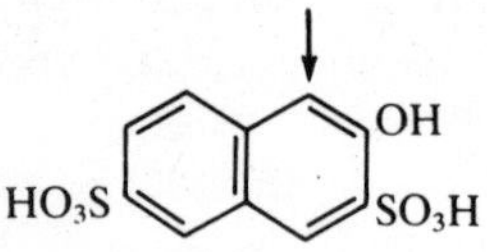

R acid 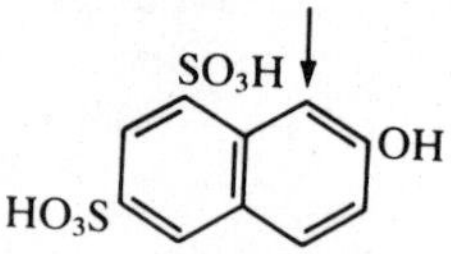   G acid   Fig. 4.27

Dihydroxynaphthalenesulphonic acids.

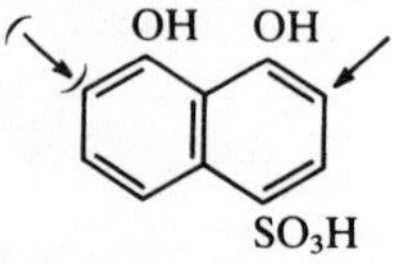

4,5-dihydroxynaphthalene-   Chromotropic acid
1-sulphonic acid   Fig. 4.28

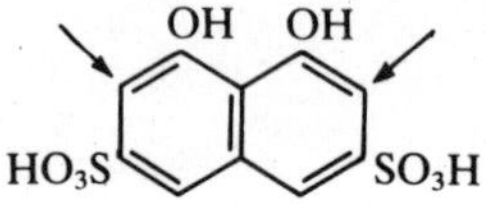

Naphthylaminesulphonic acids. As noted previously, the presence of a primary amino group in a coupling component makes possible the formation of an additional azo group and use is made of this in synthesising disazo and trisazo dyes of the types

$$A \rightarrow M \rightarrow E$$

and

$$A \rightarrow M \rightarrow M' \rightarrow E$$

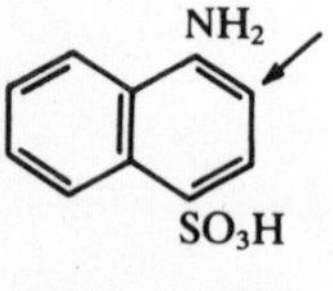

naphthionic acid 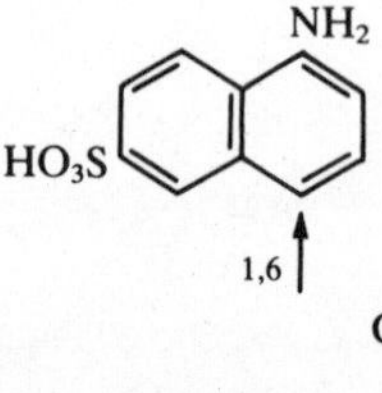 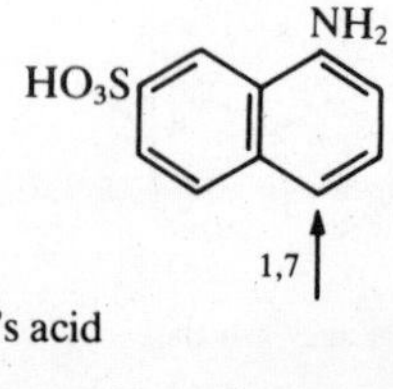   Cleve's acid   Fig. 4.29

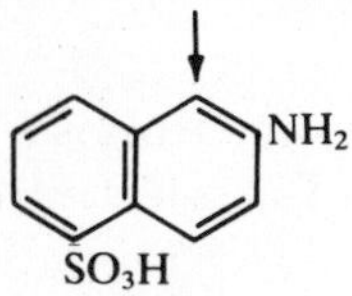

2-aminonaphthalene-
5-sulphonic acid

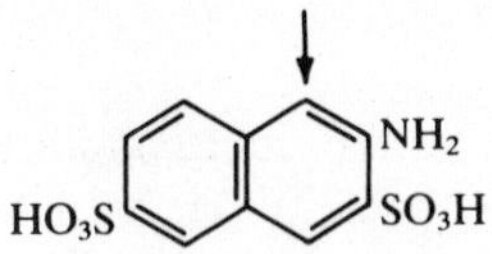

2-aminonaphthalene-
3,6-disulphonic acid

Fig. 4.30

Aminonaphtholsulphonic acids. One of the most important of this class is H acid, 1-amino-8-naphthol-3, 6-disulphonic acid, from which is derived hundreds of azo dyes, among them widely used wool, cotton and leather dyes. The annual consumption of H acid by United States dye makers is believed to exceed 2000 tons per annum. H acid couples twice, first acid then alkaline:

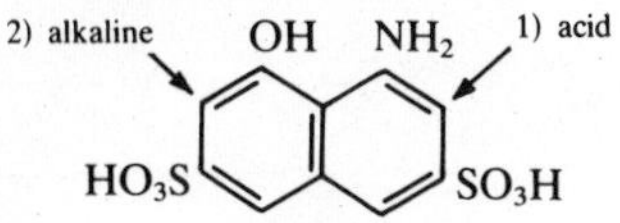

H acid

Fig. 4.31

A coupling component outstanding in its ability to induce cotton substantivity in the dyes obtained from it is J acid, a component which couples twice, as does S acid which is also used in significant quantities:

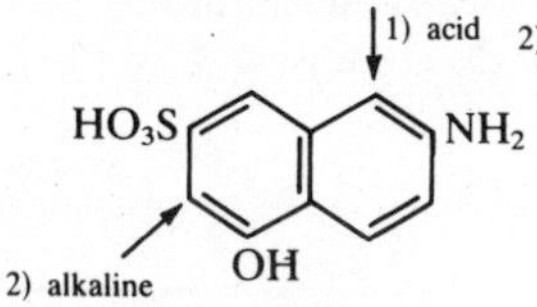

J acid

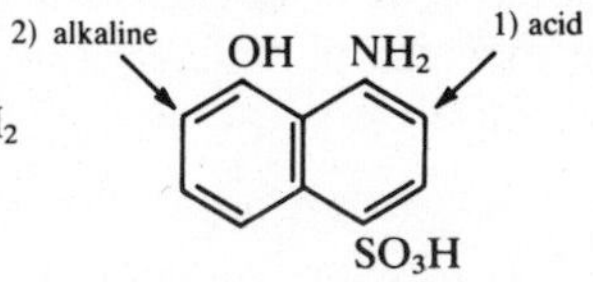

S acid

Fig. 4.32

Two other well-known coupling components are Chicago acid:

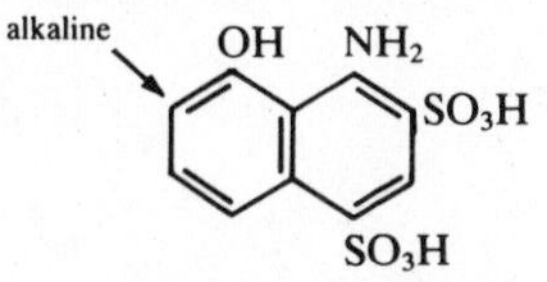

Fig. 4.33

which couples once, and Gamma acid:

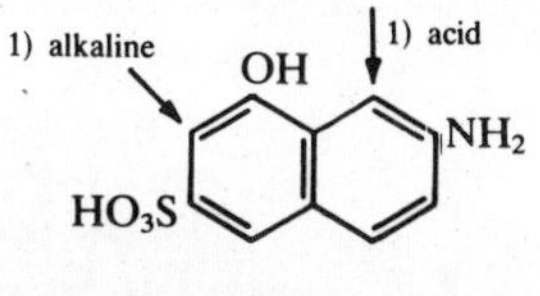

Fig. 4.34

which couples in the positions indicated.

Methylphenylpyrazolone

One of the most versatile heterocyclic coupling components is 3-methyl-1-phenyl-5-pyrazolone shown here in the enol form in which it couples at position 4. It is used in the manufacture of a number of direct and acid dyes and

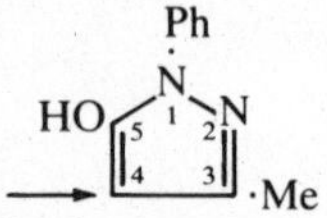

Fig. 4.35

especially in mordant dyes, including metal azo dyes and pigments. Other pyrazolones in which phenyl is substituted by Cl, SO_3H, etc., or is replaced by H, and where groups other than —Me are present at position 3, are used to some extent as coupling components.

Acetoacetanilide

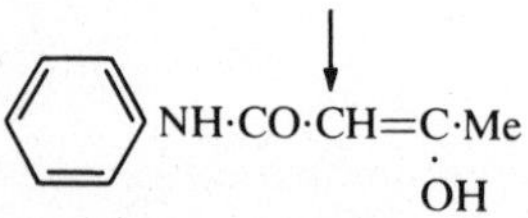

Fig. 4.36

This intermediate forms a number of direct and acid dyes and has important uses in pigment syntheses. It is also used as an azoic coupling component. Acetoacetarylamides in which phenyl is variously substituted by Cl, OMe and other groups are also important.

Quinoline-2,4-diol (2,4-dihydroxyquinoline)

This intermediate undergoes coupling in the 3-position and, like some of the components mentioned above, is useful for the preparation of dyestuffs

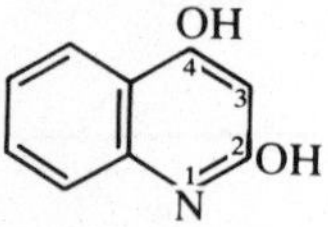

Fig. 4.37

from which chromium and other metal complexes may be derived. The dihydroxypyridines, of which two examples are given here, are employed similarly:

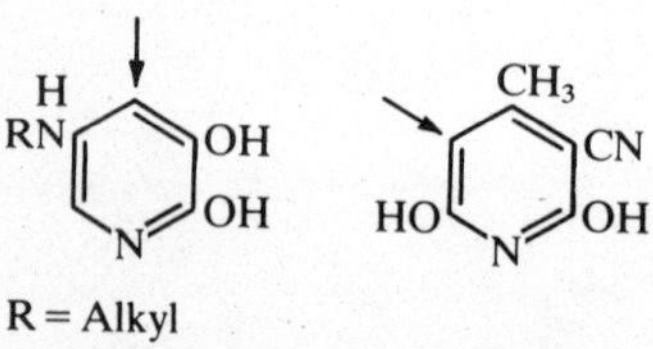

R = Alkyl

Fig. 4.38

The tautomeric hydroxypyridone structure e.g.

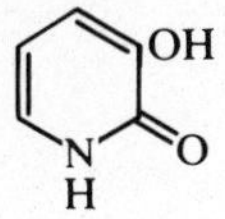

Fig. 4.39

is the form usually given in the patent literature.

5
Azo Dyes—II

Monoazo dyes

The monoazo dyes are a large group covering many important applications. They are of the type

   A → E

where   A = a diazo component, i.e. a diazotized arylamine,
         E = a coupling component coupled with one molecule
             of a diazo component.

It is convenient to consider first those dyes, the molecules of which contain no solubilizing groups.

Dyes without —CO₂H or —SO₃H groups

This group is a source of solvent, pigment, basic (cationic), mordant and disperse dyes.

Solvent dyes. These are among the simplest dyes, C.I. Solvent Yellow 1, 11000 being obtained by coupling diazotized aniline with anilinomethanesulphonic acid, the product finally being hydrolysed to give

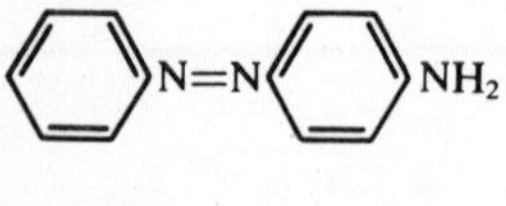

Fig. 5.1

Solvent dyes derived from phenols are exemplified by C.I. Solvent Orange 1, 11920:

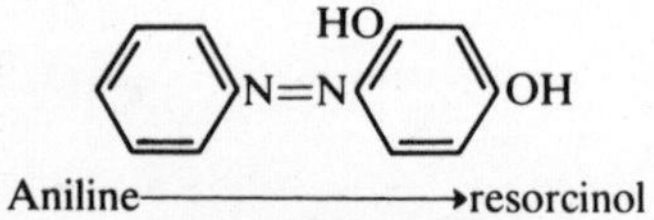

Aniline————————→resorcinol
(Sudan Orange G)

Fig. 5.2

and C.I. Solvent Red 17, 12155:

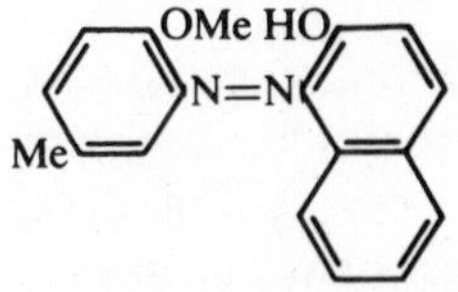

2-Amino-1-methoxy-4-methylbenzene———▸2-naphthol
(cresidine)
(Sudan Red R)

Fig. 5.3

The yellow dye:

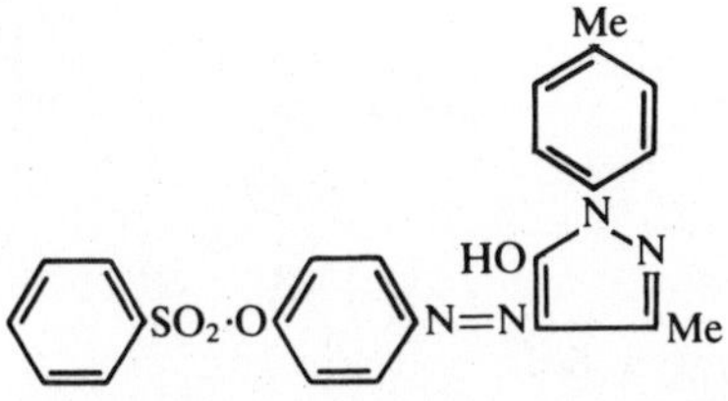

4-Aminophenylbenzene sulphonate→3-methyl-1-*p*-tolyl-5-pyrazolone

Fig. 5.4

according to the claims of B.P. 966 800 (CIBA) is suitable for the mass coloration of cellulose acetate and has good fastness to light and washing.

Pigments. Certain insoluble monoazo dyes are used as pigments. These are dealt with in Chapter 15.

Basic or cationic dyes. The basic dyes are among the earliest synthetic dyes and have been used in many different applications concerned with natural fibres. In general their fastness properties were inferior, light fastness being especially poor. They are usually the hydrochlorides of bases, having moderate solubility in water, the chromophoric system being present as a cation. An example is Chrysoidine, C.I. Basic Orange 2, 11270:

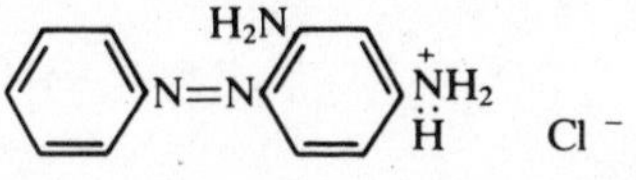

Fig. 5.5

In recent years a new range of cationic dyes has emerged with the development of polyacrylonitrile or acrylic fibres on which these dyes have superior light fastness compared with that on natural fibres. Such dyes are known under various commercial names, e.g.

Basacryl (BASF)	Calcozine (CCC)
Astrazone (FBy)	Lyrcamine (Fran)

Deorlene (CIBA)   Sandocryl (S)
Maxilon (Gy)   Noracryl (YDC)

It is estimated that 50–100 different cationic dyes, drawing chiefly on the azo, anthraquinone and triarylmethane chromophoric systems are now commercially available. The constitutions of the new cationic dyes have not so far been disclosed but the following monoazo dyes have been selected from the recent patent literature: B.P. 993 593 (Gy) claims that the dye obtained by coupling diazotized 2,4-dinitroaniline with 5-imino-3-methyl-1-phenyl-2-pyrazoline, followed by methylation and isolation as zinc chloride double salt:

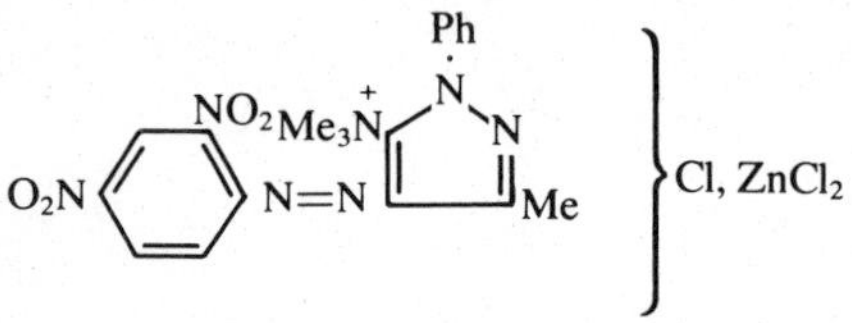

Fig. 5.6

gives reddish-yellow dyeings on polyacrylonitrile of good fastness to steaming, decatizing and pleating.

CIBA, in B.P. 957 364, describe the scarlet dye obtained from 2-chloro-4-nitroaniline → 4-N,N-dimethylamino-diphenylamine followed by quaternization as having excellent fastness properties on acrylic fibres.

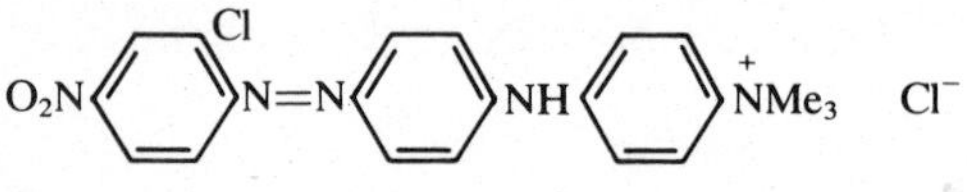

Fig. 5.7

A bright red cationic dye covered by U.S.P. 3 151 106 (CCC) is of interest since the azo link is formed by a method other than by diazotization and coupling, viz. the condensation of an amine with a nitroso compound:

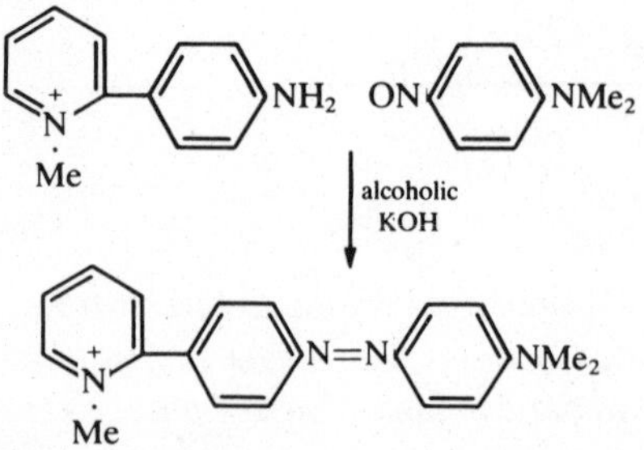

Fig. 5.8

In the above cases the cationic, positive charge is an integral part of the chromophoric system and the dyes are termed *delocalized* cationic dyes. These are generally of bright shade and high tinctorial strength (see oxazines, triarylmethane dyes, Chapter 11). Dyes in which the positive charge is insulated from the chromophoric system, e.g. by an alkylene link are known as *pendant* cationic dyes (see also anthraquinone cationic dyes, Chapter 7). Though somewhat dull in shade the dyes have high light-fastness on PAC fibres. Pechiney Ugine Kuhlmann, in B.P. 1 355 352, describe the dye:

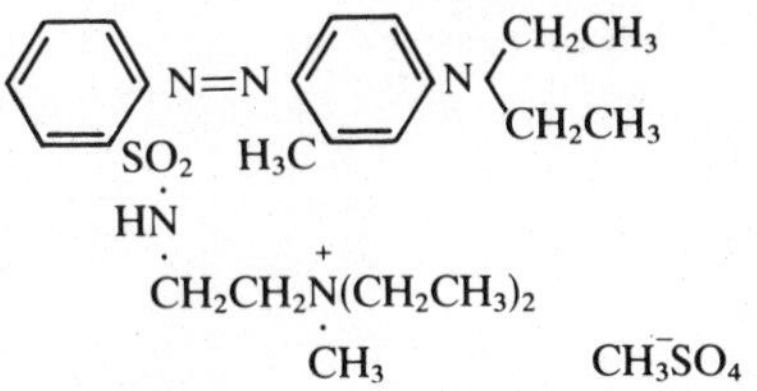

Fig. 5.9

as dyeing PAC fibres orange-red of good fastness to light.

Dyes in a third category are called *amine salts*. They have structures similar to monoazo disperse dyes but carry pendant unquaternized amino alkyl groups which, under the acidic conditions of dyeing, act as cationic groups. The dyes are said to have high light-fastness on PAC and have good substantivity for other synthetic fibres.

Mordant dyes. Only a few mordant dyes are represented. These dyes are characterized by the presence of an *ortho* hydroxy group relative to the azo linkage allowing metal complex formation when dyed material is treated with, e.g. bichromate (see Azo-metal complexes, pp. 108–9).

In C.I. Mordant Red 28, 11170 picramic acid, which has —OH *ortho* to —NH$_2$, is the diazo component, the dye having the structure:

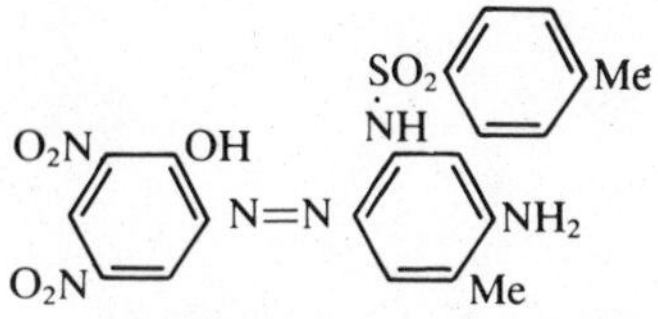

Fig. 5.10

Pyrogallol is the coupling component in C.I. Mordant Brown 54, 11965:

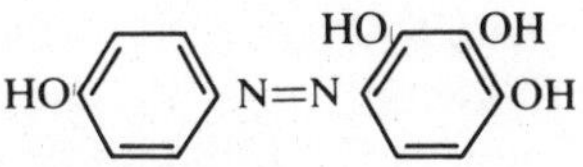

Fig. 5.11

Disperse dyes—See Chapter 14.

Soluble dyes, containing —CO₂H, or —SO₃H groups

Acid, Mordant and a few Direct dyes, are represented in the water-soluble monoazo dyes. It is convenient to deal with the soluble dyes according to the coupling component —E involved, in the manner of the Colour Index.

Arylamines

Acid dyes. The solubilizing —SO₃H group may be present in the diazo component as in C.I. Acid Orange 5, 13080, known as Orange IV, an old dye not now used to any extent:

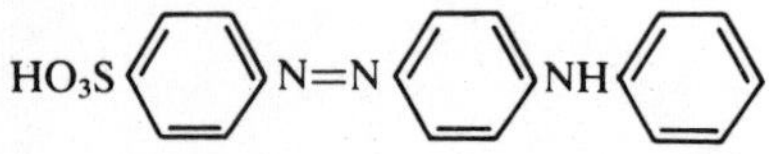

Sulphanilic acid→diphenylamine

Fig. 5.12

It may also be present in the coupling component as in C.I. Acid Red 74, 13355:

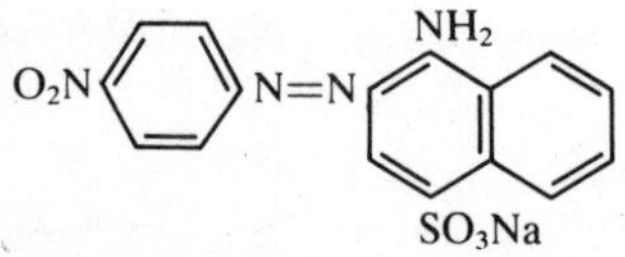

p-nitroaniline→naphthionic acid

Fig. 5.13

or in both as in C.I. Acid Blue 135, 13385:

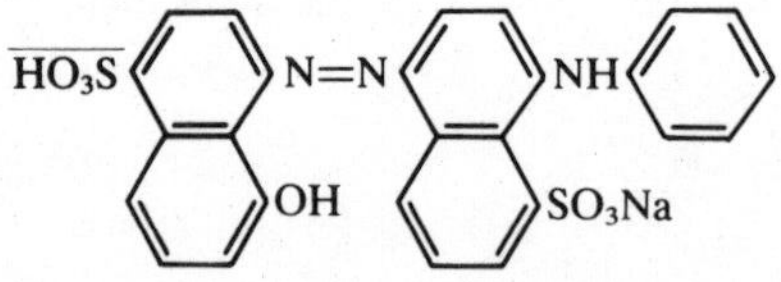

S acid→*N*-phenyl-Peri acid

1-amino-8-hydroxynaphthalene-4-sulphonic acid→1- phenylaminonaph-
thalene-8-sulphonic acid

Fig. 5.14

Mordant dyes. There are only a few mordant monoazo dyes in which the coupling component is an arylamine, the necessary hydroxy group *ortho* to the subsequent azo group to bring about co-ordination with chromium being present in the diazo component. A typical example is C.I. Mordant Brown 13, 13225 obtained by coupling diazotized 2-aminophenol-4-sulphonic acid on to *m*-phenylenediamine:

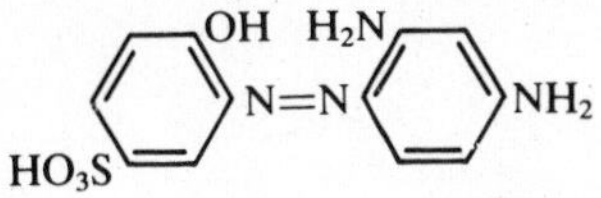

Fig. 5.15

Salicylic acid

This important coupling component is used in the manufacture of a large number of azo dyes including a number of yellow and orange monoazo mordant dyes. An example of a yellow is Eriochrome Yellow 2G *m*-nitroaniline → salicylic acid, the coupling being done under alkaline conditions

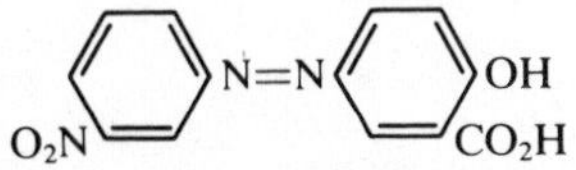

C.I. Mordant Yellow 1, 14025

Fig. 5.16

The property of co-ordination resides in the adjacent carboxy and hydroxy groups, a situation met with in other classes of mordant dyes, e.g. the triaryl-methane dye Eriochromazurol B.

1-Naphthol and 1-naphtholsulphonic acids

Acid dyes. The monoazo acid dyes as a whole are a group of relatively cheap dyes of good levelling properties but of rather low wet fastness. They dye wool from an acid bath, are bright and are of moderate to good light fastness. A simple example is Orange I (sulphanilic acid → 1-naphthol), C.I. Acid Orange 20, 14600:

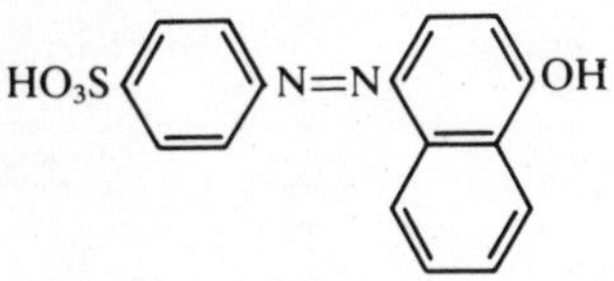

Fig. 5.17

C.I. Acid Red 14, 14720, Azo Rubine, is naphthionic acid → Nevile and Winther's acid:

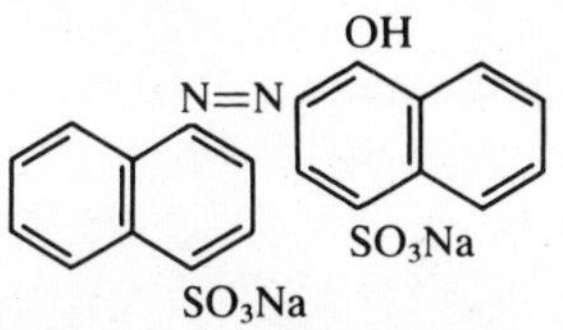

Fig. 5.18

Couplings with naphthols are carried out under alkaline conditions especially where amino groups are present to activate alternative coupling positions under neutral or acid conditions.

Mordant dyes. An outstanding example is C.I. Mordant Black 11, 14645 (Eriochrome Black T) used in large quantities on account of its high light and wet fastness.

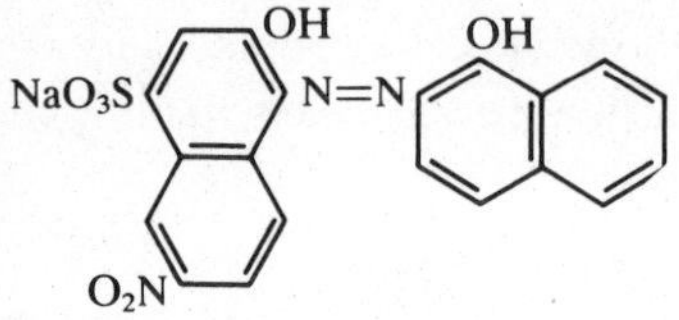

Fig. 5.19

1-amino-6-nitro-2-naphthol-4-sulphonic acid → 1-naphthol.

Coupling of the diazo-oxide in the 2- instead of the 4-position is probably the result of the strongly alkaline conditions employed.

2-Naphthol and 2-naphtholsulphonic acids

C.I. Mordant Black 1, 15710, is a very important dye obtained from 2-naphthol by coupling with diazotized 1-amino-6-nitro-2-naphthol-4-sulphonic acid:

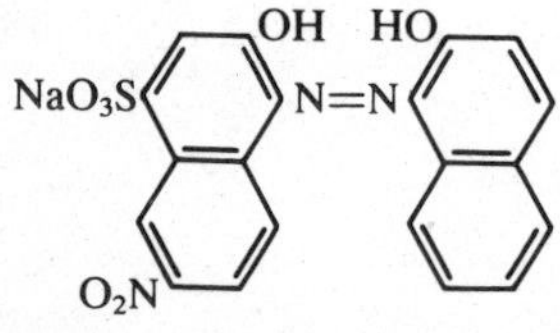

Fig. 5.20

It is used also as the chromium complex, 2 Cr: 3 moles dye, Neolan Black WA, C.I. Acid Black 52, 15711, for polyamide fibres.

C.I. Acid Red 25, 16050, uses crocein acid as coupling component:

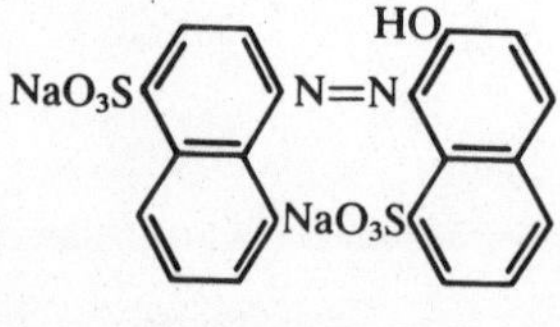

naphthionic acid ⟶ crocein acid

Fig. 5.21

C.I. Acid Orange 10, 16230, is aniline → G acid:

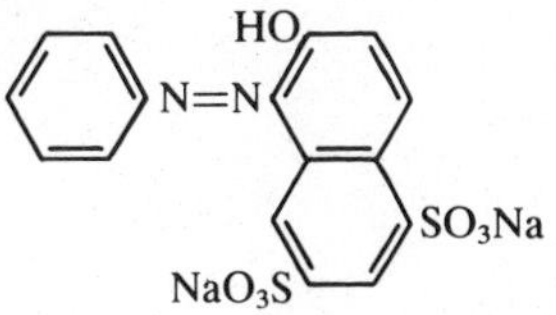

Fig. 5.22

Among the direct dyes C.I. Direct Red 70, 16081, employs Primuline as diazo component and Schäffer's acid as coupling component:

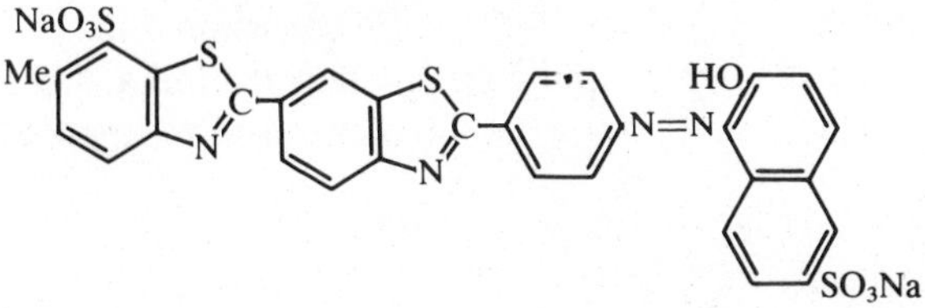

Fig. 5.23

The sulphurization products of *p*-toluidine, primuline base and dehydrothio-*p*-toluidine are used, as their sulphonic acids, in the manufacture of some valuable cotton dyes, the thiazole structure being responsible for the substantivity of such dyes.

Naphthalenediolsulphonic acids

The dyes stemming from 1,8-dihydroxynaphthalene-3,6-disulphonic acid (chromotropic acid) are the most interesting examples among this class, e.g. C.I. Acid Red 29, 16570:

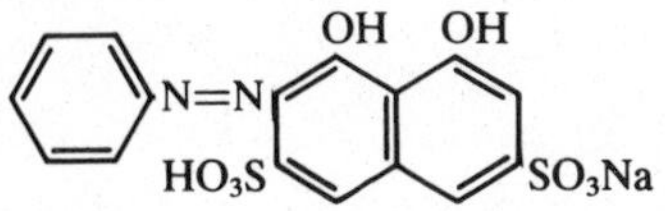

Fig. 5.24

C.I. Acid Red, 176, 16575 (*p*-nitroaniline → chromotropic acid) gives rise, on reduction of the nitro group, to C.I. Acid Violet 3, 16580. Chromotropic acid has to a large extent been replaced by cheaper intermediates, chiefly *N*-acetyl-H acid, the dyes obtained being more stable to light.

Aminonaphtholsulphonic acids and their derivatives

There are over a hundred dyes of known constitution listed in the C.I. as being derived from the aminonaphtholsulphonic acids and their *N*-alkyl, *N*-aryl and *N*-acyl derivatives.

Acid dyes. C.I. Acid Red 231, 17040, is a leather dye derived from *p*-aminoacetanilide by acid coupling on to Gamma acid:

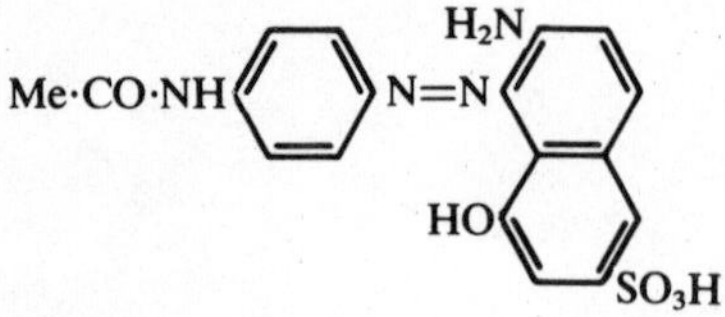

Fig. 5.25

C.I. Acid Violet 1, 17025, is 2-amino-5-nitrobenzene sulphonic acid diazotized and coupled (acid) on to Gamma acid. By reduction of the 5-nitro group with sodium sulphide C.I. Acid Red 34, 17030, is obtained.

Examples of acid and alkaline coupling on *N*-phenyl-gamma acid are: C.I. Acid Black 31, 17580 (acid coupling) with diazotized *p*-nitro-*o*-anisidine:

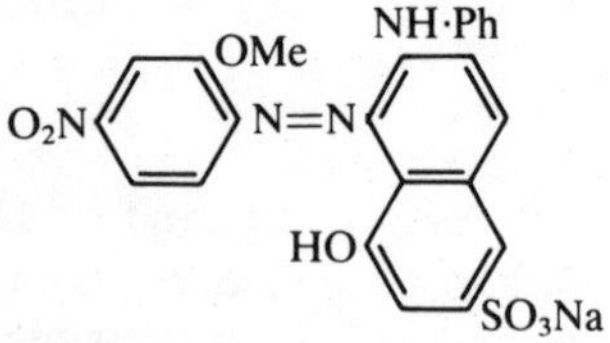

Fig. 5.26

and C.I. Acid Brown 88, 17595 (alkaline coupling) with diazotized sulphanilic acid.

H acid. This intermediate is a prolific source of azo dyes of many classes. An example of a wool dye is C.I. Acid Blue 6, 17185:

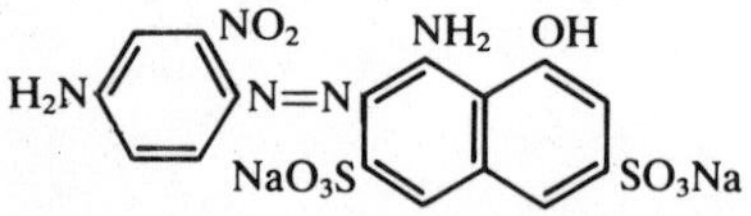

Fig. 5.27

obtained by acid coupling diazotized 4-amino-3-nitroacetanilide on to H acid, the acetylamino being subsequently hydrolysed.

Acetyl-H acid. By the alkaline coupling of diazotized *N*-dodecylaniline on *N*-acetyl-H acid, a member of the classical carbolan range, Carbolan Crimson B (C.I. Acid Red 138) is obtained:

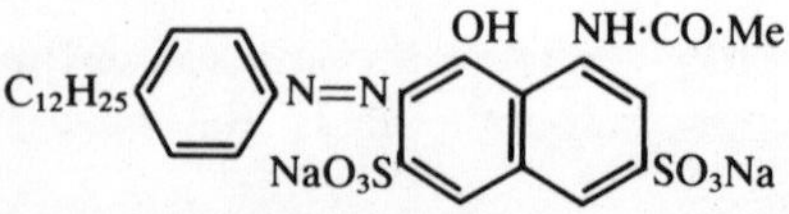

Fig. 5.28

This series was developed by ICI and is characterized by high milling fastness, a property conferred on the molecule by the long chain hydrocarbon group. The milling fastness of Carbolan Crimson B is 5, whereas that of C.I. Acid Red 1, 18050 (Azo Geranine 2G, aniline → N-acetyl-H acid) is only 1.

Mordant dyes. The mordant dyes are represented, among others, by C.I. Mordant Black 38, 18160 (Metachrome Black Blue G):

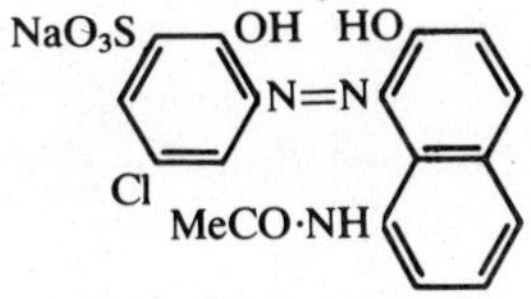

Fig. 5.29

the diazo component being 1-amino-4-chlorophenol-6-sulphonic acid and the coupling component being 1-acetylamino-7-hydroxynaphthalene.

Direct dyes. A number of useful red and orange direct cotton dyes are obtained from J acid derivatives. Most are development dyes, being finally diazotized on the fibre and coupled with 2-naphthol as second coupling component. In effect a disazo dye is produced and the substantivity of the series may be ascribed to the ability of the J acid molecule to form a linear disazo-dye molecule. Typical examples are: C.I. Direct Red 118, 17780:

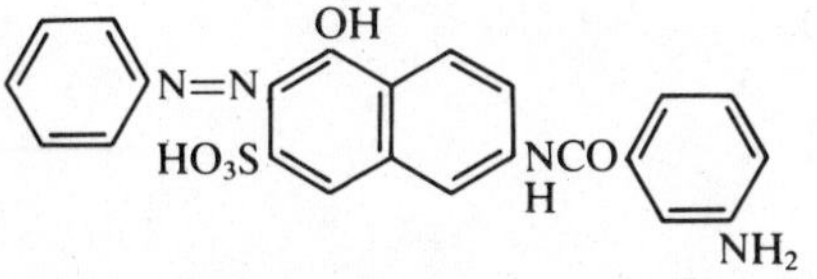

Fig. 5.30

the coupling component being N-m-aminobenzoyl-J acid. The dye is developed on the fibre with 2-naphthol.
C.I. Direct Orange 75, 17840 (developed with 2-naphthol):

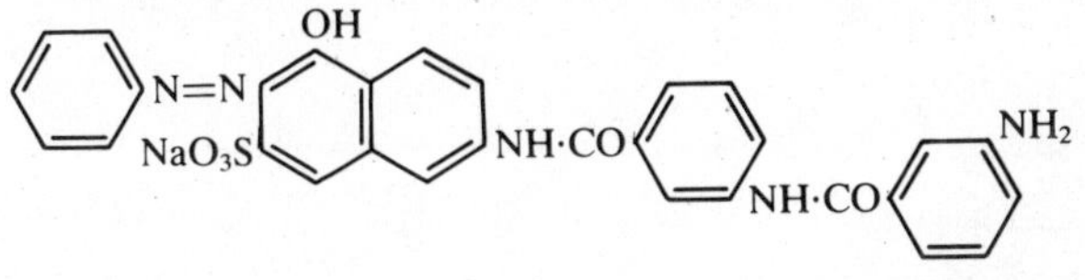

Fig. 5.31

contains two —NH·CO— linkages. The amide group also confers cotton substantivity.

In C.I. Direct Red 65, 17870, both amide and urea linkages are present:

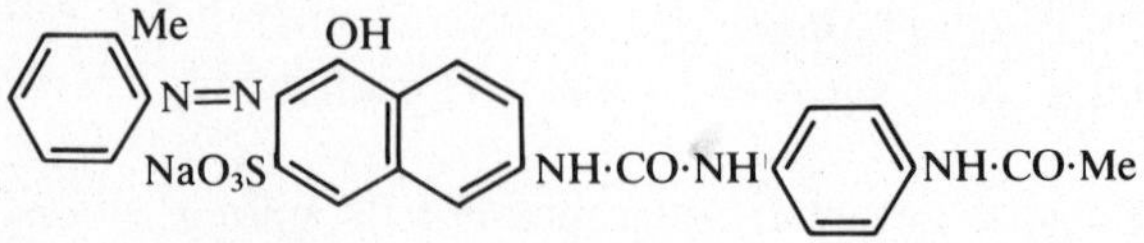

Fig. 5.32

Pyrazolones

Acid dyes. Two of the most widely used monoazopyrazolone dyes are C.I. Acid Yellow 17, 18965 (Kiton Fast Yellow 2GL) sulphanilic acid → 1-(2′,5′dichloro-4′sulphophenyl)-3-methyl-5-pyrazolone used for dyeing wool and nylon:

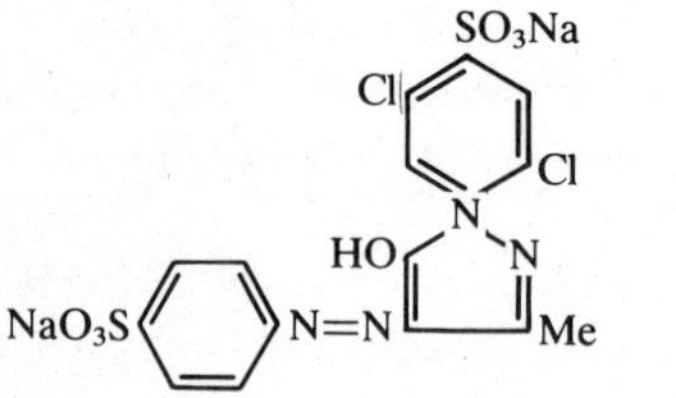

Fig. 5.33

and the classical dye Tartrazine (C.I. Acid Yellow 23, 19140), sulphanilic acid → 1-(4′-sulphophenyl)pyrazolone-3-carboxylic acid:

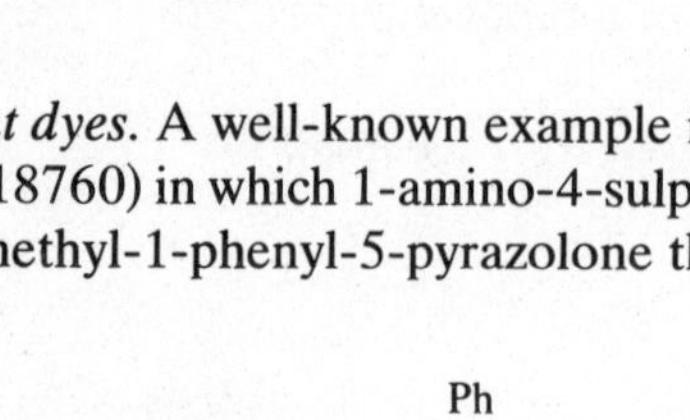

Fig. 5.34

Mordant dyes. A well-known example is Chrome Fast Red 2B (C.I. Mordant Red 7, 18760) in which 1-amino-4-sulpho-2-naphthol is the diazo component and 3-methyl-1-phenyl-5-pyrazolone the coupling component:

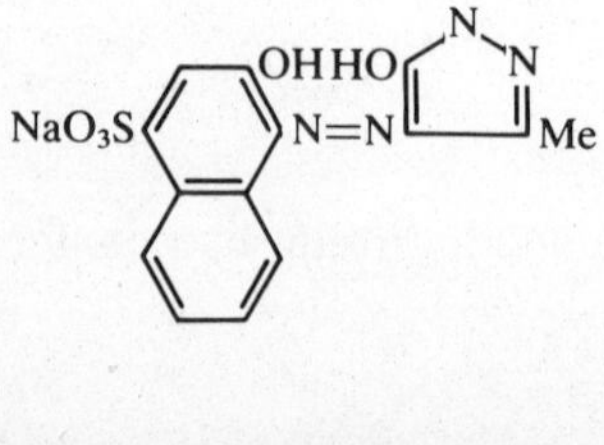

Fig. 5.35

Direct dyes. The few listed are primuline derivatives and owe their substantivity to the presence of thiazole rings. An example is C.I. Direct Yellow 14, 18780 (primuline → 3-methyl-1-phenyl-5-pyrazolone).

Hydroxyquinolines

Certain quinoline derivatives are used, to a limited extent, as coupling components. C.I. Mordant Orange 26 19325 is 5-chloroaniline-2-sulphonic acid → 8-hydroxyquinoline:

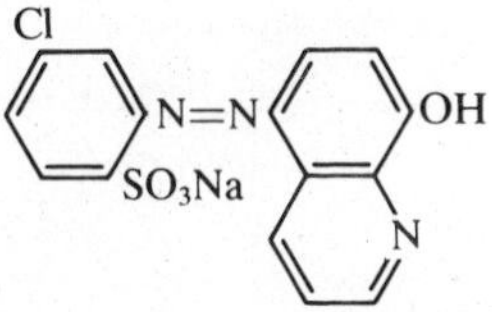

Fig. 5.36

the hydroxy group and adjacent tertiary nitrogen acting as salt-forming and chelating groups respectively in the chroming process. The dye, Palatine Fast Red BEN (C.I. Acid Red 214, 19355), is a preformed chromium complex of

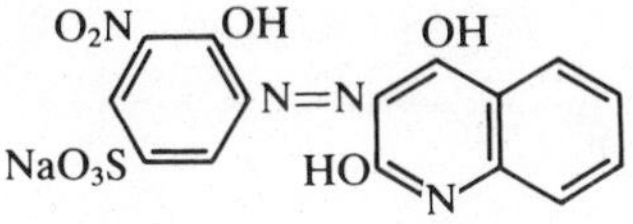

Fig. 5.37

Disazo dyes

There are four subdivisions in the Colour Index among the disazo dyes, each of which can be assigned a general formula using the symbols introduced by Winther. Thus:

(1) $A \rightarrow Z \rightarrow A'$

(2) $D \nearrow^{E} \searrow_{E'}$

(3) $A \rightarrow M \rightarrow E$

(4) $A \rightarrow Z \cdot X \cdot Z \leftarrow A'$

where   A is a diazo component,
        D is a tetrazo component
        E is a coupling component coupled with one molecule of a diazo
           component,

M is an aromatic amine which after coupling with a diazo component provides an amino group for further diazotization,

Z is a coupling component coupled with two or more molecules of a diazo component or with one molecule of each of two or more different diazo components.

In Z·X·Z, X may be —NH—, —NH·CO·NH— or more complex linkages.

Disazo dyes of the type A→ Z ← A'

There are relatively few dyes in this class; almost all the water-soluble ones are either acid or mordant dyes. They are mostly dull blues, greens, browns and blacks. A few are derived from resorcinol of which an example is C.I. Direct Orange 18, 20215:

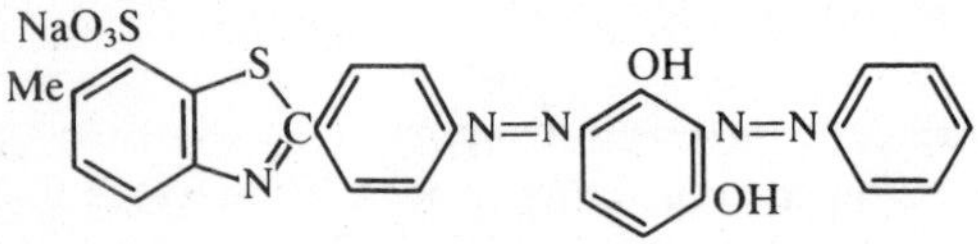

Fig. 5.38

which is

dehydrothio-*p*-toluidinesulphonic acid (1)

resorcinol

aniline (2)

In this case the suitability as a direct dye is determined by the first diazo component. In most dyes of this class it is the coupling component Z that determines the general properties of the dye.

Among the acid dyes may be mentioned C.I. Acid Green 19, Mordant Green 11, 20440, 2,5-dichloroaniline → H acid ← 1-naphthylamine:

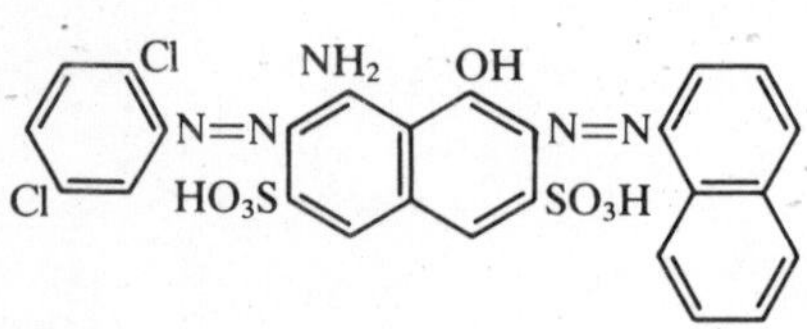

Fig. 5.39

Diazotized 2,5-dichloroaniline is coupled first under acid conditions; the second coupling is done under alkaline conditions.

In C.I. Acid Black 17, 20350 (Wool Black 6BG) S acid is the coupling component and sulphanilic acid and 1-naphthylamine are the diazo components:

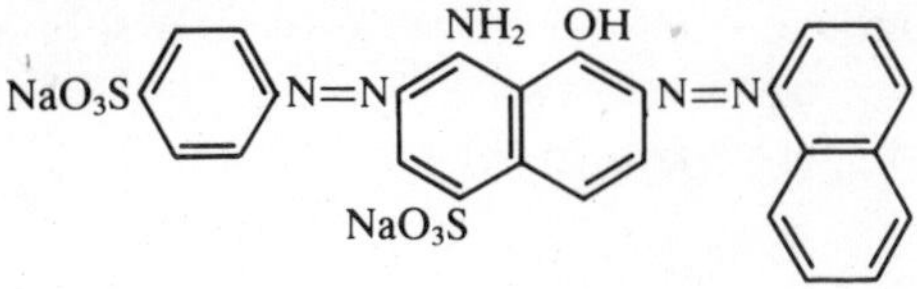

Fig. 5.40

Disazo dyes of the type D $\nearrow$ E $\searrow$ E′

This group, the largest sub-division of the disazo series, makes important contributions in the pigment field and provides a large number of direct dyes together with a smaller number of acid and mordant dyes. In contrast to the preceding type, it is the tetrazo component D that usually determines whether a dye belongs to the acid or direct series. Thus it is convenient to consider various examples under the heading of the parent diamine.

Benzidine

As already noted, benzidine and dyes derived therefrom are no longer manufactured or used for any purpose. Related substances such as dichlorobenzidine are not yet proscribed but research efforts continue to discover new direct dyes of novel structures. The benzidine dyes are of considerable historical significance in dye chemistry and their continued inclusion in this chapter would seem to be justified on that account.

Direct dyes. Congo Red, C.I. Direct Red 28, 22120, is obtained by coupling tetrazotized benzidine with sodium naphthionate in the presence of a buffer such as sodium acetate. The dye was discovered by Böttiger (1884), a university professor, who sent a specimen to a dye manufacturer; the latter found it useless as a wool dye, since it turned bright blue in the acid dyebath, and rejected it. A second manufacturer tested the dye on cotton and made the discovery that it dyed cotton directly, i.e. without the use of a mordant, from a neutral bath. Many thousands of tons of this dye were made for the dyeing of cotton, mostly in the countries of the Far East. It may be mentioned in passing that history records more than one such cautionary tale and in consequence coloured substances coming from research laboratories and elsewhere are nowadays apt to receive very thorough testing indeed.

The success of Congo Red naturally led to the development of other direct dyes since benzidine and its derivatives, in common with other middle components such as J acid and diaminostilbenedisulphonic acid give rise to dye molecules that are greatly extended in one direction (linear configuration) since recognized as one of the characteristics which confer cotton substantivity. Further examples of direct dyes are as follows:

C.I. Direct Brown 2, 22311 (Direct Brown M),

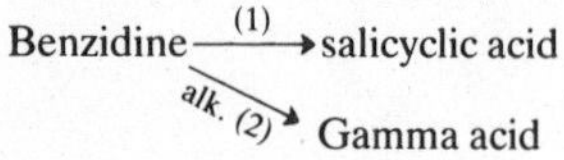

Benzidine $\xrightarrow{(1)}$ salicyclic acid
$\xrightarrow[alk. (2)]{}$ Gamma acid

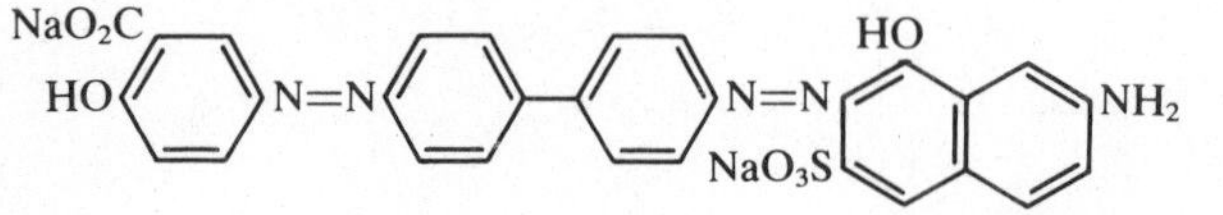

Fig. 5.41

and C.I. Direct Blue 2, 22590 (Chlorazol Black BH)

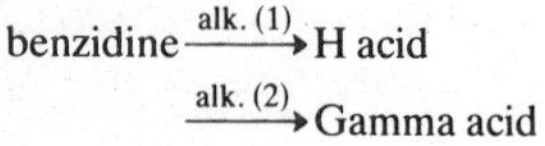

benzidine $\xrightarrow{alk. (1)}$ H acid
$\xrightarrow{alk. (2)}$ Gamma acid

Substituted benzidines. A very clear, blue dye is obtained from *o*-dianisidine (3,4′-dimethoxybenzidine) by tetrazotization and coupling (alkaline) with 2 moles of Chicago acid to give C.I. Direct Blue 1, 24410 (Direct Sky Blue GS):

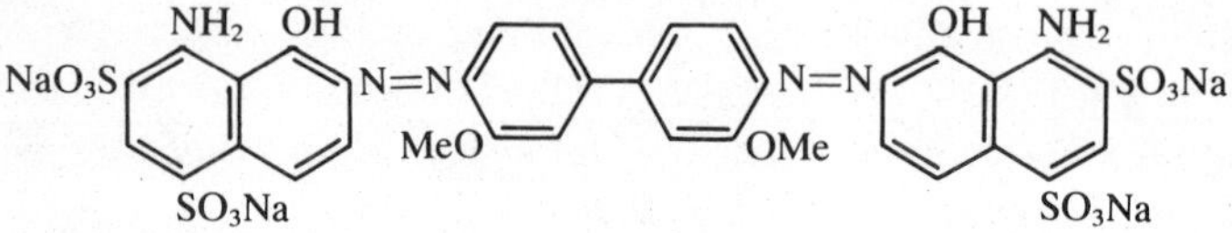

Fig. 5.42

C.I. Acid Red 99, 23285 is obtained as follows:

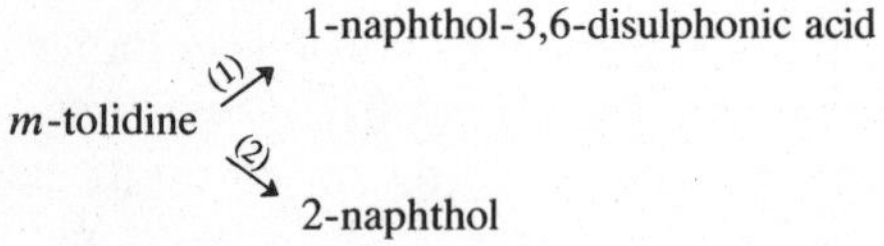

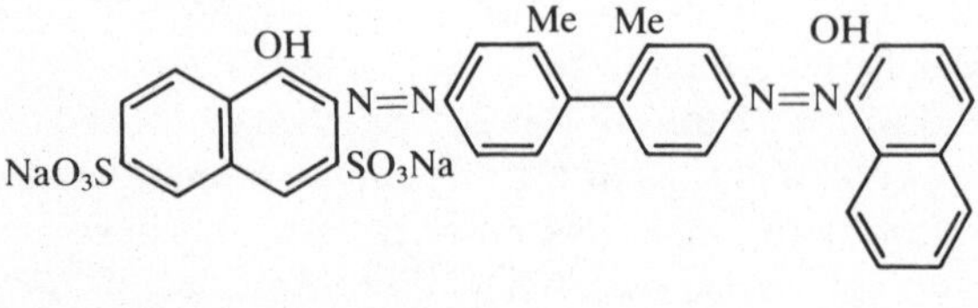

m-tolidine $\overset{(1)}{\underset{(2)}{\nearrow\searrow}}$

1-naphthol-3,6-disulphonic acid

2-naphthol

Fig. 5.43

Benzidine-2,2′-disulphonic acid

Acid and mordant dyes. The best example of an acid dye is probably C.I. Acid Yellow 42, 22910 (Benzyl Fast Yellow RS) which is benzidine-2,2′-disulphonic acid $\rightleftarrows$ 3-methyl-1-phenyl-5-pyrazolone (2 moles):

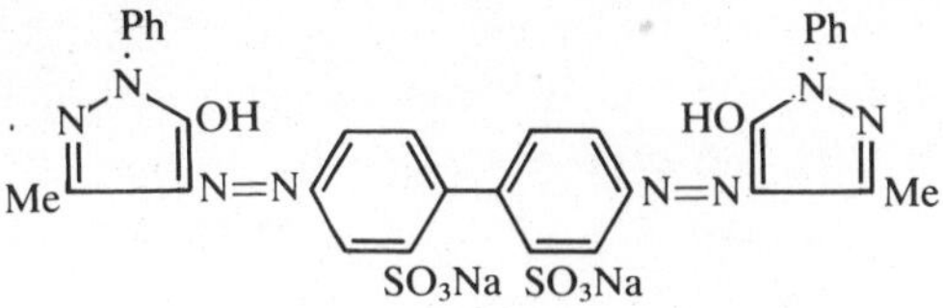

Fig. 5.44

C.I. Mordant Yellow 26, 22880 (Chrome Fast Yellow RB), is benzidine-2,2'-disulphonic acid ⇉ salicylic acid (2 moles).

A few important direct dyes of the type $D \begin{smallmatrix} \nearrow E \\ \searrow E' \end{smallmatrix}$ are derived from the bi-nuclear diamines of general formula:

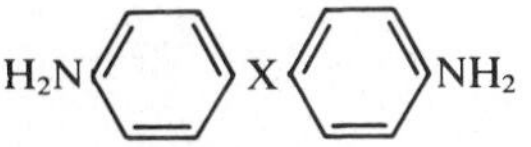

X = ·NH·CO·NH   H
    ·CH=CH·   ·N·; ·CONH·; ·S·   Fig. 5.45

The last three groups especially are currently being explored to find diamines alternative to benzidine in direct dye manufacture. A particularly important example is C.I. Direct Yellow 12, 24895 (Cotton Yellow CH, Chrysophenine G) which is obtained from 4,4'-diamino-2,2'-stilbenedisulphonic acid ⇉ phenol (2 moles) (Brilliant Yellow) followed by ethylation giving:

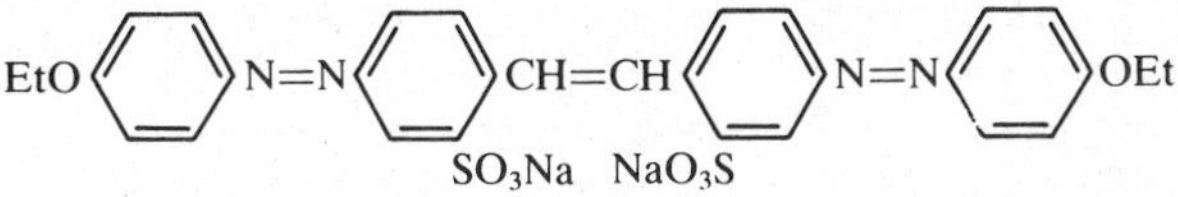

Fig. 5.46

Brilliant Yellow itself has poor alkali fastness giving a bright red colour with sodium carbonate. The ethylated product is stable towards alkali and is widely used as a cotton dye.

Disazo dyes of the type A → M → E

The constitutions are known of about 250 of the dyes in this group, known also as the secondary disazo dyes. About half are direct dyes; the remainder are mostly acid dyes together with a few mordant dyes.

Direct dyes. An example in which a monoazo dye containing a diazotizable amino group is the diazo component is afforded by Chlorazol Fast Red K, C.I.

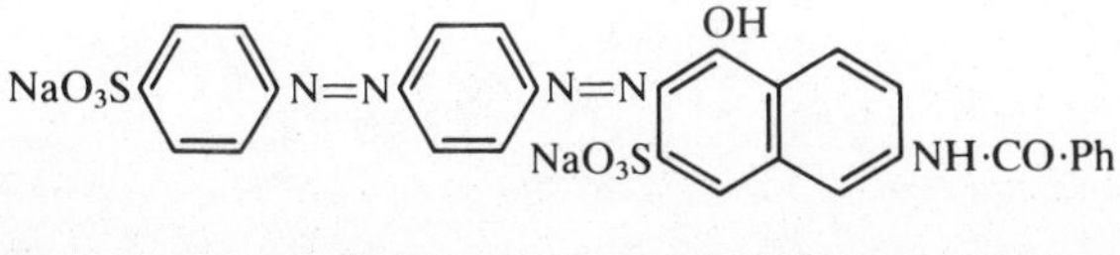

Fig. 5.47

Direct Red 81, 28160, 4-(p-aminophenylazo)benzenesulphonic acid → N-benzoyl-J acid. A recent example in which N-p-aminobenzoyl-J acid is used as middle component is the orange dye:

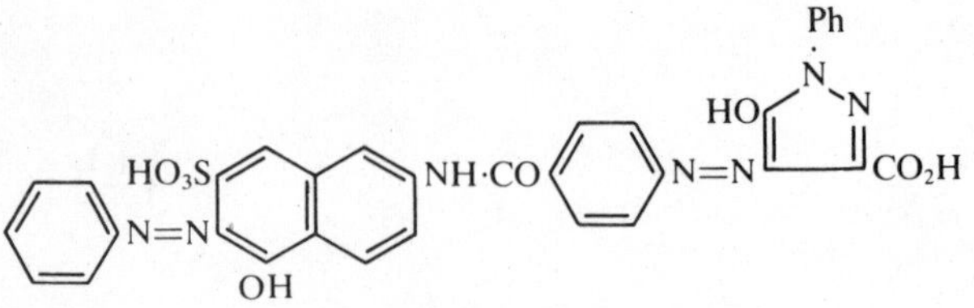

aniline→N-p-aminobenzoyl-J acid→1-phenyl-5-pyrazolone-3-carboxylic acid.

Fig. 5.48

Among the acid dyes, C.I. Acid Red 148, 26665 (Cloth Red B) has the constitution:

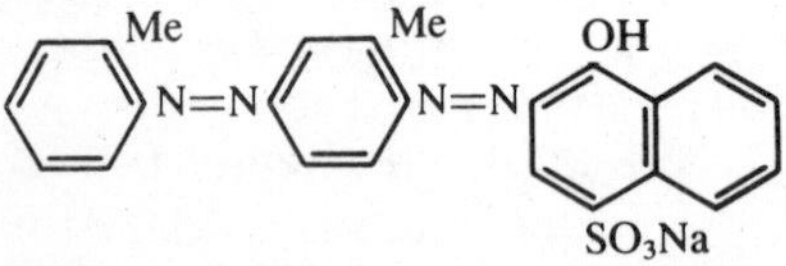

Fig. 5.49

The important Diamond Black F, C.I. Mordant Black 5, 26695, is obtained by acid coupling aminosalicylic acid with 1-naphthylamine, the resulting monoazo dye being coupled alkaline with Nevile and Winther's acid.

Disazo dyes of the type A → Z·X·Z ← A'

This very important group is almost entirely composed of direct dyes. They are of two main kinds:

1. Those resulting from the phosgenation of monoazo dyes containing a primary amino group, a urea derivative —NH·CO·NH—, being formed.
2. Those resulting from the use of J acid urea (or carbonyl-J acid) as middle (coupling) component.

Fig. 5.50

the two coupling positions being indicated by X. A typical dye of the first category is C.I. Direct Yellow 49, 29035 (Sirius Yellow G), Fig. 5.51,

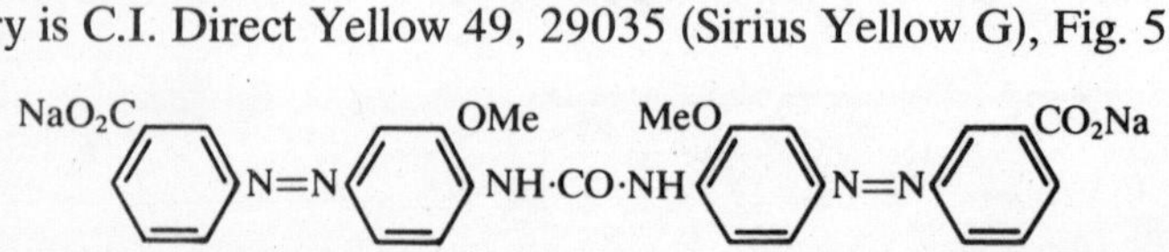

Fig. 5.51

made by the action of phosgene on the monoazo dye *m*-aminobenzoic acid → *o*-anisidine, Fig. 5.52:

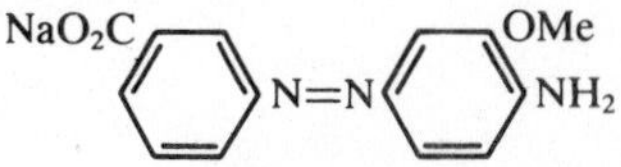

Fig. 5.52

Such reactions are often carried out by passing phosgene gas through an alkaline, aqueous solution of the dyestuff, when the reaction

$$2R \cdot NH_2 + COCl_2 \rightarrow R \cdot NH \cdot CO \cdot NH \cdot R + 2HCl$$

takes place, the acid liberated being taken up by excess of alkali. In some cases an equimolecular mixture of two different monoazo dyes is phosgenated and an unsymmetrical urea and two different symmetrical ureas are theoretically possible and in fact mixtures are formed.

J acid urea. A widely used dye derived from J acid urea is Chlorazol Scarlet 4BS, C.I. Direct Red 23, 29160 in which aniline and *p*-aminoacetanilide are the two diazo components employed:

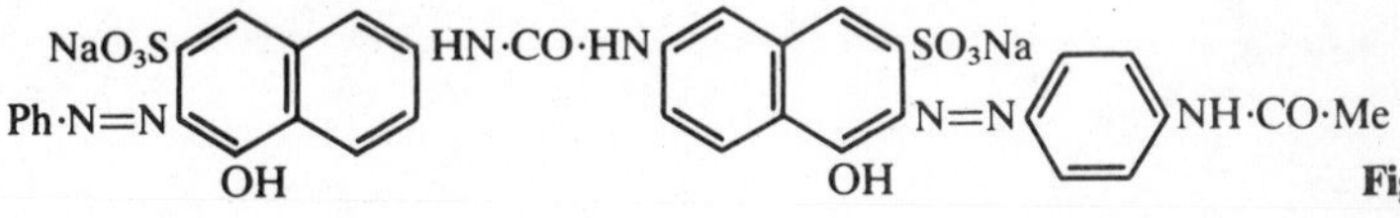

Fig. 5.53

Trisazo dyes

The trisazo dyes can be subdivided into five groups, of which only the following three are commercially important, using the Winther symbols as before. These and the higher polyazo dyes are mostly direct dyes some of which are used as leather dyes also.

Trisazo dyes of the type D

The dyes in this subdivision are chiefly browns and blacks, a widely used example being C.I. Direct Black 38, 30235 (Carbide Black E) obtained by three coupling operations as follows:

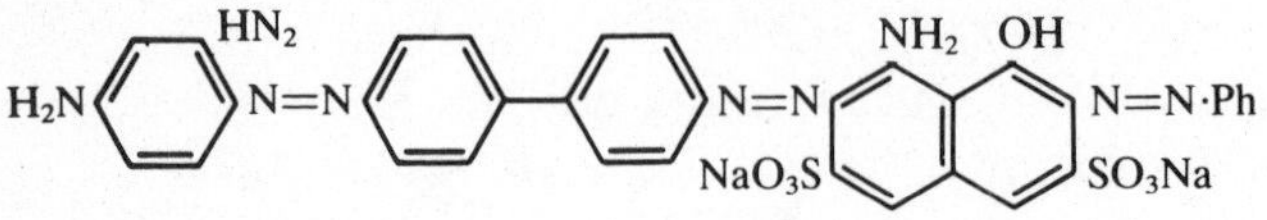

Fig. 5.54

Type D

E
↗
M → E′

The dyes of this kind are chiefly browns, blues, olives and blacks. The subdivision is numerically the largest of the five. An example of a brown is C.I. Direct Brown 54, 31735:

benzidine
↗ salicylic acid
↘ Cleve's acid → phenol

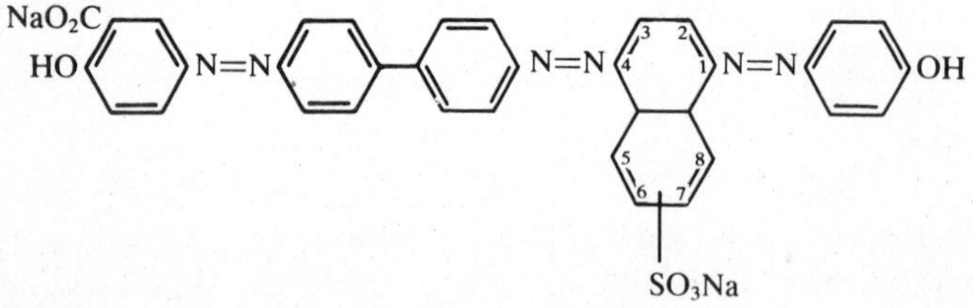

Fig. 5.55

Type A → M → M′ → E

These direct dyes are described in the Colour Index as making an important contribution to the blue to grey range in contrast to the drabness of the preceding trisazo types. Where E is J acid or N-phenyl-J acid the dyes are usually of good shade, good substantivity for cellulose fibres and good light fastness. Two widely used examples are:

C.I. Direct Blue 71, 34140 (Chlorantine Fast Blue GLL), 3-amino-1,5-naphthalenedisulphonic acid → 1-naphthylamine → 1,7-Cleve's acid —(alk.)→ J acid

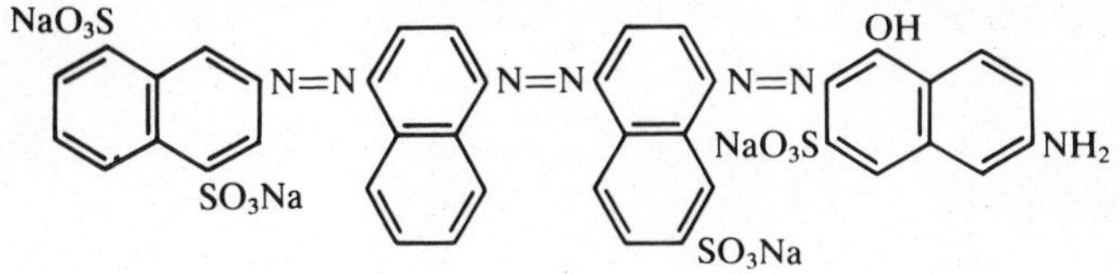

Fig. 5.56

and C.I. Direct Blue 78, 34200 (Chlorantine Fast Blue 4GL), 2-amino-1,4-benzenedisulphonic acid → 1,7-Cleve's acid → 1-naphthylamine $\xrightarrow{\text{(alk.)}}$ N-phenyl-J acid

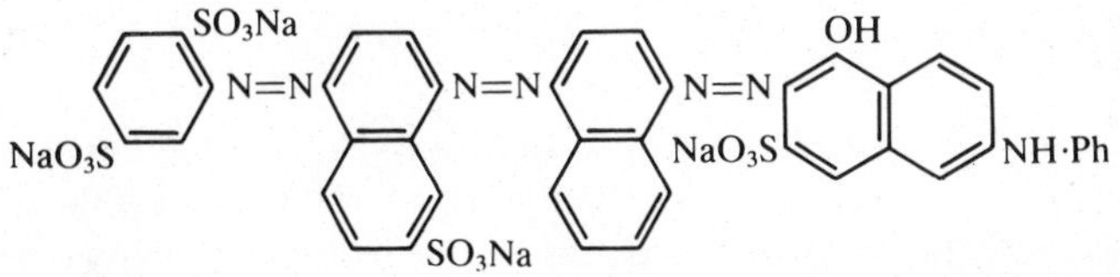

Fig. 5.57

Polyazo dyes

The tetrakisazo dyes and azo dyes of greater complexity are mixed products, their structural formulae being mainly conjectural. The dyes are direct and leather dyes, chiefly of black or dark brown hue. There are, however, some reds and one example, a bright bluish-red of some importance, is C.I. Direct Red 80, 35780 (Chlorantine Fast Red 5BRL), a symmetrical urea of structure:

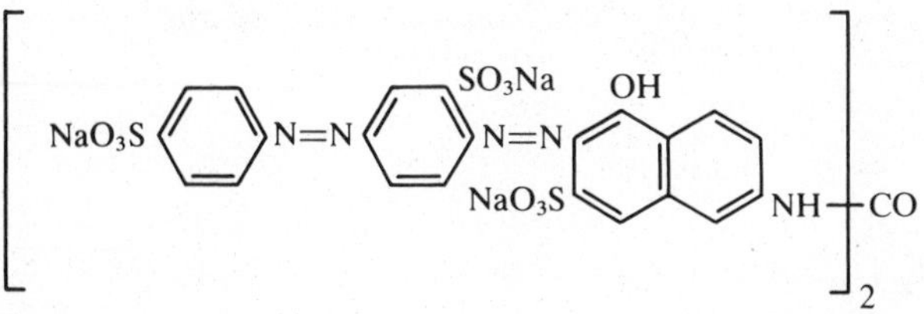

Fig. 5.58

obtained by phosgenation of the appropriate disazo dye. This last is obtained by diazotizing 6-amino-3,4′-azodibenzenesulphonic acid and coupling with N-acetyl-J acid. The acetyl group is hydrolysed prior to the phosgenation stage.

6
Azo Dyes—III

Metal–azo dye complexes

From the earliest days of dyeing the addition of certain metallic salts to the dyebath, or the 'after-treatment' of the dyed material with such metallic salts, were steps known to produce fast dyeings. For instance polyhydroxyanthraquinone dyes, on being after-chromed with a chromium salt or bichromate, formed a lake on the fibre, the dyeings being of superior light-fastness and washing-fastness.

In the case of certain azo dyes having hydroxyl groups in each of the two *ortho* positions relative to the azo group, stable chromium complexes are formed relatively easily. The electronic configuration of the chromium atom is $3d$ (5), $4s$ (1) and $4p$ (0). On losing three electrons in salt formation the Cr^{3+} ion is formed having the configuration $3d$ (3), $4s$ (0) and $4p$ (0). In complex formation the stable outer shell in the case of chromium consists of twelve electrons, i.e. its co-ordination number is 6. A simple complex with one molecule of a dihydroxyazo dye can be formulated thus, X being an anion:

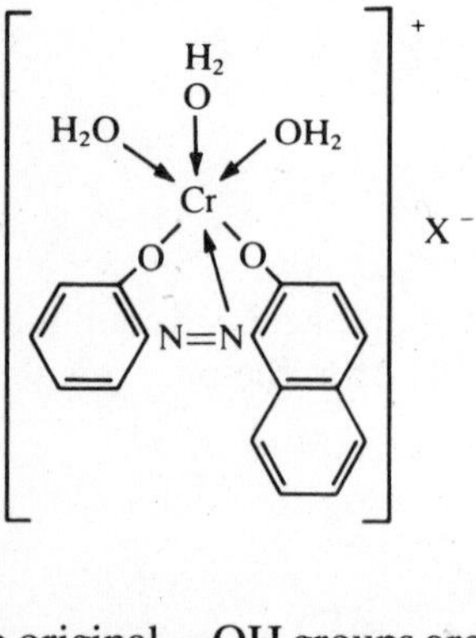

Fig. 6.1

The two original —OH groups are salt-forming changing Cr^{3+} to Cr^+, the lone pair of a nitrogen atom of the azo link donating two electrons, the other six electrons coming from the lone pairs of the oxygen atoms of three water molecules. Such donor atoms or groups are called 'ligands'.

1:1 Metal–azo complexes

The 1:1 complexes, introduced by CIBA in 1919, are obtained from azo dyes in which sulphonic acid groups are present in the molecule to confer water-solubility and in which, for example, there are two hydroxyl groups in the two *ortho* positions relative to the azo group. They are mostly chromium complexes manufactured by the dye-maker and used as such by the dyer. These complexes are made, as a rule, by heating the dyestuff with a chromium salt (often the formate) in aqueous solution at 120–130 °C, i.e. under a pressure of 1–2 atm.

The dyes are classed as acid wool dyes and must be used at a pH of 2 or thereabouts. It is necessary therefore to employ large amounts of sulphuric acid, up to 8% on the weight of wool to be dyed, in the dyebath. Too little acid causes skittery, i.e. unlevel, dyeings whereas excess acid corrects this by modifying the fibre so that level dyeings result, but sometimes causes damage to the wool with consequent deterioration in mechanical strength.

Bird[38], in summarizing the findings of Rattee and others in regard to the theory of dyeing with 1:1 complexes, points out that where only one $-SO_3H$ group is present in the molecule, a zwitterion $-SO_3^-$ Cr^+ is set up. If a second $-SO_3H$ group is present then combination with basic centres in the wool can occur just as with ordinary acid dyes (see Chapter 2). The most important factor controlling dyeing is considered, however, to be the ability of the $\ce{>N\!\!:}_H$ group occurring in wool to act as a ligand thus:

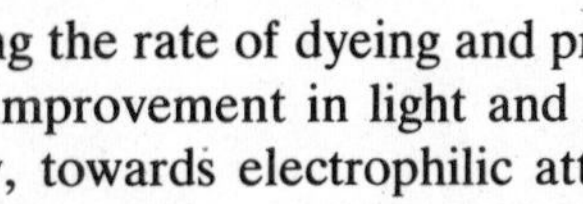

Fig. 6.2

Excess of acid suppresses this effect by protonation of $\ce{>N\!\!:}_H$ giving $\ce{>N^+H_2}$ thus retarding the rate of dyeing and producing a levelling action.

The improvement in light and general fastness is ascribed to the greater stability, towards electrophilic attack, of the azo group acting as ligand in complex formation compared with an azo group not so involved. Thus azo dyes derived from salicylic acid, while able to form complexes with metals by virtue of the adjacent $-CO_2H$ and $-OH$ groups, do not as chromium complexes show greatly improved fastness in comparison with the unmetallized dye, since the azo group is not involved in complex formation.

The Neolan (CIBA) and Palatine (BASF) dyes are prominent among the commercial 1:1 complexes of which the following are some examples.

C.I. Acid Orange 74, 18745, Neolan Orange R, is obtained from 6-amino-4-nitro-1-phenol-2-sulphonic acid → 3-methyl-1-phenyl-5-pyrazolone, the dye

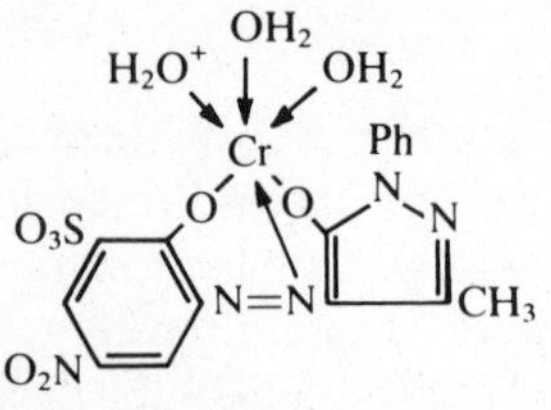

C.I. Acid Orange 74.   **Fig. 6.3**

being finally heated with aqueous chromium formate at 125 °C for several
hours. In subsequent examples the formula of the parent, chelating molecule,
either as free acid or sodium salt will be given. The 1 : 1 chromium complex C.I.
Acid Yellow 99, C.I. Solvent Yellow 19 (Neolan Yellow GR) is obtained from:

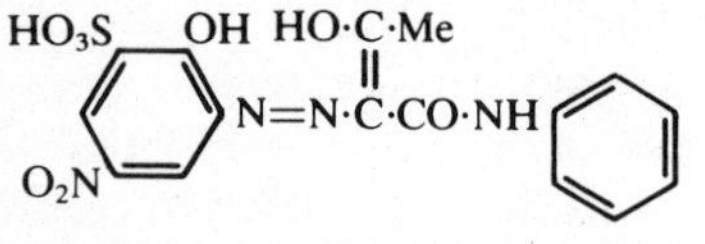

Fig. 6.4

2-amino-4-nitrophenol-6-sulphonic acid→acetoacetanilide

by heating with an aqueous solution of chromium fluoride.

The chromium complex of 2-amino-4-chlorophenol-6-sulphonic
acid → 2,4-dihydroxyquinoline:

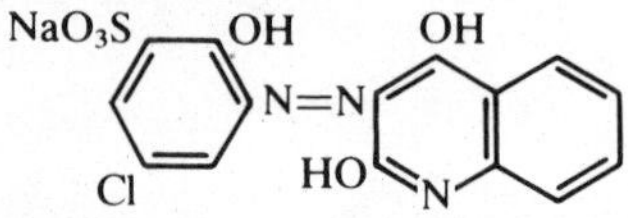

Fig. 6.5

is Neolan Bordeaux R, C.I. Acid Red 179, 19351.

C.I. Acid Black 54, 14885, Neolan Black 2G, Palatine Fast Black GGN has
the structure:

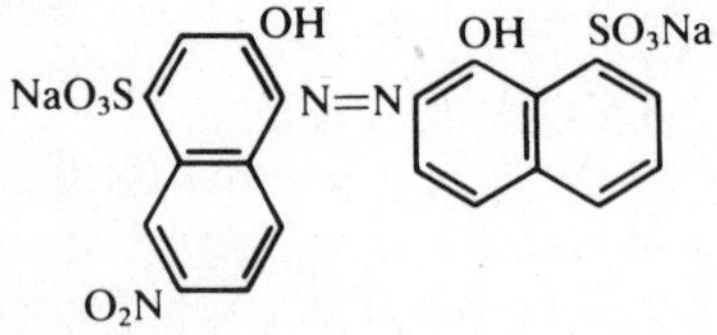

Fig. 6.6

and is obtained from the same diazo component as the important mordant dye
Chrome Black T already noted (p. 94).

1 : 2 Metal–azo complexes

It was found in 1927 that the 1 : 1 metal complexes could, under certain
conditions, react with another molecule of the same or a different dye to give a

complex in which a chromium atom is combined with two dye molecules. In 1951, following the work of G. Schetty, the neutral-dyeing 1:2 metal–azo complexes, outstanding in fastness to light and wet treatments, were introduced by Geigy as the Irgalan range. They have become one of the most important groups of wool dyes now in use. They are mostly chromium complexes, though a few cobalt complexes are employed also, and differ from 1:1 complexes in that the metal atom, e.g. Cr, is the centre of an anion, i.e. it carries a negative charge. This is brought about since the four hydroxyl or other acidic groups alter the original Cr^{3+} to Cr^-, the two azo groups acting as ligands to complete the twelve-electron system. Thus the 1:2 chromium complex derived from the dye 2-aminophenol → 2-naphthol has the structure

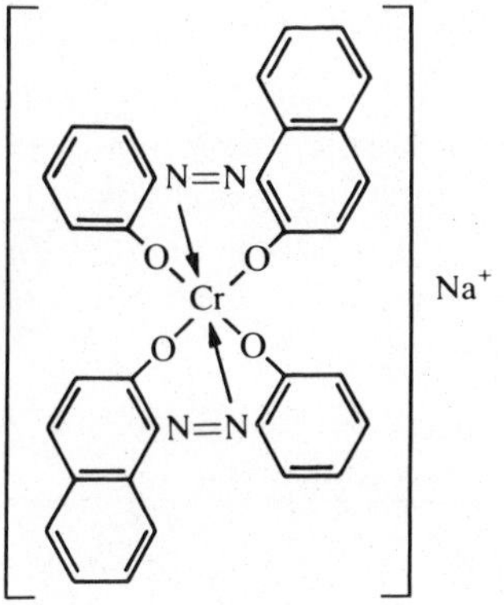

Fig. 6.7

This dye was found by Schetty to be homogeneous, i.e. chromatographic analysis showed it to be a single substance and not a mixture of isomers. In contrast, the 1:2 chromium complex:

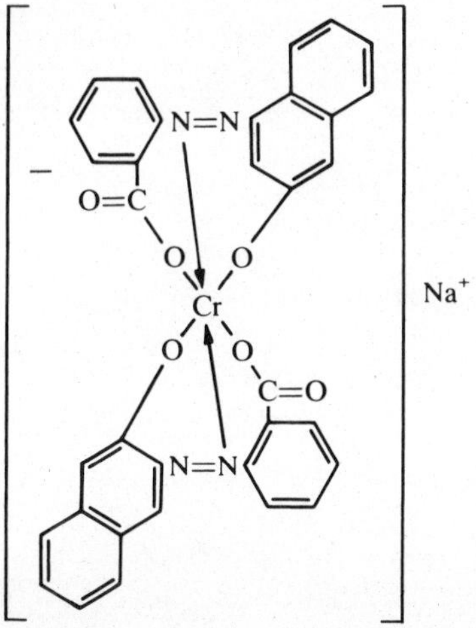

Fig. 6.8

was found by the same worker to be separable into four isomeric forms. These and other facts have been accounted for on stereochemical grounds. The Drew–Pfitzner or MER configuration explains the absence of isomerism in the cases where the two tridentate ligands are *o, o'*-dihydroxyazo- or *o*-amino-*o'*-hydroxyazo dyes and the 1 : 2 complexes obtained are homogeneous.

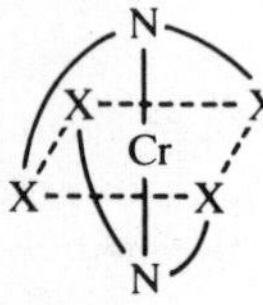

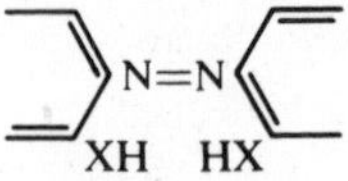

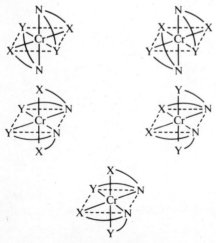

Meridial or MER form

Where XH = OH
or one XH = OH
the other = NH$_2$

Fig. 6.9

It will be seen that the two azo dye molecules are orientated at right angles to each other. For simplicity, only the ligand atoms are shown in Figs. 6.9 and 6.11, those belonging to the same azo dye molecule being linked by curved lines. In all cases N denotes one of the nitrogen atoms of the azo link. To account for stereoisomerism in 1 : 2 chromium complexes of dyes of the type:

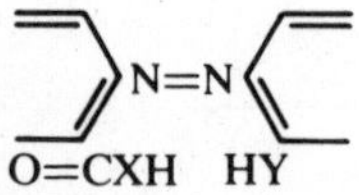

Where XH = OH
YH = OH or NH$_2$

Fig. 6.10

the Pfeiffer–Schetty or FAC configuration, sometimes called the sandwich form, postulates that the complexed chromium atom lies between parallel planes occupied by the two tridentate ligand dye molecules. This gives rise to five theoretical isomers as follows:

Facial or FAC forms

Fig. 6.11

The results from X-ray crystallographic studies on separated isomers or homogeneous products support these views. It should be noted that MER and certain FAC configurations are chiral, i.e. they may exist in enantio-morphic forms as *dl* mixtures. Such *d* and *l* forms do not differ in physical properties with the exception of their behaviour towards plane-polarized light.

According to Bird[38] chromium complexes having the FAC configuration are less soluble in water, and when dyed on wool are brighter in hue and have higher light-fastness but lower wet-fastness than otherwise comparable com-plexes having the MER configuration.

The mechanism of wool dyeing with the 1:2 complexes (Bird) is concerned partly with the bond between dye anion and positively-charged centres in the wool:

$$\text{Complex}^- \qquad H_3\overset{+}{N}{-}\big\rangle$$

but mainly with the van der Waals' forces between the large molecules of the metal–dye complex and the fibre. These van der Waals' forces being large, the rate of dyeing is low and fastness to wet-treatments is high. It should be noted that none of the bonds formed by the ligands and by the replacement of hydrogen atoms of the hydroxyl or other acidic groups, is replaceable by a 'donor' bond from $\big\rangle\!\!\begin{smallmatrix}N\\H\end{smallmatrix}$: groups in the wool molecule. The 1:2 complex wool dyes are superior to the older 1:1 type in several respects. They dye wool from neutral or very slightly acid baths, the wool being unimpaired under such mild conditions. As a class they are characterized by very good all-round fastness properties and as a further result of their low rates of dyeing they have excellent levelling properties. They are also important dyes for silk, polyamide fibres and other hydrophobic fibres.

Only in a few cases has the constitution of individual dyes been disclosed. From the few given in volume 5 (Supplement) of the Colour Index and from the examples published in the patent literature it is clear that solubilizing groups such as $-SO_3H$ and $-CO_2H$ are not present in the molecule. In practice such groups lead to dyes of poor levelling properties and of poor fastness to wet treatments. Certain non-ionic solubilizing groups such as $-SO_2CH_3$, $-SO_2NH_2$, $-SO_2NH$ alk, $-NH\cdot CO\cdot$alk and others are employed to improve solubility and to raise the rate of dyeing to the desired level. In contrast to dyes that are sulphonic acids the new dyes are not fibre selective, i.e. the presence of natural variations in the wool fibres does not give rise to 'tippy' or irregular dyeings.

Irgalan Violet DL (Gg) C.I. Acid Violet 78 has the structure:

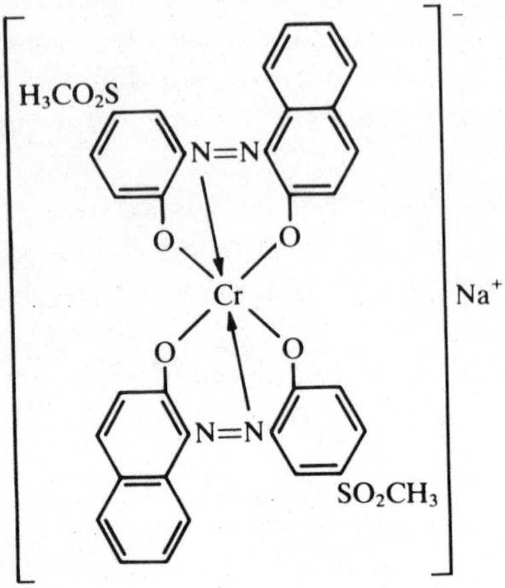

Fig. 6.12

In the following examples only the unmetallized molecules or pair of molecules are given.

C.I. Acid Orange 99 (Supplement), 12696, Solilan Orange RL (FDN) uses 3-methyl-5-pyrazolone as coupling component and is the 1:2 chromium complex of

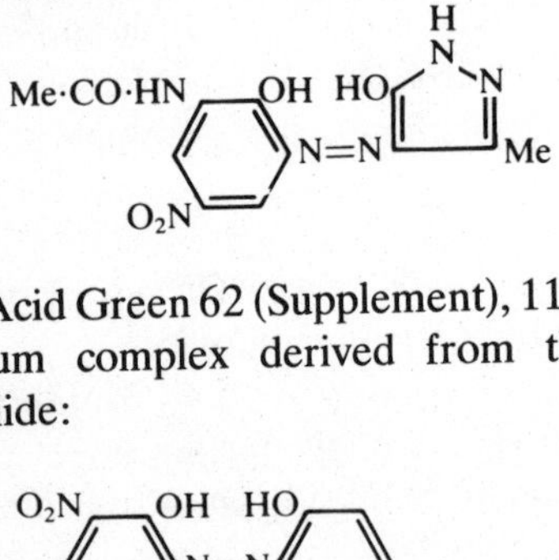

Fig. 6.13

C.I. Acid Green 62 (Supplement), 11836, Solilan Olive GL (FDN) is the 1:2 chromium complex derived from the dye, picramic acid → p-hydroxy-acetanilide:

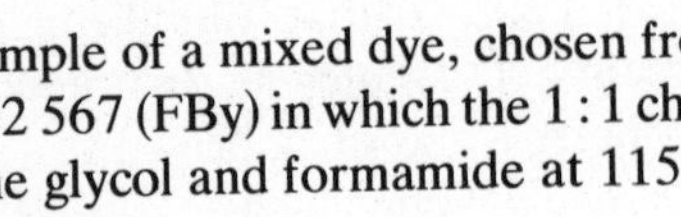

Fig. 6.14

An example of a mixed dye, chosen from the patent literature, is provided by B.P. 992 567 (FBy) in which the 1:1 chromium complex of I is heated with II in ethylene glycol and formamide at 115 °C:

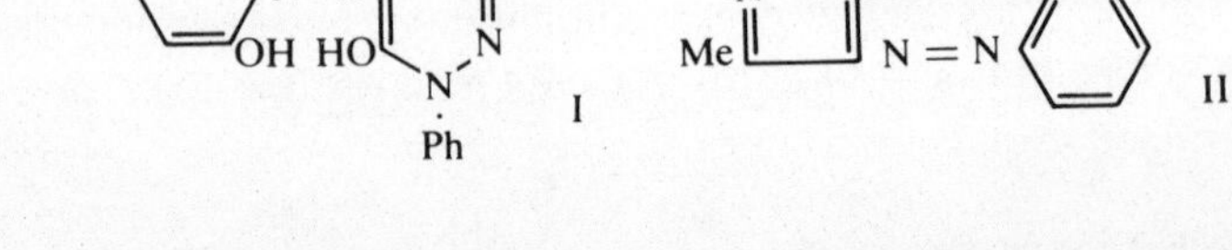

Fig. 6.15

The resulting dye is claimed to give yellow to orange dyeings on wool, polyamides and polyurethanes, of very good all-round fastness. Unlike chromium, cobalt does not form comparable 1:1 complexes but will give 1:2 complexes. The bathochromic effect of cobalt is less than that of chromium in azo metal complexes. Cobalt complexes are superior in light-fastness but have a lower rate of dyeing than corresponding chromium complexes. The 1:2 cobalt complex described in B.P. 1 008 169 (Acna) is derived from:

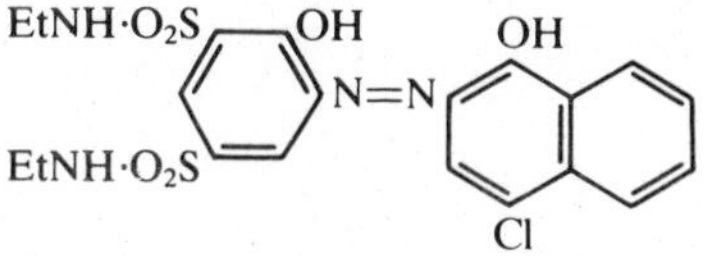

Fig. 6.16

and is stated to dye polyamides reddish-blue, of good fastness to wet treatments.

Copper–azo complexes as direct dyes

After-coppering, i.e. the treatment of certain kinds of direct dyeings with copper salts has been carried out for many years as a means of improving light fastness. Corresponding improvement in fastness towards wet treatments does not however always follow, although a number of preformed copper complexes of satisfactory light and wash fastness are in use.

A typical example is afforded by C.I. Direct Blue 95, 23150, which is obtained from tetrazotized o-dianisidine by coupling with two moles of 1-naphthol-3,8-disulphonic acid:

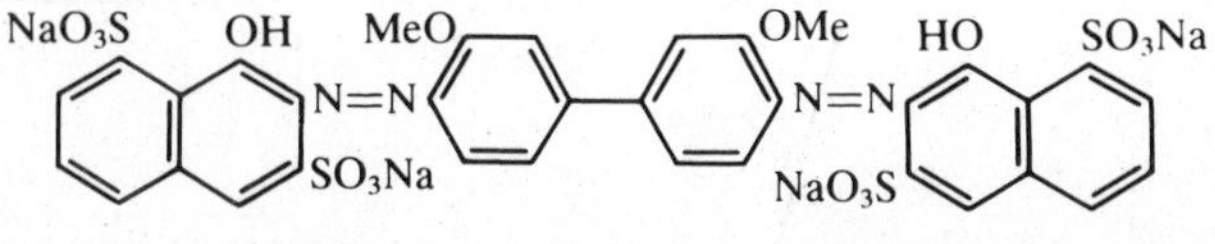

Fig. 6.17

The dye paste is intimately mixed with a solution of copper sulphate and sodium acetate and then dried at 120–125 °C in a vacuum-drier provided with a scraper agitator. The methyl groups are replaced during this process, a copper complex being formed at each o, o'-dihydroxy-azo site. This dye and the related C.I. Direct Blue 84, 23160 and C.I. Direct Blue 98, 23155, also obtained from o-dianisidine, have high washing fastness and fastness to wet treatments.

Formazan complexes

An interesting variation is provided by the formazan complexes, discovered by R. Wizinger; the parent dye is:

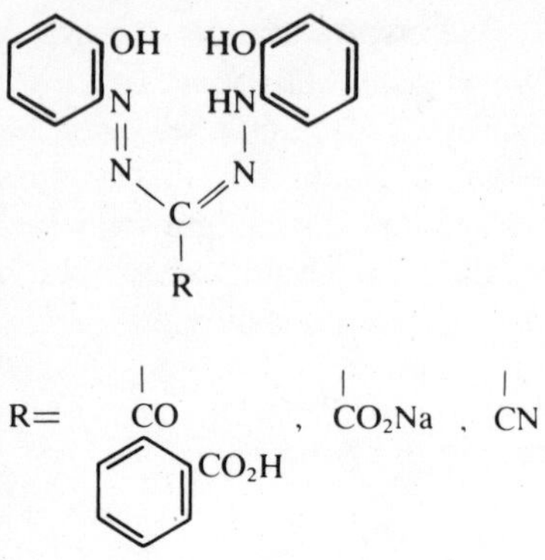

R= $\underset{\underset{CO_2H}{|}}{CO}$, $\overset{|}{CO_2Na}$, $\overset{|}{CN}$

Fig. 6.18

from which three hydrogen atoms are displaced by Cr^{3+}; the azo group and e.g. two moles of water provide the three necessary ligands:

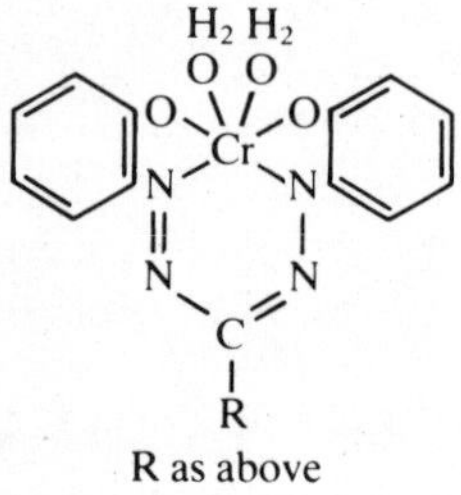

R as above

Fig. 6.19

The formazan dyes are neutral-dyeing wool dyes.

Azoic dyes

In the azoic dye system the fibre is impregnated with a coupling component, usually an alkali-soluble compound, and then separately treated with a diazo-salt solution. Coupling thus occurs *in situ*, an insoluble azo dye being formed. The principle stems from the discovery, in 1880, by the Huddersfield firm of Read, Holliday that cotton cloth padded with an alkaline solution of 2-naphthol, dried and then passed through a solution of a diazotized amine such as aniline produced an azo pigment *in situ* which was firmly fixed in the fibre.

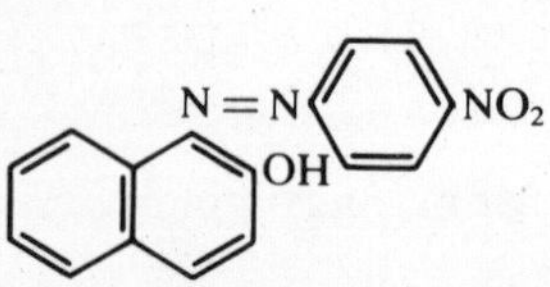

Fig. 6.20

Diazotized p-nitroaniline was recommended to dyers somewhat later (1895) by Meister, Lucius and Brüning the dye so produced being Para Red. A small range of Ice Colours, so called because the preparation of the diazo solutions by the dyer needed ice, was built up but the technique had its limitations and the dyeings so obtained were of poor light-fastness and of very poor rubbing and wash-fastness.

In 1912, Winther, Laska and Zitscher introduced the substantive naphthols, of the Naphthol AS type, which are widely used in the dyeing and printing of cellulosic fibres, especially cotton, although there is limited use, by special techniques, in the coloration of silk, wool, fur and hydrophobic fibres. The Colour Index lists about forty Azoic Coupling Components and nearly sixty Azoic Diazo Components of known constitution. In theory each coupling component could be combined with each diazo component. In practice the dyer employs a limited number of combinations of proved value. The range of hues covered by the azoic colours includes oranges, reds and maroons, the dyeings obtained being generally of very high light-fastness, some as high as 7–8 depending on structure, and of excellent fastness to wet treatments. A few dark blues and greens are known, but this range of hues is better covered by the use of vat dyes (p. 129). Certain azoic colours, manufactured in substance, are in use as pigments (see Chapter 15).

Azoic diazo components

The azoic diazo components are available commercially as stable powders, sometimes as the free base or a salt such as the hydrochloride or the sulphate, in which cases diazotization is carried out by the dyer, or as the stabilized diazo compounds, to which reference has already been made, which can be used directly. Many of the components are substituted benzene compounds, free however from solubilizing groups, e.g. C.I. Azoic Diazo Component 44, 37000, o-chloroaniline hydrochloride (Fast Yellow GC Salt), and C.I. Azoic Diazo Component 3, 37010, 2,5-dichloroaniline (Fast Scarlet GG Salt). Among the stabilized diazo compounds are C.I. Azoic Diazo Component 16, 37045 (Fast Red GGD base), derived from the amine:

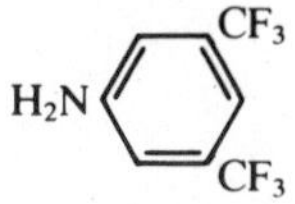

Fig. 6.21

The presence of the trifluoromethyl group in azoic combinations is said to improve clarity of shade and to increase light fastness but washing fastness is somewhat reduced (Venkataraman[10]). The $-CF_3$ group is much more stable than the $-CCl_3$ group from which it may be derived. Fast Orange GGD base is obtained by the method given on p. 42.

The sulphone group occurs in a few of the Fast Salts and, in azoic combinations, improves light fastness. An example is Fast Gold Orange GR, C.I. Azoic Diazo Component 17, 37055, the stabilized diazo salt of

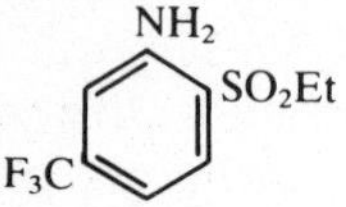

Fig. 6.22

Aminoazo compounds are used as Fast Salts since in azoic combinations the possibility of disazo (or tetrakisazo) dyes is introduced. C.I. Azoic Diazo Component 38, 37190, Fast Black Salt K is the stabilized diazo compound of the amine which is in turn the product of p-nitroaniline $\xrightarrow{\text{(acid)}}$ 2,5-dimethoxy-

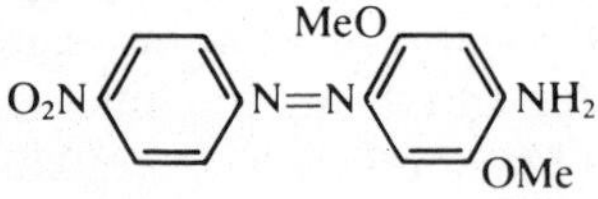

Fig. 6.23

aniline. C.I. Azoic Diazo Component 27, 37 215, Fast Garnet GC Base has the structure:

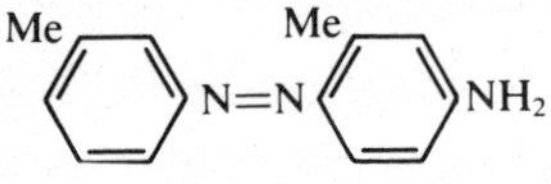

Fig. 6.24

and is marketed as free base or the hydrochloride.

Variamine Blue Salts. These are derivatives of diphenylamine of which the simplest example is C.I. Azoic Diazo Component 22, 37240, Variamine Blue Salt RT, the stabilized diazo salt of 4-aminodiphenylamine. The Blue Salts are used for producing dark blue or green shades with suitable coupling components.

Azoic coupling components

Over two-thirds of the coupling components are derivatives of 2-hydroxy-3-naphthoic acid which is made on the large scale by heating sodium 2-naphtholate in carbon dioxide (Kolbe–Schmitt reaction).

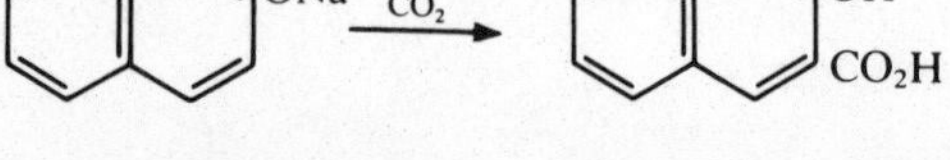

Fig. 6.25

The azoic coupling components derived from this acid are anilides of the type

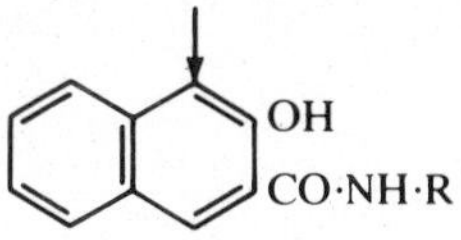

Fig. 6.26

coupling taking place in the position indicated.

R represents phenyl, naphthyl, substituted phenyl and other aromatic systems. No solubilizing groups such as —SO_3H are present. The Naphthols (Brenthols (ICI); Cibanaphthols (CIBA)) are made by the action, on a mixture of 2-hydroxy-3-naphthoic acid and the appropriate amine in an inert solvent, of phosphorus trichloride, e.g.

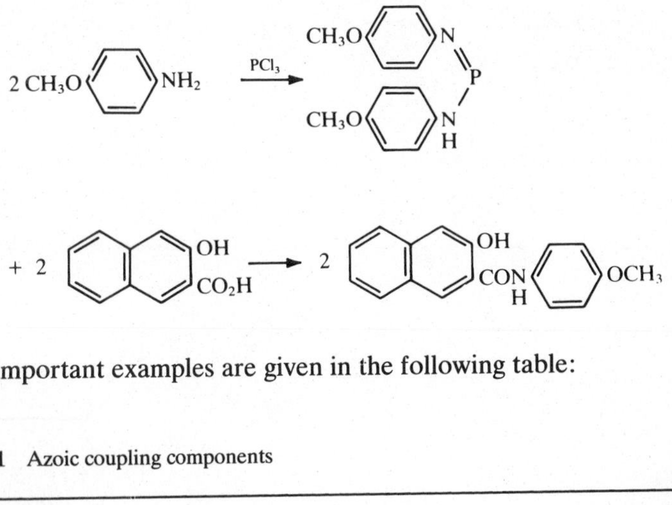

Fig. 6.27

A few important examples are given in the following table:

Table 6.1 Azoic coupling components

C.I. Azoic coupling component	Number	R=	Name
2	37505	phenyl-	Naphthol AS
27	37516	4-nitrophenyl-	Naphthol AS-AN
29	37527	2,4-dimethyl-phenyl-	Naphthol AS-MX
6	37532	5-bromo-2-methoxy-phenyl-	Brenthol BA
12	37550	5-chloro-2,4-dimethoxyphenyl-	Naphthol AS-ITR
30 and 46	37559	4-ethoxyphenyl-	Cibanaphthol RPH

Two other examples, also called 'naphthols', a term used generically rather than systematically, are a carbazole C.I. Azoic Coupling Component 15,

37600, Naphthol AS-LB:

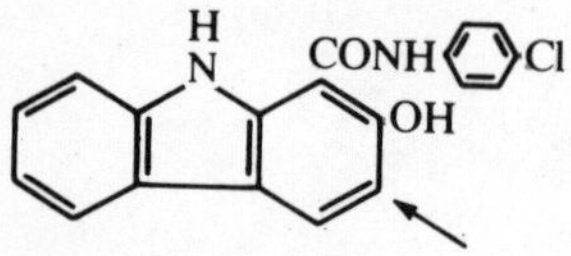

Fig. 6.28

(this compound, previously regarded as a 2-hydroxy--3-naphthyl compound was shown, in 1969, by Joshi, Kamat and Rani to be the 2-hydroxy-1-naphthoyl derivative), and a reactive methylene compound having two coupling positions, C.I. Azoic Coupling Component 35, 37615, Naphthol AS-LG:

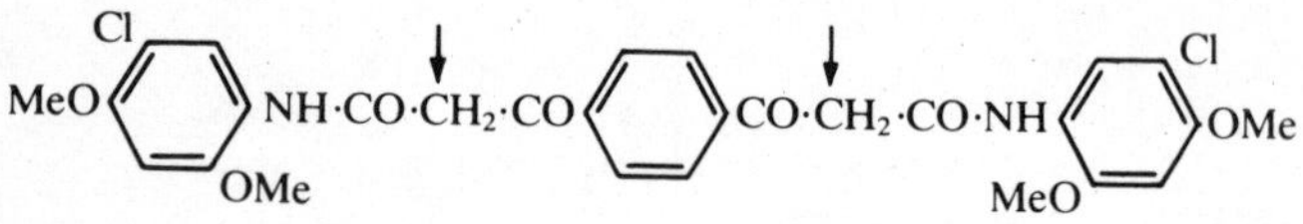

Fig. 6.29

7
Anthraquinone Dyes—I

Anthraquinone dyes and related colorants

The characteristic chromophore of the anthraquinone series consists of one or more carbonyl groups in association with a conjugated system. Amino and hydroxyl groups, their simple ·substitution derivatives such as alkylamino, arylamino, acylamino groups, and more complex heterocyclic systems may be present as auxochromes. In the case of the complex fused-ring compounds such as pyranthrone, violanthrone and others the parent carbonyl compound is coloured although no auxochrome is present.

Anthraquinone dyes and colorants make important contributions to a number of widely different usage groups, among them the acid, direct, disperse, mordant, solvent, vat, pigment and reactive dyes. This order will be observed in describing the series; pigments are described in Chapter 15, reactive dyes in Chapter 13.

Acid dyes

The anthraquinone acid wool dyes provide a number of bright, fast-to-light blues and greens not available among the azo dyes nor in fact equalled by any other class. They are the sulphonic acids of arylaminoanthraquinones, usually 1,4 derivatives and are sold and used as the sodium salt or other alkali metal salt. The sulphonic acid group may be present in the same ring of the anthraquinone system as the auxochromes as in the case of those dyes obtained by condensation of bromamine acid, 1-amino-4-bromo-anthraquinone-2-sulphonic acid (p. 41):

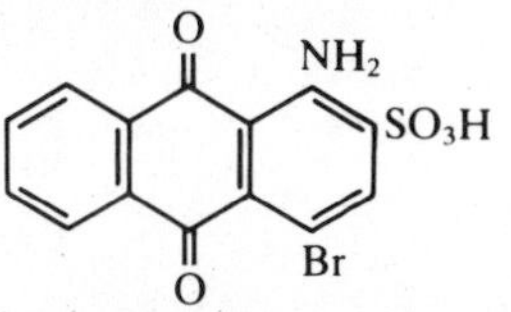

Fig. 7.1

With aromatic amines, or where sulphonation is the final stage, the sulphonic group invariably enters the aromatic ring of the arylamino group.

As a group the light fastness falls within the range 5–7 and wet fastnesses are moderate to good. The dyes are employed in general for the dyeing of woollen piece goods and yarns and many are suitable for the neutral dyeing of the wool in wool-cellulosic fibre unions. They are also useful in the dyeing of nylon. The following are important, widely used examples: C.I. Acid Blue 47, 62085, Kiton Fast Blue CR:

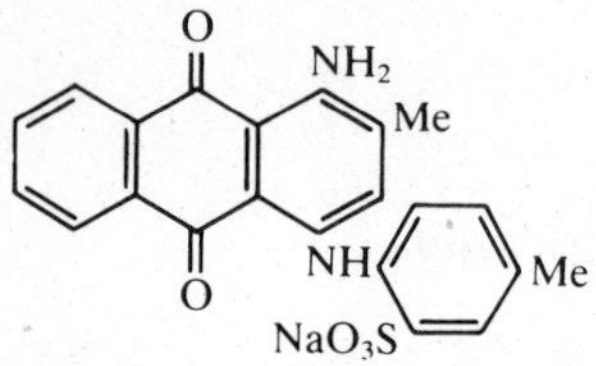

Fig. 7.2

is obtained by sulphonating the base C.I. Solvent Blue 13, in turn produced by the condensation of 1-amino-4-bromo-2-methylanthraquinone (p. 41). and p-toluidine.

C.I. Acid Blue 23, 61125, Alizarine Light Blue 4 GL results from the condensation of 1-amino-4-bromo-2,5 or 2,8-anthraquinonedisulphonic acid and p-aminoacetanilide:

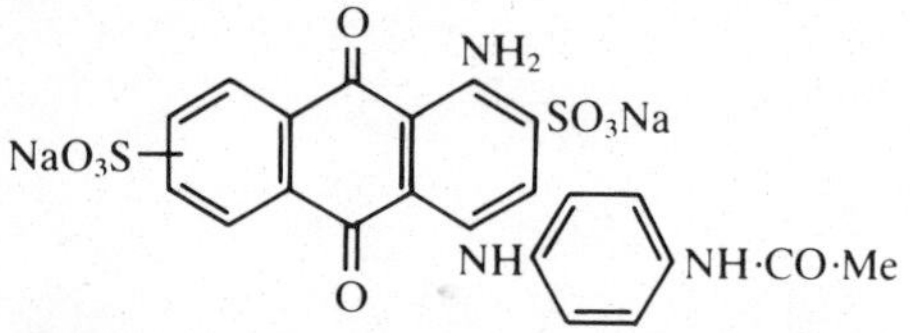

Fig. 7.3

It has very good light fastness and good fastness to wet treatments.

A number of interesting acid dyes are obtained from leucoquinizarine by condensation with two molecules of a primary aromatic amine followed by oxidation to a 1,4-diarylaminoanthraquinone which is finally sulphonated.

C.I. Acid Green 25, 61570, Alizarine Fast Green G, is an important wool dye obtained by sulphonating C.I. Solvent Green 3, 61565, (1,4-di-p-tolylaminoanthraquinone) giving:

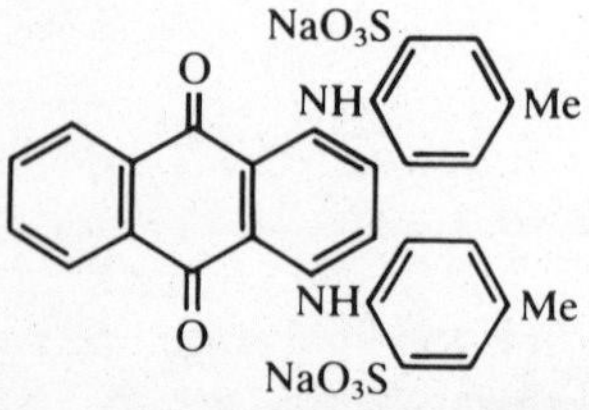

Fig. 7.4

It has a light fastness on wool of 6 but has only fair acid and alkaline milling fastness.

C.I. Acid Green 27, 61580, Carbolan Green G, is similarly obtained from *p-n* butylaniline:

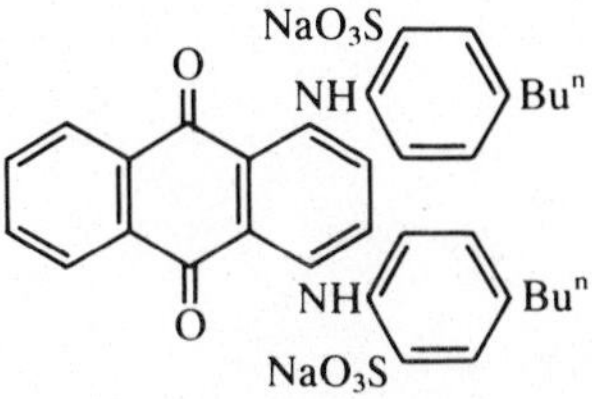

Fig. 7.5

and has a light fastness of 6 and an alkaline milling fastness of 5. Improvement in milling and potting fastness has also been achieved in the Carbolan series of I.C.I. by the introduction into the dye molecule of dodecyl or dodecyloxy groups.

C.I. Acid Blue 80, 61585, Brilliant Alizarine Milling Blue BL, is derived from mesidine, the final dye differing from the last two in having its sulphonic acid group in a different position relative to the amino groups, and also in having a 'deeper' colour (bathochromic shift):

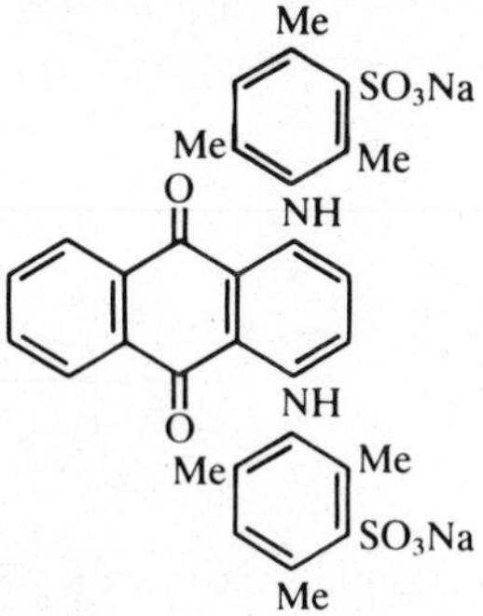

Fig. 7.6

It has a light fastness on wool of 6 and has good fastness to both acid and alkaline milling.

C.I. Acid Blue 78, 62105, Solway Blue BN, is made by condensing 1-amino-2,4-dibromoanthraquinone with 1 mole of *p*-toluidine, the resulting base, C.I. Solvent Blue 12, being sulphonated to give the dye:

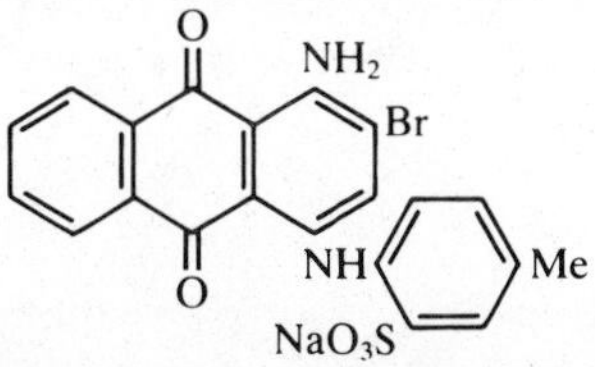

Fig. 7.7

Another widely used blue of good all-round fastness, differing from the foregoing dyes in having no arylamino groups present, is C.I. Acid Blue 45, 63010, Kiton Fast Blue CB, which is obtained by the sulphonation of 1,5-dihydroxyanthraquinone followed by nitration and sulphide reduction, leading to:

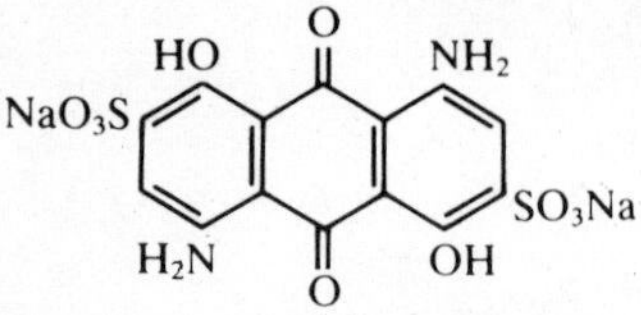

Fig. 7.8

C.I. Acid Violet 43, 60730, has the structure:

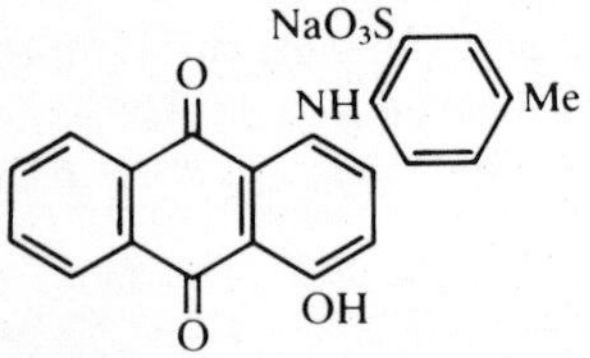

Fig. 7.9

Among the important reds is C.I. Acid Red 80, 68215, Alizarine Light Red R, which is made by ring-closure of 1-*N*-methylacetamido-4-*p*-tolylanthraquinone to give the base C.I. Solvent Red 52, which on sulphonation gives the dye

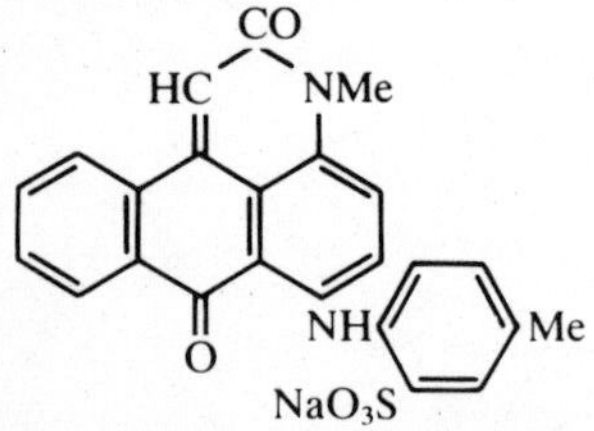

Fig. 7.10

A brown of very good light fastness and good general fastness is C.I. Acid Brown 27, 66710, which has the structure:

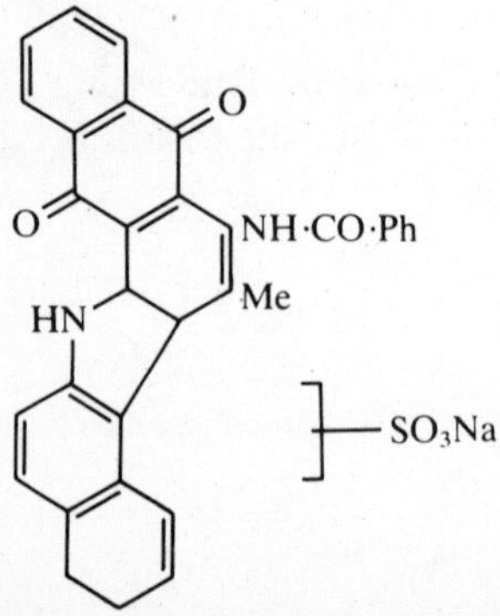

Fig. 7.11

C.I. Acid Black 48, 65005, Alizarine Fast Grey BLL, Coomassie Fast Grey 3G, is an important black of very good light fastness and good fastness to wet

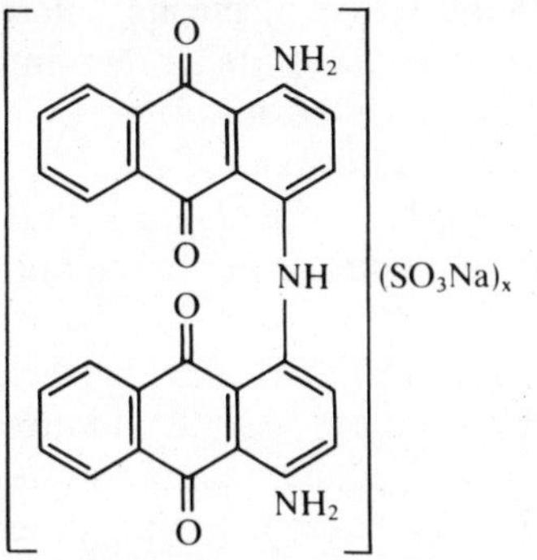

Fig. 7.12

treatments. It is the dianthraquinonyl derivative obtained by condensing 1,4-diaminoanthraquinone with 1-amino-4-bromoanthraquinone in the presence of copper and sodium acetate, the product being sulphonated with oleum in the presence of boric acid.

Direct dyes

The Chlorantine Greens, a Swiss discovery in the field of direct cotton dyes, are formed by linking two dye molecules, e.g. a blue anthraquinone dye and a yellow azo dye, each having a free amino group, by means of a substituted triazinyl ring system. An important example is C.I. Direct Green 28, 14155, Chlorantine Fast Green 5 GLL (CIBA) discovered in 1934 by Gubler and Bernasconi. It has the structure:

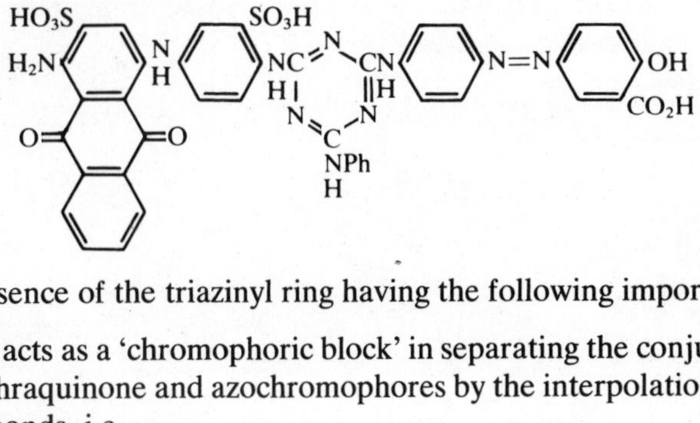

Fig. 7.13

the presence of the triazinyl ring having the following important effects:

1. It acts as a 'chromophoric block' in separating the conjugated systems of the anthraquinone and azochromophores by the interpolation of two adjacent single bonds, i.e.

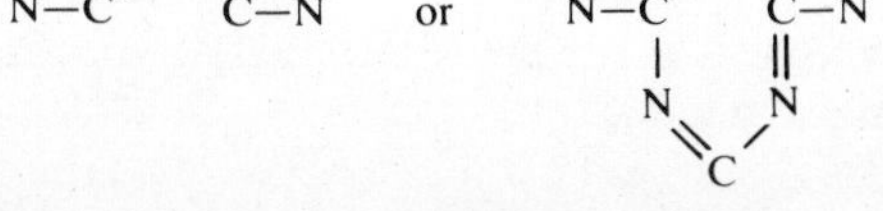

Fig. 7.14

If the conjugated chain is not interrupted in this manner electronic interaction ensues, the absorption characteristics are altered and an indifferent bluish-green hue results. By using a chromophoric block, electronic interaction is prevented, the absorption characteristics of the two systems remain virtually unaltered, and a clear green is produced by a simple additive effect.

2. It increases the substantivity of the dye for cotton.

3. It produces, in linking the two dye molecules, a dye of comparatively high molecular weight less prone, in consequence, to diffuse out of the fibre once it has been dyed.

Chlorantine Fast Green 5GLL is synthesized by the serial replacement of the three chlorine atoms in cyanuric chloride by reaction with the appropriate amino compounds, i.e. aniline, 1-amino-4-p-aminophenylaminoanthra-quinone-2-sulphonic acid and p-aminophenylazosalicylic acid, a process used in principle in the manufacture of certain reactive dyes and optical brightening agents (pp. 180, 185). The presence of the salicylic acid residue permits the after-treatment of dyeings with a copper salt, a process employed where a good standard of light and water fastness is needed.

Disperse dyes

Anthraquinone derivatives make a major contribution to the range of disperse dyes available for the dyeing of acetate, polyester, polyamide and other synthetic fibres. This class of dyes is dealt with in Chapter 14.

Cationic dyes (basic dyes)

Anthraquinone dyes in which there is a quaternary ammonium group, insulated by an alkylene chain from the chromophoric system, are of considerable interest for dyeing polyacrylonitrile fibres.

An example is the dye:

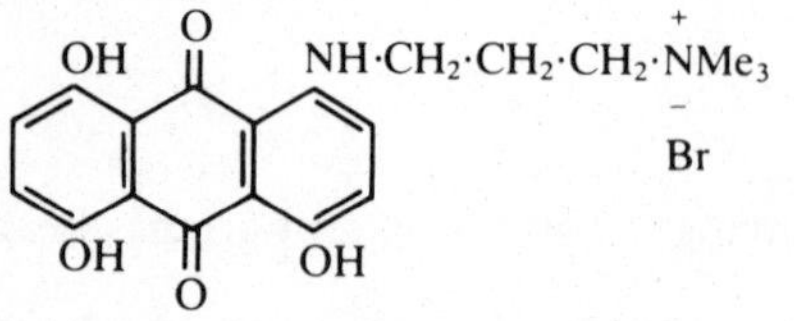

Fig. 7.15

B.P. 939 573 (General Aniline) prepared by condensing leuco-1,4,5,8-tetrahydroxyanthraquinone with 1-amino-3-dimethylaminopropane and oxidizing the product with m-nitrobenzenesulphonic acid. Quaternization with methyl bromide gives a dye which, it is claimed, dyes acrylic fibres bright, greenish-blue of excellent fastness to light.

Mordant dyes

The di- and trihydroxyanthraquinones are very old mordant dyes, some originally obtained from natural sources, e.g. madder root, morinda root, and later produced synthetically from coal tar chemicals such as naphthalene and anthracene. These mordant dyes were formerly used extensively in printing, being fast to light but having inferior fastness to washing, wet-treatments and perspiration. In consequence they have been largely replaced by vat dyes, azoic colours, reactive dyes and soluble azo colours.

The simplest and most important of this group is C.I. Mordant Red 11, 58000, Alizarin or 1,2-dihydroxyanthraquinone. It is listed in the Colour Index, under Natural Organic Colouring Matters, as C.I. Natural Red 6, 8, etc., and occurs in madder as the glucoside, alizarin-2-β-primeveroside. Alizarin is sometimes described as a polygenetic mordant dye on account of its ability to develop a variety of colours on different mordants as shown in Table 7.1 (after Trotman[41]).

Table 7.1

Mordant	Colour
Aluminium	Red
Tin	Pink
Iron	Brown
Chromium	Puce brown
Copper	Yellowish brown

Nowadays the chief use of the hydroxyanthraquinones is as intermediates for the manufacture of other anthraquinone dyes.

Solvent dyes

A number of comparatively simple anthraquinone derivatives, devoid of —SO$_3$H groups, serve as solvent dyes, the range of hues covered being chiefly violets and blues together with a red, C.I. Solvent Red 52 (p. 124) and the important C.I. Solvent Green 3 (p. 122).

C.I. Solvent Blue 11, 61525, Sudan Blue GA, is obtained by condensing 4-bromo-1-N-methylaminoanthraquinone and a molecule of p-toluidine, the product being:

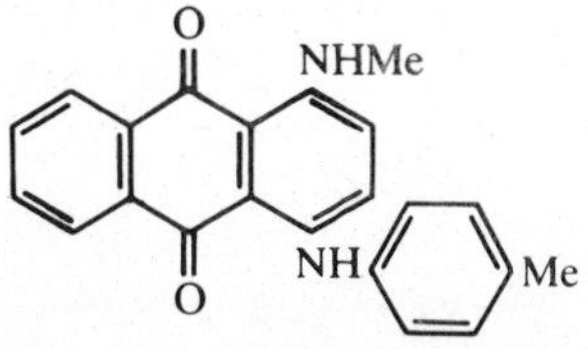

Fig. 7.16

C.I. Solvent Blue 18 (used also as a disperse dye, C.I. Disperse Blue 1) 64500, is the tetra-amino derivative, Oracet Sapphire Blue G:

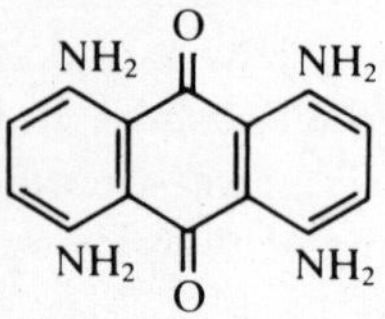

Fig. 7.17

C.I. Solvent Violet 13, 60725, Waxoline Purple A, (p. 17) is 4-hydroxy-1-p-tolylaminoanthraquinone.

Disperse dyes of the anthraquinone series, that are used in solvent dyeing, are described in Chapter 14.

8
Anthraquinone Dyes—II

Vat Dyes

In 1901 René Bohn, a chemist at the famous Badische Anilin- und Soda-Fabrik, in trying to make diphthaloyindigo by the then new glycine-sodamine indigo synthesis, obtained the blue vat dye indanthrone (Indanthren Blue, C.I. Vat Blue 4, 69800). The new dye, which was unrelated to indigo as a chemical structure, was found to have extraordinarily high light fastness on cotton (7–8) and, as a result of a period of intense research activity, the Indanthrene range (BASF) of vat colours was introduced in 1923. This range included as its members only those dyes of the highest fastness and the description Indanthrene Fast became current. Other leading dye-making firms have made great efforts in this field, an outstanding example being the discovery in 1920 of Caledon Jade Green by Davies, Fraser-Thomson and Thomas of Scottish Dyes Ltd.

In addition to Indanthren (BASF) and Indanthrene (G) other brand names, also reserved for the fastest vat dyes, are

Ahcovat (AH)	Paradone (LBH)
Amanthrene (AAP)	Ponsol (DuP)
Benzadone (YDC)	Sandothrene
Caledon (ICI)	Tinon (Gy)
Cibanone(CIBA)	

Anthraquinone vat dyes are mostly sold in the insoluble oxidized form, sometimes as dry solids but more often as aqueous pastes. They are applied in the reduced form as 'vats', the reduction being effected by the use of sodium hydrosulphite under strongly alkaline conditions. In consequence the use of vat dyes is mainly confined to cellulosic fibres though, in suitable cases, vat dyes serve as pigments (Chapter 15). Ease of vatting is naturally influenced by the state of division of the suspended vat dye and in order to achieve a satisfactory degree of fineness recourse is frequently made to the fractional or total precipitation of the dye from concentrated sulphuric acid solution. This step is usually part of the manufacturing process and is a useful and cheap method of purification or modification.

The widely practised operation of 'vatting' calls for a high degree of skill from the dyer. The 'vats' or leuco compounds, which have a characteristic colour in contrast to the leuco-indigoid compounds (p. 144) which are colourless and relatively stable, vary considerably in degree of stability. The development in 1921 by Bader and Sunder of the Swiss firm of Durand and Huguenin, in preparing a stable sulphuric ester from leucoindigo (Indigosol O, C.I. Solubilized Vat Blue 1, 73002) led the chemists of Scottish Dyes Ltd. to devise a process for making stable leuco esters (Soledons) from the more complicated anthraquinone vat dyes. This process consists in treating the parent vat dye in dry pyridine containing sulphur trioxide with a metal such as iron, zinc or more usually copper or brass powder, the copper–pyridine complex being finally converted into the sodium salt of the leuco sulphate ester. In application the original vat dyes are regenerated on the fibre by the use of an oxidizing agent, e.g. nitrous acid:

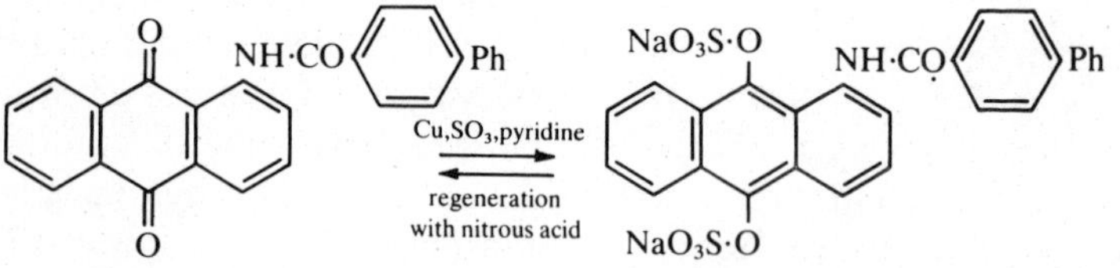

C.I. 60530   C.I. 60531   **Fig. 8.1**

These water-soluble vat dye derivatives are used mainly for the dyeing and printing of cellulosic fibres but may also be applied to wool, silk and nylon. They are generally sold as spray-dried powders and, being expensive, are used mainly for pale shades and special applications. Their use on protein fibres is rather restricted since there is no dearth of satisfactory acid wool colours and, in general, equally good results can be obtained with metal-azo complexes.

In the brief account of the anthraquinone vat dyes the various groups are arranged according to chemical structure or parent ring structure.

Acylaminoanthraquinones

The substance 1-aminoanthraquinone, although coloured is of no use as a dye since its leuco compound has little or no affinity for cotton and the reddish dyeing obtained is weak and unsatisfactory. When this substance is condensed with biphenyl-4-carboxylic acid in the presence of thionyl chloride, the acylamino compound thus formed is the useful vat dye Anthrasol Yellow V, C.I. Solubilized Vat Yellow 7, 60531 (Fig. 8.1). As a group the acylaminoanthraquinones are easily vatted and in general give level shades. They have good fastness to light and chemical agencies, substantivity increasing with increase in molecular size. The range of hues covered is mainly confined to yellows and reds though two important violets are known. Among the simpler examples is C.I. Vat Yellow 3, 61725, Cibanone Yellow FGK, Indanthrene Yellow GK:

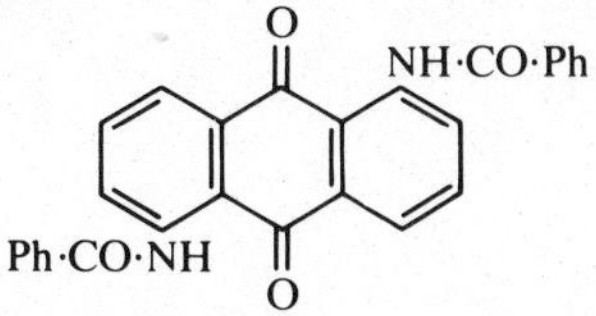

Fig. 8.2

obtained by benzoylating 1,5-diaminoanthraquinone. This dye is vulnerable to hydrolysis and care is needed in application.

The corresponding 1,4-dibenzoylaminoanthraquinone is C.I. Vat Red 42, 61650, Indanthrene Red 5GK. Two other examples of diacylaminoanthraquinones which appear to show promise as pigments are mentioned in Chapter 15.

By condensing 1-amino-5-benzoylaminoanthraquinone (2 moles) with terephthaloyl chloride, C.I. Vat Yellow 13, 65425, Caledon Yellow 5GK is

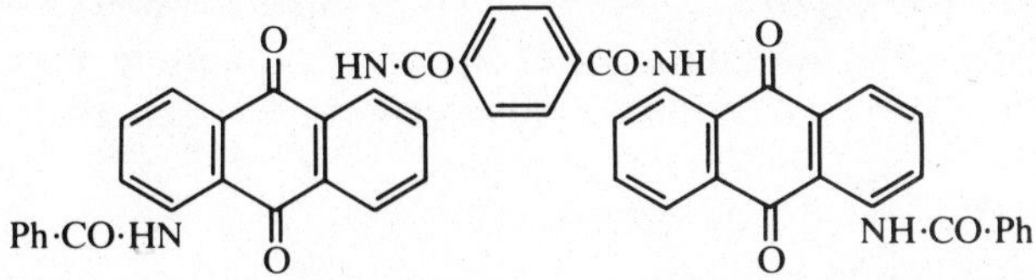

Fig. 8.3

obtained. The presence of two hydroxyl groups has a strong bathochromic effect in giving rise to C.I. Vat Violet 15, 63355 (R = Ph·) and C.I. Vat Violet

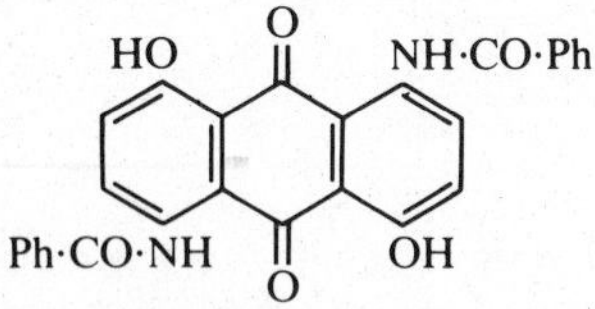

Fig. 8.4

17, 63365 (R = p-anisyl). The presence of the hydroxyl groups in these molecules is said to diminish washing and chlorine fastness.

Some important dyes in which aminoanthraquinones are linked through triazine and other residues, have been developed by CIBA. A good example is Cibanone Orange 6R, C.I. Vat Orange 18, 65705, which has the constitution:

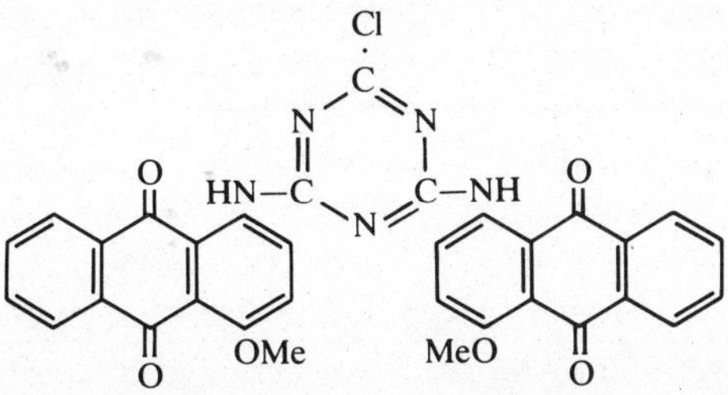

Fig. 8.5

In a recent patent (B.P. 1 006 157, CIBA) dyes of structure:

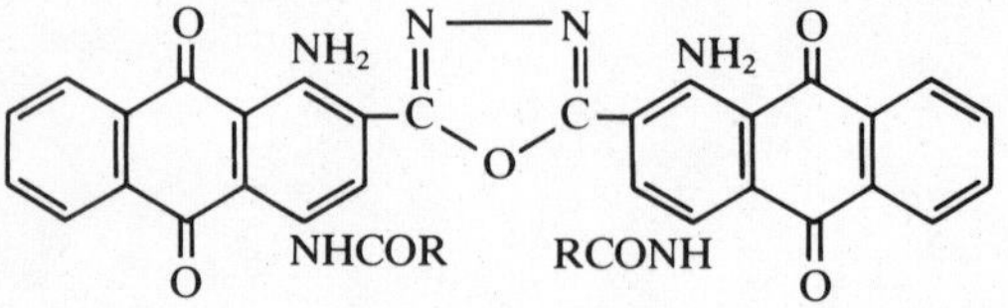

Fig. 8.6

where one R is a heterocyclic ring, the other a heterocyclic or an aromatic ring, are claimed to give strong greenish to reddish-blue dyeings, on cellulosic fibres, of excellent fastness to light, washing, kier-boiling, chlorine and water spotting.

Anthraquinone anthrimides

The term anthrimide is applied to those compounds in which two anthraquinone rings are linked by $>$NH (dianthrimides) or where three such rings are linked by two $>$NH groups. As a general rule only those compounds in which the linkage is made with one of the alpha (1, 4, 5 or 8) positions in one ring with the beta (2, 3, 6 or 7) position in the second ring, are usable as dyes. In fact the anthrimides are no longer important as vat dyes but serve, together with α,α' dianthrimides, as intermediates for carbazole dyes. One example, that of a trianthrimide, will therefore suffice:

C.I. Vat Red 48, 65205, Indanthrene Orange 7RK:

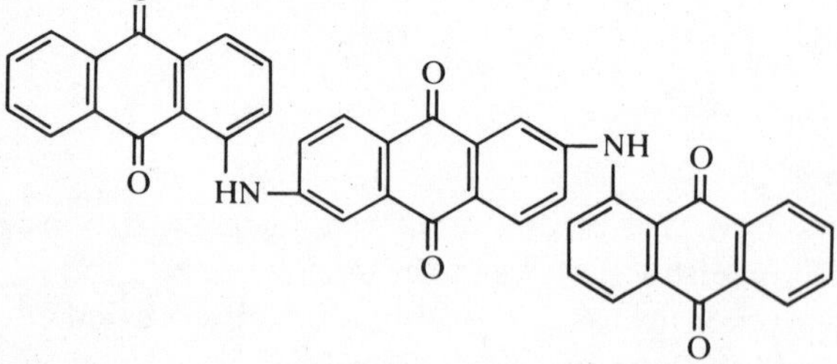

Fig. 8.7

which is obtained by condensing 2,6-dichloroanthraquinone with two molecules of 1-aminoanthraquinone in the presence of cuprous chloride and sodium acetate in boiling nitrobenzene. The dye has good all-round fastness (light fastness 6–7) but suffers from the disadvantage, shared by other yellow and red anthraquinone vat dyes of causing deterioration especially when exposed to sunlight on the cotton on which it is dyed (tendering). Where this property is unacceptable the dyer may employ suitable direct azo dyes or azoic combinations for his yellow to red shades.

Anthraquinonecarbazole dyes

This group formed by oxidative ring closure of appropriate di and tri-anthrimides, is sometimes referred to as the anthraquinonylpyrrole group and sometimes as the diphthaloylcarbazole group according to viewpoint. The carbazole grouping confers outstanding wet fastness and, among others, the following examples are widely used dyes of high quality.

C.I. Vat Orange 15, 69025, Indanthrene Golden Orange 3G, is obtained by the ring closure, in concentrated sulphuric acid of 5,5'-dibenzamido-1,1'-dianthrimide to give:

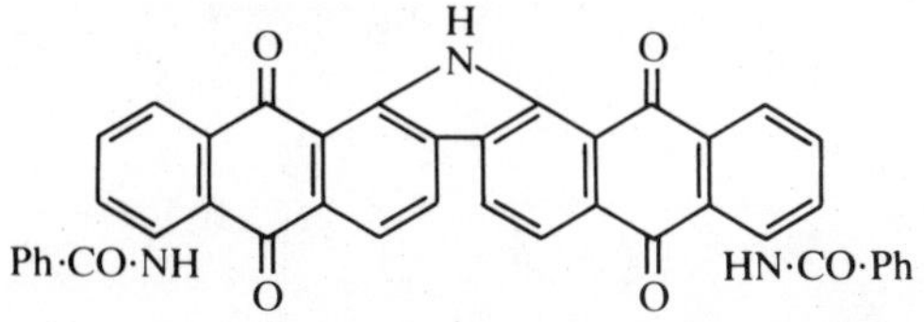

Fig. 8.8

By the condensation of 3-bromobenzanthrone (p. 140) and 1-aminoanthraquinone in the presence of sodium carbonate and copper oxide in boiling naphthalene followed by ring closure with caustic potash in isobutanol, C.I. Vat Green 3, 69500, Cibanone Olive FB, is obtained and has the structure:

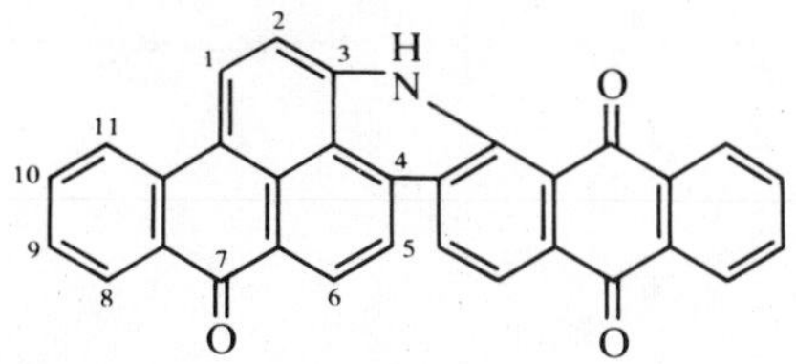

Fig. 8.9

It is of outstanding light fastness (7–8) and is much used for curtains and furnishings.

C.I. Vat Brown 1, 70800, Indanthrene Brown GR has very good fastness to light and washing and has the structure:

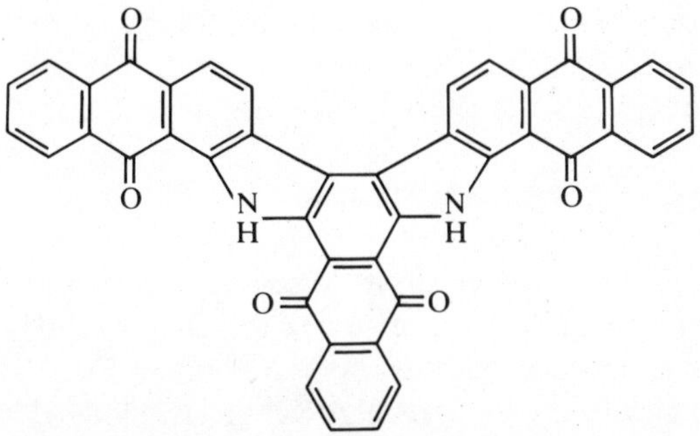

Fig. 8.10

and is obtained by the condensation of 1,5-diaminoanthraquinone with 2 moles 1-chloroanthraquinone followed by ring-closure in an aluminium chloride or a caustic potash melt and final oxidation with hypochlorite.

Anthrapyrazolones

A very important grey vat dye, C.I. Vat Black 8, 71000, Indanthrene Grey M, which has a light fastness of 7, good all-round fastness and is stable towards hypochlorite is obtained by the following route: 1-hydrazinoanthraquinone, made by reducing the diazonium salt derived from 1-aminoanthraquinone, is treated with concentrated sulphuric acid to give anthrapyrazolone:

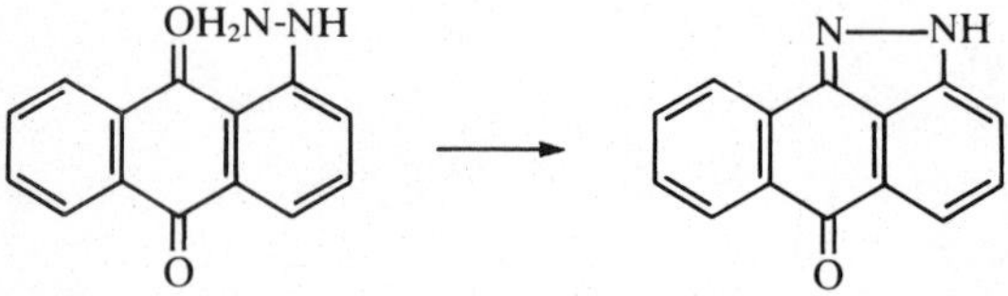

Fig. 8.11

This substance, together with an equimolecular proportion of 1-aminoanthraquinone, is condensed with 3,9-dibromobenzanthrone in the presence of caustic potash to give:

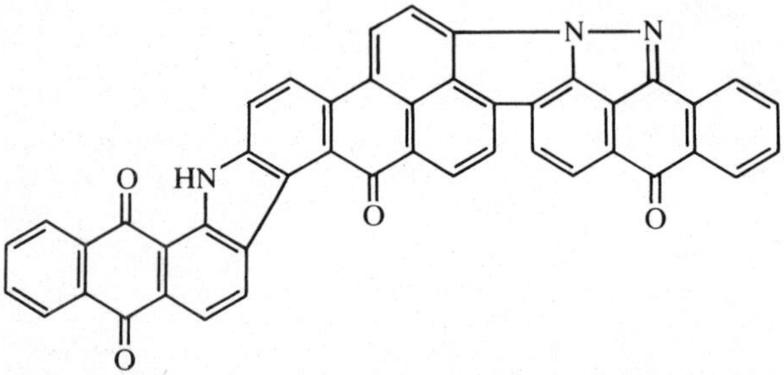

Fig. 8.12

it will be seen that the carbazole ring system is also present in this case. Examples in which the only heterocyclic system in the molecule is the pyrazole system are C.I. Vat Red 13, 70320, and the important C.I. Vat Blue 25, 70500, Indanthrene Navy Blue R.

Indanthrones

Indanthrone itself and the manner of its discovery have already been mentioned in the preamble to the vat dyes section of this chapter and is referred to also in Chapter 15 in connection with its use as a pigment C.I. Vat Blue 4, 69800. As a vat dye, however, in spite of its high light fastness it is not entirely satisfactory since it is readily oxidized to a yellow azine, especially by hypochlorites. This tendency can be considerably lessened by the introduction of two chlorine atoms by the action of sulphuryl chloride on indanthrone in an inert solvent, or by passing chlorine through a solution of indanthrone in concentrated sulphuric acid containing a little manganese dioxide. The resulting dye, C.I. Vat Blue 6, 69825 (Caledon Blue XRC, Cibanone Blue GF and other brands) has the structure:

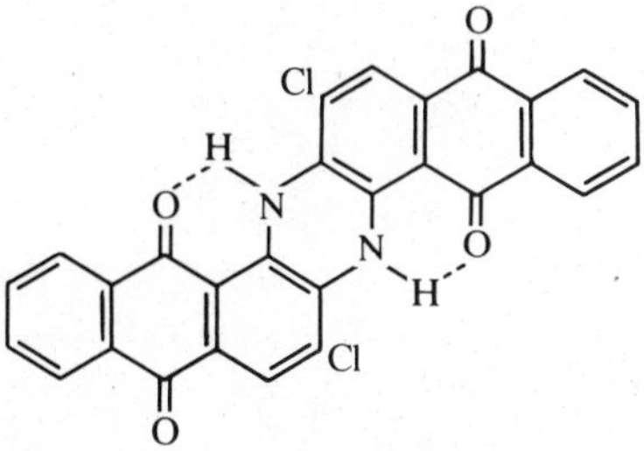

Fig. 8.13

and is used in large quantities for the production of bright blues of outstanding light fastness and very good general fastness including bleach fastness.

Flavanthrones

The only significant member of this group is flavanthrone itself C.I. Vat Yellow 1, 70600, Indanthren Yellow G. It is a by-product in the potash fusion of 2-aminoanthraquinone for the manufacture of Indanthrone, but it is usually produced by an Ullmann reaction, involving two molecules of 2-amino-1-chloroanthraquinone by heating with copper powder. The resulting dianthraquinonyldiamine is converted into either the dianil, by condensation with two molecules of benzaldehyde, or more usually into the diphthalimido derivative by condensing with phthalic anhydride. The product:

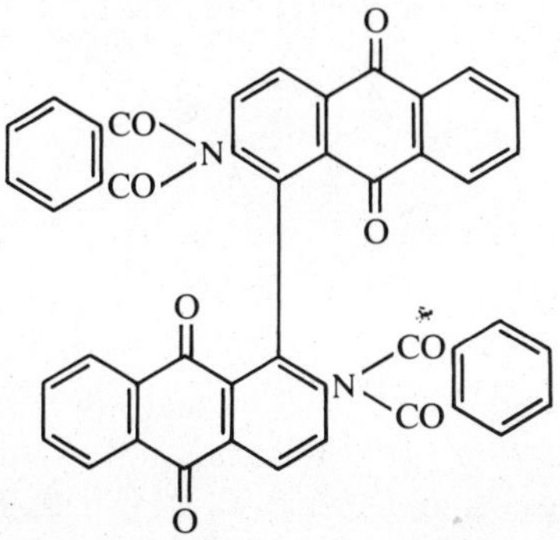

Fig. 8.14

on boiling with aqueous sodium hydroxide gives the dye:

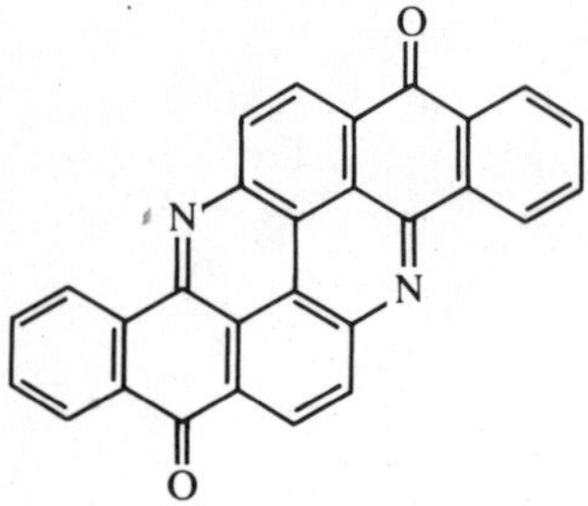

Fig. 8.15

A simplified process giving an 80%, yield is described in B.P. 1 278 914 (CGY) whereby 2-amino-1-bromoanthraquinone is heated with copper powder in dimethylformamide at 120 °C. The reaction product is oxidized with aqueous sodium chlorate and hydrochloric acid. Flavanthrone serves as a useful yellow component of fast to light greens, olives, etc. It is phototropic, i.e. it undergoes a change in shade by severe exposure to light, the effect being readily reversible, however, by contact with air, or by a mild soap treatment.

Anthraquinoneacridones

This important group of dyes, of relatively simple molecular structure, covers a wide range of hues, orange, red, violet, and blue. They are of good general fastness, especially light fastness, but possess only moderate substantivity. Three examples are given here:

C.I. Vat Red 35, 68000, is obtained by condensing 2-amino-1-naphthalenesulphonic acid (Tobias acid) with 1-chloroanthraquinone-2-carboxylic acid, ring closure being effected by heating to 200–210 °C when the sulphonic acid group is eliminated:

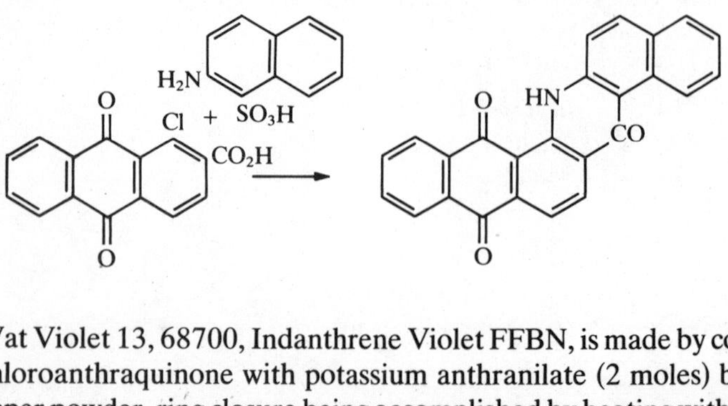

Fig. 8.16

C.I. Vat Violet 13, 68700, Indanthrene Violet FFBN, is made by condensing 1,5-dichloroanthraquinone with potassium anthranilate (2 moles) by heating with copper powder, ring closure being accomplished by heating with sulphuric acid, chlorosulphonic acid or certain acid chlorides with or without a solvent:

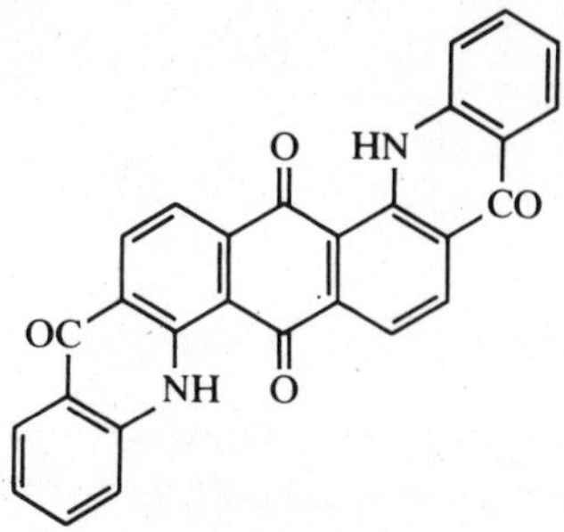

Fig. 8.17

C.I. Vat Blue 21, 67920, Indanthrene Printing Blue HFG, is used for direct prints and resist styles on cotton, viscose and acetate. The molecule contains the acridone ring system as well as having a benzoylamino group in the 4-position:

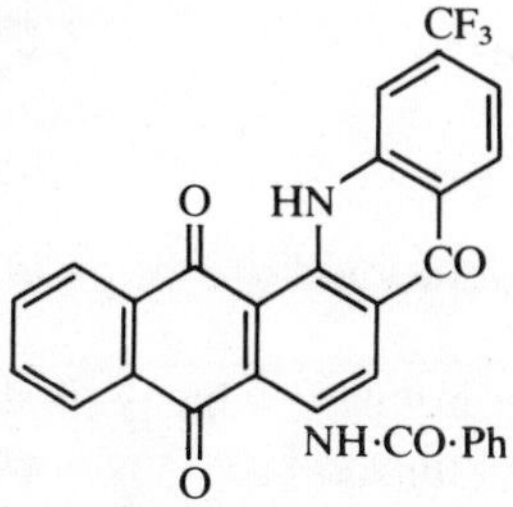

Fig. 8.18

The starting materials are 1-amino-4-bromoanthraquinone-2-sulphonic acid and a substituted anthranilic acid. As previously noted, the presence in the molecule, in a suitable position, of the $-CF_3$ group confers clarity of shade on the dye.

Polycyclic systems

The remainder of the vat dyes that will be considered in this chapter consist of fused-ring, polycyclic systems containing keto groups, some also contain halogen atoms, but the molecules do not contain any obvious auxochromes, at any rate of the kind essential to other chemical classes of dyes. Nevertheless, some of the brightest dyes of the highest light fastness are to be found among this group.

Dibenzpyrenequinones

C.I. Vat Yellow 4, 59100, Indanthrene Golden Yellow GK, is formed by the oxidative ring-closure of 1,5-dibenzoylnaphthalene by fusion with a mixture of aluminium and sodium chlorides:

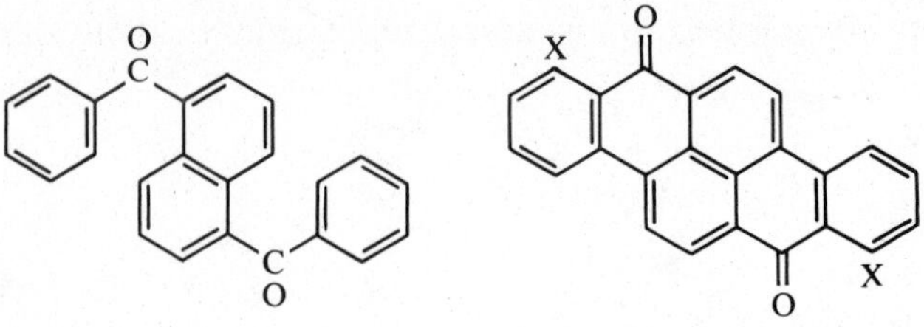

X=H   Fig. 8.19

C.I. Vat Orange 1, 59105, Indanthrene Golden Yellow RK, (X = Br) is obtained by direct bromination to a bromine content of 28%, the light fastness, washing and bleach fastness being thereby improved.

Anthanthrones

There are two dyes of interest in this group, namely

C.I. Vat Orange 19, 59305 (Z = Cl)

and

C.I. Vat Orange 3, 59300 (Z = Br)

Both are of brilliant hue and high tinctorial value and are of good general fastness.

The synthesis of anthanthrone starts from naphthalene which is first sulphonated giving 1-naphthalenesulphonic acid, then nitrated, the product being a mixture of 5-nitro and 8-nitronaphthalene-1-sulphonic acid. This mixture is then reduced and 1-naphthylamine-8-sulphonic acid is precipitated from an aqueous solution of the two isomers at pH 4.5. The synthesis then proceeds as follows:

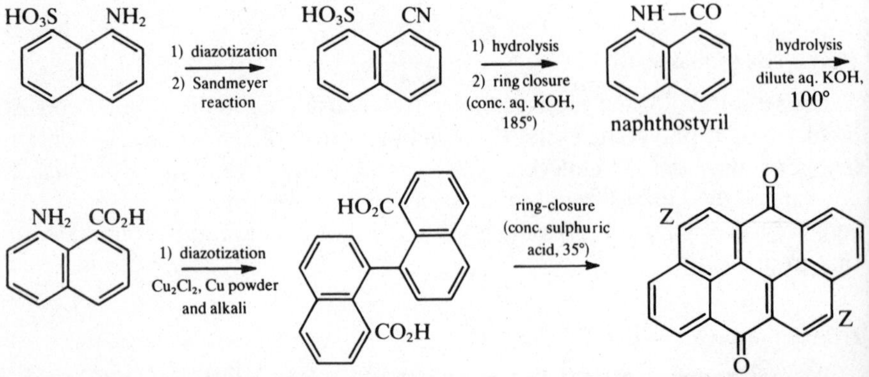

Anthanthrone (Z=H)

Fig. 8.20

Chlorination or bromination is often carried out directly as an extension of the ring-closure stage, i.e. without isolation of anthanthrone.

Pyranthrones

Pyranthrone itself is C.I. Vat Orange 9, 59700, a vat dye of moderate light fastness, good washing fastness and good bleach fastness: it has a tendering action on cellulosic fibres. The dye is manufactured by the following synthetic route:

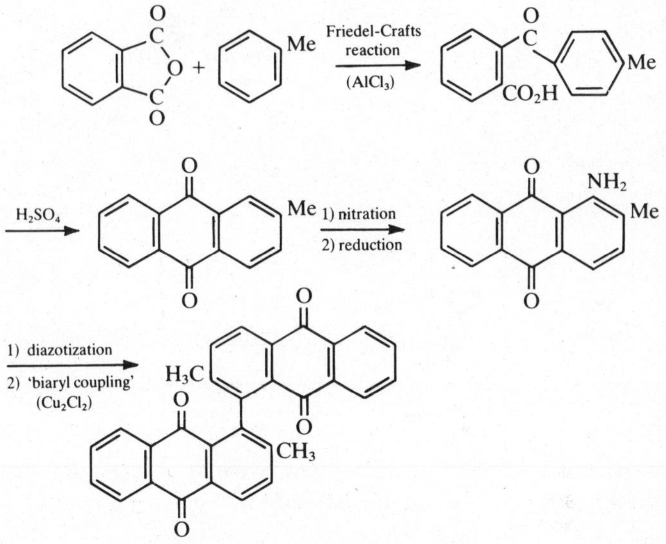

Fig. 8.21

The 2,2'-dimethyl-1,1'bianthraquinone thus obtained gives pyranthrone:

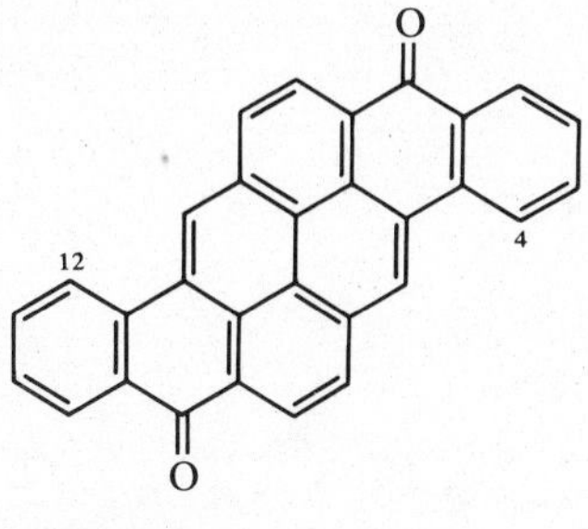

Fig. 8.22

by fusing with potash.

By the action of bromine in chlorosulphonic acid at 60 °C in the presence of catalytic quantities of iodine, 4,12-dibromopyranthrone is obtained and is the dye C.I. Vat Orange 2, 59705, Cibanone Gold Orange 2R. It has a light fastness of 6–7 and has very good all-round fastness. it is used both in printing and dyeing.

Benzanthrone derivatives

Reference has already been made to 3-bromobenzanthrone in connection with the anthraquinonecarbazole dyes. Benzanthrone itself is manufactured by adding a mixture of glycerol and iron borings to anthraquinone in 80–85% sulphuric acid at 130–140 °C.

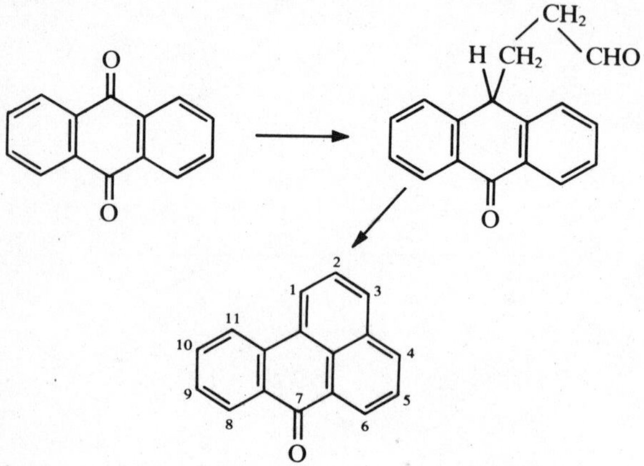

O
O
H CH2
CH2
CHO
O
1
2
3
4
5
6
7
8
9
10
11
O

Fig. 8.23

Bromination occurs in the 3-position, an excess of bromine giving 3,9-dibromobenzanthrone; nitration occurs in the 3-position, sulphonation at position 9.

Benzanthrone can be converted into 4,4′-bibenzanthrone in the following manner:

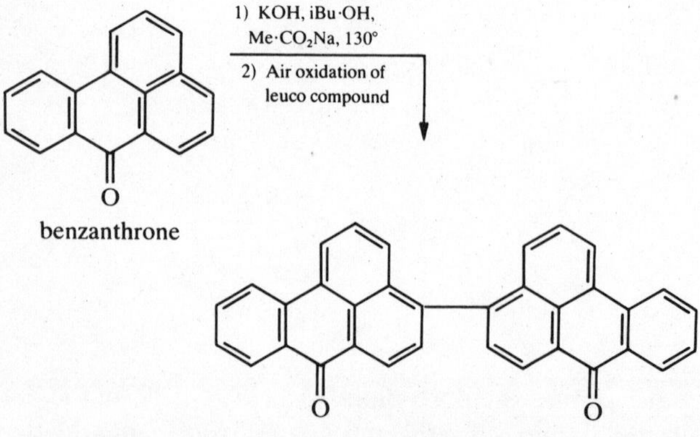

1) KOH, iBu·OH,
Me·CO2Na, 130°
2) Air oxidation of
leuco compound
O
benzanthrone
O
O

4,4′-bibenzanthrone (2)

Fig. 8.24

By treating the product (2) with manganese dioxide in sulphuric acid at 20 °C Violanthrone C.I. Vat Blue 20, 59800, (3) is obtained. It has good general fastness but is a poor 'leveller'.

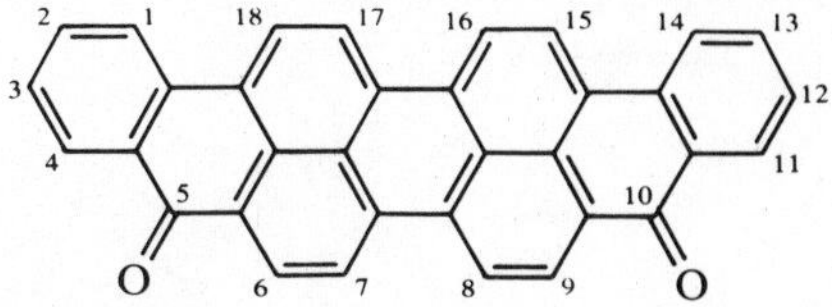

(3)

Violanthrone

Fig. 8.25

When 4,4′-bibenzanthrone is treated with sulphuric acid and manganese dioxide at 35 °C then keto groups are formed at carbon atoms 16 and 17. These keto groups can be reduced to hydroxyl groups by means of 35% aqueous sodium bisulphite. The resulting green dyestuff is not alkali fast but it was found in 1920, by Davies, Fraser-Thomson and Thomas, that methylation of the hydroxyl groups gave a green vat dye, C.I. Vat Green 1, 59825, Caledon Jade Green XBN of unique brilliance of shade and of outstanding general fastness including fastness to alkali:

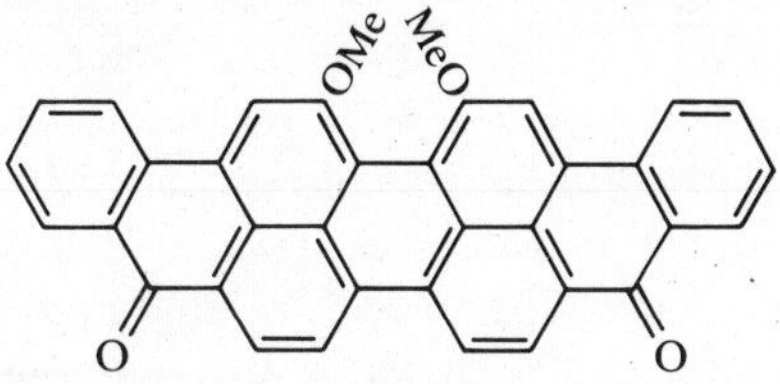

Caledon Jade Green XBN

Fig. 8.26

As will be understood, the 16,17-dihydroxyviolanthrone must be in a high state of purity, i.e. free from violanthrone and related substances otherwise an unsatisfactory product, dull in shade, results. Methylation is carried out in trichlorobenzene using methyl p-toluenesulphonate.

Perinone and perylene vat dyes

References to these, together with examples, are to be found in Chapter 15 (Pigments), p. 225.

9
Indigoid, Thioindigoid and Sulphur Dyes

Natural indigo has been known for centuries. It occurs as the glucoside indican together with indirubin in various species of *Indigofera* formerly cultivated in the Far East and is also present in Woad, *Isatis tinctoria*, and in other plants. Although the processes needed for the reduction of the natural indigo to the soluble leuco form necessary for dyeing were complicated, protracted and uncertain as to the final result, the chemical conditions were comparatively mild and so the dyeing of wool as well as cotton was feasible, fast dyeings, especially on wool, being obtained. Such was the interest in indigo that, following Adolf von Baeyer's pioneer work on the chemistry of indigo, the German firm, Badische Anilin- und Soda-Fabrik spent in the region of £1 000 000 on research, an enormous sum in those days, before being able in 1897, to enter the market with synthetic indigo. By 1901 the Meister, Lucius and Brüning sodamide process was introduced and the production of natural indigo rapidly declined. It has been pointed out by Paine[47] that the return on the vast outlay needed to solve the indigo problem was probably overestimated at the time but that the discovery of indanthrone and the opening up of the high-grade vat dyes field was achieved by the Badische Company as a direct outcome of the indigo work.

Indigo C.I. Vat Blue 1, 73000, has the structure:

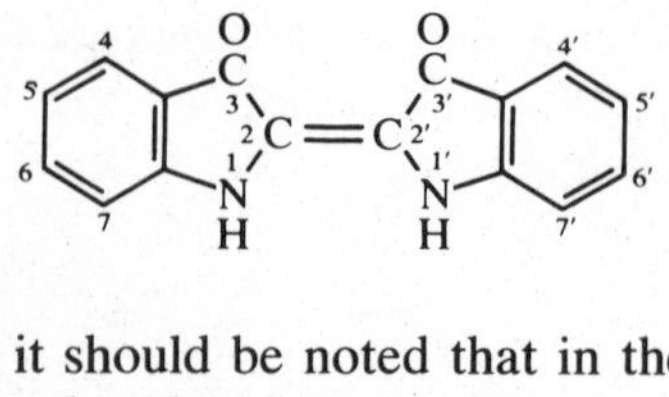

Fig. 9.1

though it should be noted that in the solid state, at any rate, there is good evidence that the isomeric *trans*- form predominates:

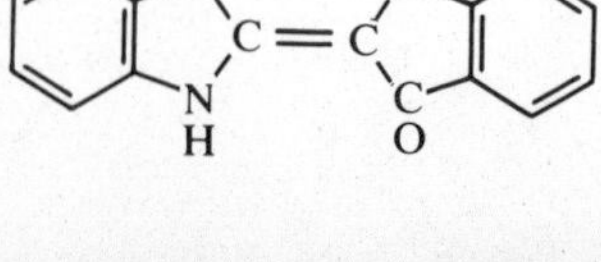

Fig. 9.2

Indigo Syntheses

Heumann processes (1890). In the original Heumann synthesis, phenylglycine was fused with a mixture of sodium and potassium hydroxides. The high temperature required, however, had an adverse effect on the yield and the first commercially successful process depended on the use of anthranilic acid, which was formed when phthalimide was treated with aqueous sodium hydroxide followed by sodium hypochlorite or hypobromite (Hofmann reaction). Thereafter the synthesis proceeded as follows:

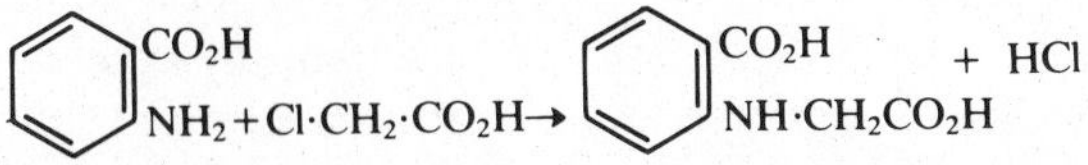

anthranilic acid   chloroacetic acid   phenylglycine-*o*-carboxylic acid

I

Fig. 9.3

Unlike phenylglcine itself, the *o*-carboxylic acid (I) readily gave indigo by fusion with caustic alkali followed by oxidation as follows:

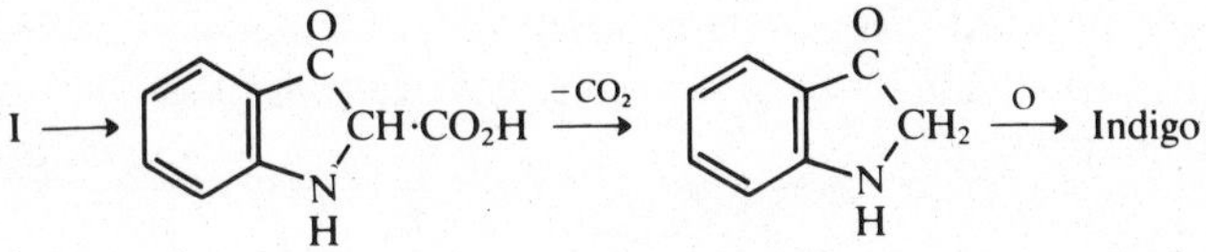

indoxyl-2-carboxylic acid   Indoxyl   Fig. 9.4

Sodamide process (1901). As mentioned earlier Meister, Lucius and Brüning introduced a highly economic process in which the much cheaper phenylglycine was fused with a mixture of sodamide ($NaNH_2$) and potassium hydroxide, the reaction taking place at a lower temperature with consequent improvement in yield.

Sandmeyer process. The discoverers of an important route to a valuable dye naturally protect their invention by patenting it where possible in as many countries as necessary for complete safeguard. Competitors must therefore draw on their resources and their ingenuity to devise other routes which may in their turn be patentable. Such a case is the Sandmeyer route to indigo in which aniline was heated with carbon disulphide to give thiocarbanilide (*N,N*-diphenylthiourea). By heating with lead carbonate and sodium cyanide, sulphur was eliminated and there was obtained a cyano compound of structure:

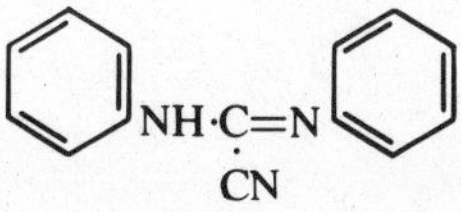

Fig. 9.5

which was taken through the following stages:

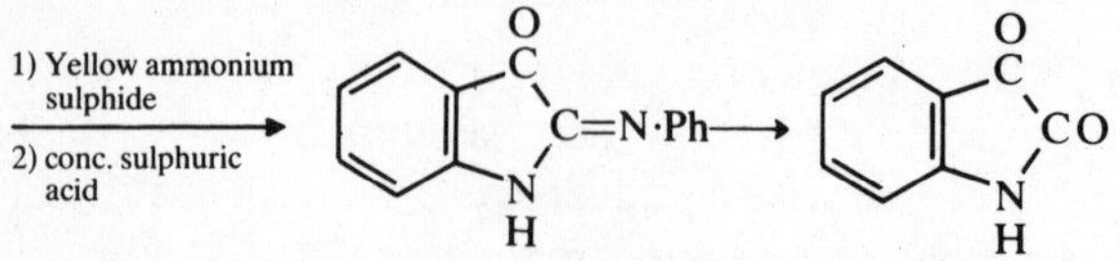

Isatin   **Fig. 9.6**

When isatin is treated with sodium hydrosulphide, 2-thioisatin is produced and on treating this with aqueous alkali indigo is obtained. The process is now no longer used, the sodamide process being the main technical method. Phenylglycine can be made relatively cheaply from aniline by condensing it with formaldehyde bisulphite and sodium cyanide solution; the resultant phenylaminoacetonitrile is then hydrolysed with alkali:

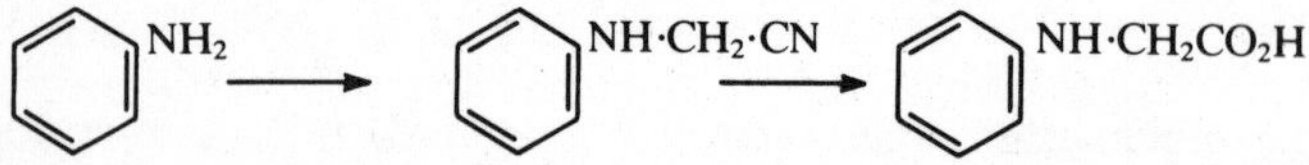

Fig. 9.7

Indigo is easily reduced by sodium hydrosulphite under mildly alkaline conditions to give a yellow vat, the isolated sodium salt of which is relatively stable and is sold for cotton dyeing as Indigo White, C.I. Reduced Vat Blue 1, 73001, and has the structure:

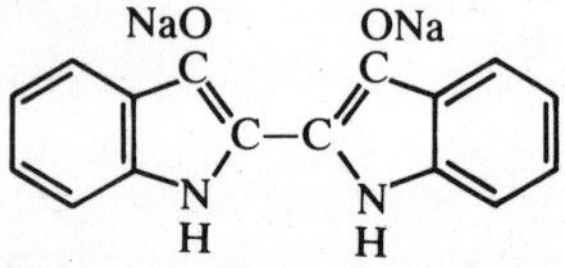

Fig. 9.8

The dye is developed on the fibre with nitrous acid in the cold.

For wool dyeing the soluble leuco sulphuric acid ester, the original Indigosol O (Bader and Sunder, 1921) is employed.

C.I. Solubilized Vat Blue 1, 73002:

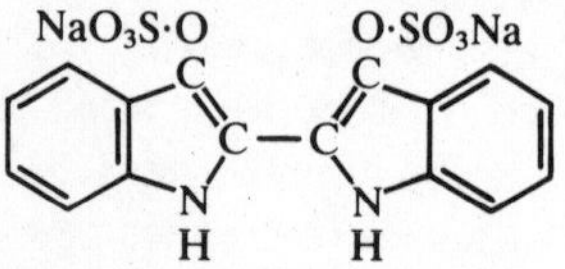

Fig. 9.9

The most important derivative of Indigo is Ciba Blue 2B, C.I. Vat Blue 5, 73065, obtained by the bromination of indigo in nitrobenzene:

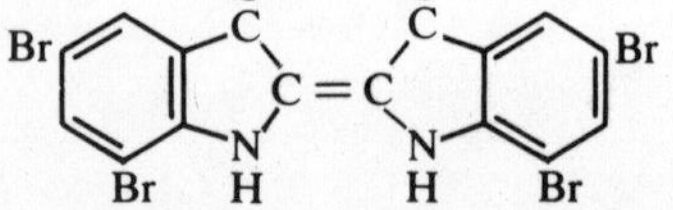

Fig. 9.10

It is essential to the economic running of the process that the hydrogen bromide evolved is recovered and oxidized to bromine for re-use. It is of interest to note that Tyrian Purple, known to the ancients and extracted at great cost from a species of shell-fish, *Murex brandaris*, is the 6,6′-dibromo derivative. Ciba Blue 2B is brighter in shade and is more easily reduced to the leuco form than is indigo itself. It is used chiefly in textile printing by direct, discharge and resist styles.

Thioindigoid dyes

The thioindigoid dyes, in which —NH of indigo is replaced by S, are insoluble orange, red and brown vat dyes which, like indigo, must be applied in the reduced condition and developed on the fibre or printed, with suitable additives containing a reducing agent, and then developed. The problem of introducing the sulphur atom into the molecule has been solved in a number of ingenious ways. Thioindigo Red B, C.I. Vat Red 41, 73300, can be made by the Friedländer synthesis (1905). When diazotized anthranilic acid is treated with sodium sulphide (Na_2S_2) a disulphide is formed which is converted into the thioglycollic acid by the following steps:

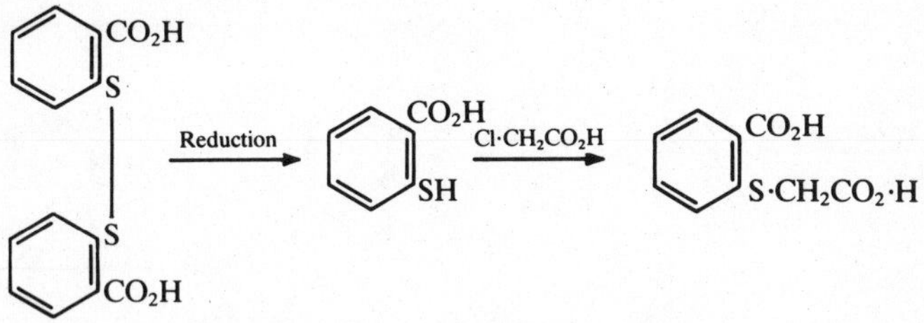

Fig. 9.11

This, on potash fusion, yields 2-carboxythioindoxyl and then thioindoxyl:

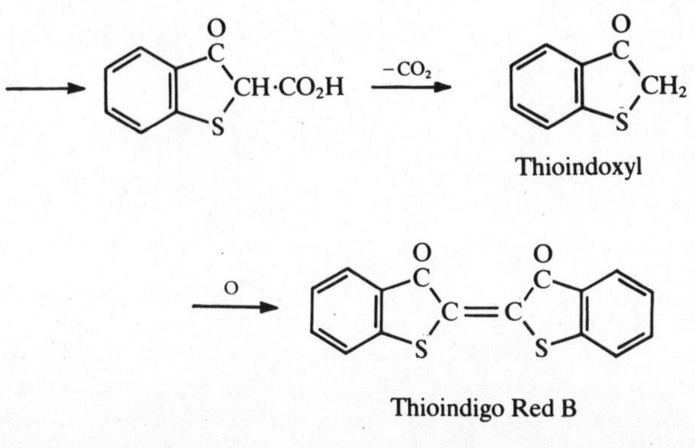

Thioindoxyl

Thioindigo Red B

Fig. 9.12

the thioindoxyl is finally oxidized usually with the sodium polysulphide corresponding in composition to $Na_2S_{4.7}$, with other oxidizing agents such as ferricyanide, or with air in presence of a copper salt to give the dye.

Two very important printing colours are:

C.I. Vat Orange 5, 73335:

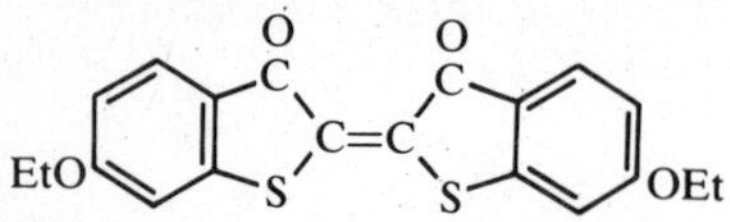

Fig. 9.13

obtained from p-phenetidine using the Herz reaction, and

C.I. Vat Red 1, 73360, obtained from o-toluidine also using the Herz reaction as follows:

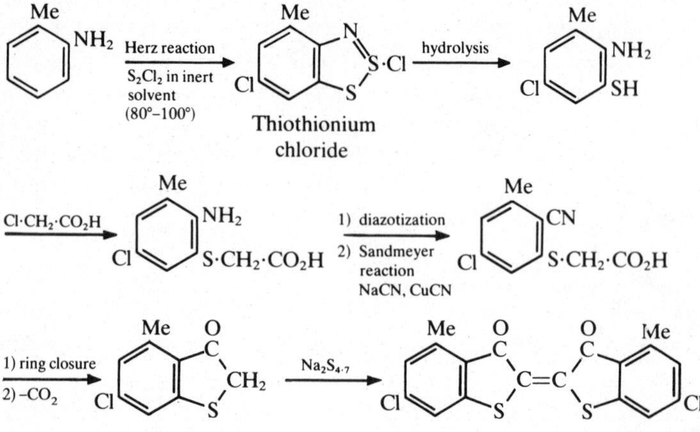

Fig. 9.14

Work by Hope and Wiles indicates that the nuclear substitution which occurs in this and other cases, where the *para*- position of the aromatic amine is unoccupied, is brought about by elemental chlorine generated under the conditions of the Herz reaction.

C.I. Vat Brown 5, 73410, can be prepared from naphthalene-2-sulphonyl chloride as follows:

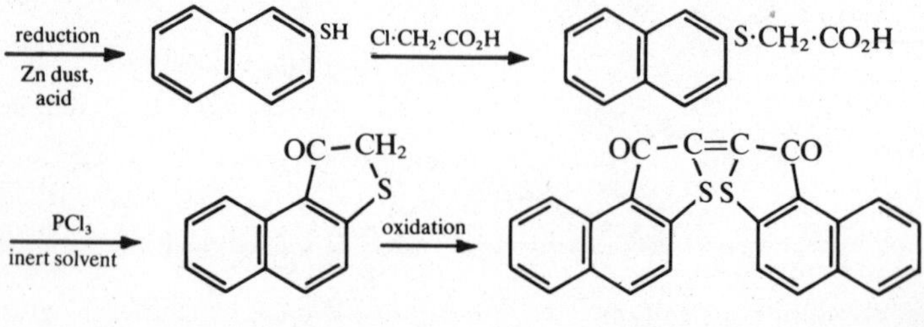

Fig. 9.15

In spite of its being a 'tenderer' this is a widely used vat dye especially for textile printing.

Thioindigo Bordeaux is 4,7,4',7'-tetrachlorothioindigo and has special properties as a pigment (Chapter 15, p. 227).

Indole–Thianaphthene dyes

A number of interesting, mixed dyes are known in which one half of the molecule is indigoid while the other half is thioindigoid, intermediate shades, i.e. violets, being produced. Such a case is C.I. Vat Violet 5, 73595, which is obtained by condensing a chloro-isatin derivative with a thianaphthenone:

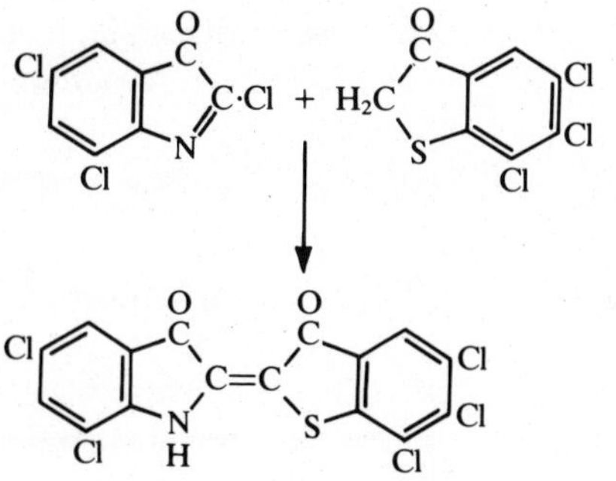

Fig. 9.16

Miscellaneous

A scarlet, of very clear shade, is obtained by the condensation of acenaphthenequinone with thioindoxyl:

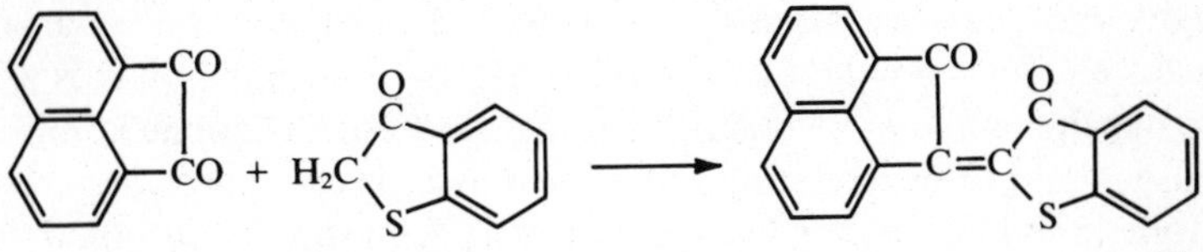

Fig. 9.17

the product being C.I. Vat Red 45, 73860, Ciba Scarlet G.

Sulphur Dyes

The sulphur dyes have been in use as cotton dyes for over ninety years. They are complex mixtures of uncertain composition and to which it has not so far proved possible to assign precise chromophores. As far as the application is concerned, the sulphur dyes are akin to the vat dyes since they are water-insoluble substances which must first be reduced to a soluble form, in this case by means of sodium sulphide, which is applied to the cotton fibre, the dye being regenerated by oxidation (in air). This group of dyes is produced by heating relatively simple aromatic substances with sulphur or a sulphur compound whereby aromatic rings are linked by disulphide or disulphoxide bridges. These links are converted, by the action of sodium sulphide, into —SNa groups, smaller, water-soluble molecules being produced. On oxidation in air the molecules are linked together once more as sulphides.

Sulphurization or thionation is brought about in a number of ways:

1. By heating a stirred, dry mixture of the organic material and sulphur ('sulphur-bake' process).
2. As (1) except that sodium polysulphide is used in place of sulphur.
3. By heating the organic compound or compounds with an aqueous solution of sodium polysulphide under reflux conditions or sometimes under pressure.
4. As (3) except that butanol or other solvent is employed instead of or together with water.

In all four cases hydrogen sulphide is evolved and is usually absorbed directly in sodium hydroxide solution for use elsewhere in the dye-making factory, e.g. for the reduction of nitro compounds. The lethal effects of hydrogen sulphide, not always as well known as they should be, make a leak-free plant and efficient absorption methods essential for safe working. In addition to the method of sulphurization the nature of the substance or substances acted upon determines the general type and properties of the end-product. Thus the Colour Index lists sulphur colours according to the chemical class of the starting materials, e.g. amines, nitro compounds, phenols, indophenols, carbazoles and so on.

The sulphur colours provide a full range of hues from yellows to black. None is bright and reds are almost absent apart from a few dull maroons and bordeaux shades. General fastness is fairly good especially towards wet treatments but they have poor bleach and light fastness. Although still important their use is said to be declining: their great asset is cheapness.

Before individual examples are considered, it should be noted that solubilized forms of sulphur dyes are marketed. In some cases these are simply the dyes 'vatted' in sodium sulphide solution and sold as such. In other cases the commercial product consists of a mixture of the dye and a small proportion of suitable reducing agent, the product being thereby stable and sufficiently reduced on contact with water to dissolve. Further reduction by sulphide is finally needed for satisfactory application to cotton in the dyebath.

The main representative among the sulphur colours is Sulphur Black T, C.I. Sulphur Black 1, 53185, discovered by Vidal in 1896. It is made by heating 2,4-dinitrophenol (or 2,4-dinitrochlorobenzene hydrolysed *in situ*) with aqueous sodium polysulphide under reflux during 2–3 days or for a somewhat shorter period at 130–140 °C under pressure. In either method the 'melt' is diluted with water and air blown to oxidize reduced forms to insoluble dye, During air blowing sodium thiosulphate is formed and remains in the mother-liquors. Its recovery therefrom, and its sale, e.g. as a 'fixative' in photography, is said to be essential if a competitive low price for the dye is to be reached. It is of interest to note that Sulphur Black T, used annually in very large quantities, gradually replaced Vidal's original discovery C.I. Sulphur Black 3, 53180, Vidal Black, obtained from *p*-phenylenediamine or *p*-aminophenol by a polysulphide bake-process at a temperature of 180–210 °C.

Among the greens is C.I. Sulphur Green 11, 53165, an olive dye obtained by sulphurizing *p*-nitrosophenol or *p*-nitrophenol or *p*-aminophenol by boiling with sodium polysulphide solution under reflux or by a polysulphide-bake at 290–300 °C. As with all such dyes final isolation of the insoluble dye is brought about by air-oxidation.

An example of a red is C.I. Sulphur Red 2, 53260, which has in fact a dull bordeaux shade. It is made by sulphurizing the substituted diphenylamine

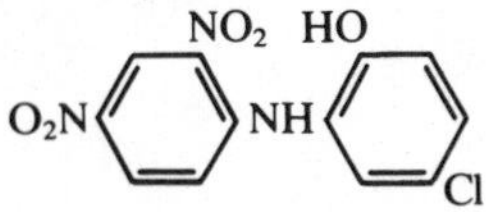

Fig. 9.18

obtained from the ready condensation of 2,4-dinitrochlorobenzene and 2-amino-4-chlorophenol.

C.I. Sulphur Blue 14, 53400, is an example of a dye obtained from an indophenol. This starting material is produced by the action of bleach on a mixture of phenol and *p*-aminophenol:

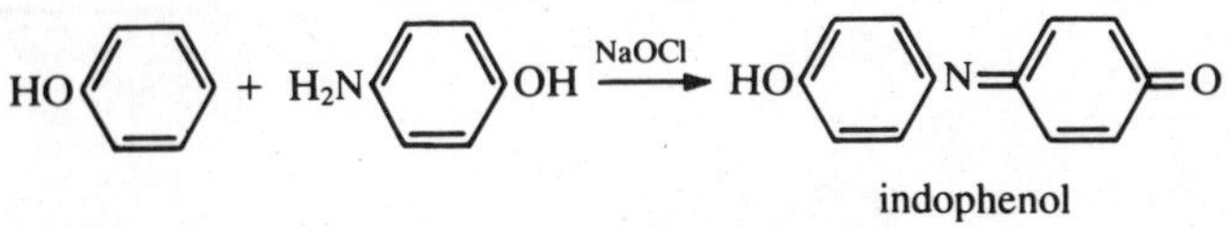

indophenol   Fig. 9.19

Hydron Blue R, C.I. Vat Blue 43, 53630. When carbazole is treated with *p*-nitrosophenol in concentrated sulphuric acid at −20 to −23 °C and the product reduced, the compound:

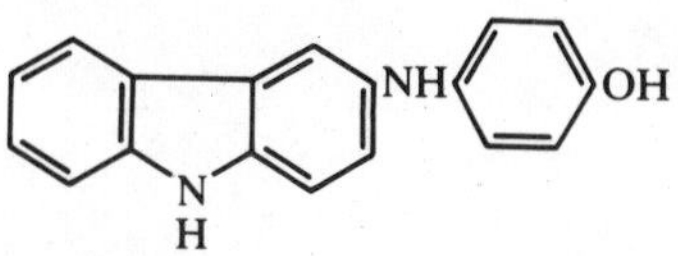

Fig. 9.20

is obtained. When this is refluxed at 127 °C for 24 hours with a butanol solution of sodium polysulphide, sodium nitrite added, and the butanol then distilled off in a current of steam, a blue dye can be isolated, after air-blowing, by the addition of salt. This dye has competed successfully with indigo for many years and, when demand for the dye began to exceed the available supplies of carbazole, synthetic methods were devised for the manufacture of this other-wise not very valuable coal-tar by-product.

Hydron Blue and the dye obtained from N-ethylcarbazole C.I. Vat Blue 42, 53640, Hydron Blue G, are reduced by the dyer with sodium hydrosulphite and are thus classed as vat dyes. They possess superior fastness, compared with other sulphur colours, especially towards chlorine. A great deal of work has been done by Fierz-David,[9] Venkataraman,[10] their co-workers and others on the constitution of the Hydron Blues which suggest that it is polymeric, the molecular unit having the thiazine structure:

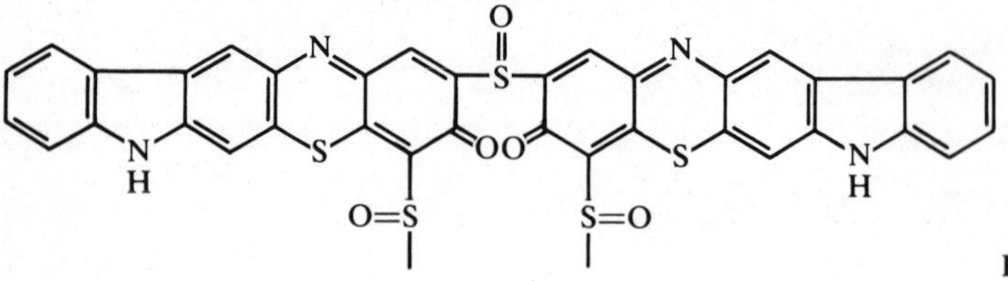

Fig. 9.21

An alternative suggestion by Zerweck postulates sulphide and not sulphone linkages:

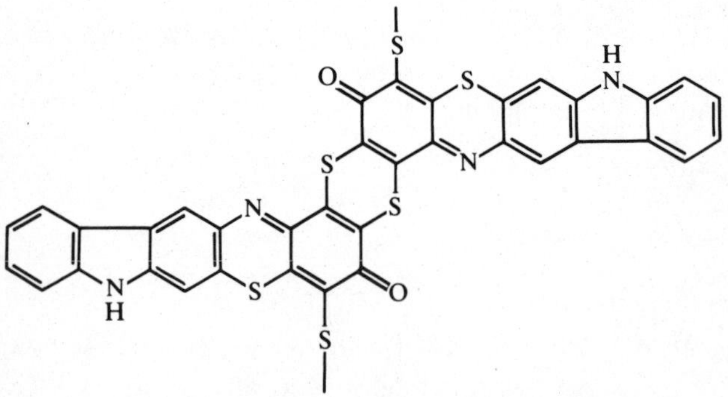

Fig. 9.22

10
Triarylmethane and Related Dyes

Triarylmethane dyes

The triarylmethane dyes are among the oldest synthetic dyes. They are of brilliant hue, the range covered including reds, violets, blues and greens. The chromophoric system consists of a central carbon atom joined to three aromatic rings, the hue and properties depending on the number and nature of the auxochromes —OH, or —NR$_2$ where R=H, alkyl, aryl or a combination, in the three *para* positions. Where no acidic groups are present in the molecule the di- and triaminotriarylmethane dyes are termed cationic. The presence of sulphonic acid groups confers water-solubility, the dye being anionic; a —SO$_3$H group *ortho* to the central carbon atom usually increases alkali-fastness. Where hydroxyl groups are present as auxochromes, adjacent car-boxy groups confer mordant dyeing properties. Thus the class includes cationic (the Colour Index uses the term 'basic') acid, direct, mordant, solvent and pigments (see Chapter 15).

Cationic dyes (basic dyes)

The chief representative among the diaminotriphenylmethane dyes is C.I. Basic Green 4, 42000, Malachite Green. It is manufactured by heating benzal-dehyde under reflux with an excess of *N,N*-dimethylaniline in water containing two-thirds the quantity of hydrochloric acid to form the hydrochloride. After 8–10 hr, i.e. when all the benzaldehyde has been consumed, sodium carbonate is added to liberate the dimethylaniline and leuco-base. The dimethylaniline is distilled off in steam and the white granular leuco-base is filtered off and washed. The reaction may be represented:

$$2Me_2N \cdot Ph + Ph \cdot CHO \longrightarrow$$

leuco-base

The leuco base is now dissolved in dilute hydrochloric acid, the temperature adjusted to 0 °C by the addition of ice, and with vigorous mechanical agitation the theoretical quantity of lead dioxide (freshly prepared, by the action of hypochlorite on lead nitrate solution) is added as quickly as possible. A solution of sodium sulphate is added to precipitate lead sulphate which is removed by filtration. The strongly coloured green filtrate, which contains the dye hydrochloride, is now treated with sodium carbonate solution to precipitate the 'carbinol base':

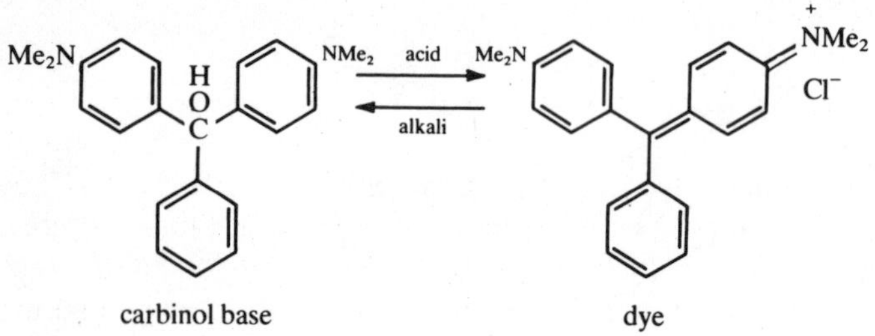

carbinol base   dye   Fig. 10.2

The base is converted into the dye once more by the addition of acid and is isolated as the zinc chloride double salt.

Note: In this structure and in that of the other dyes described in this chapter the central carbon atom is omitted and only one of the canonical, mesomeric forms will be shown (see Chapter 1).

Malachite Green is used in the dyeing of bast fibres and cotton, especially in Asiatic countries. It has a light fastness of 1 on cotton and its general fastness is poor. On polyacrylonitrile, however, its light fastness increases to 3–4, milling to 5, alkaline perspiration to 5 and washing to 4. The enhancement of fastness properties in association with polyacrylonitrile is common to most cationic dyes and, though so far largely unexplained, its importance has caused a revival of interest in the synthesis of this class of dyes especially those containing cyano groups.

C.I. Basic Violet 3, 42555, Crystal Violet, is an example of a triamino-triphenylmethane dye. Its method of synthesis illustrates a second method of introducing the central carbon atom, i.e. by the use of phosgene:

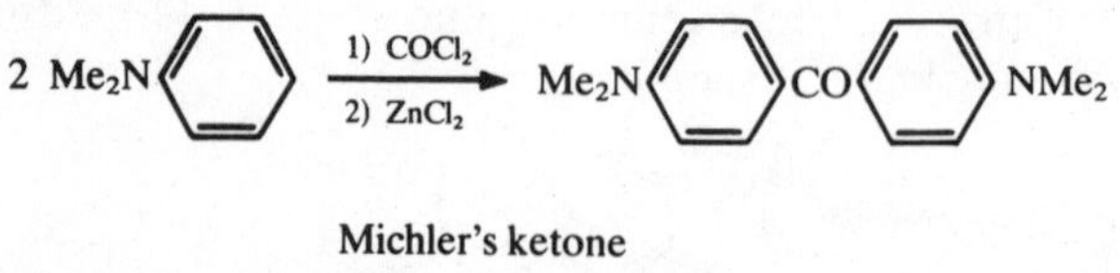

Michler's ketone   Fig. 10.3

Michler's Ketone, 4,4'-bis-dimethylaminobenzophenone is produced by the condensation of a molecule of phosgene with a molecule of dimethylaniline giving *p*-dimethylaminobenzoyl chloride; condensation with a second molecule of dimethylaniline requires the presence of a Lewis acid, usually zinc chloride or aluminium chloride.

Further treatment with phosgene causes condensation, via a reactive chloro compound, with a second molecule of dimethylaniline to give Crystal Violet:

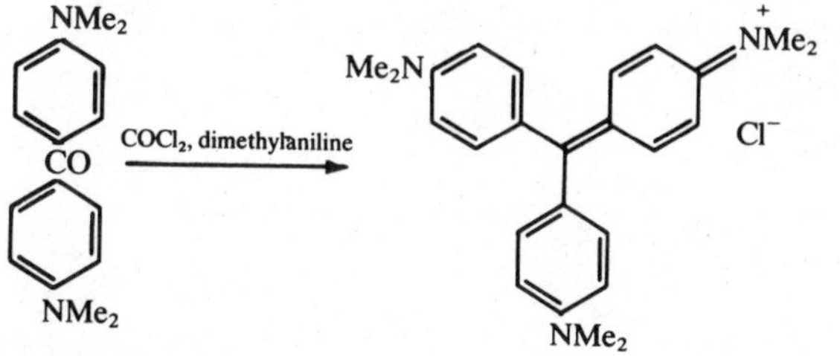

Crystal violet

Fig. 10.4

Its light fastness and other fastness properties are poor and it is used only where brilliance of shade is required regardless of fastness. When treated with sodium hydroxide solution, crystal violet forms the colourless carbinol base:

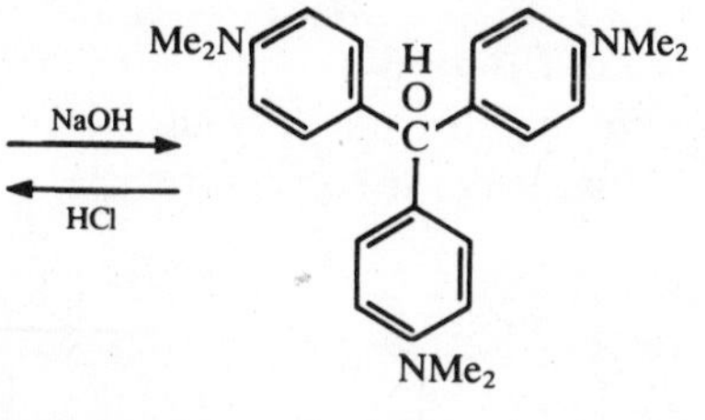

Fig. 10.5

This product is sold as a solvent dye C.I. Solvent Violet 9, 42555B, since with, for example, oleic acid, it gives a solvent soluble colorant.

Although the step is unnecessary in the manufacture of Crystal Violet, the Ketone can be isolated by dissolving out unchanged dimethylaniline in dilute hydrochloric acid, which treatment also takes out basic organic impurities and zinc compounds. The feebly basic Michler's Ketone remains undissolved at the acid concentration employed and is filtered off as a grey-blue crystalline solid m.p. 171–172 °C. In the purified state it is colourless.

The technical product is used in the manufacture of a number of cationic dyes notably the Victoria Blues:

C.I. Basic Blue 26, 44045, Victoria Blue B is produced by condensing Michler's Ketone with N-phenyl-1-naphthylamine in the presence of phosphorus oxychloride:

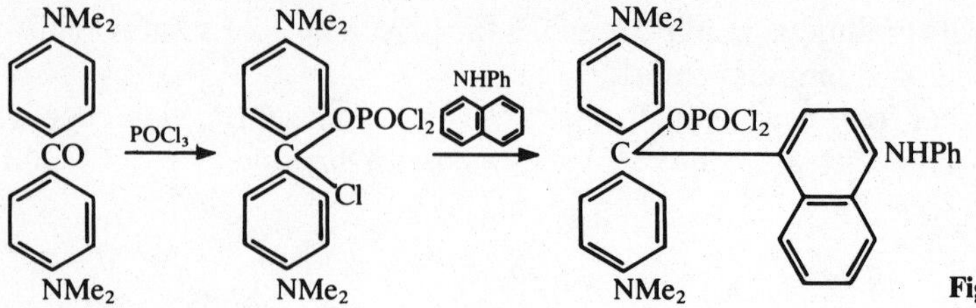

Fig. 10.6

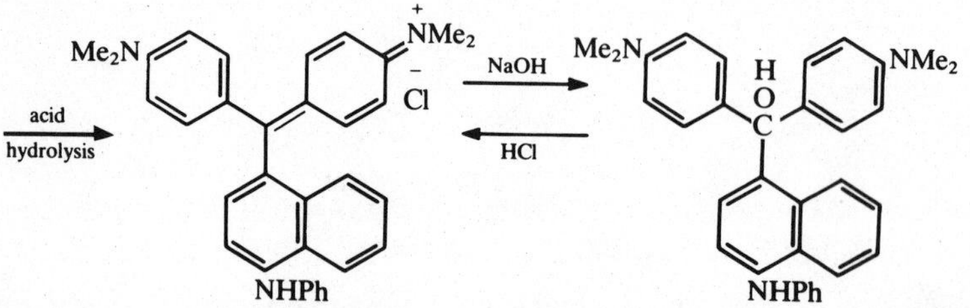

Victoria Blue B

Fig. 10.7

The corresponding carbinol base is C.I. Solvent Blue 4, 44045B which is colourless when pure.

C.I. Basic Blue 7, 42595, Victoria Pure Blue BO, is made by condensing 4,4′-bis(diethylamino)benzophenone (obtained from N,N-diethylaniline and phosgene) and N-ethyl-1-naphthylamine. It has the structure:

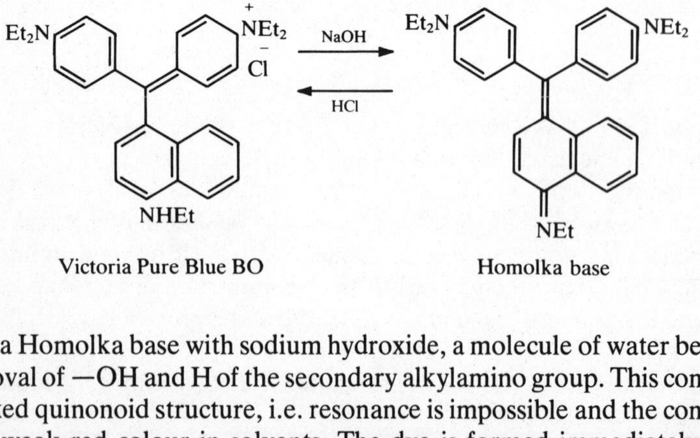

Victoria Pure Blue BO   Homolka base   Fig. 10.8

It gives a Homolka base with sodium hydroxide, a molecule of water being lost by removal of —OH and H of the secondary alkylamino group. This compound has a fixed quinonoid structure, i.e. resonance is impossible and the compound gives a weak red colour in solvents. The dye is formed immediately on the addition of acid. The Victoria Blues are used chiefly as paper dyes and, in the form of their carbinol or Homolka bases, as solvent dyes.

The colourless compound:

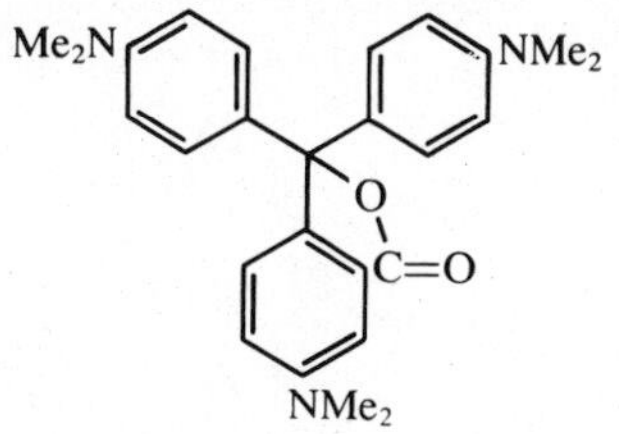

Fig. 10.9

known as Crystal Violet Lactone (CVL) is a 'colour-former' used in the carbonless copying system invented and developed by the National Cash Register Company in the USA and later the subject of research by British, European and Japanese firms. In this system the action of typing or writing causes the rupture of minute gelatine capsules, containing a solution of CVL in an organic solvent, coated on the underside of the top sheet. The oily solution, released wherever pressure is applied, comes into contact with the undersheet coated with an amphoteric substance such as sodium aluminium silicate with which CVL reacts instantly to give the coloured form:

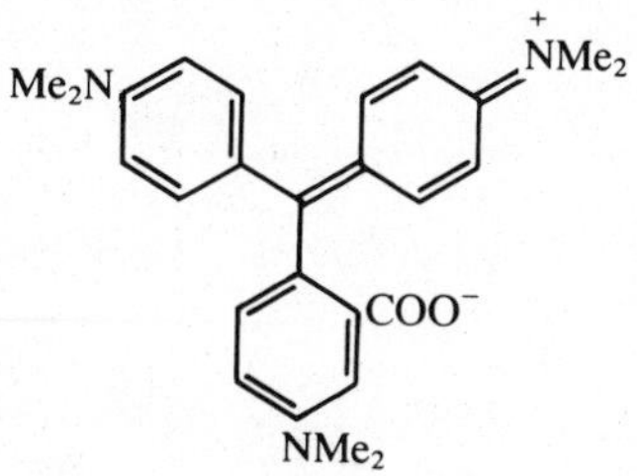

Fig. 10.10

This image gradually fades however, and it is usual to employ a second, slower-acting colour former together with CVL in the capsules. (See Benzoyl leuco Methylene Blue—Chapter 11).

Acid dyes

The direct method from Michler's Ketone is only rarely used in the manufacture of acid dyes. An important case is that of C.I. Acid Violet 15, 43525, in which the ketone is condensed with 3-ethoxy-4'-methyldiphenylamine to give the hydrochloride of the base which is then sulphonated with oleum to give the dye:

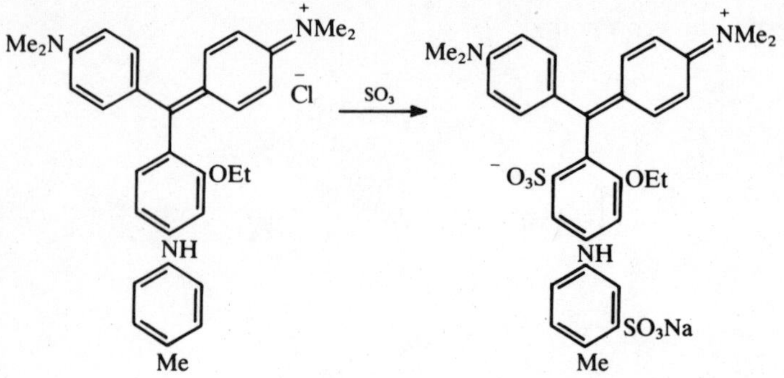

C.I. Acid Violet 15   **Fig. 10.11**

Its fastness properties as a wool dye are rather poor, nevertheless it is used as a shading colour, i.e. to correct an undesirable nuance such as yellowness or greenness in a main wool dye. It is employed also for the neutral dyeing of wool in wool–cotton unions.

Dyes containing two auxochromic dialkylamino groups in the molecule provide two important greens:

C.I. Acid Green 16, 44025, Naphthalene Green V, has the structure:

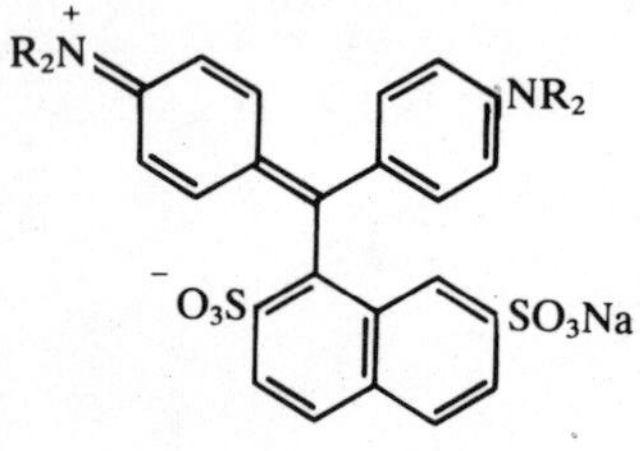

Fig. 10.12

where R = Me or Et; the tetraethyl compound gives yellower shades than the tetramethyl compound.

C.I. Acid Green 50, 44090 (Food Green 4), Wool Green S, has the structure:

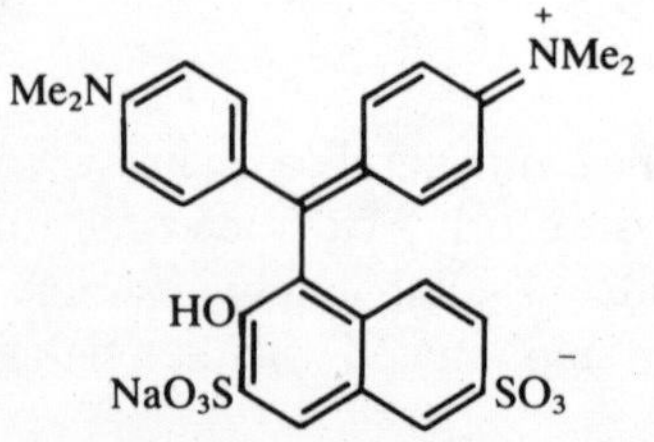

Fig. 10.13

Both dyes are made by a similar method, illustrated below:

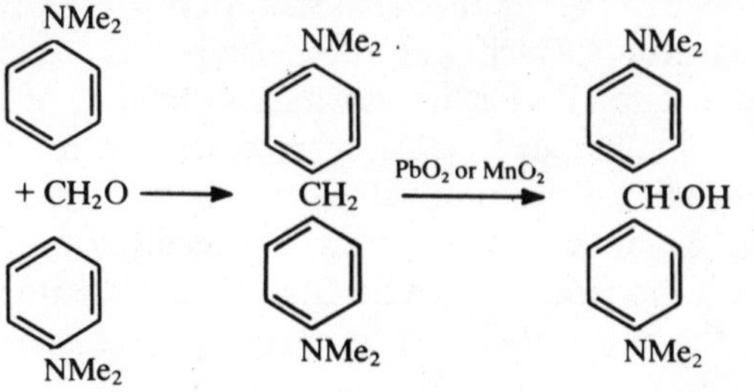

Michler's hydrol   **Fig. 10.14**

The product, known as Michler's hydrol, is very unstable especially towards heat. Moreover it causes severe dermatitis in susceptible persons. Accordingly it is almost always used as a moist filter-cake, superfluous water being removed where reaction conditions demand this by spinning in a centrifuge. Michler's hydrol readily condenses with 2-naphthol-3,6-disulphonic acid in moderately concentrated sulphuric acid with the elimination of a mole of water to give the leuco compound which, on oxidation with manganese dioxide in weakly acid solution, gives the dye:

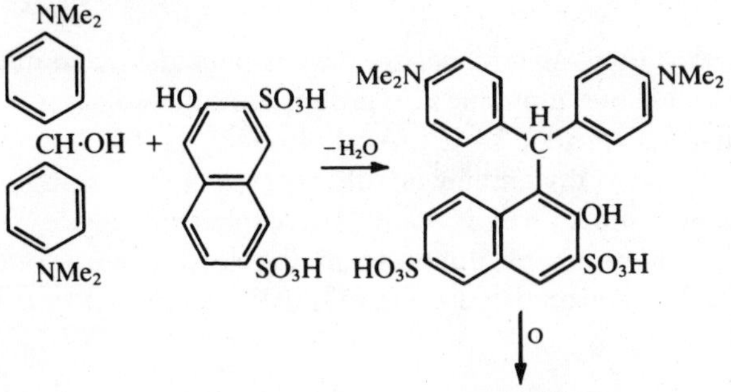

Wool green S   **Fig. 10.15**

Patent blues

The original Patent Blue V, C.I. Acid Blue 3, 42051, was obtained by condensing 3-hydroxybenzaldehyde with 2 moles N,N-diethylaniline, oxidizing the leuco compound and sulphonating the product, the dye:

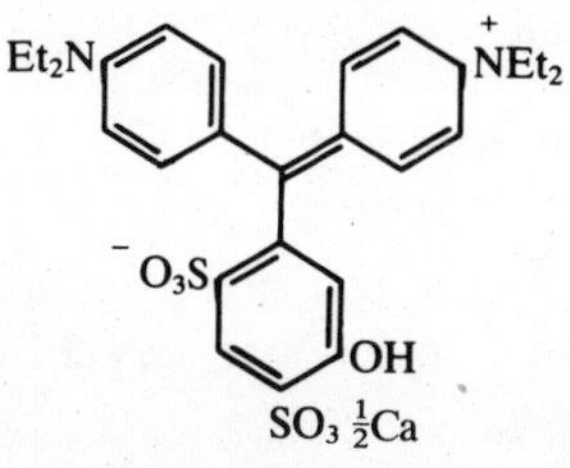

Fig. 10.16

being the calcium salt. The superior fastness towards alkali was at first ascribed to the presence of the *m*-hydroxy group though it was afterwards shown that it was the *o*-sulphonic acid group which was responsible. C.I. Acid Blue 1, 42045, Erioglaucine Supra, Kiton Pure Blue V, which is obtained by condensing benzaldehyde-2,4-disulphonic acid (see Intermediates) with 2 moles of *N,N*-diethylaniline and oxidizing the product with sodium bichromate and aqueous oxalic acid, has good all-round fastness especially towards alkali, though light-fastness is only moderate. C.I. Acid Blue 7, 42080, Kiton Blue A, Disulphine Blue AN has the structure:

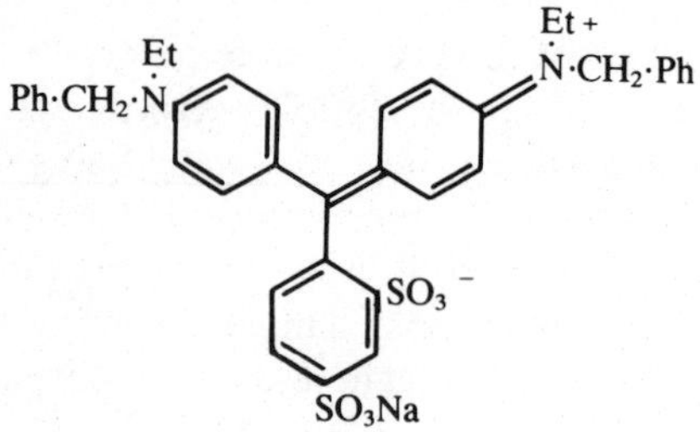

Fig. 10.17

and is reasonably fast to alkali and wet-treatments including acid milling.

An example in which the sulphonic acid groups are situated other than in the parent benzaldehyde is afforded by C.I. Acid Green 9, 42100, Xylene Milling Green 6B. *N,N*-Benzyl-ethylaniline is sulphonated and a solution of the sodium salt is boiled under reflux with *o*-chlorobenzaldehyde and, after removing excess aldehyde in a current of steam, the isolated leuco compound is dissolved in weak alkali and oxidized with sodium dichromate and acetic acid:

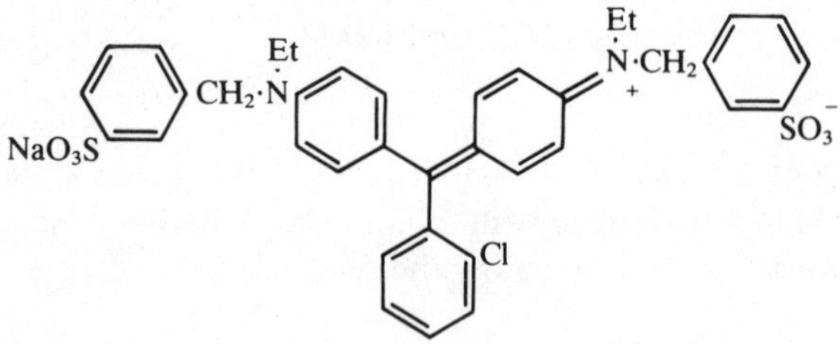

Xylene Milling Green 6B

Fig. 10.18

C.I. Acid Violet 17, 42650, Formyl Violet S4B is obtained by condensing a molecule of formaldehyde with two moles of *N*-ethyl-*N*-(3-sulphobenzyl)aniline:

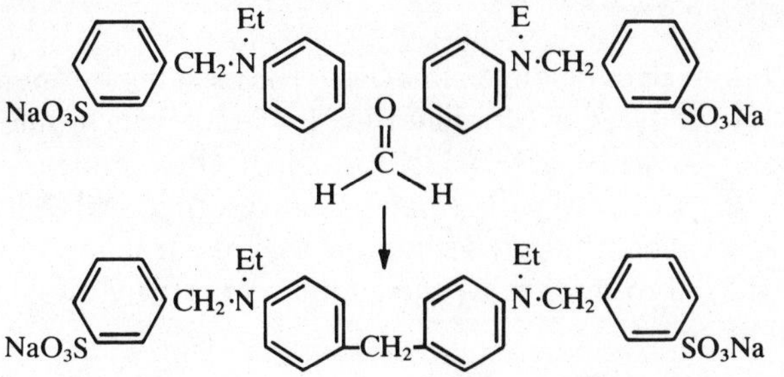

Fig. 10.19

followed by condensation with 1 mole N,N-diethylaniline under oxidative conditions giving the dye:

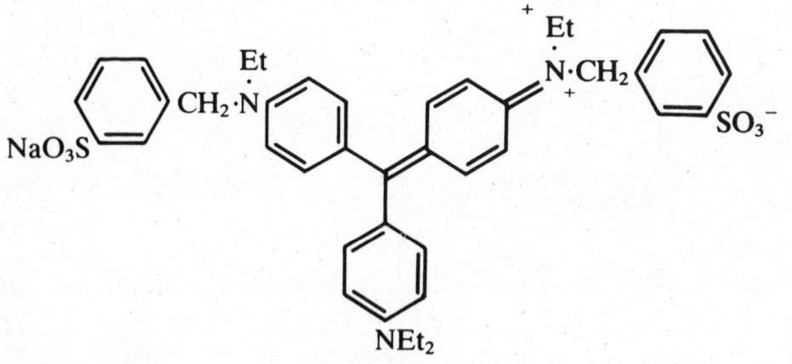

Formyl violet S4B

Fig. 10.20

The light-fastness is rather low and the chief use of this dye is as the phosphotungstomolybdic acid lake (see Pigments).

C.I. Acid Blue 83, 42660, Brilliant Indocyanine 6B, Benzyl Cyanine 6B, is prepared by condensing p-chlorobenzaldehyde with N-3-sulphobenzyl-N-ethylaniline. The leuco compound is oxidized to a green dyestuff and finally condensed with p-phenetidine when the nuclear chlorine atom is replaced:

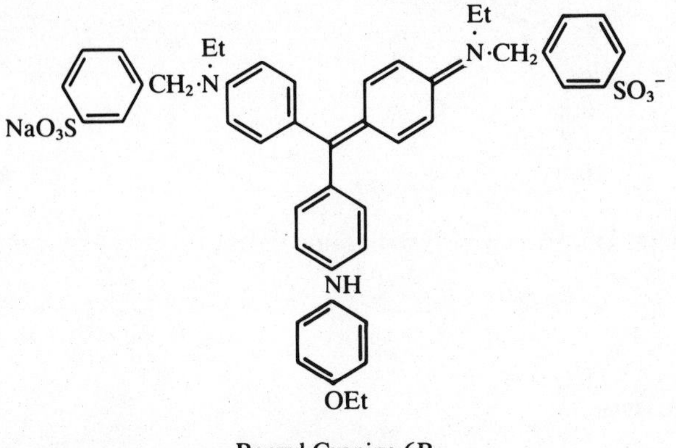

Benzyl Cyanine 6B

Fig. 10.21

The dye is used for both wool and nylon.

Hydroxytriarylmethane dyes

Certain useful chrome dyes belong to this class. The most important member is the bright blue chrome dye, C.I. Mordant Blue 1, 43830, Eriochrome Azurol B, Naphthochrome Azurine 2B, which is made by condensing 2,6-dichlorobenzaldehyde (see p. 63) with 2 moles of *o*-cresotinic acid (2-hydroxy-3-methylbenzoic acid) in concentrated sulphuric acid, the leuco compound so produced being oxidized to the dye by the addition of nitrosylsulphuric acid followed by aeration:

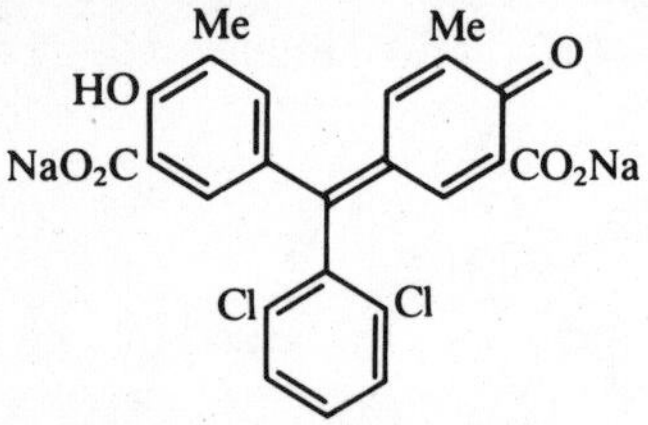

Eriochrome Azurol B   Fig. 10.22

Dyeings on wool are a dull maroon colour; on treatment with a chromium compound a bright blue shade is produced. Its light fastness is moderate (4–5), but it has good wet fastness properties.

An example of a dye containing a dimethylamino group as auxochrome in addition to hydroxyl groups is C.I. Mordant Violet 15, 43560, Metachrome Violet RR, obtained in an analogous manner to the preceding dye from *o*-cresotinic acid and *p*-dimethylaminobenzaldehyde (see p. 63). It has the structure:

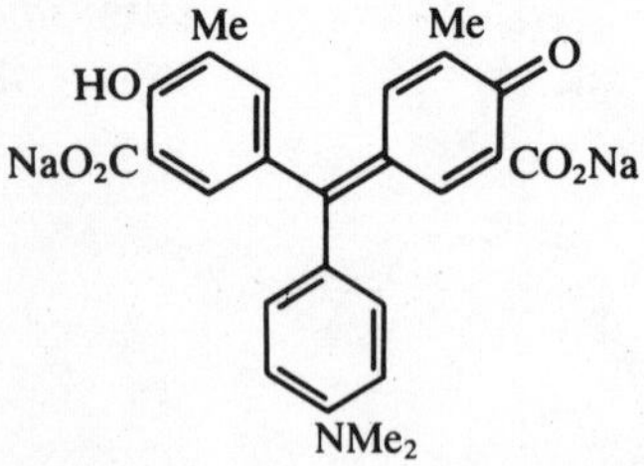

                                                       Fig. 10.23

and has a light fastness on wool of 5 with good fastness to wet treatments.

Related dyes

Diphenylmethane dyes

The diphenylmethane dyes are usually classed with the triarylmethane dyes but have in fact very little in common with them. Only two such dyes are of any significance, the more important being C.I. Basic Yellow 2, 41000, Auramine O, which is obtained by heating 4,4′-bis(dimethylaminophenyl) methane (see p. 157) with sulphur, ammonium chloride and salt in an atmosphere of ammonia at 175 °C. It may also be synthesized by heating Michler's ketone (see p. 152) with ammonium chloride and zinc chloride at 150–160 °C though this is not an economic method. The dye has the structure:

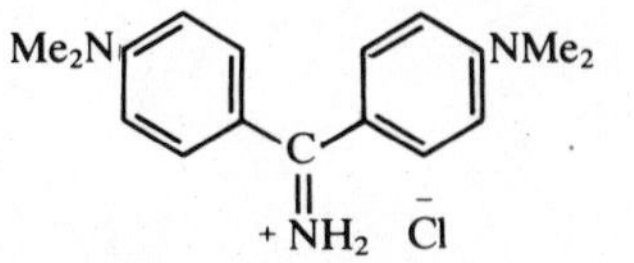

Auramine O   Fig. 10.24

and, being cheap, is used largely as a paper dye. The manufacturing process, though not the dye itself, is suspected as being a source of carcinogenic risk and is controlled by Government Regulations. Auramine G, C.I. Basic Yellow 3, 41005 has the structure:

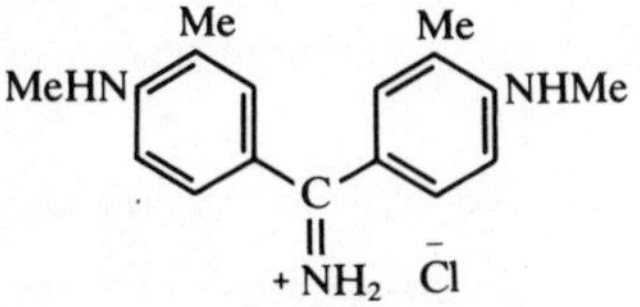

Auramine G   Fig. 10.25

Xanthene dyes

The parent heterocyclic ring system characteristic of this class is xanthen:

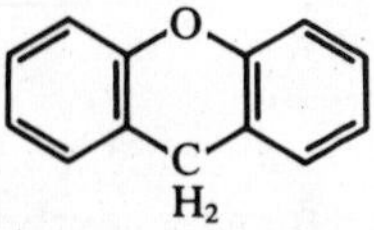

Fig. 10.26

The nature of the individual dyes is dependent on the nature of the auxochromes present and on that of the other substituents present in the molecule.

As a whole the group gives rise to brilliant, fluorescent dyes, red to greenish-yellow in hue. General fastness, in particular light fastness, is poor. An interesting dye, made by fusing 3-diethylaminophenol (p. 55) with succinic anhydride and isolating as the zinc chloride double salt, is C.I. Basic Red 11, 45050:

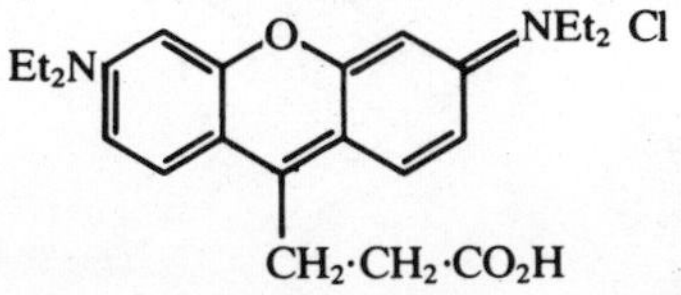

Fig. 10.27

In the dyes discussed in the remainder of this section the xanthene system contains an additional aromatic ring forming a group analogous to the triaryl-methane dyes already considered.

A very important dye, classed in the colour index as a 'Rosamine', is C.I. Acid Red 52, 45100, Sulpho Rhodamine B:

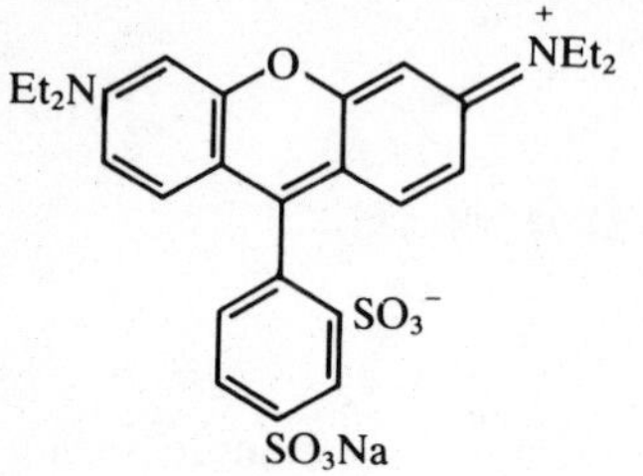

Fig. 10.28

The structure shown is only one of the possible resonating forms of the 'zwitter-ion'. In addition to that involving the second alkylamino group, the oxygen atom may also be the site of a positive charge, two o-quinonoid structures involving each aromatic ring carrying a diethylamino group becoming contributing forms of which the following is one:

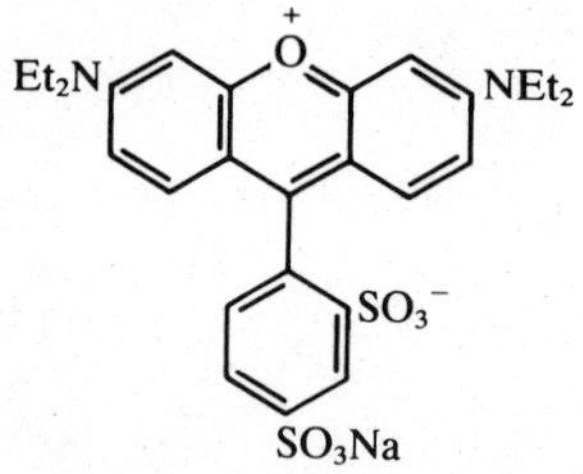

Fig. 10.29

The dye is made by condensing benzaldehyde-2,4-disulphonic acid with 3-diethylaminophenol to give the leuco compound which then passes through the following stages:

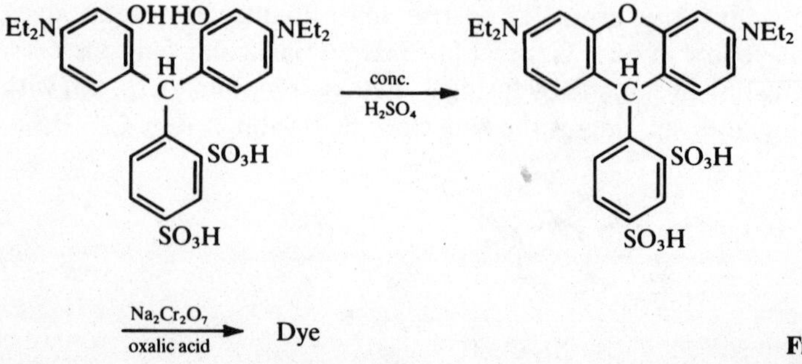

Fig. 10.30

Rhodamines

The Rhodamines are made by fusing phthalic anhydride with a 3-alkylaminophenol.

C.I. Basic Violet 10, 45170, Rhodamine B:

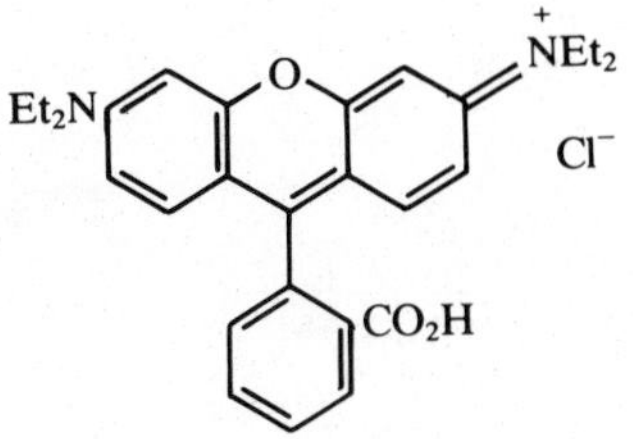

Fig. 10.31

is obtained from phthalic anhydride and 3-diethylaminophenol and is used in the preparation of lakes (see Pigments, Chapter 15) and in leather and paper dyeing. It is also used as a solvent dye, i.e. after dissolving the base, a lactone derived from the corresponding carbinol base, in stearic acid:

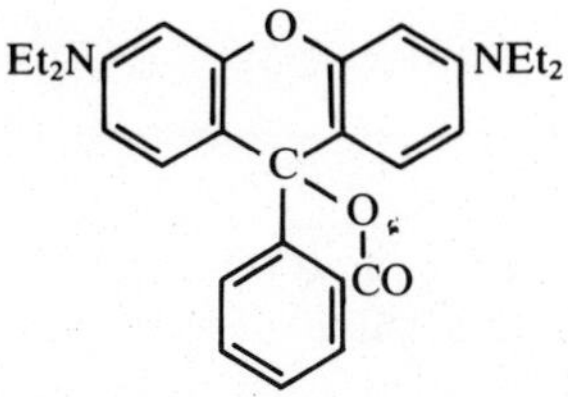

Fig. 10.32

The use of Rhodamine B as a food colour has been discontinued for a number of years on account of its suspected carcinogenic nature.

C.I. Basic Red 1, 45160, Rhodamine 6G, is made from N-monoethyl-o-toluidine and phthalic anhydride, the fusion product finally being esterified with ethanol and mineral acid:

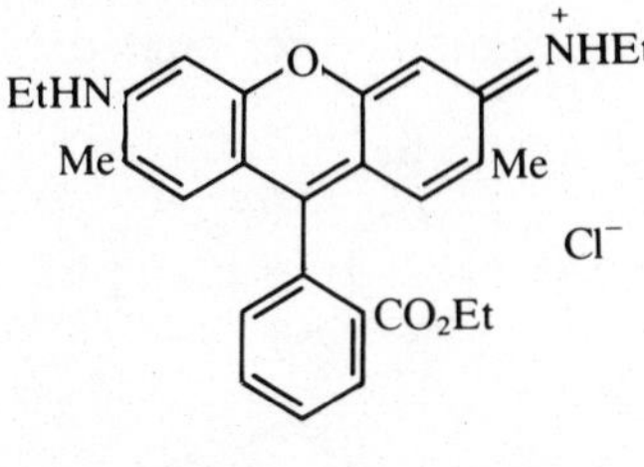

Fig. 10.33

C.I. Acid Violet 9, 45190, Kiton Fuchsine A2R, is a wool dye of some importance obtained by condensing 3',6'-dichlorofluoran with o-toluidine (12

moles) and sulphonating the product

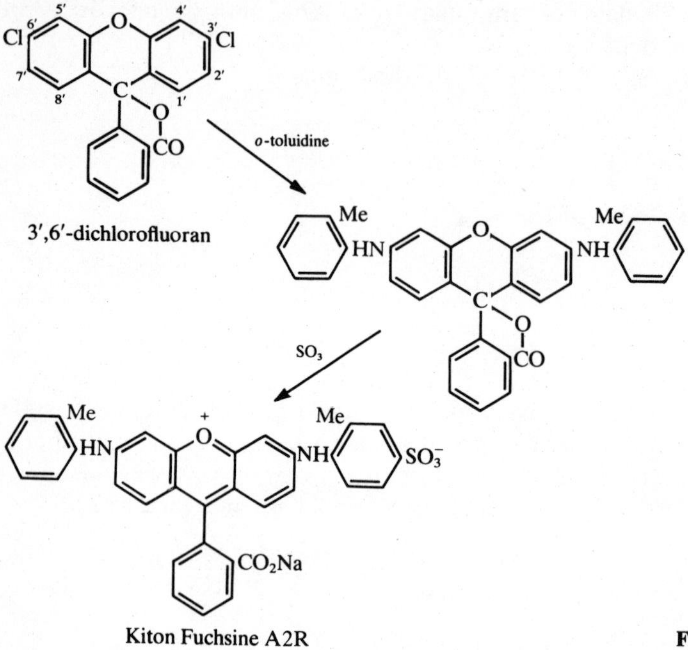

Kiton Fuchsine A2R   **Fig. 10.34**

The dye has a beautiful bright reddish-violet hue of moderately good all-round fastness and has a light fastness on wool of 4. It is widely used in dyeing and in paper coloration.

Fluorescein and derivatives

Fluorescein C.I. Acid Yellow 73, 45350 is the familiar, strongly-fluorescing substance produced when phthalic anhydride, resorcinol and a small quantity of sulphuric acid (or zinc chloride) are heated together and the product made alkaline with dilute sodium hydroxide solution. When the solution is acidified fluorescence disappears and 3′,6′-dihydroxyfluoran is precipitated:

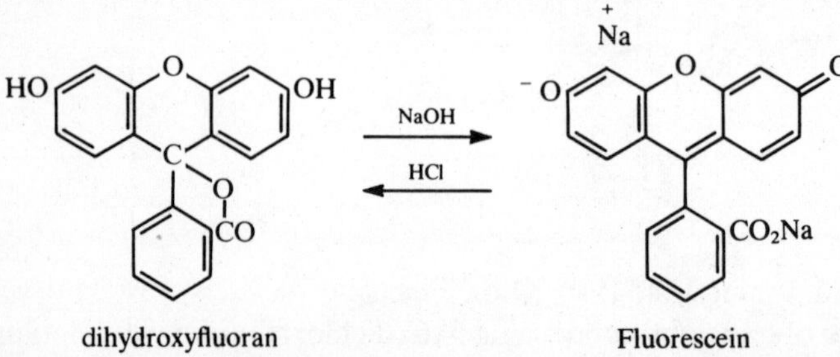

dihydroxyfluoran   Fluorescein   **Fig. 10.35**

When this substance is treated with phosphorus trichloride $3',6'$-dichlorofluoran, mentioned above, is obtained. By reason of its powerful fluorescence, fluorescein is used as a sea marker in rescue operations and also for tracing underground streams, rivers, etc.

C.I. Acid Orange 11, 45370, Eosin, the dye used in red ink, is obtained by brominating fluorescein in aqueous sodium hydroxide. The dye is the sodium salt, the anion being a resonance hybrid of a number of contributing forms, one being:

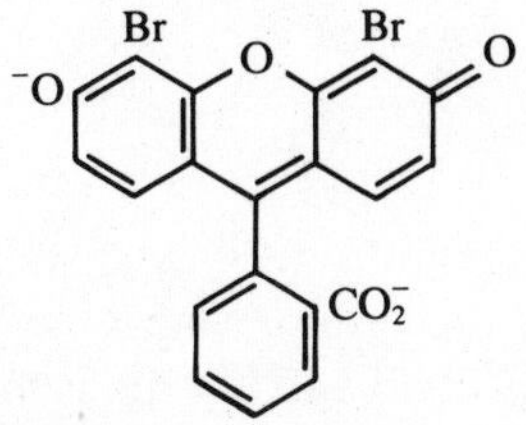

Fig. 10.36

Fluorol 5G, C.I. Solvent Green 4, 45550, used for colouring mineral oils, is obtained by condensing p-cresol (2 moles) with phthalic anhydride to give $2',7'$-dimethylfluoran which is then treated with 24% oleum and finally with zinc dust and ammonia under pressure:

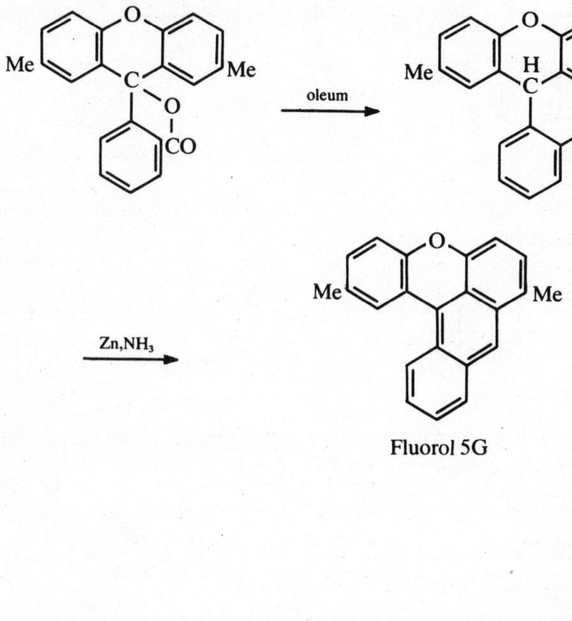

Fluorol 5G

Fig. 10.37

11
Miscellaneous Dyes

Azines

The azines are among the oldest of the synthetic dyes, Mauveine, now obsolete, being the most famous member of the group. Safranine T, used extensively as a red paper-dye, is C.I. Basic Red 2, 50240 (4) and is manufactured from *o*-toluidine and aniline by the following route:

1. *o*-Toluidine is diazotized and coupled with a second molecule to give aminoazotoluene.
2. The aminoazotoluene solution is run into a well-stirred mixture of hydrochloric acid and iron-filings at 80 °C, the reduction product being an equimolecular mixture of *o*-toluidine and toluylene-2,5-diamine:

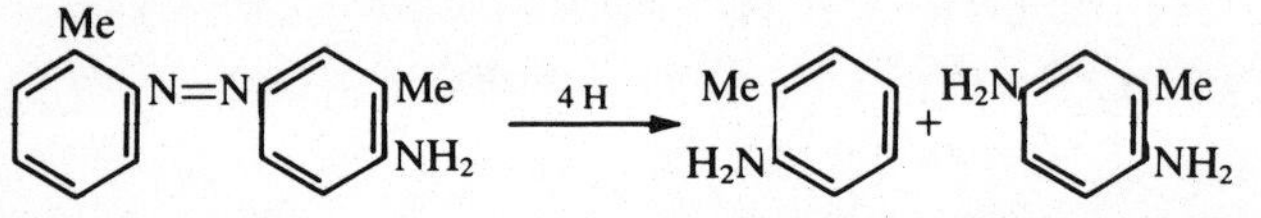

o-toluidine   toluylene-2,5-diamine   **Fig. 11.1**

3. The filtered solution of the amines is oxidized with dichromate at 10 °C giving an indamine

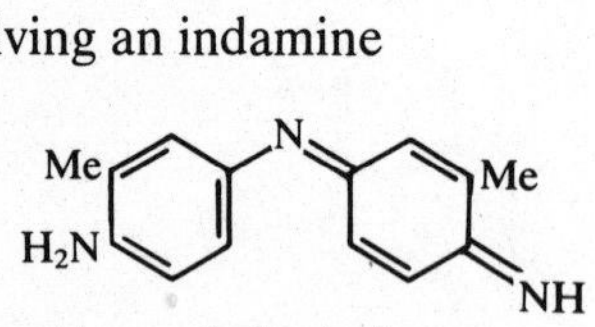

'indamine'   **Fig. 11.2**

4. Aniline is then added, 2 minutes after addition of dichromate, leading to the formation of a substituted diphenylamine:

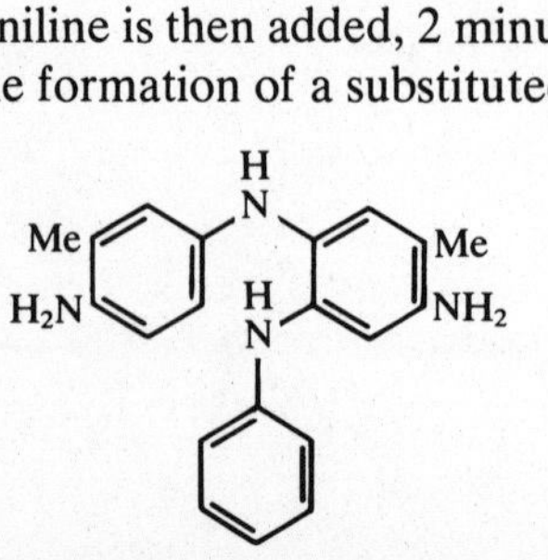

Fig. 11.3

5. The solution is partly neutralized with calcium carbonate to precipitate 'chromium sludge' which is filtered off. The filtrate is acidified, heated to 80 °C and oxidized with a further quantity of sodium dichromate giving the dye

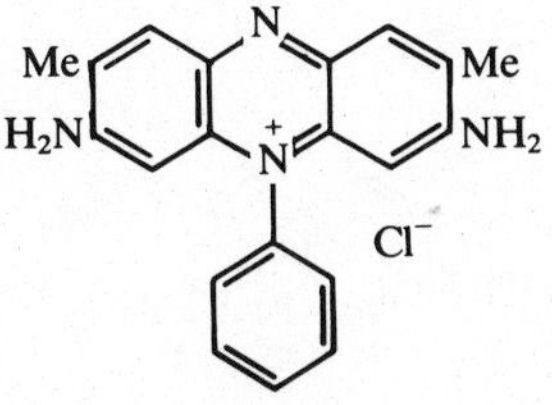

Safranine T

Fig. 11.4

6. After neutralization, the solution is treated with a small quantity of sodium sulphide to reduce any remaining dichromate and after the sludge has been removed by filtration the dye is 'salted-out' by the addition of 25% brine.

C.I. Acid Blue 59, 50315, Xylene Fast Blue BL, is an important acid dye of the azine class having high tinctorial power giving bright navy blues on wool of good all-round fastness; it is also suitable for nylon. The dye is made by passing air or oxygen through an aqueous-alcoholic solution containing equimolecular proportions of 1,3-di(phenylamino)-naphthalene-8-sulphonic acid (diphenyl-epsilon acid) and 4-aminodiphenylamine-2-sulphonic acid, and a small quantity of ammoniacal copper sulphate solution:

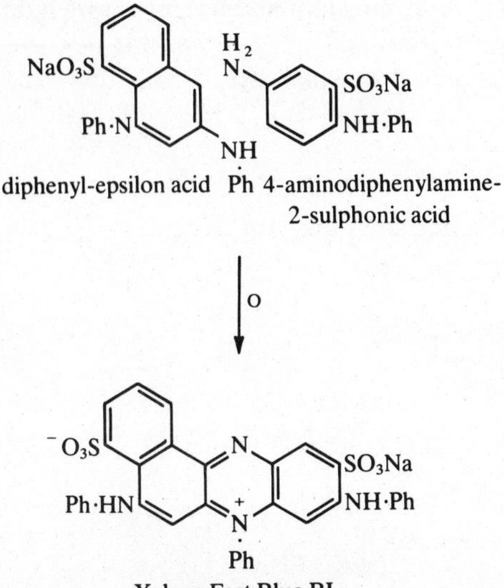

diphenyl-epsilon acid   Ph 4-aminodiphenylamine-
                              2-sulphonic acid

Xylene Fast Blue BL

Fig. 11.5

Oxazines

The oxazines are manufactured by condensing 4-nitroso-*N*,*N*-dimethylaniline with a suitable phenol such as 2-naphthol in alcoholic solution in the presence of zinc chloride. The dye, C.I. Basic Blue 6, 51175, Meldola's

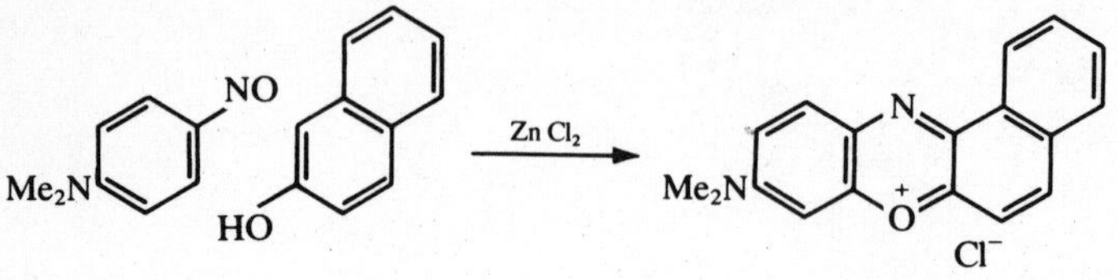

Meldola's Blue   Fig. 11.6

Blue, is isolated as the zinc chloride double salt and, among other applications, is used as a leather dye.

C.I. Mordant Blue 45, 51045, Gallamine Blue, is prepared similarly from the gallamide and has the structure:

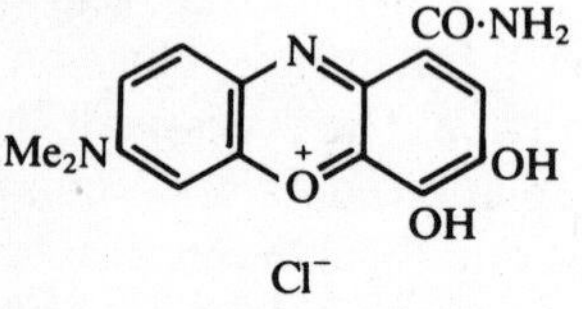

Gallamine Blue   Fig. 11.7

It is used for navy blues on a chrome mordant and has moderate light fastness (5), with outstanding fastness to chlorine (5) and to washing (4–5).

A modern example of a cationic dye, which dyes PAC fibres blue of good fastness to light and washing is provided by B.P. 1 339 300 (FH):

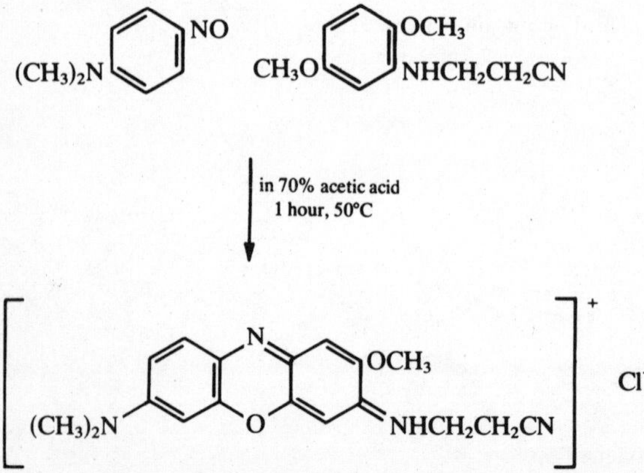

Fig. 11.8

Thiazines

The chief member of this group is C.I. Basic Blue 9, 52015, Methylene Blue, produced from the simple starting material N,N-dimethylaniline by means of a number of interesting chemical stages. The first step is the nitrosation of dimethylaniline followed by reduction with zinc dust or aluminium powder and acid to diamine. The diamine is now oxidized in aqueous solution with sodium dichromate in the presence of sodium thiosulphate giving the 'thiosulphonic acid'. Further oxidation in the presence of an equimolecular proportion of dimethylaniline gives an indamine:

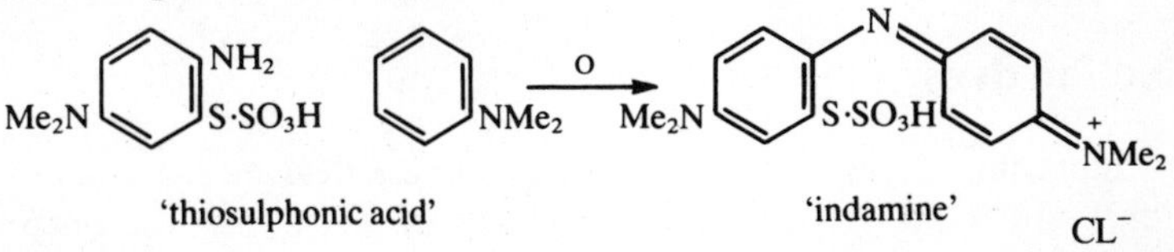

'thiosulphonic acid'   'indamine'

CL⁻

Fig. 11.9

On still further oxidation, ring-closure takes place with formation of the dye:

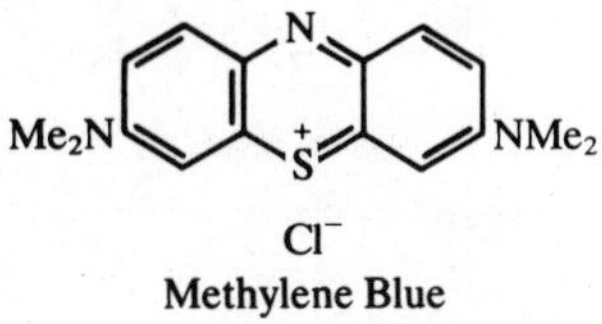

Cl⁻
Methylene Blue

Fig. 11.10

None of the intermediates is isolated; the dye itself is obtained by isolation as the zinc chloride double salt. It is used for dyeing bast fibres, in printing, as a leather dye, and, in the purified zinc-free form, as an antiseptic and for other medicinal purposes. The N-benzoyl derivative of the leuco dye is used as colour former in the so-called colourless carbon paper system of duplication.

Acridines

C.I. Basic Orange 14, 46005, Acridine Orange R is a typical acridine dye and is obtained from 4,4'-bis(dimethylamino) diphenylmethane by nitration giving the 2,2'-dinitro derivative, followed by reduction with, zinc dust and 30% hydrochloric acid, to the diamine:

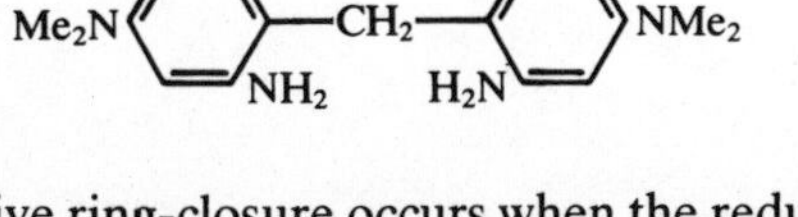

Fig. 11.11

Oxidative ring-closure occurs when the reduction mixture is heated to the boil

(115–120 °C) giving the dye which is isolated as the zinc chloride double salt:

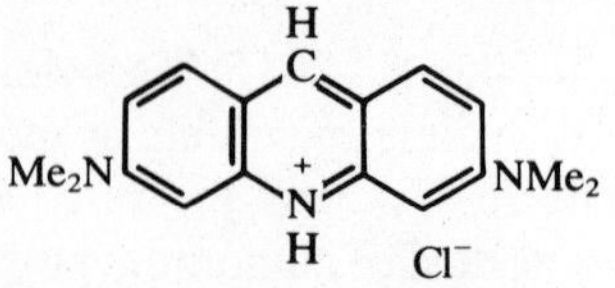

Acridine Orange R   **Fig. 11.12**

The dye, which has poor fastness properties, is used for dyeing bast fibres, for leather dyeing and in spirit ink manufacture.

Quinoline dyes

The more important members of this group are derived from quinaldine by condensation with phthalic anhydride at 200 °C in the presence of zinc chloride.

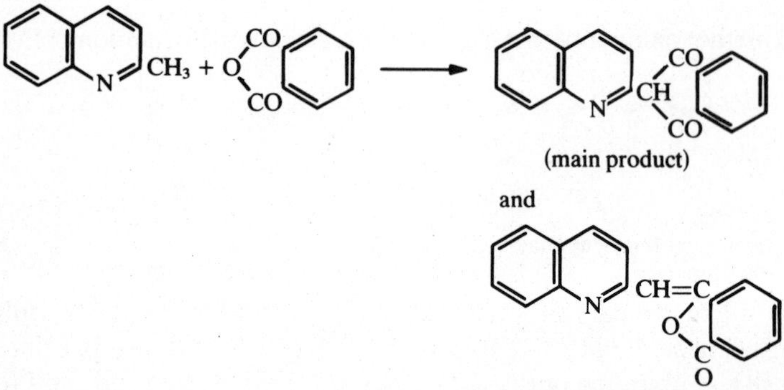

(main product)

and

C.I. Solvent Yellow 33   **Fig. 11.13**

In this way, a yellow, spirit-soluble dye used as a solvent dye and for coloured 'smokes' is obtained (C.I. Solvent Yellow 33, 47000) which on sulphonation affords C.I. Acid Yellow 3, 47005, Quinoline Yellow, used as a paper dye. It is a mixture of mono and di-sulphonic acids, the sulphonic groups being present in the quinoline ring system.

A quinophthalone dye of the 'amine salt' type (see Chapter 91) which dyes PAC fibres yellow of good fastness to washing and light is described in B.P. 1 324 389 (S) and has the structure:

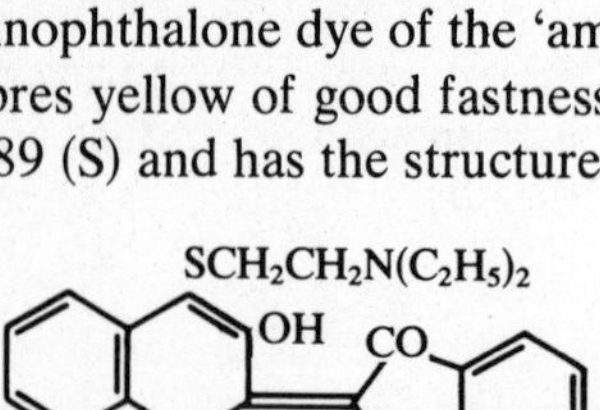

Fig. 11.14

The quinophthalone system also figures in disperse dyes (see Chapter 14).

Thiazole dyes

This group of dyes contains the thiazole ring system:

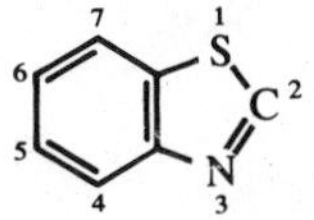

Fig. 11.15

the presence of which enhances substantivity for cellulosic fibres. In consequence the thiazole has been incorporated into a number of dyes including azo, anthraquinone and certain methine and polymethine dyes.

The parent substance is dehydrothio-*p*-toluidine or 2-(4'-aminophenyl)-6-methylbenzthiazole obtained by heating *p*-toluidine with sulphur and a little sodium carbonate to 175 °C. Hydrogen sulphide is evolved and is recovered by absorption in sodium hydroxide solution for re-use in sulphide reductions of nitro bodies to amines. The crude reaction mass is distilled at 1–5 mm Hg; after forerunnings, almost pure dehydrothio-*p*-toluidine distils over, less volatile material remains as a tarry still-residue. The product may be sulphonated to give a useful diazo component for the manufacture of direct azo colours, or may be methylated by heating with methanol and hydrochloric acid at 160–170 °C under pressure. The fully methylated product is C.I. Basic Yellow 1, C.I. Pigment Yellow 18, 49005:

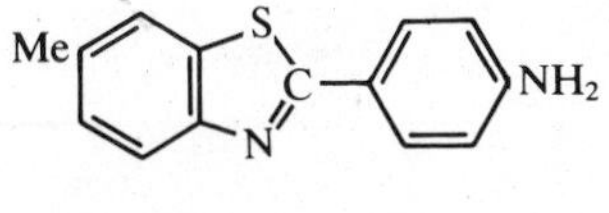

dehydrothio-*p*-toluidine 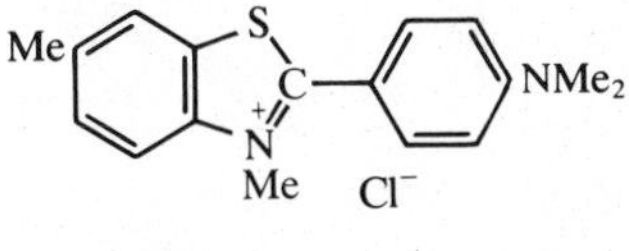   C.I. Basic Yellow I   **Fig. 11.16**

The dye is a beautiful, clear yellow used in quantity for the manufacture of the phosphotungstomolybdic acid lake (see Pigments, Chapter 15).

C.I. Direct Yellow 59, 49000, Primuline, is made by sulphonating Primuline Base, the product of high-temperature (200–280 °C) sulphurization of *p*-toluidine. The constitution given in the Colour Index is as follows:

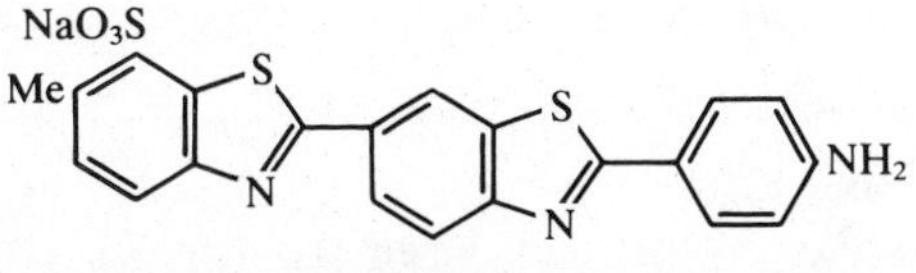

(main product)

and

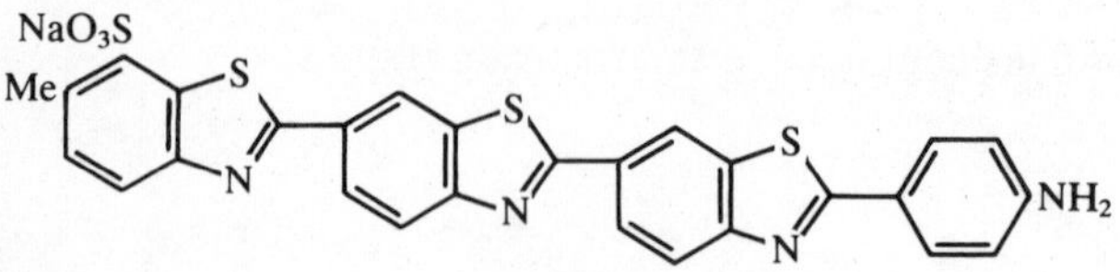

Primuline

Fig. 11.17

It dyes cotton greenish-yellow but is more usually diazotized on the fibre and developed with 2-naphthol, a red being produced. Varied shades can be obtained by the use of other developers, e.g. resorcinol (orange-red) or by treatment with hypochlorite (yellowish-orange). Primuline is used for cotton and viscose when a good standard of washing and water fastness is the primary requirement and where low light fastness (1) can be tolerated (hypochlorite development produces dyeings of relatively high light fastness, i.e. 4–5).

Nitro dyes

A number of useful dyes are known and used in which the sole chromophore is the nitro group. A well-known example is C.I. Acid Yellow 1, 10316, Naphthol Yellow S. It has the structure:

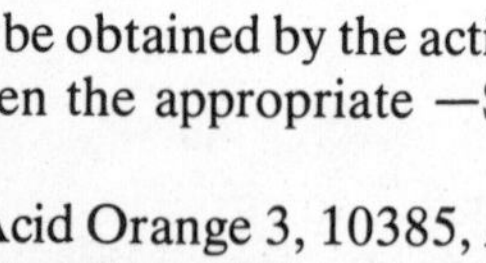

Naphthol Yellow S

Fig. 11.18

and can be obtained by the action of nitric acid on naphthol-2, 4,7-trisulphonic acid when the appropriate $-SO_3H$ groups are smoothly replaced by $-NO_2$ groups.

C.I. Acid Orange 3, 10385, Amido Yellow E, is a brownish-yellow wool dye of good levelling properties and excellent light fastness. It has the structure:

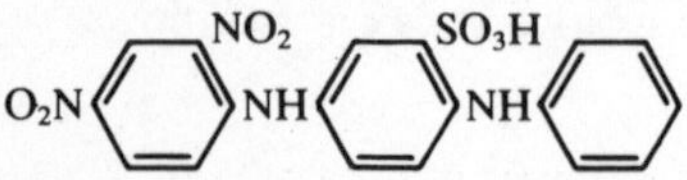

Fig. 11.19

and arises from the condensation of 1-chloro-2,4-dinitrobenzene and 4-aminodiphenylamine-2-sulphonic acid.

Nitro dyes, devoid of sulpho groups, are used as disperse dyes (see Chapter 14).

Ingrain dyes

Strictly speaking, the term ingrain is applicable to all dyes formed *in situ*, i.e. in or on the substrate by the development or coupling of one or more intermediate compounds which are not themselves true, finished dyes. Thus azoic dyes are ingrain dyes as are the oxidation dyes briefly mentioned later in this chapter. In the Colour Index the sub-section designated Ingrain is limited to tetra-azaporphin derivatives or precursors.

The outstanding light fastness and high tinctorial strength of copper phthalocyanine makes it unique among pigments (see Chapter 15) and from the time of its discovery dye manufacturers all over the world directed their efforts to the discovery of a solubilized form suitable for textile dyeing and printing. It is true that sulphonation gives a soluble product of excellent strength and light fastness but it is not fast to water-treatments especially washing. In Alcian Blue 8GS (ICI) C.I. Ingrain Blue 1, 74240 solubilization was achieved by the introduction of a so-called onium group. When copper phthalocyanine is heated with aluminium chloride and a tertiary base such as triethylamine, a 'melt' is obtained in which the copper phthalocyanine, being dissolved, will react with dichlorodimethyl ether to give chloromethyl derivatives. In this way three, four or even more chloromethyl groups can be introduced into the aromatic rings of the phthalocyanine molecule and, by quaternization with suitable bases, water-soluble derivatives are obtained. The use of dichlorodimethyl ether has, however, been discontinued by reason of its carcinogenicity.

Phthalogen dyes

A quite different approach to the problem of dyeing and printing using tetra-azaporphins is that of the phthalogen dyes (Farbenfabriken Bayer) in which the precursor diiminoisoindoline:

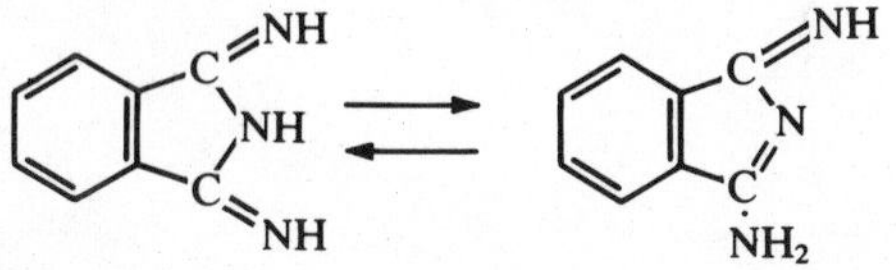

Fig. 11.20

in admixture with certain organic solvents and a copper compound, is printed or padded on to cotton and then dried. In this way a metal complex is formed which, at 130–150 °C (by steaming or by dry heating) and in the presence of certain solvents having a reducing action, is converted into copper phthalocyanine *in situ*. C.I. Ingrain Blue 2, 74160, Phthalogen Brilliant Blue IF3G, is formed in this way. In textile printing a printing paste is prepared containing the precursor, a special solvent and a copper or nickel salt. The textile is printed, dried, steamed and fixation then completed by treatment with an aqueous mixture of formic and oxalic acids.

Oxidation colours

The chief member of this small but important group of dyes is Aniline Black discovered in 1863 by Lightfoot and undoubtedly produced, as a by-product, by Perkin during the oxidation of crude aniline to give Mauveine. In the Aniline Black process cotton is treated with aniline and its hydrochloride and oxidized with suitable reagents, among them dichromates and chlorates in the presence of a catalyst such as a copper or vanadium salt. The dyeings or printings so produced have good all-round fastness properties. According to the conditions employed, so the properties of the dye, or rather complex mixture of colorants, vary. A good deal of work has been done by Willstätter, Green and others on the mode of oxidation of aniline and the structure of the resulting products. For details of this and other work more extensive textbooks should be consulted. It is sufficient here to say that structural units such as the following:

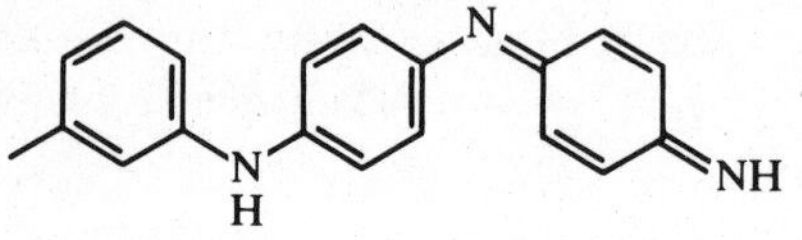

Fig. 11.21

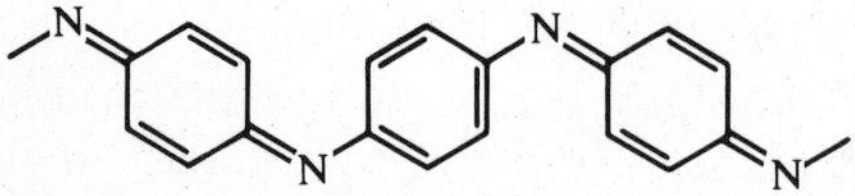

Fig. 11.22

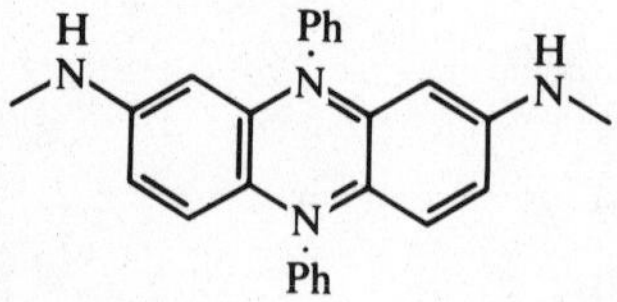

Fig. 11.23

occur in the products at various stages in the course of oxidation.

Certain diamines are extensively used for the dyeing of fur, hair, etc., by oxidation processes. Among these are:

C.I. Oxidation Base 12, 76050, 1-methoxy-2,4-phenylenediamine.
C.I. Oxidation Base 10, 76060, 1,4-phenylenediamine.
C.I. Oxidation Base 6, 76550, 4-aminophenol.

Indulines and nigrosines

When aminoazobenzene is heated with aniline and aniline hydrochloride at 150–160 °C Induline Spirit Soluble, C.I. Solvent Blue 7, 50400, is produced. The product is a mixture containing the azines:

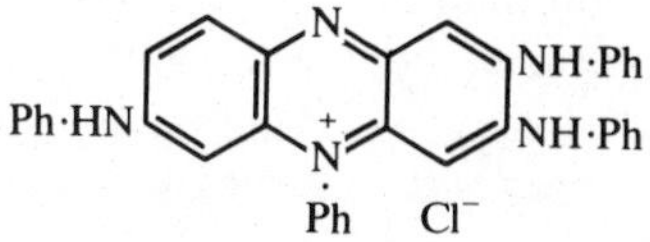

Fig. 11.24

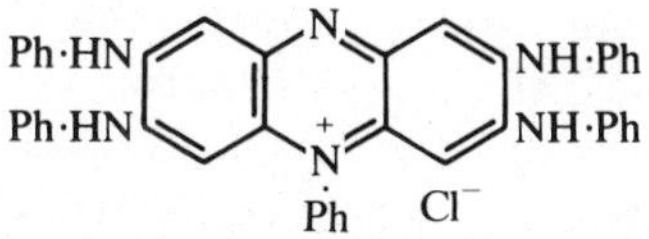

Fig. 11.25

The base is used as a solvent dye for colouring waxes, polishes, etc., while the product of sulphonation, C.I. Acid Blue 20, 50405, is used as a paper and leather dye.

C.I. Solvent Black 5, 50415, Nigrosine Spirit Soluble is a complex dye made by heating together nitrobenzene, aniline and aniline hydrochloride with iron or copper at 180–200 °C. Compounds containing the oxazine and diazine ring systems are thought to be present. The chief use of Nigrosine Spirit Soluble is as the black in shoe polish. The sodium salts of the sulphonation products are employed as paper and leather dyes.

Methine and polymethine dyes

The characteristic of this group of dyes, known also as the cyanines, is the presence in the molecule of the methine group —CH= or a conjugate chain of such groups. The nature of the terminal groups, which may or may not be similar, influences the nature of the dye with regard especially to its light absorptive properties.

The main use of these dyes is as photographic sensitizers. In general they have poor fastness to light and have therefore only limited application in dyeing and printing. A few dyes of this group are used as disperse dyes (see Chapter 14).

Cationic dyes

In all the cyanine dyes at least one of the terminal groups is a quaternary nitrogen grouping and individual dyes are resonance hybrids of forms such as

$$>N-C=C-C=N< \leftrightarrow >N=C-C=C-N>$$

The dyes in use as photographic sensitizers, of which many hundreds have been synthesized, contain various heterocyclic systems including pyridine, quinoline, indole, thiazole and others. They cover the full range of hues; the term cyanine owes its origin to the blue colour of the first members. Larger works should be consulted for a detailed account of those cyanine dyes in use for photographic purposes. It is worth mentioning that the study of this group by Brooker and others has led to important theoretical advances in the relationship of colour and constitution.

Hamer[43] has pointed out that those cyanines of the indolenine series are the most stable towards oxidative fading and those listed as Basic Colours in the Colour Index, Volume III, are mostly of this type.

C.I. Basic Yellow 11, 48055, Astrazone Yellow 3G is of very good fastness to wet treatments and has a light fastness on acetate of 4–5 and on poly-acrylonitrile of 6. It is made by condensing 1,3,3-trimethylindolenine-ω-aldehyde, Fischer's aldehyde with 2,4-dimethoxyaniline, the product being converted into a salt (chloride):

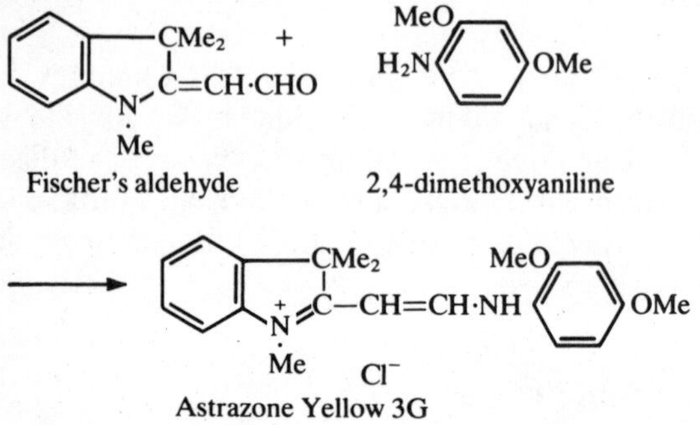

Fischer's aldehyde   2,4-dimethoxyaniline

Astrazone Yellow 3G   Fig. 11.26

C.I. Basic Violet 7, 48020, Astrazone Red 6B, has good general fastness but only moderate light fastness on acetate (4) and polyacrylonitrile (4). It is obtained by condensing 4-(N-β-chloroethyl-N-ethylamino)-2-methyl-benzaldehyde with 1,3,3-trimethyl-2-methyleneindoline:

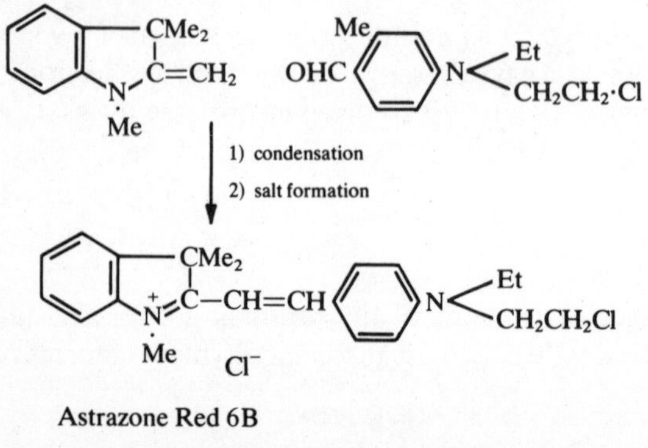

1) condensation
2) salt formation

Astrazone Red 6B   Fig. 11.27

The indole derivative is obtained, by Fischer's indole synthesis, from the phenylhydrazone of isopropyl methyl ketone followed by methylation.

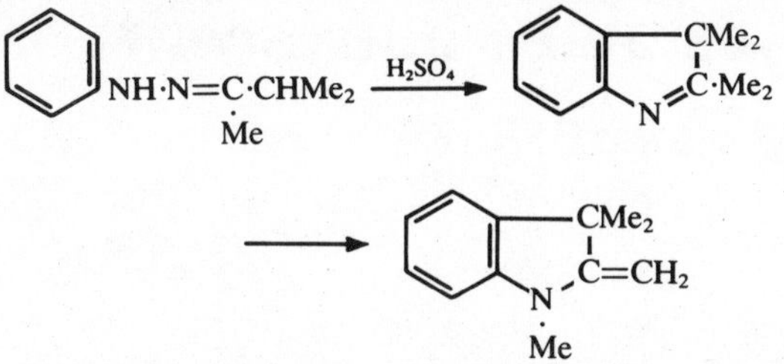

Fig. 11.28

Fischer's aldehyde is obtained from the above methylated indole derivative by direct formylation using *N*-methylformanilide and phosphorus oxychloride (Wilsmeier reaction).

Only occasional references to cyanines as textile dyes occur in recent patent literature. Nevertheless, the supplement to the Colour Index lists more than a dozen new basic yellows, oranges, reds and violets that are classed as either methines or polymethines, though none of the individual constitutions is disclosed. It seems at least likely that interest will continue in this group especially as dyes for polyacrylonitrile.

Naphthostyryl dyes

Dyes derived from naphthostyril by condensing with *N*-substituted aromatic amines using phosphoryl chloride and a Lewis acid such as zinc chloride, serve as cationic dyes for PAC fibres. Useful blue dyes of good fastness to light and washing are exemplified by

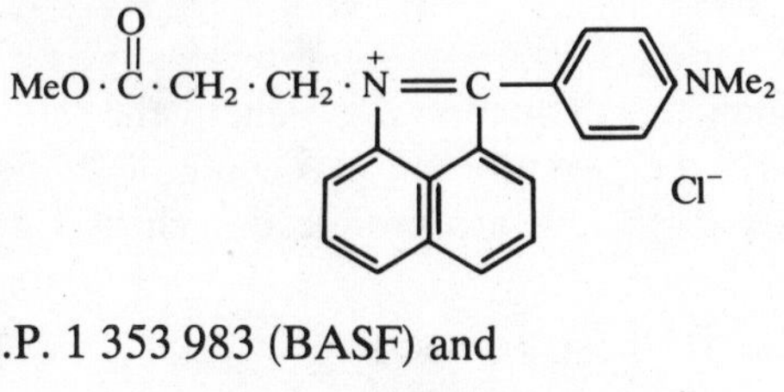

Fig. 11.29

B.P. 1 353 983 (BASF) and

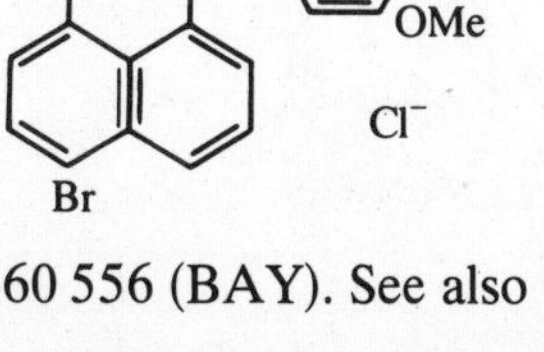

Fig. 11.30

B.P. 1 360 556 (BAY). See also Chapter 14, naphthostyryl disperse dyes.

12
Stilbene Dyes and Fluorescent Brightening Agents

The stilbene dyes are a small but extensively used group of direct dyes, the members of which are mixtures of substances which owe their colour to the presence of azo and azoxy groups as chromophores. They arise from the condensation of 4-nitrotoluene-2-sulphonic acid in aqueous sodium hydroxide solution either alone or together with other aromatic compounds usually arylamines or aminoazo compounds.

The first of the stilbene dyes C.I. Direct Yellow 11, 40000, was discovered by Walter, 1883, and was manufactured shortly afterwards by Geigy. It results from heating 4-nitrotoluene-2-sulphonic acid (1) with aqueous sodium hydroxide; the mixture of yellow dyes varies according to the alkali concentration, the length of time of heating and the temperature. In all such condensations it is most probable that the condensation of two molecules of 4-nitrotoluene-2-sulphonic acid occurs giving 4,4'-dinitro-stilbene–2,2'-disulphonic acid:

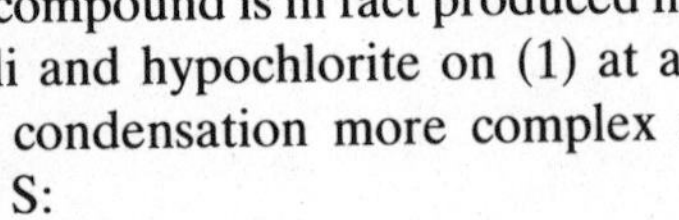

4,4'-dinitrostilbene-2,2'-disulphonic acid

Fig. 12.1

This compound is in fact produced in almost quantitative yield by the action of alkali and hypochlorite on (1) at a temperature not exceeding 50 °C. By further condensation more complex molecules are produced such as Curcumine S:

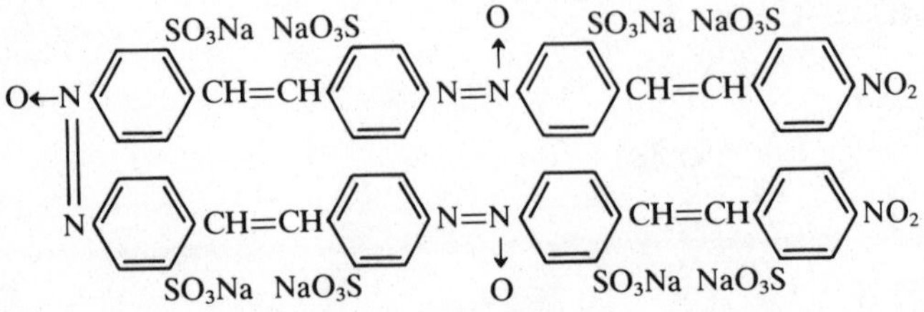

Curcumine S

Fig. 12.2

which is usually considered to be the main constituent in Sun Yellow.

The Colour Index lists a dozen or so direct reds and oranges that are derived from the condensation of 4-nitrotoluene-2-sulphonic acid (or 4,4′-dinitrostilbene-2,2′-disulphonic acid) with aminoazo compounds.

C.I. Direct Orange 34, 39, 44, 46 and 60, Sirius Supra Orange 7GL is obtained by heating an alkaline solution of 4-nitrotoluene-2-sulphonic acid and the monoazo dye, sulphanilic acid → aniline (C.I. 13010), under reflux. Various brands are produced by using different proportions of the reactants; in some cases the product is treated, in a final stage, with glucose and sodium hydroxide solution. C.I. Direct Orange 34 (Chlorantine Fast Orange TGLL) has excellent light-fastness (6–7) on cotton and is used in dyeing and printing (direct style) and also as a leather and paper dye.

Large quantities of 4,4′-dinitrostilbene-2,2′-disulphonic acid are manufactured annually by dye makers for conversion into 4,4′-diaminostilbene-2,2′-disulphonic acid. This important intermediate is used to a relatively minor extent in the manufacture of Cotton Yellow CH and in very large quantities in the manufacture of fluorescent stilbene derivatives.

Fluorescent brightening agents

Synthetic products having the power of absorbing radiation of wavelengths lying between 330 and 380 nm (u.v. region) and of re-emitting light within the range 430–490 nm, i.e. in the blue region of the visible spectrum, have been in use as 'optical brighteners' from 1940 onwards. They are in effect applied to textiles like dyes and they enhance the whiteness by adding the emitted blue light to the white light already being reflected from the surface in the normal way. Fluorescent brightening agents have in fact largely replaced ultramarine and other blueing agents formerly used to counteract the yellowness of textiles. Large quantities are consumed annually as ingredients in soap and washing powders. The principal textile application is on cotton, though fluorescent brightening agents suitable for wool, nylon and other synthetic fibres are of increasing importance. According to Lanter the annual sales of fluorescent brightening agents amount, at the present time, to almost 10% of the total value of world dye sales. Some of the commercial names under which these products are sold are:

Blankophor	FBy	Photine	HWL
Calcofluor	CCC	Pontamine White	DuP
Fluolite	ICI	Tinopal	Gy
Fluorosol	NAC	Ultraphor	BASF
Fluotex	Fran	Uvitex	CIBA
Leucophor	S		

Adams[42] has pointed out that for high fluorescent activity and cotton substantivity the molecule must possess a conjugated system, it must be planar, and must contain electron-donating groups such as —OH and —NH₂. For maximum whitening effects the re-emitted light should have a wavelength of 450 nm.

Stilbene derivatives

Over 80% of the fluorescent brightening agents in use at the present time are stilbene derivatives obtained from 4,4′-diaminostilbene-2,2′-disulphonic acid. One of the early examples is C.I. Fluorescent Brightening Agent 30, 40600, Blankophor R, made by the action of phenyl isocyanate (2 moles) on 4,4′-diaminostilbene-2,2′-disulphonic acid, the product being:

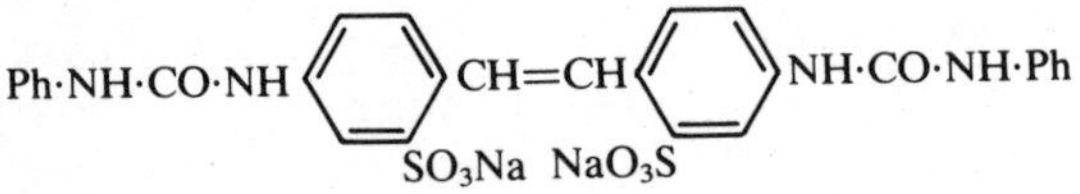

Blankophor R   Fig. 12.3

More modern examples contain substituted triazinyl rings and have the general formula:

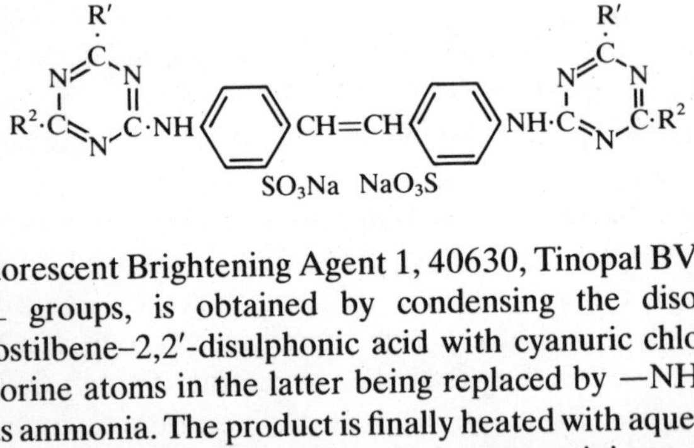

Fig. 12.4

C.I. Fluorescent Brightening Agent 1, 40630, Tinopal BV, in which R′, R² are —NH₂– groups, is obtained by condensing the disodium salt of 4,4′-diaminostilbene–2,2′-disulphonic acid with cyanuric chloride, the remaining two chlorine atoms in the latter being replaced by —NH₂ by treatment with aqueous ammonia. The product is finally heated with aqueous formaldehyde at 80 °C when high molecular weight products containing methylol groups result. The serial replacement of the three active chlorine atoms in cyanuric chloride is by no means an easy process. The alkalinity must be very carefully controlled as the chlorine atoms are readily replaced by hydroxyl groups at pH values greater than 6.5–7.0.

The brightening agents of this class are mostly symmetrical products, each of the two triazine rings being identically substituted. Unsymmetrical compounds are more difficult and more costly to manufacture. Various symmetrical compounds have been claimed, e.g. R′ can be phenylamino, tolylamino, methoxyphenylamino or 3-sulphophenylamino and R² may be methylamino, ethylamino or 2-hydroxyethylamino. These changes have relatively minor influence on the intensity of fluorescence while the main effect is in altering physical properties, in particular solubility and substantivity. As a class the bistriazines are not stable to the action of hypochlorite especially in solution. The use of 4,4'-diamino-5,5'-dichlorostilbene-2,2'-disulphonic acid as starting material is said to give bistriazines that are more resistant to hypochlorite.

Stilbene triazoles

B.P. 683 895 (FBy) describes the bistriazole:

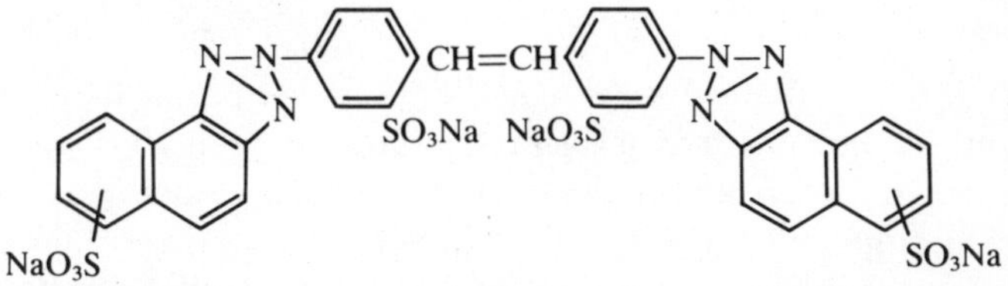

Fig. 12.5

obtained by oxidizing the disazo dye 4,4'-diaminostilbene-2,2'-disulphonic acid ⇄ naphthylaminesulphonic acid (2 moles) with hypochlorite. The product has a greenish fluorescence, useful in shading products have a reddish fluorescence and is very stable to hypochlorite. Blue fluorescence and hypochlorite stability is displayed in the unsymmetrical product described in B.P. 717 889 (Gy):

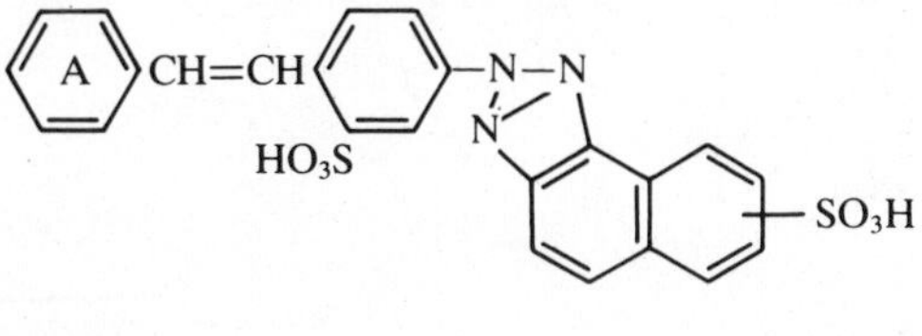

Fig. 12.6

in which ring A may contain a substituent such as Me—, MeO—, —Cl, or —SO₃H.

Miscellaneous products

C.I. Fluorescent Brightening Agent 48, 40640, Blankophor WT, is obtained by condensing benzoin and urea and sulphonating the product. It has the structure:

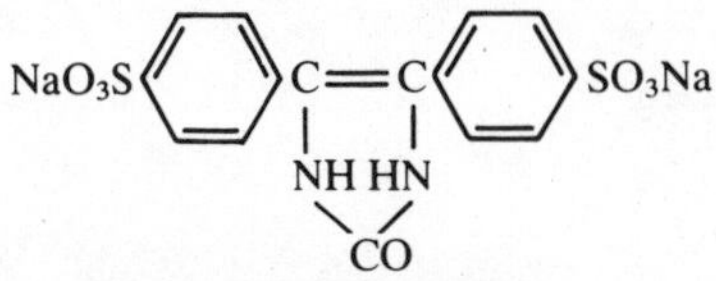

Blankophor WT

Fig. 12.7

and has moderate bleach fastness.

Coumarin derivatives
   Compounds of the type:

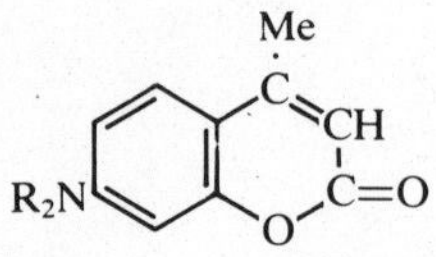

Fig. 12.8

where R is alkyl, are suitable for nylon and wool. These products are employed from aqueous solution either as acid salts or, where one R is alkyl and the other H, as the aldehydebisulphite (methane-ω-sulphonate) compound.

   Fluorescent brightening agents, whose molecules contain no sulpho groups or other water-solubilizing groups are of interest for application to polymer fibres and for the mass-brightening of polymers, especially polyesters and polyamides. Resistance to high temperatures, compatibility with various additives and low tendency to sublime are among the special requirements of this class, of which the following are a few representatives:

Benzthiazoles, benzoxazoles and benziminazoles

   CIBA have investigated compounds of general formula

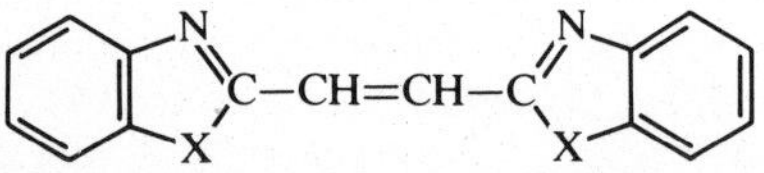

Fig. 12.9

where X may be S, O, NH or NR (R = e.g. $-CH_2-CH_2OH$). Such compounds have good fastness to hypochlorite an substantivity for nylon. Quaternary derivatives of this series are claimed to possess improved substantivity for nylon, polyester and cellulose acetate. The compounds

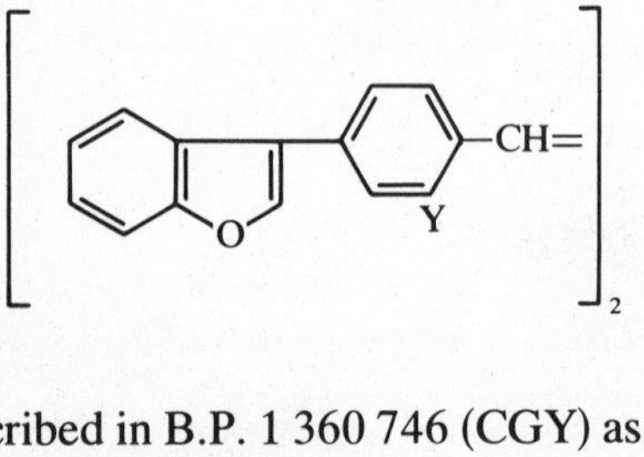

Fig. 12.10

are described in B.P. 1 360 746 (CGY) as being useful for the mass coloration of polyesters and nylons.

An example in which the ethylenic link is replaced by a thiophene residue is described in Belgian P. 641 607 (CIBA) in which the compound

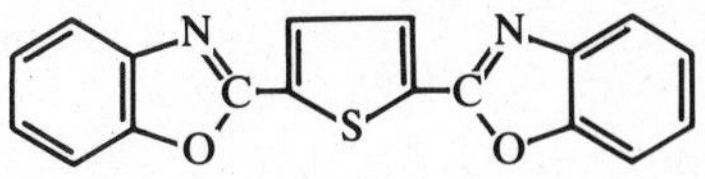

Fig. 12.11

is stated to be suitable for plastics and hydrophobic fibres.

Naphthalimide derivatives

BASF claim in B.P. 741 798 that compounds of the type

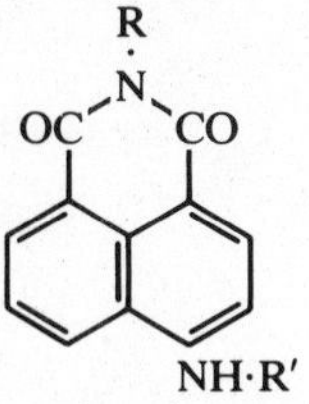

Fig. 12.12

where

R = alkyl or aryl, R' = —COMe, —CONHPh

are suitable fluorescent brightening agents for synthetic materials such as polyesters and polyamides. Other naphthalimide derivatives have been similarly claimed.

Ultraviolet absorbers

Certain plastics are known to deteriorate on prolonged exposure to an ultraviolet light source such as sunlight. It has been found that some fluorescent brightening agents tend to improve the stability to light of the plastics with which they are incorporated, i.e. they prevent or delay discoloration. Substances have been developed which act as stabilizers in this way and among them are derivatives of benzophenone of which a recent example is given in B.P. 947 686 (CCC).

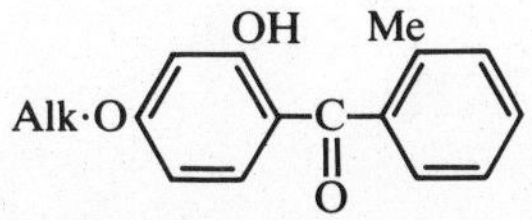

Fig. 12.13

Substituted styrenes of the type

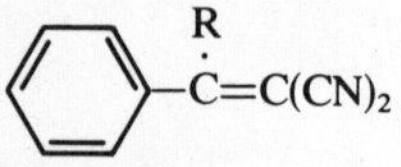

Fig. 12.14

are described in two General Aniline patents, Belgian P. 633 103 (R = heterocyclic residue) and Belgian P. 642 224 (R = H), as being suitable for epoxides and melamine plastics.

Many other kinds of substances have been investigated as potential ultraviolet absorbers, among them substituted triazines. It has been pointed out that although most stabilizers are u.v. absorbers, their efficiency does not appear to be directly related to their absorptive power. Further, such stabilizers are influenced by the presence of other compounds and suitable combinations of u.v. absorbers and antioxidants may show synergistic effects.

13
Reactive Dyes

A reactive dye, according to a useful definition by Rys and Zollinger,[34] is a coloured compound which has a suitable group capable of forming a covalent bond between a carbon atom of the dye ion or molecule and an oxygen, nitrogen or sulphur atom of a hydroxy, an amino or a mercapto group respectively of the substrate. They point out that this definition excludes mordant dyes and 1:1 chromium azo dye complexes which, in dyeing protein fibres, may form covalent bonds between metal ion and nucleophilic groups of the fibre.

The idea that the establishment of a covalent bond between dye and substrate would result in improved wash fastness compared with that of ordinary dye–substrate systems where weaker forces were operative is an old one. Attempts were made by various dye firms from about 1906 onwards to achieve this aim but it was not until 1956 that the first successful reactive dyes, the Procions, were introduced by ICI for the dyeing and printing of cellulose fibres, following the work of Rattee and Stephen from 1954 onwards. The invention consisted in the synthesis of dyes containing a reactive group, the 2,4,6-dichlorotriazinylamino group which has two labile chlorine atoms activated by the electron-withdrawing action of the three N atoms, and the

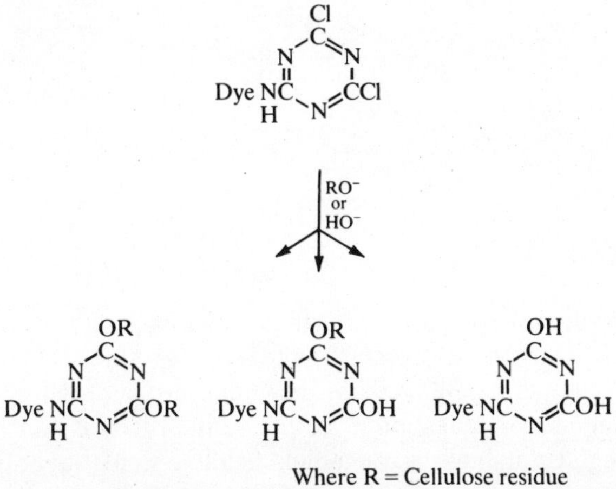

Where R = Cellulose residue   **Fig. 13.1**

devising of dyebath conditions which, while bringing about the formation of a covalent bond, were mild enough to avoid serious damage to the fibre. The dyeings were carried out at ordinary temperatures, 'fixation' being brought about by the addition of sodium bicarbonate, thus raising the pH. The reaction with cellulose may be represented as nucleophilic substitution by the attacking species RO^- or HO^- where R = cellulose moiety. Attack by HO^-, derived from the water of the dyebath, occurs simultaneously, but that of cellulose anion predominates since the dye is absorbed by the cellulose fibres and dye–substrate reaction is therefore facilitated. It is necessary to remove hydrolysed unfixed dye by thorough soaping and washing otherwise inferior fastness to wet treatments results. An example of a Procion M dye is the following:

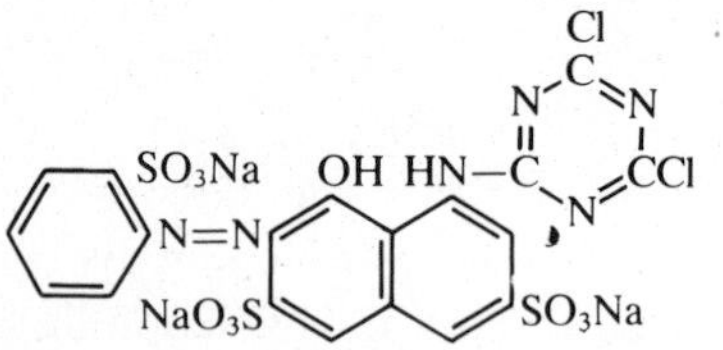

Fig. 13.2

Procion Red MX-2B ICI

These dichlorotriazinyl dyes, being relatively easily hydrolysed, tend to be unstable in storage.

The Swiss Company CIBA had been interested from 1930 onwards in the introduction of triazinyl groups into dye molecules (see Chlorantine Fast Green GLL, Chapter 7) and had patented, manufactured and marketed monochlorotriazinyl dyes, though not as reactive dyes. In 1957 ICI and CIBA jointly introduced the Procion H and Cibacron ranges which require a higher temperature (60–90 °C) and a higher pH to bring about fixation, but are more stable in storage. An early example is:

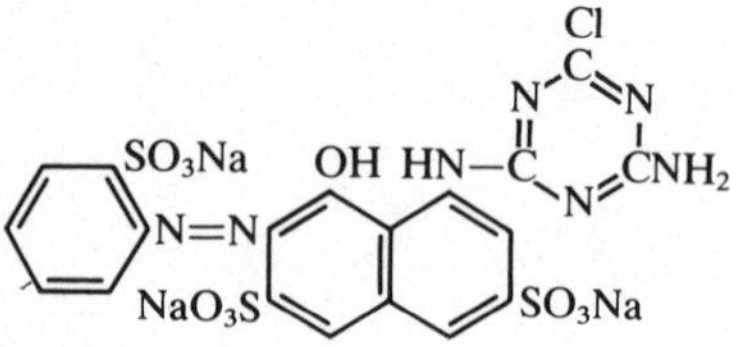

Fig. 13.3

Cibacron Brilliant Red B (CGY)

The chlorotriazinyl reactive dyes are by far the most important class and have proved a serious rival to the vat dyes as regards wash-fastness and in other ways. The main chromogens employed are azo, metal-azo, anthraquinone and phthalocyanine systems. The question of cotton substantivity is an important one. It should be high enough to ensure a high 'fixation-yield' but at the same time the substantivity of the unfixed, hydrolysed dye should be low enough to permit easy removal by soaping and rinsing to ensure maximum fastness to wet treatments in the finished dyeing. Structural modifications to the molecule which (a) inhibit coplanarity or (b) increase the water-solubility, tend to reduce substantivity.

Since their introduction reactive dyes have been the subject of a very large number of patents comparable only with the numbers granted for inventions in the disperse dye field and in that of synthetic organic pigments. Most dye manufacturers have invested heavily in research programmes concerning new reactive systems and variations of molecular structure to achieve optimum fastness and other properties. Attention has naturally turned to reactive dyes for substrates other than cellulose and dyes have been developed which are suitable for wool and polyamides. Water-insoluble disperse dyes having reactive groups (Procinyl dyes, ICI) have been introduced principally for the dyeing of polyamide fibres on which they show improved washing and heat fastness. Reactive systems may be divided into two main types:

(1) those involving nucleophilic substitution
(2) those involving nucleophilic addition.

Nucleophilic substitution systems

The monochloro and dichlorotriazinyl dyes, of which early examples have already been given, account for 50% of all reactive dyes used in commerce. The dye:

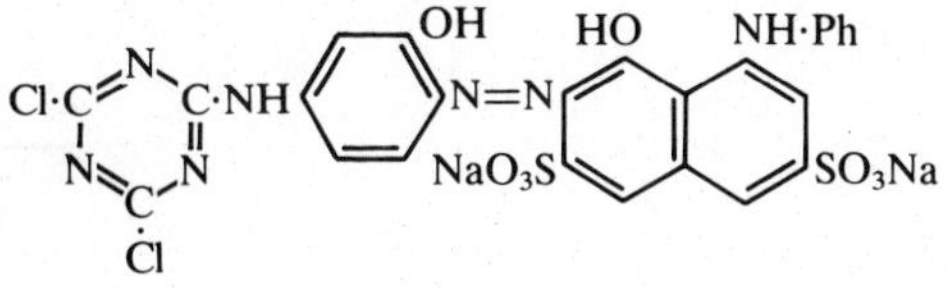

Fig. 13.4

as the $1:2$ chromium complex, is claimed in B.P. 938 125 (ICI) to dye cotton dark-green of excellent all round fastness. An example of a copper phthalocyanine dichlorotriazinyl dye is afforded by:

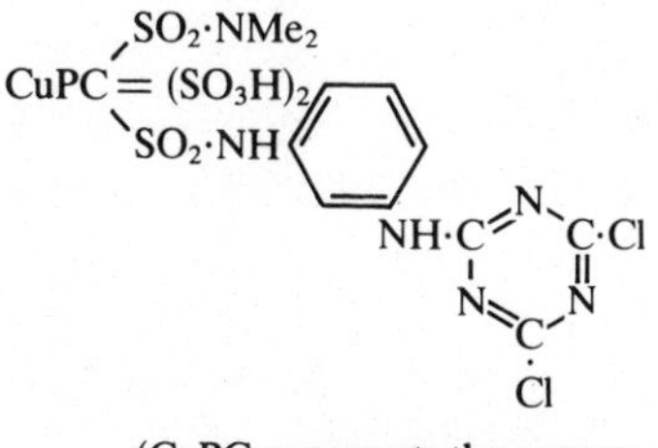

(CuPC represents the copper phthalocyanine molecule)

Fig. 13.5

which, according to B.P. 948 256 (ICI), dyes cotton a bright greenish-blue of excellent fastness to wet treatments.

The blue monochlorotriazinyl dye

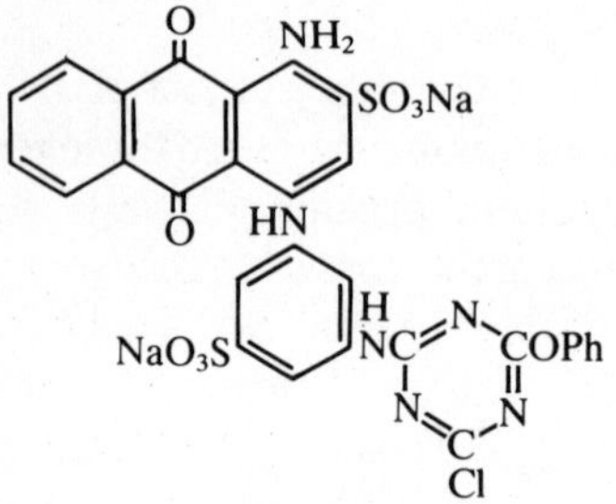

Fig. 13.6

B.P. 1 230 722 (CGY) is said to have good light fastness and outstanding wet fastness. Dyes stemming from sulphonyl chloride derivatives of copper phthalocyanine by reaction with N-(β-hydroxyethyl)ethylenediamine, followed by condensation with 2,4-dichloro-6-methoxy-3-triazine are described in B.P. 1 227 538 (ICI).

It should be noted that improved fixation can be obtained by introducing a second monochlorotriazinyl group into the reactive dye molecule. Such dyes form the basis of the Procion Supra range of ICI.

Trichloropyrimidine dyes

These are derived from tetrachloropyrimidine:

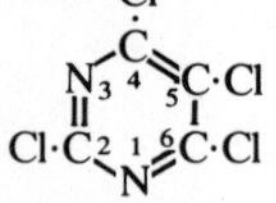

Fig. 13.7

The electron-withdrawing properties of the two nitrogen atoms render the chlorine atoms in positions 2, 4 and 6 labile; that in position 5 is unreactive. The trichloropyrimidine dyes do not equal the dichlorotriazines in reactivity and their fixation on the fibre requires higher temperatures. The dyes themselves are stated to be less sensitive to hydrolysis. Trichloropyrimidine dyes are marketed as Drimarenes (S) and Reactones (Gy) and are of the general structure

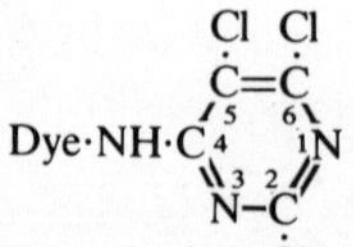

Fig. 13.8

Fluorine atoms replace chlorine atoms in other pyrimidine systems e.g.

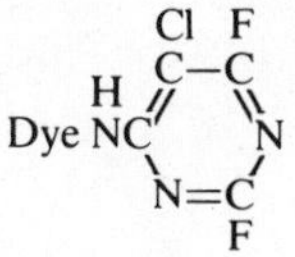

Drimalan (S)
Verafix (FBy)
Levafix (FBy)

Fig. 13.9

Among other heterocyclic systems are the 2-chlorobenzthiazole system:

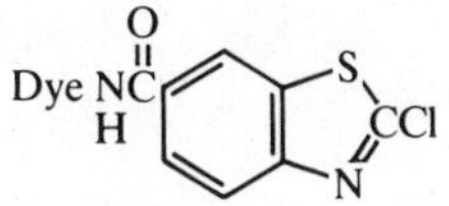

Reatex (Fran)

Fig. 13.10

the chloropyridazine systems:

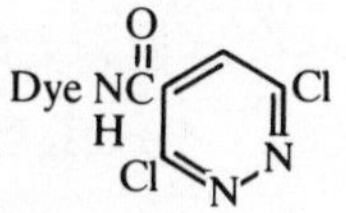

Solidazol (Fran)

Fig. 13.11

and   Dye NC... Reatex (Fran)

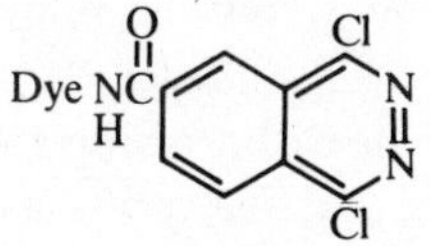

Fig. 13.12

Quinoxaline derivatives

The use of various quinoxaline derivatives is covered by B.P. 995 796 (FBy):

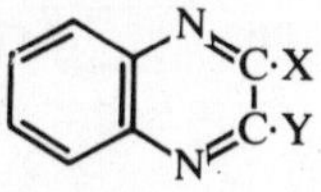

Fig. 13.13

where X = halogen, Y = H, Cl, Br, Oalk and other groups.
An example of a typical dye is given in B.P. 993 747 (FBy):

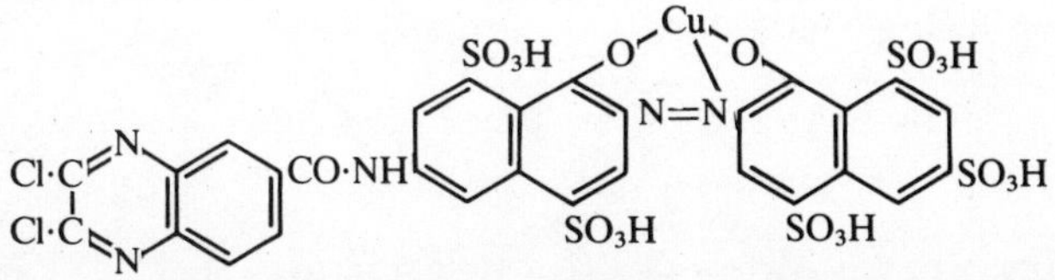

Fig. 13.14

The acid chloride of the quinoxaline is condensed with the free amino group at position 6 in the monoazo copper complex at 40 °C and pH 6.5–7.0 under which conditions neither chlorine atom undergoes hydrolysis. This class of reactive dyes is marketed as the Levafix E range (FBy).

Chloroacetyl and bromoacetyl derivatives

The Drimalan (S) dyes employ α-halogenoacetyl groups as reactive centre and this group occurs (along with monochlorotriazinyl dyes) in the Cibalan Brilliant dyes (CIBA). In both cases the main application is in wool dyeing. The principle has been applied to disperse dyes as in B.P. 977 222 (S):

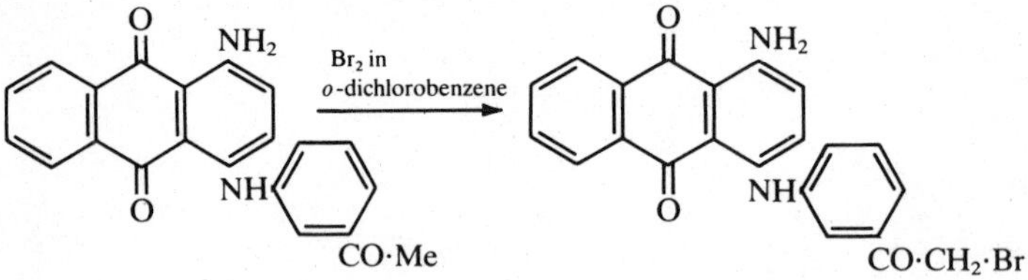

Fig. 13.15

The resulting reactive disperse dye gives blue dyeings on polyamides of excellent fastness to wet treatments.

Nuclear halogen, activated by electron-withdrawing groups such as $-NO_2$ in *o*- or *p*-positions, can also serve as a reactive centre as in:

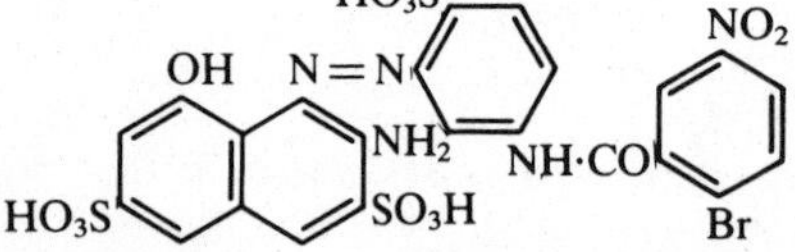

Fig. 13.16

which is claimed in B.P. 982 583 (CFM) as giving bluish-red prints on cotton of very good wet fastness and dischargeability.

Vinylsulphonyl dyes

The Remazol (FH) dyes employ the vinylsulphone group as in $Dye \cdot SO_2 \cdot CH = CH_2$ or compounds giving the vinyl group on treatment with alkali, i.e. under dyeing conditions:

$$Dye \cdot SO_2 \cdot CH_2 \cdot CH_2 OSO_3 Na + NaOH \rightarrow Dye \cdot SO_2 CH = CH_2 + Na_2 SO_4 + H_2 O$$

or

$$Dye \cdot SO_2 CH_2 CH_2 Cl + NaOH \rightarrow Dye \cdot SO_2 CH = CH_2 + NaCl + H_2 O$$

The reaction mechanism leading to the formation of a covalent link with the substrate concerns the formation of a carbonium ion, facilitated by the electron-withdrawing properties of the sulphone group, followed by interaction with the anionic centre in the cellulose fibres:

$$Dye \cdot SO_2-CH=CH_2 + O-Cellulose \rightarrow Dye \cdot SO_2 \cdot CH_2-CH_2 \cdot O-Cellulose$$

The mechanism is thus essentially one of **nucleophilic addition**. The Cavalites (DuP) also employ the vinylsulphonyl group (and also the chloroquinoxalines) while in the Levafix (FBy) range the vinylsulphonamides

$$Dye \cdot SO_2NHCH_2CH_2OSO_3Na$$

are the reactive groups, $SO_2NH \cdot CH=CH_2$ being formed under the conditions of dyeing or printing. The 'dye' portion of the molecule is a water-insoluble pigment, the molecule of which contains no $-SO_3H$ or other solubilizing group. It is of interest also that β-thiosulphatoethylsulphones, $-SO_2CH_2CH_2 \cdot S \cdot SO_3H$, are converted by bases into vinylsulphones. The Bunte salts or organic thiosulphate salts derived from dye molecules are capable of reacting directly with the thiol groups in wool fibres

$$\begin{array}{l} -SH + SCH_2CONH\,Dye \\ \underset{SO_3Na \rightarrow}{|} \qquad\qquad -S \cdot S \cdot CH_2CONH\,Dye \end{array}$$

Acrylamide dyes

The Primazin (BASF) dyes embody the acrylamide group $-NH \cdot CO \cdot CH=CH_2$ or a precursor such as $-NH \cdot CO \cdot CH_2CH_2OSO_3Na$. As with the vinyl sulphones the mechanism is primarily concerned with nucleophilic addition. The Procilan dyes for wool (ICI) embody the acryloylamino group attached to a 1:2 nickel or cobalt azo complex. The Lanasol dyes (CGY) have as reactive centre the α-bromoacryloylamino group $-NHCOC=CH_2$.
$$\;\underset{}{\text{Br}}$$

Evidence for chemical combination

Cellulose

Stamm, Zollinger and co-workers have endeavoured to obtain experimental evidence of the formation of a covalent link and to demonstrate its position in the D–glucose unit of cellulose. Cotton dyed with a Remazol dye was subjected to microbiological hydrolysis, a mixture of oligomers being formed. Further degradation, with dilute sulphuric acid, gave a glucose derivative in which one hydroxyl group was blocked by a dye molecule. Methylation of this under very mild conditions, followed by alkaline treatment to remove the dye molecule, and then acid hydrolysis to remove the glucosidic methyl group gave finally a known trimethylglucose. Stamm later showed that a glucoside is normally formed by Remazol dyes acting on cellulose and concluded that the earlier findings were ambiguous.

Cellulose dyed with a chlorotriazinyl reactive dye however will not dissolve in cuprammonium solution, whereas cellulose dyes with direct dyes will dissolve.

Work on the attachment of reactive disperse dyes to polyamides has shown that both $-CO \cdot NH-$ groups and terminal $-NH_2-$ groups are most probably involved. There is good evidence that chemical combination does indeed occur in that polyamides dyed with reactive disperse dyes cannot be 'stripped' by solvents in contrast to the same substrate dyed with conventional disperse dyes or azoic combinations, from which the colorant can be removed by solvents. Another striking demonstration is afforded by diluting a solution of dyed polyamide in o-chlorophenol. In the case of a reactive dye a coloured precipitate is obtained while the aqueous phase is colourless; with conventional dyes, coloration of the aqueous phase occurs.

It is clear from the number of published patents relating to reactive dyes that this field is regarded as being of the highest importance by the dye-maker and dye-user. Much work is also being done on the kinetics and physical chemistry of dyeing and printing processes in which reactive dyes are involved; in this, as in other fields of dye technology, progress is thereby accelerated.

14
Disperse Dyes

Introductory

Disperse dyes came into existence two or three years after the introduction of (secondary) cellulose acetate rayon by the British Celanese Company in 1920. None of the existing dyes then in use for natural fibres was suitable. The water-soluble anionic dyes had little substantivity for the new fibres; a few cationic dyes could be used, the effective dyeing species being the free base which was gradually absorbed. The alkaline conditions needed for the application of vat dyes brought about rapid hydrolysis of the acetyl groups with severe impairment of properties, e.g. loss in tensile strength, deterioration in appearance and 'handle'. It soon emerged that certain dyestuffs of relatively simple structure, containing no water-solubilizing groups such as sulpho groups, would 'dye' cellulose acetate simply by being brought into physical contact with the textile. Efforts were accordingly concentrated on devising a practical method of application in which water could be used as a vehicle.

The earliest invention was that of Green and Saunders, 1923, who prepared the sodium methane-ω-sulphonates of selected dyes having in their molecules, primary or secondary amino groups. These 'temporarily solubilized' dyes were marketed as the Ionamines, the example given here being Ionamine Red KA (BDC), C.I. 13040.

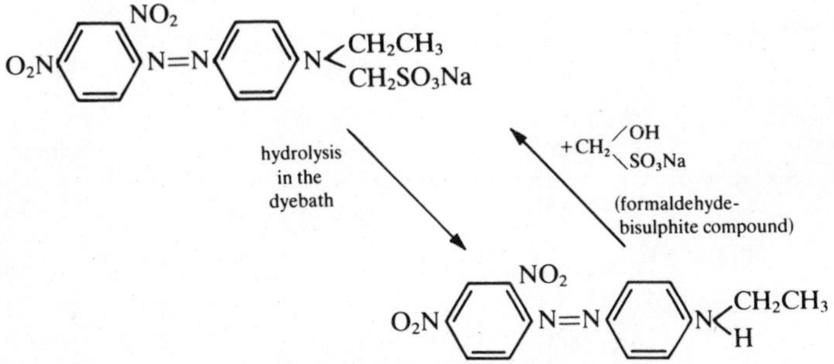

Fig. 14.1

In the dyebath the colorant underwent hydrolysis, the original insoluble dye being slowly precipitated in finely divided form. Contact between dye and hydrophobic fibre was thus greatly facilitated and finally a solid solution of dye in the cellulose acetate resulted. The dyes proved difficult to apply however since the rate of hydrolysis varied from one dye to another and unsatisfactory results were obtained when mixtures, e.g. to produce a green shade, were used. The range was soon replaced by the 'acetate' dyes which were fine aqueous dispersions (particle size range $1-4\,\mu$) which would dye acetate rayon in conventional dyebaths at temperatures up to 80 °C. Both the discovery and subsequent development of the disperse dyes, a name suggested in 1953 by C. M. Whittaker, were the work of several groups, prominent among whom were Holland Ellis and co-workers (British Celanese) and Baddiley and Shepherdson (BDC). Early methods of producing dispersions included precipitation techniques and various forms of milling with surface-active agents. Nowadays the use of small glass ballotini or certain kinds of sand in specially designed milling apparatus is the favoured method. The dyes are sold as stable aqueous paste dispersions or as dried granular products which break down readily in the dyebath to give satisfactory, stable dispersions.

It should be noted here that disperse dyes are required to have a minute but definite solubility in water. The classical experiments of Vickerstaff and Waters[21] showed that acetate was slowly dyed by an aqueous dispersion even though insulated by a cellophane membrane impermeable to the dispersed particles themselves but not to a solution of the dye. It was also shown by Bird (1953) that the presence of dispersing agents needed both for the preparation of the dispersion and for its subsequent stabilization by preventing or delaying aggregation or crystal growth in the dyebath, enhanced the 'natural solubility of the dyes'. Three examples of common acetate dyes are given in the table (after C. L. Bird, *J.S.D.C.* **70**, 68). Solubility is considered to have a bearing on the rate of dyeing and to govern levelling power to a marked extent. Manufacturing procedures for producing dye dispersions are largely secret but it is

Table 14.1 Acetate dyes

Commercial name	C.I. reference numbers	Chemical class	Solubility at 25 °C, mg/l. in	
			Water	1% Lissapol NS (purified)
Dispersol Fast Scarlet B	Disperse Red 1, 11110	Monoazo	0.3	138
Cibacet Yellow GBA	Disperse Yellow 3, 11855	Monoazo	1.2	276
Duranol Red 2B	Disperse Red 15, 60710	A/Q	0.2	46

known that modern dispersing agents include long chain alkyl sulphates, alkaryl sulphonates, fatty amine/ethylene oxide condensates, fatty alcohol/ethylene oxide condensates, formaldehyde/naphthalene sulphonic acid condensation products, and, from natural sources, lignins sulphonated to various degrees according to the solubility class of the disperse dye concerned.

As with other classes, various properties are expected of disperse dyes according to dyeing conditions, subsequent stages in textile processing and the conditions that will be encountered in use. Disperse dyes for acetate are required to have brightness and fastness of shade, good build-up and levelling properties. Some dyes, otherwise satisfactory, show a tendency to sublime under domestic ironing conditions. Others, having free amino, alkylamino or arylamino groups are sensitive, especially on acetate, to traces of oxides of nitrogen in the atmosphere leading to marked deterioration in shade (see page 26, fastness to burnt gas fumes). Research efforts were accordingly made to overcome these defects and to discover structural features which would confer improvements in properties. The volume of research work and the number of patents increased greatly from 1950 onwards with the introduction by ICI of polyester fibre (see page 19, i.e. Terylene © ICI. Once more difficulties in application arose. Dyes suitable for the relatively open-structured cellulose acetate were found unsuitable for the even more hydrophobic polyester fibres, the dyeing of which called for disperse dyes of generally more complex structure and for more vigorous dyeing conditions in their application.

The use of dyebath additives or 'carriers' and dyebath temperatures up to 100 °C, was one of the first effective methods discovered. Among others Tumescal D (ICI), an emulsified preparation of biphenyl, and Tumescal OP (ICI), a water-soluble form of o-phenylphenol, are used as carriers. These organic substances are absorbed by the polyester and, in loosening the tight binding between the long fibre molecules, facilitate the entry of dye molecules (Bird[38]). A second and very important method is high-temperature (H·T·) dyeing in which temperatures of 130 °C are achieved by dyeing in totally enclosed pressure vessels. More recently thermofixation processes, solvent dyeing and transfer-printing have been introduced as alternative means of dyeing hydrophobic fibres. These methods are dealt with later in this chapter.

According to Müller[23] the annual world production of polyester fibre increased during the period 1956–1966 from 22 500 to 585 900 metric tons. The corresponding figures for acetate (including cellulose triacetate) were 208 800 to 350 550 metric tons. It may be inferred from these figures, with reasonable accuracy, that quantities in excess of 20 000 metric tons disperse dyes per annum would be needed for the coloration of the 1966 totals. The contribution of the various chemical classes to commercial dye ranges is shown in the following table (adapted from Müller).

Chemical class	Contribution as % total
Monoazo	50
Anthraquinone	25
Disazo	10
Methine	6
Aroylenebenzimidazole	3
Quinoline (quinophthalone)	3
Nitro	1
Miscellaneous	2

Among the commercial names under which disperse dyes are sold are:

Amacel (AAP)	Foron (S)
Artisil (S)	Levafix (FBy)
Celanthrene (DUP)	Palanil (BASF)
Celliton (BASF)	Serisol (YCL)
Cibacet (CGY)	Serilene (YCL)
Dispersol (ICI)	Setacyl (CGY)
Duranol (ICI)	Setaron (CGY)
Esterophile (Fran)	Supracet (LBH)
Fenacet (G)	Terasil (CGY)

Monoazo dyes

This group, the largest in the disperse dye class, now provides an almost complete range of hues and properties. Secondary acetate (CA) and especially polyester (PES) including blends with natural fibres are the chief substrates, though sizeable quantities of polyamides (PA), poly(acrylonitrile) (PAC) and triacetate (CT) are also dyed with disperse dyes. The early acetate monoazo dyes, mostly reds with some yellows, were relatively simple structures of small molecular size and thus able easily to pass into the fibre structure. Examples are:

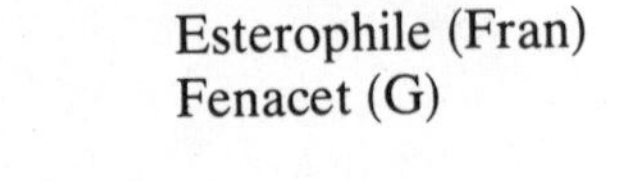

Fig. 14.2

Cibacet Yellow GBA (CGY) C.I. Disperse Yellow 3, 11855, which has a light fastness on CA of 5–6 and good all-round fastness properties including sublimation, and:

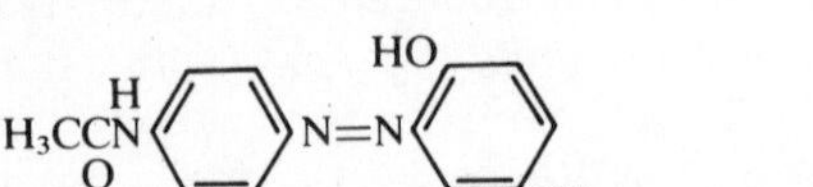

Fig. 14.3

X = H: Dispersol Fast Scarlet B, C.I. Disperse Red 1, 11110, light fastness on CA of 5.

X = Cl: Dispersol Fast Crimson B, C.I. Disperse Red 13, 11115, light fastness on CA of 6.

Both these dyes have poor sublimation fastness (1–2) but are satisfactory towards burnt-gas fumes (4–5). It is interesting to note that the presence of the chlorine atom in position 2 (diazo component) brings about a minor shade change from scarlet to crimson and improves the light fastness by a whole point. This is an early example illustrating the effect of structural variations on the properties of dyes, a highly important and interesting branch of colour chemistry. Though a certain body of knowledge exists in the technical literature and is open to all, dyemakers are understandably reluctant to publish the large volume of data and information concerning structure and properties accruing from years of costly research. Fortunately a few excellent monographs and reviews have appeared recently which give useful information on disperse dyes, e.g. Straley;[24] Müller;[23] Clark and Hildreth,[25] and Dawson.[26] Frequent allusion to these and other sources will be made in the course of this chapter.

An example of a development dye is afforded by:

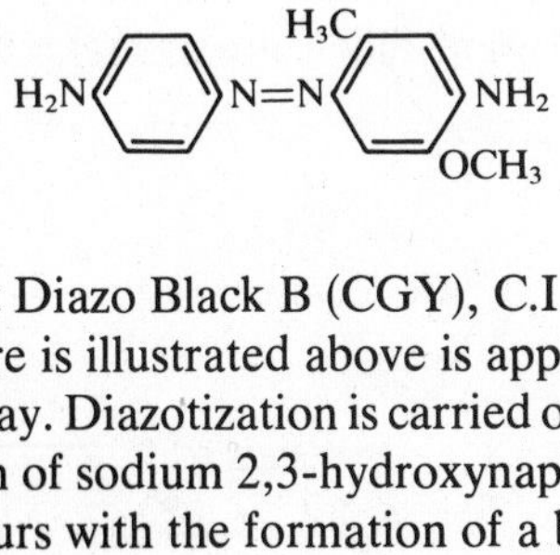

Fig. 14.4

Cibacet Diazo Black B (CGY), C.I. Disperse Black 2, 11255. The dye whose structure is illustrated above is applied to CA as a dispersion and dyed in the usual way. Diazotization is carried out on the fibre followed by the addition of a solution of sodium 2,3-hydroxynaphthoate to the dyebath, whereupon coupling occurs with the formation of a black of excellent fastness properties.

Structural variations and bathochromic effect

Many of the monoazo disperse dyes are derived from 4–aminophenylazobenzene variously substituted. In general the presence of chlorine, bromine and electron-withdrawing groups such as NO_2 and CN in the diazo component tends to cause a shift of λ_{max} towards the longer wavelengths (bathochromic effect) so that the hue of the dye is deepened, i.e. moves from the red to the blue end of the spectrum. This effect is enhanced and the colour intensified by variations in nuclear substituents and non-nuclear substituents attached to nitrogen. Where the effect on electron mobility is at a maximum full blue hues are achievable. For many purposes the bright blues afforded by the 1,4- and 1,4,5,8-substituted anthraquinones (see pp. 201–2) are quite satisfactory. The addition of satisfactory blues to the monoazo dyes range becomes desirable however for two main reasons. In contrast to aminoanthra-quinones the monoazo dyes are (a) less prone to change in shade on CA when exposed to burnt-gas fumes and (b) can be satisfactorily discharged under the conditions used by the textile printer (see Chapter 2, Textile printing). In Fig. 14.5 a selection of the examples given by Müller[23] shows the effect on hue of progressive substitution in the 2, 4 and 6 positions of the diazo component. A

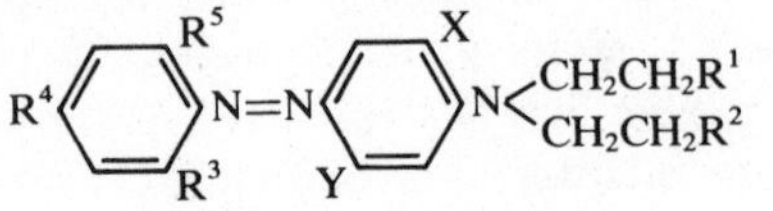

Groups R^1, R^2, X and Y
are the same in each case

$R^3 = $ H; H; H;   H;   H;   H;   H; NO_2; CN;
$R^4 = $ H; Cl; CN; NO_2; NO_2; NO_2; NO_2; NO_2; NO_2;
$R^5 = $ H; H; H;   H;   Cl; NO_2; CN;   Cl; NO_2;

Deepening of hue ⟶ Blue

Fig. 14.5

similar effect results from the use of various heterocyclic amines as diazo components. The examples, also selected from Müller, are again arranged in progressive order.

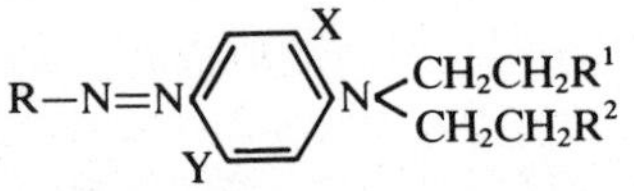

Groups R^1, R^2, X and Y
are the same in each case

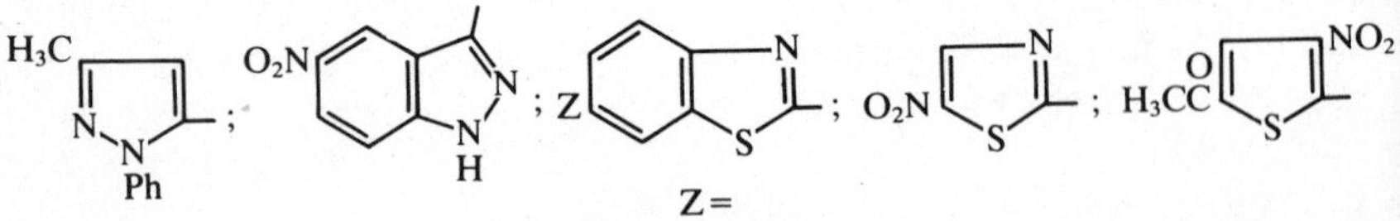

$Z = $
$(CH_3)_2NSO_2$; CH_3SO_2

Deepening of hue ⟶ Blue

Fig. 14.6

The following, fairly typical dyes have recently been disclosed in the patent literature:

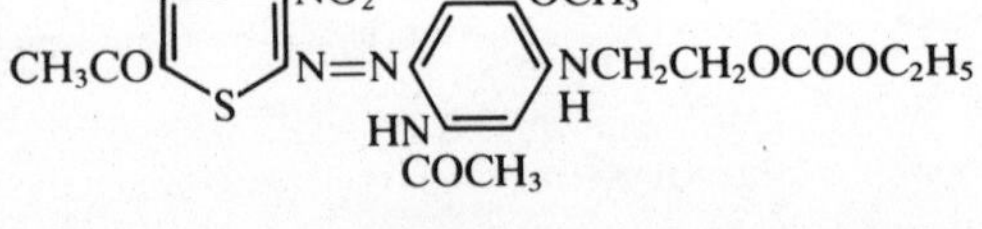

Fig. 14.7

B.P. 1 351 382 (ICI) claims that CA is dyed bluish-green of good fastness properties. Eastman Kodak, U.S.P. 3 816 391 also claim a green (Fig. 14.8) of very good fastness properties when dyed on PES:

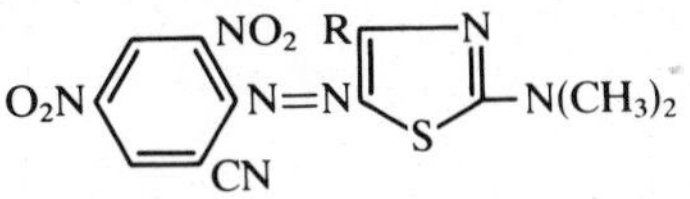

Fig. 14.8

It should be mentioned here that, for many years, there was no satisfactory single green in the disperse dye range, a mixture of yellow and blue dyes being used.

Two further examples of blue dyes, both described as having excellent fastness to light and sublimation on PES are:

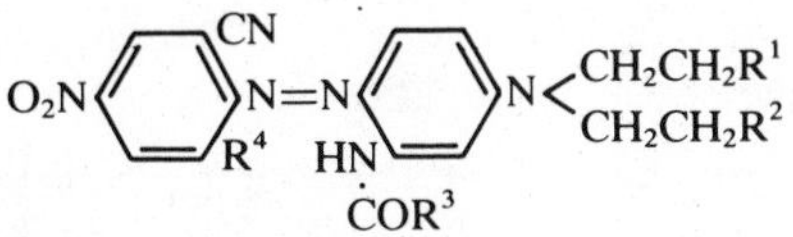

Fig. 14.9

B.P. 1 370 034 (NSK) wherein $R^1 = R^2 = OCH_3$; $R^3 = CH_3$; $R^4 = Br$ and B.P. 1 374 022 (ICI) wherein $R^1 = H$; $R^2 = OH$; $R^3 = CH_3$; $R^4 = NO_2$.

Structural variations and fastness properties

The acetate dyes are in general unsuitable for PES fibres by reason of rather poor build-up and lack of fastness to thermofixation and other finishing processes which involve high temperatures. In the thermofixation process the dispersion is padded onto the fabric at ordinary temperatures, dried at 60 °C and briefly subjected (e.g. 45 seconds) to high temperatures in the range 190–210 °C. (see also Transfer Printing, p. 209). Simpler molecules sublime appreciably at these temperatures and structural variations in more complex molecules have been studied to correct this drawback, as well as to achieve improved light fastness. The effects of different groups in substituted diethylamino dyestuffs is shown in Fig. 14.10 (adapted from Müller).

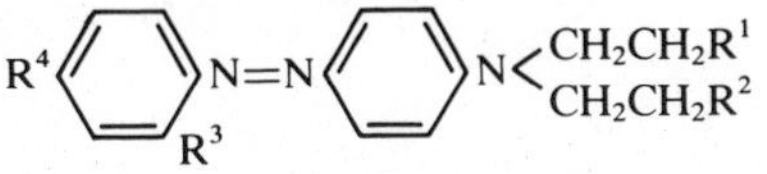

$R^3 = Cl$ $\quad R^4 = NO_2$

$R^1 =$ H;H;OH;OCOMe;CN $\quad$ Me = CH_3

$R^2 =$ OH;H;CN; $\quad\quad$ CN;CN

LF = $3;3\frac{1}{2};$ $\quad 4\frac{1}{2};$ $\quad\quad 7;7$ $\quad\quad$ LF = Light fastness

TF = $2\frac{1}{2};1\frac{1}{2};$ $\quad 4;$ $\quad\quad 4;4\frac{1}{2}$ $\quad\quad$ TF = Thermofixation fastness

(PES)

Fig. 14.10

The cyanoethyl group is strikingly effective here, as in other cases, in improving both light and thermofixation. A quite different case is that described in B.P. 1 349 003 (S) where, in the structure of Fig. 14.9, $R^1 = R^2 =$ H; $R^3 = (CH_2)_3OCH_3$; $R^4 = CN$. The product dyes PES blue with good fastness to light, sublimation and thermofixation. In other dyes also sublimation fastness is increased by an acetylamino group in position 3 of the coupling component.

Disazo dyes

The disazo dyes are not much used in the dyeing of acetate but are useful for the more hydrophobic fibres, especially triacetate (CT) and PES. In a recent review Dawson[26] gives examples of two monoazo dye molecules linked by, e.g. an alkylene group, with improvement in sublimation fastness by reason of the increase in molecular weight. However the conjugation is interrupted by such linkages and the range of hues obtainable is in consequence limited. Recent patents describe disazo dyes where the conjugation is unbroken and hence a full shade range is possible by appropriate substitution. The dyes have excellent fastness properties on PES and are especially suitable for application by the thermofixation process.

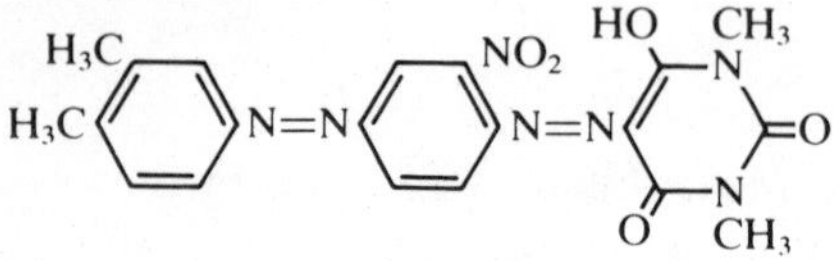

Fig. 14.11

B.P. 1 348 591 (CGY)—golden yellow on PES.

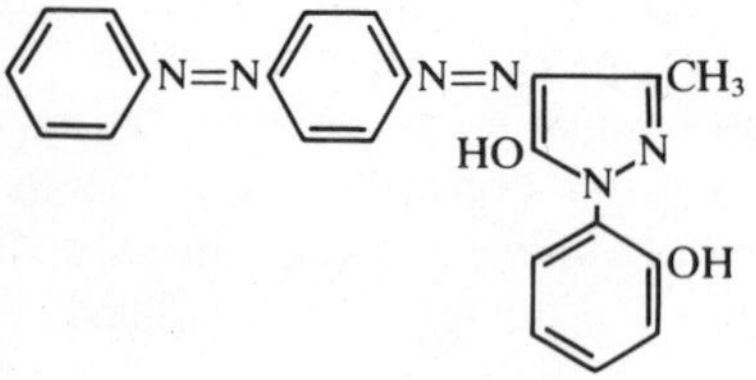

Fig. 14.12

B.P. 1 171 803 (FH)—orange on PES.

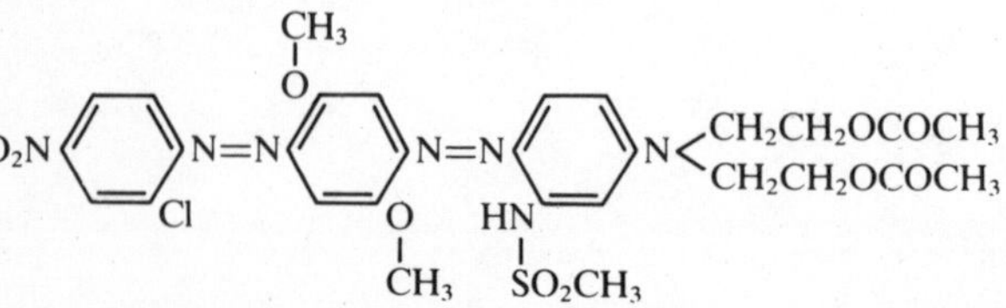

Fig. 14.13

B.P. 1 205 326 (DUP)—navy on PES.

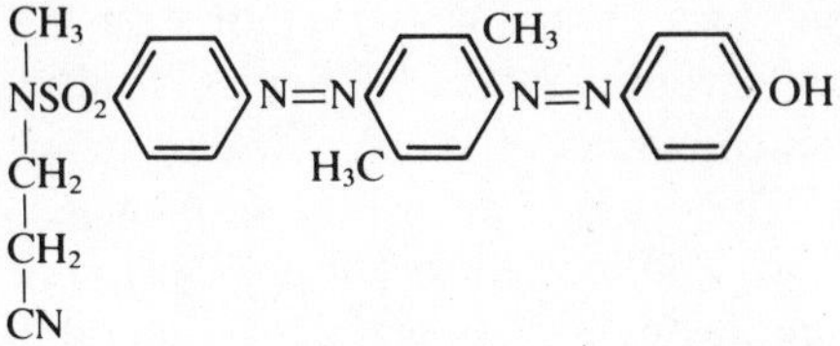

Fig. 14.14

B.P. 1 163 918 (S)—yellowish-brown on PES.

The presence in the molecule of substituted sulphonamido groups, especially of those containing 2-cyanoethyl groups, has a beneficial effect both on sublimation and thermofixation fastness.

Anthraquinone disperse dyes

This group makes an important contribution to the range of violets and blues; anthraquinone derivatives were among the earliest acetate dyes. C.I. Disperse Red 15, 60710, Duranol Red 2B (ICI) has the structure:

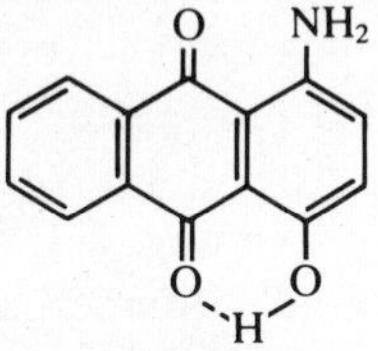

Fig. 14.15

and is interesting in having been known as a chemical compound almost fifty years before the discovery, by Baddiley and Shepherdson in 1923, that it could be used as a disperse dye. It has a light fastness on CA of 6, moderate burnt-gas fume fastness (3–4) and excellent sublimation fastness (5). The 1,4-diaminoanthraquinones provide a red (Fig. 14.16; X = OMe) Celliton Fast Pink FF 3B (BASF), C.I. Disperse Red 11, 62015. C.I. Disperse Violet 1,

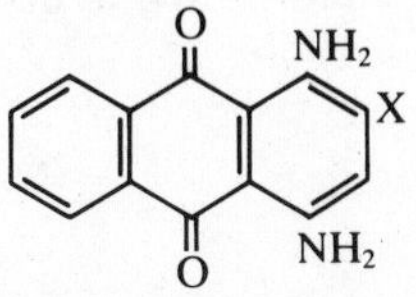

Fig. 14.16

61100, (Fig. 14.16; X = H) has a light fastness of 6 on acetate, but poor fastness to gas fume fading (2). The presence of strongly electron-withdrawing groups in the molecule (e.g. Fig. 14.16; X = CF_3) reduces the basicity of amino groups in the 1 and 4 positions and inhibits nitrosation or diazotization by atmospheric oxides of nitrogen thus increasing the fastness. The burnt-gas fumes fastness of

202 DISPERSE DYES

dyeings on CA can be increased by treatment of the fabric during or after dyeing with substances which preferentially take up oxides of nitrogen, e.g. *N,N'*-diphenyl-1,6-hexamethylenediamine.

C.I. Disperse Blue 3, 61505, Cibacet Brilliant Blue BG New (CGY) is an important acetate dye used as such and in mixtures to produce navy blues. It has good build-up, moderate light fastness (5–6) and good general properties apart from burnt-gas fume fastness (1–2). It is obtained by condensing leuco-quinizarine with a mixture of methylamine and 2-hydroxyethylamine in butanol followed by oxidation (c.f. the similar nucleophilic substitution described on p. 126, Chapter 7). The main product has the structure:

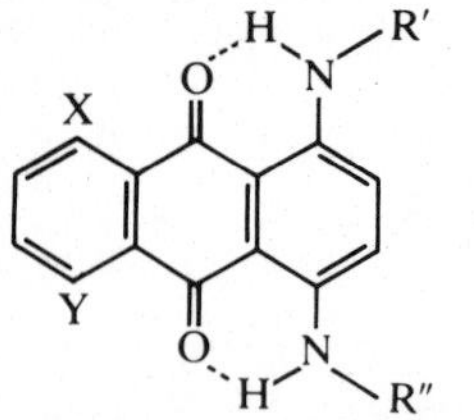

Fig. 14.17

$X = Y = H$; $R' = CH_3$; $R'' = CH_2CH_2OH$, though the 1,4-*bis*-(methylamino)- and 1,4-*bis*-(2-hydroxyethyl)anthraquinone compounds are also present. A related dye is C.I. Disperse Blue 7, 62500, Setacyl Turquoise Blue G (Gy)— Fig. 14.17; $X = Y = OH$; $R' = R'' = CH_2CH_2OH$. The 1,4,5,8-tetramino derivative of anthraquinone is an acetate dye of long standing, C.I. Disperse Blue 1, 60710, and the product of part methylation with methanol and sulphuric acid, C.I. Disperse Blue 31, Celliton Blue Extra (IG), is also used for dyeing CA.

Structural modifications and properties

As with the monoazo series the advent of PES fibres and the technical advances in application and after-treatment called for more elaborate structures than those used in dyeing CA. The patent literature provides a number of instances where groups in one or both β positions confer improved fastness and suitability for PES dyeing. The following are all blue dyes:

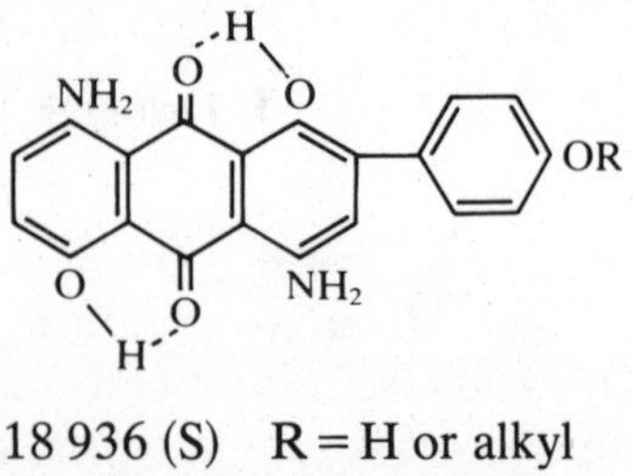

Fig. 14.18

F.P. 1 218 936 (S)   R = H or alkyl
F.P. 1 373 758 (ICI)   R = COCH₃

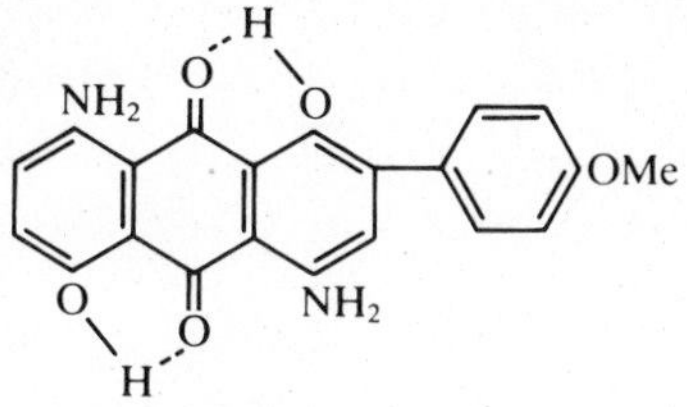

Fig. 14.19

F.P. 1 345 377 (FBy)

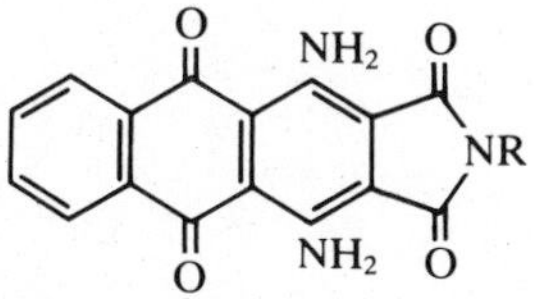

Fig. 14.20

B.P. 1 288 157 (NSK) $R = CH(CH_3)_2$
U.S.P. 3 835 540 (DUP) $R = CH_2CH_2CH_2N(Et)Ph$
B.P. 1 296 774 (BASF) $R = CH_2CH_2OH$ or CH_2CH_2CN

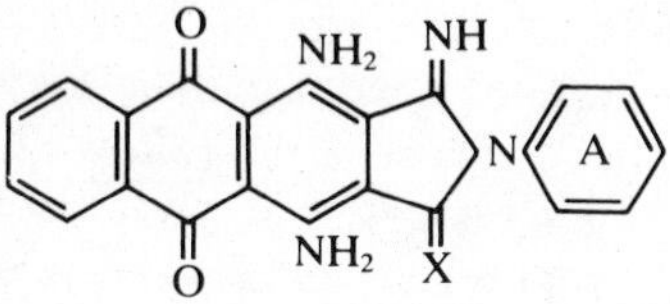

Fig. 14.21

in which ring A may carry one or more alkyl or hydroxyalkyl groups.

U.S.P. 3 801 595 (BASF) $X = O$
B.P. 1 379 450 (BASF) $X = NH$

The effect on thermofixation fastness of various groups in the 2-position on the simple dye molecule 1-amino-4-hydroxyanthraquinone has been discussed by Müller.[23] A selection of these groups arranged in increasing order of thermofixation fastness (PES) is given in Fig. 14.22.

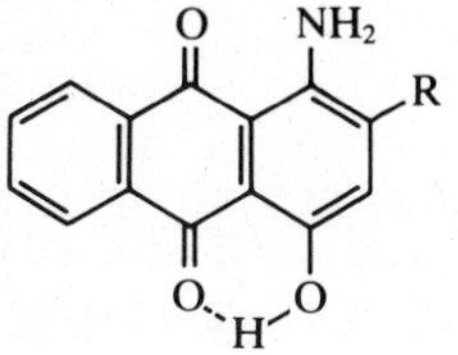

$R =$

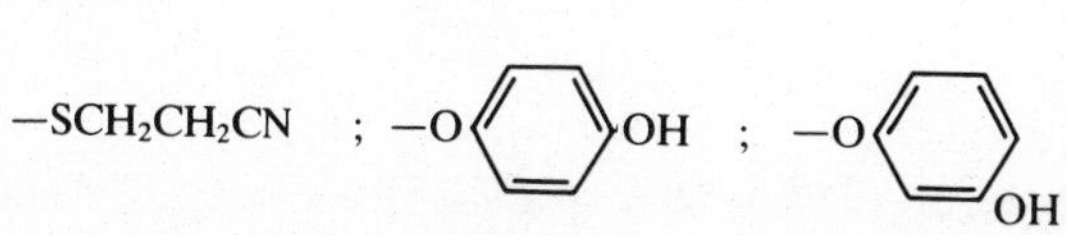

$-SCH_2CH_2CN$; $-O$⟨⟩OH ; $-O$⟨⟩OH

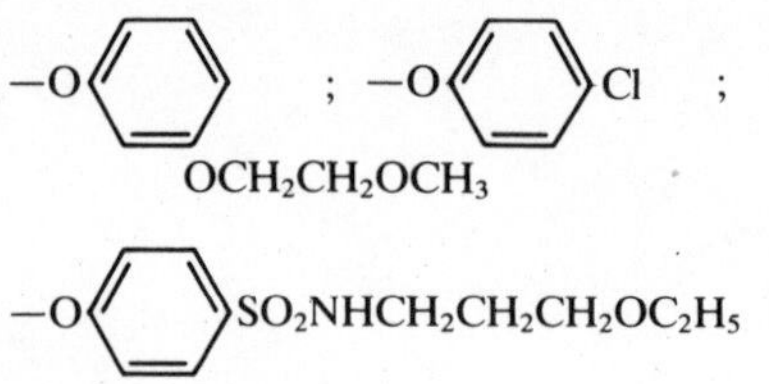

OCH$_2$CH$_2$OCH$_3$

Fig. 14.22

Miscellaneous disperse dyes

Nitro dyes

C.I. Disperse Yellow 14, 10340, discovered by Holland Ellis in 1923 is obtained by nucleophilic attack by 4-aminophenol at the C—Cl link in 1-chloro-2,4-dinitrobenzene to give:

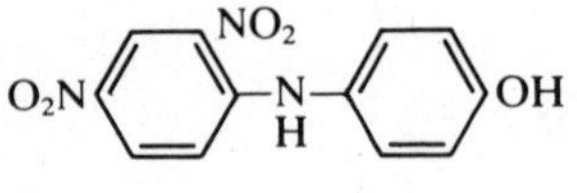

Fig. 14.23

It is used chiefly on CA for pale to medium shades where high fastness to light is not important. C.I. Disperse Yellow 9, 10375, Serisol Fast Yellow PL (YCL), (Fig. 14.24) in contrast has excellent light fastness but poor sublimation fastness on CA. Dawson has pointed out[26] that the dye obtained by diazotizing

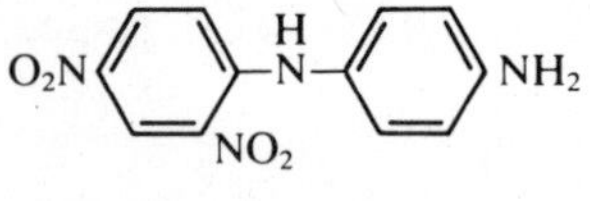

Fig. 14.24

(14.24) and coupling with 2-hydroxybiphenyl has greatly improved sublimation fastness on CA. The structure is:

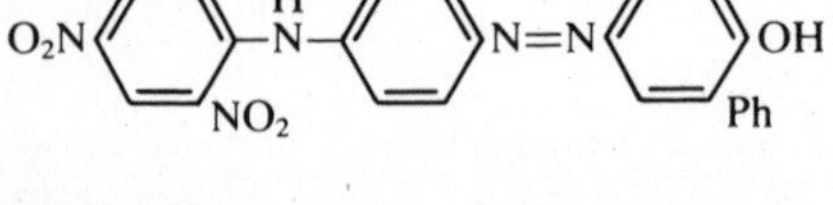

Fig. 14.25

the brand name being Serilene Golden Yellow RFS (YCL).

There are a small number of modern nitrodiphenylamine dyes suitable for the dyeing of PES. A substituted sulphonamido group is effective in increasing fastness to sublimation. Light fastness is higher with the nitro group in the 2-position since hydrogen bonding is possible with stabilization of the charge-transfer o-quinoid form, compared with the 4-position in which hydrogen bonding is not possible. This is the case for a number of dyes represented by:

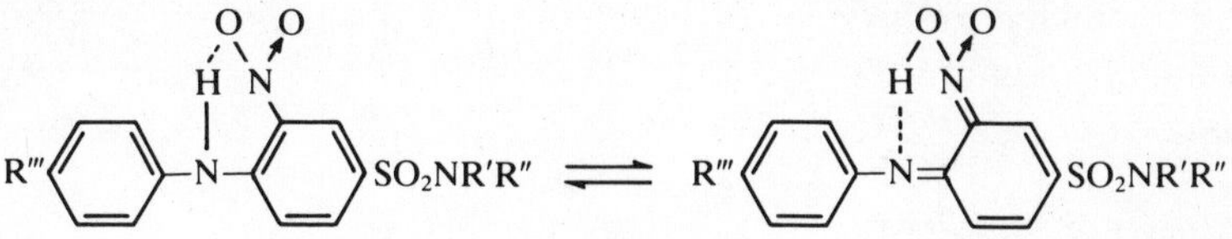

Fig. 14.26

$R' = R'' =$ alkyl or substituted alkyl, but the light fastness is diminished where $R''' = NO_2$ also. Allied Chemical Corporation in B.P. 998 918 claim that in (14.26) where $R' = R'' = CH_2CH_2CH$, and $R''' = H$, yellow dyeings on PES of excellent fastness are obtained.

Methine (or Styryl) dyes

A very good example in this class is C.I. Disperse Yellow 31, 48000, Celliton Fast Yellow 7G, which has exceptionally good light fastness (7) and fastness to burnt-gas fumes (5), in both cases on CA. It is synthesized by condensing 4-(N-n-butyl-N-chloroethylamino)-benzaldehyde, obtained via Wilsmeier reaction (p. 63), with ethylcyanoacetate and has the structure:

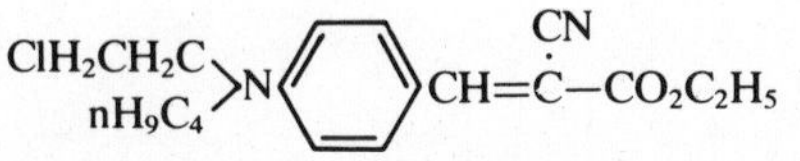

Fig. 14.27

A similar example from the patent literature is:

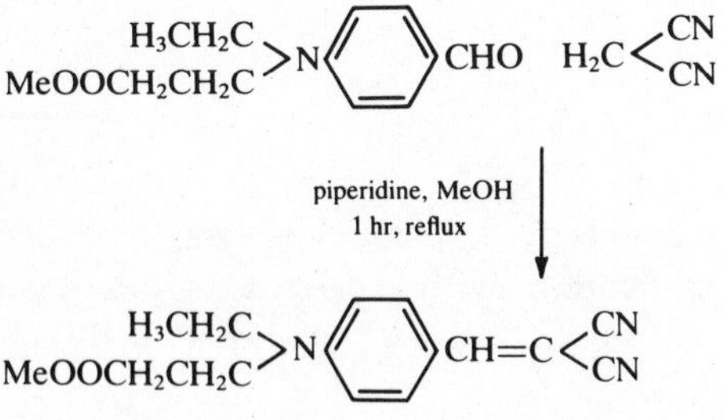

Fig. 14.28

B.P. 1 226 370 (BASF); the product of the reaction dyes hydrophobic fibres yellow of very good fastness to light, washing and sublimation and does not stain wool in blends.

Coumarin dyes

An interesting dye is described in B.P. 1 121 947 (Gy) useful for dyeing PES fibres in fluorescent yellow shades, having very good fastness properties. It is synthesized from 4-(N,N-diethylamino)-2-hydroxybenzaldehyde and 2-

cyanomethylbenzothiazole by reaction in a glacial acetic acid/dimethyl-formamide mixture.

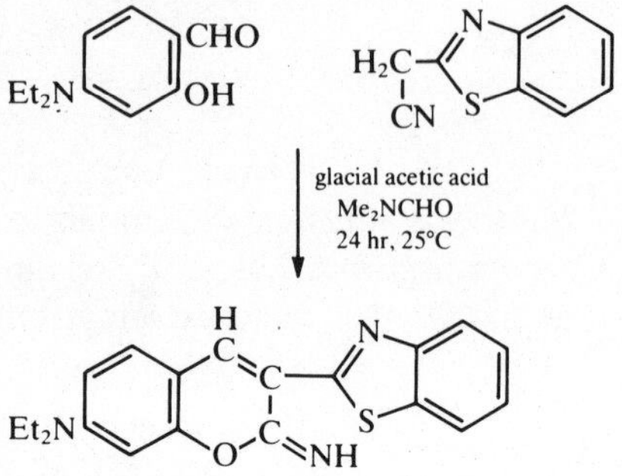

Fig. 14.29

Naphthostyril dyes

A relatively simple dye giving yellow/orange shades on hydrophobic fibres, of good fastness to light and sublimation is the subject of B.P. 1 234 688 (NSK):

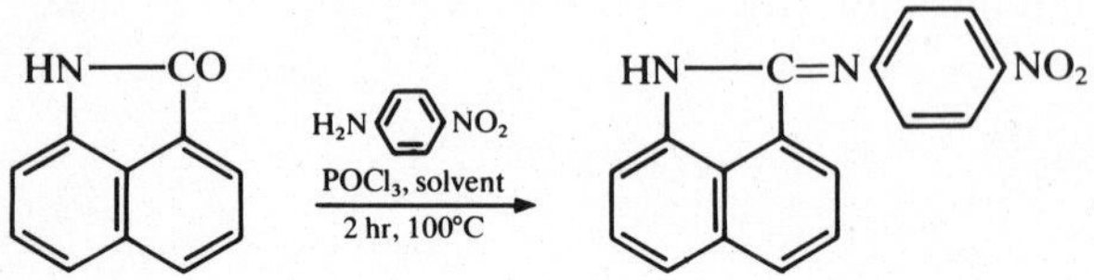

Fig. 14.20

The starting point in the synthesis is naphthostyril, already discussed under anthanthrones, Chapter 8.

Quinophthalone dyes

This group of mostly yellow dyes is of some importance in the dyeing of PES materials especially by thermofixation methods. An example illustrative of these dyeing methods is afforded by U.S.P. 3 399 028 (TRC); B.P. 1 071 187 (S):

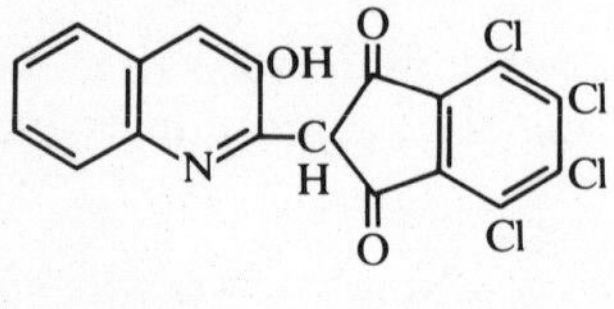

Fig. 14.31

which is padded on to PES fabric as an aqueous dispersion, dried at 60 °C and fixed by baking at 200 °C for a period of 60 seconds. Another dye of good fastness properties on PES and suitable for thermofixation procedures is described in B.P. 1 350 201 (YCL):

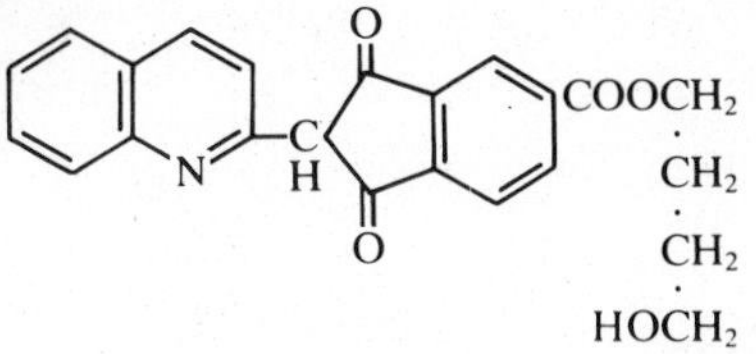

Fig. 14.32

The introduction of a phenylsulphone group by nucleophilic attack of sodium phenylsulphinate on 4-bromo-3-hydroxyquinophthalone is covered in B.P. 1 251 547 (FH) the dye so produced having very good fastness properties including thermofixation and solvent fastness.

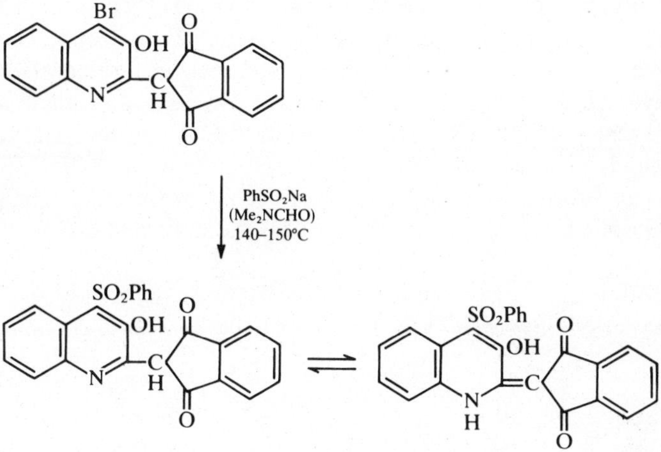

Fig. 14.33

Formazan dyes

Neutral-dyeing wool dyes of the formazan class have already been mentioned in Chapter 6. The patent literature provides cases where the formazan system has been exploited in the disperse dye field. U.S.P. 3 655 637 (TRC) claims blue dyes typified by

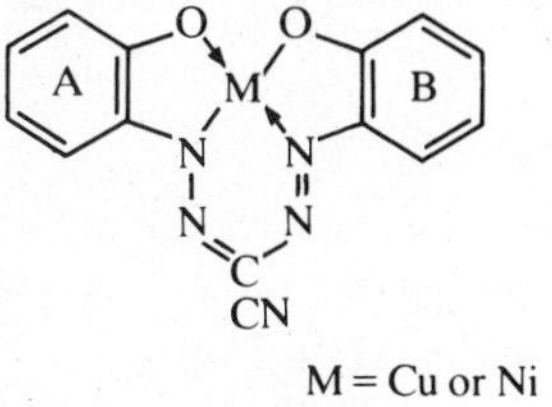

M = Cu or Ni

Fig. 14.34

wherein rings A and B may also carry one or more substituent groups, e.g. NHCOCH₃, SO₂Alk, SO₂NR'R" (R' and R" may be the same or different alkyl groups). Such dyes are claimed to be particularly suitable for nylon having very good fastness to light and excellent levelling properties. They are also applicable to PES by pad/thermofix methods.

Dyeing by non-aqueous methods

Solvent dyeing

In recent years attention has been directed to the possibility of using an easily recoverable solvent, having low toxicity, as an alternative to water in the dyeing of synthetic hydrophobic fibres and possibly other kinds of textiles. So far there have been no disclosures of structures of dyes used for this purpose except in a small number of patent examples. The dyes used have the structural features of disperse dyes and are soluble in solvents such as perchloroethylene (PEC; 1,1,2,2-tetrachloroethylene). Such dyes need only be ground and milled to ordinary standards, the costly time- and energy-consuming milling operations essential to the production of fine dispersions being unnecessary. The use of 1-lauroylamino-4-phenylaminoanthraquinone is the subject of U.S.P. 3 741 720 (FBy):

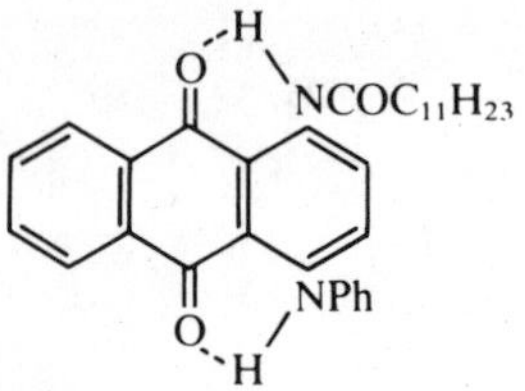

Fig. 14.35

PES fabric is impregnated with a 1% solution of the dye in PCE, dried at 80 °C (60 seconds), 'fixed' at 190–220 °C (45 seconds) and finally rinsed with cold solvent. Dyeings are reddish-blue of good general properties, especially light fastness, though this property is impaired by adsorbed solvent. This is a general phenomenon and care must be taken to remove solvent completely. An example of an monoazo dye, also a blue applicable to PES by a similar method is afforded by B.P. 1 282 246 (FBy).

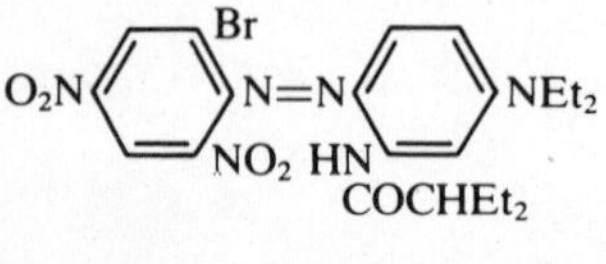

Fig. 14.36

It is not yet clear to what extent solvent dyeing methods will be adopted in preference to aqueous dyeing procedures. Effluent problems are however reduced and there are significant savings in water usage. Other advantages include rapid wetting and increased speed of drying compared with aqueous methods.

Heat transfer printing

The principle of this revolutionary method of coloration of textiles may be briefly stated as the transfer by sublimation from pre-printed paper in contact with a substrate which may be a continuous roll of fabric or an undyed made-up garment. No solvent is involved, the dyestuff entering the fibre as vapour. Typical conditions are: temperature, 200–210 °C, duration 30–40 seconds. Suitable substrates include PES (main), PAC, PA, CA, CT and blends of these fibres. There is a limit to the depth of shade achievable on PAC and fastness on PA may not be adequate for some purposes. The transfer paper is printed in the conventional way with a non-aqueous printing ink in which sublimable dyes are used in place of normal pigments. There are many advantages, both economic and technical, in heat transfer printing. Savings in time and expense accrue from the elimination of all the complicated stages inherent in traditional textile printing and there are no effluent difficulties since the only stage in the process is that of transfer of dyes by sublimation. Here again expensive milling of the dyes to a highly-dispersed state is unnecessary. There is very little information concerning the constitutions of the dyes used in this method but there is a specific reference to a dye usable in transfer printing in B.P. 1 334 114 (CGY):

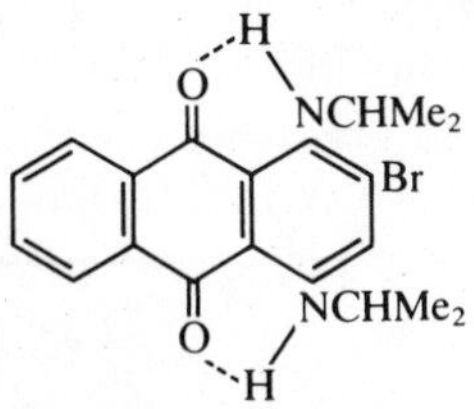

Fig. 14.37

which gives blue shades on PES and PA fibres. The principle of heat transfer printing has been applied, in the Fastran© process, to wool and other substrates. The process is not one of sublimation, reactive dyes being employed. Fixation time is longer (20 minutes) and an aqueous environment is necessary. Temperatures of up to 100 °C are employed and heating methods include the use of microwave (radio frequency) energy at 27.2 megahertz. Details of the dyes employed have not been disclosed.

15
Pigments

Introductory

Insoluble colouring matters, mostly of mineral origin, have been used from earliest times for the coloration of metal, wood, stone, plaster and other surfaces as paints in association with oil or water. Such insoluble colorants or pigments, e.g. certain oxides of iron, chromium, lead and other inorganic materials, presented a limited range of hues generally of very good fastness to light but of variable behaviour towards other agencies, e.g. the sulphur compounds present in urban and industrial atmospheres which blacken painted surfaces in which lead compounds are present.

As the synthetic dye industry grew, a range of organic pigments of great brilliance, but not invariably of outstanding durability, emerged. The introduction in 1935 of the phthalocyanine pigments, embodying a completely new chromophoric system, set such high standards of all-round fastness that extensive research has been directed towards the discovery of comparable pigments of other hues to complete the chromatic range. In this some success has already been achieved and a fairly full range of high-grade pigments is available.

Uses of synthetic organic pigments

Pigments find wide application in coating compositions, a term covering application in aqueous and non-aqueous paints, printing inks, leather finishing, paper coating and similar processes. The pigment may be used alone or incorporated with a white pigment such as zinc oxide, titanium dioxide or white lead as a means of controlling the opacity and the depth of shade required.

Most printing inks contain pigments and are used in various techniques for the printing of metal-foil, tin-plate, paper, cardboard wrapping materials and so on. Pigments are used in certain of the pastes used in textile printing and are of great importance in the modern technique of pigment printing, using a resin binder, mentioned in Chapter 2.

Pigments are used in paper coloration by coating methods, and also by mixing with the cellulose pulp in the 'beater' during papermaking. Pigments are also used for colouring cosmetics, soaps, wax compositions and for the manufacture of chalks, crayons, artists' colours and so on.

The mass coloration of rubber and of plastics of many kinds is done by the incorporation of pigments. Another application of importance is in the spin-dyeing of viscose, cellulose acetate and synthetic fibres produced by extrusion through spinnerets or minute dies, the pigment being mixed with the 'dope' (i.e. polymer in solvent) or molten polymer, prior to extrusion.

In all applications, the physical form, shape and size of the pigment particles are of the highest importance. Great care is needed in manufacture to ensure consistency of operation as comparatively minor variations in procedure can cause alterations in crystalline structure or may result in a quite different modification from that desired, with deleterious effects on shade, covering power and other properties. It is necessary also to clarify each reagent solution by filtration and in some cases to remove soluble, coloured impurities by absorbing on active charcoal followed by filtration, to ensure that a bright pigment of maximum tinctorial strength is obtained. The entry of extraneous matter, especially pieces of metal, must be avoided on safety and other grounds (see Chapter 16).

Fastness

As with dyes, the resistance of a pigment to the various agencies which it must withstand during processes of manufacture and in use is of great importance. Ratings are analogous to those current in textile dyeing and printing and are similarly designed to help the user decide on the suitability of a pigment for a given purpose.

The more important criteria by which pigments are evaluated are fastness to light, heat, solvents, water, alkalis, acids and other chemical agencies.

Light

Although there are no internationally accepted standard conditions for carrying out tests, nor fully accepted numerical standards, in practice the leading firms employ the blue wool scale described in Chapter 2. After exposure to daylight, or to artificial light in the 'Fadeometer', alteration in visual effect of a test strip is assessed against the blue standards by the grey scale method. As with dyes, the highest light fastness is rated 8, the scale descending to 1 (poor). Assessments of light fastness are commonly made not only in full depths but also in pale depths, i.e. after dilution or reduction with a white pigment such as titanium oxide.

Heat

It is most important, in modern applications, that a pigment be stable to relatively high temperatures. This applies especially in surface coatings 'cured' or polymerized by heat and in thermoplastic coloration, i.e. the mixing of pigments and molten polymer, a process which may require temperatures up to 300 °C. With inferior pigments chemical decomposition may result from such heat treatment, or physical change from one modification to another may occur causing deterioration in hue and in other properties.

Solvents

The solvents most frequently employed in lacquers, printing inks, automobile finishes and many other pigment applications are ethanol, 'cellosolve' (ethyleneglycol monoalkyl ether), aliphatic and aromatic hydrocarbons, ketones, esters and the mixed nitrocellulose solvents (mixtures of acetone, butyl acetate, cellosolve and toluene). 'Insoluble' is the highest grade and is applied where no 'bleeding', i.e. coloration of the solvent, occurs. Solvent bleeding is a serious defect in a pigment and can give rise to unpleasant effects, e.g. when a second colour is over-sprayed on to the first. Solubility in vehicle or solvent may bring about crystallization of the pigment causing a change in the colour properties of the paint.

Linseed oil and oleic acid

The degree of bleeding in these widely used media or 'vehicles' for pigments is important. The highest grading, i.e. 'insoluble', is reserved for cases where no bleeding occurs; 'very good' indicates slight bleeding.

Flocculation

Certain pigments, among them copper phthalocyanine, show the undesirable property, in association with titanium dioxide in paint mixtures, whereby marked differences in strength can occur with variations in the applied shearing forces, i.e. in brushing or spraying. The effect is reversible and has been ascribed to 'flocculation' which occurs during storage, the pigment aggregates being broken down according to the applied shear. Evidence has however been adduced by Carr[30] that the effect is concerned with the optical characteristics of the pigment and disappears when the pigment is milled below a certain particle size. In the case of copper phthalocyanine the critical particle diameter is $0\cdot18\,\mu$.

Water

Complete insolubility in water is rated as excellent (5), the remainder of the descending scale being respectively very good, good, fair and poor. Where pigments have a slight degree of solubility in water or other liquid media they are said to show 'bleeding'. 'Absence of bleeding' is synonymous with insolubility in this connection.

Alkalis

The usual test reagent is 5% sodium carbonate solution at room temperature (sodium hydroxide solution is used for special cases). The highest grade on the usual scale of 5 is 'unaffected' and indicates that there is neither bleeding nor alteration in colour. Good fastness to alkalis is an essential property of pigments for use in the manufacture of distempers or the coloration of plaster surfaces.

Acids

The usual test reagent is 5% hydrochloric acid at room temperature; otherwise, as for 'alkalis'.

Types of pigments

Lakes of cationic dyes

Dyes of the type D^+X^-, where D is a chromophoric system embodying one or more basic groups and X is a chlorine atom or similar salt-forming group, may form insoluble products on double decomposition with tannic acid or with certain inorganic polyacids. Certain of these insoluble products or lakes are

Table 15.1   PTMA Lakes of cationic dyes

Colour Index		Parent cationic dye	
Name	Number	Name	Class
Pigment Yellow 18	49005	Basic Yellow T	Thiazole
Pigment Green 4	42000	Malachite Green	Triarylmethane
Pigment Blue 9	42025	—	Triarylmethane
Pigment Violet 4	42510	Magenta	Triarylmethane
Pigment Violet 3	42535	Methyl Violet	Triarylmethane
Pigment Blue 2	44045	Victoria Blue B	Triarlymethane
Pigment Red 82	45150	Rhodamine B	Xanthene

useful as pigments on account of their high tinctorial value and other properties. The best examples are the 'Fanal' or permanent pigments produced by BASF by precipitating a cationic dye with phosphotungstomolybdic acid (PTMA). These lakes, though generally superior in fastness properties to the parent dyes, do not attain the all-round high standards of the modern pigments typified by phthalocyanine (p. 218).

Lakes of anionic dyes

These insoluble colorants are precipitated from solutions of anionic dyes, of the type D^-X^+ where X is usually a sodium atom, by double decomposition with the soluble salts of heavy metals such as calcium or barium:

$$2Dye\text{-}SO_3Na + BaCl_2 \rightarrow [Dye\text{-}SO_3^-]_2Ba^{++} \downarrow + 2NaCl$$

Table 15.2 Lakes of anionic dyes

Colour Index		Parent anionic dye		Lake-forming metal
Name	Number	Description	Class	
Pigment Red 48 (Permanent Red 2B)	15865	1-Amino-5-chloro-4-methylbenzene-2-sulphonic acid → 3-hydroxy-2-naphthoic acid	Monoazo	Calcium, Barium or Manganese
Pigment Red 57 (Permanent Red 4B)	15850	1-Amino-4-methylbenzene-2-sulphonic acid → 3-hydroxy-2-naphthoic acid	Monoazo	Calcium
Pigment Red 53 (Lake Red C)	15585	1-Amino-4-chloro-5-methylbenzene-2-sulphonic acid → 2-naphthol	Monoazo	Barium
Pigment Red 49 (Lithol Red R)	15630	2-Aminonaphthalene-1-sulphonic acid → 2-naphthol	Monoazo	Calcium and Barium
Pigment Blue 24	42090	Patent Blue	Triarylmethane	Barium
Pigment Red 90	45380	Eosin	Xanthene	Lead

Such metallic salts or lakes have the useful property of being relatively resistant to solvents but are of poor general fastness; they are, for instance, very sensitive to acids and alkalis.

Metal complexes

This small group has excellent light fastness but is inferior in other fastness properties. These pigments are coordination or chelate compounds and require for their formation dye molecules which contain oxygen or nitrogen atoms able to donate electrons to the metal atom. A good example is C.I. Pigment Green 8, 10006 (Pigment Green B), which is the tervalent iron complex of 1-nitroso-2-naphthol (see Chapter 2, p. 13). Three moles of the oxime form a complex with Fe(III):

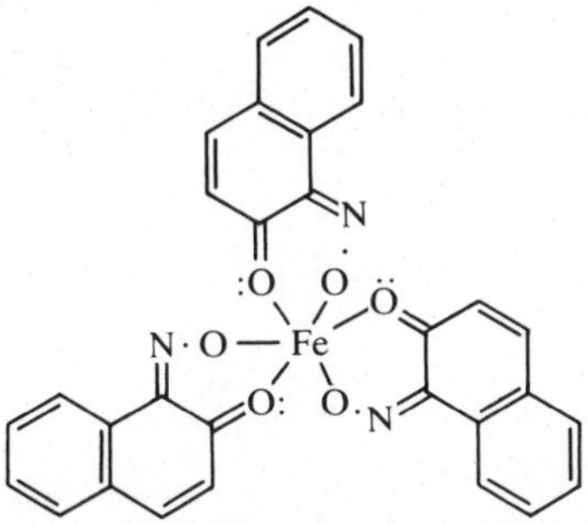

Fig. 15.1

C.I. Pigment Brown 2, 12071, is the copper complex derived from the monoazo dye *p*-nitroaniline→2-naphthol and has the structure:

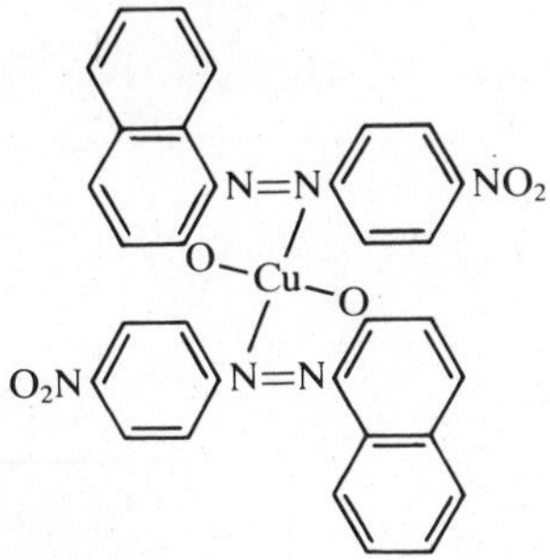

Fig. 15.2

C.I. Pigment Red 83, 58000. Metal complexes of alizarin (1,2-dihydroxyanthraquinone) have been used as pigments for many years. The aluminium/calcium lake is bluish-red, chromium dull bluish-red and iron dull purple, and they are all used either as such or formed on the fibre as in dyed-style printing (p. 32).

Neutral, metal-free compounds

This is the largest and most widely used group of pigments and draws largely on monoazo and disazo dyes, with a few representatives from azine, indigo and anthraquinone classes. The neutral metal-free pigments can be regarded as classical dye molecules devoid of solubilizing groups such as —SO₃H, —COOH. They provide a fairly full range of hues, being especially well represented among yellows, reds and oranges. They have, in general, good resistance to alkalis and acids but inferior fastness to solvents and plasticizers. The following is a selection of mono and disazo pigments in common use.

Monoazo pigments

C.I. Pigment Yellow 1, 11680, Hansa Yellow G, 4-amino-3-nitrotoluene → acetoacetanilide:

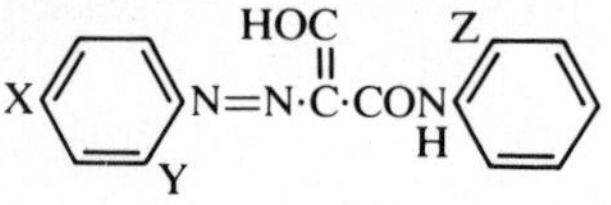

$X = CH_3$; $Y = NO_2$; $Z = H$;   **Fig. 15.3**

for the manufacture of this pigment see Chapter 16.

Another important 'Arylamide' Yellow is C.I. Pigment Yellow 3, 11710, Hansa Yellow 10G, 4-chloro-2-nitroaniline → 2-chloro-acetoacetanilide (Fig. 15.3; $X = Cl$, $Y = NO_2$, $Z = Cl$). Although greener and somewhat weaker than Hansa Yellow G, the 10G brand is of superior light fastness.

C.I. Pigment Yellow 7, 12780, 2-nitroaniline → 2,4-dihydroxyquinoline, is a bright, reddish-yellow:

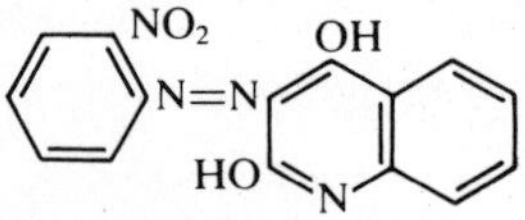

C.I. Pigment Yellow 7   **Fig. 15.4**

C.I. Pigment Orange 6, 12730, 4-amino-3-nitrotoluene → 3-methyl-1-phenyl-5-pyrazolone, is an example of the large class of pyrazolone pigments:

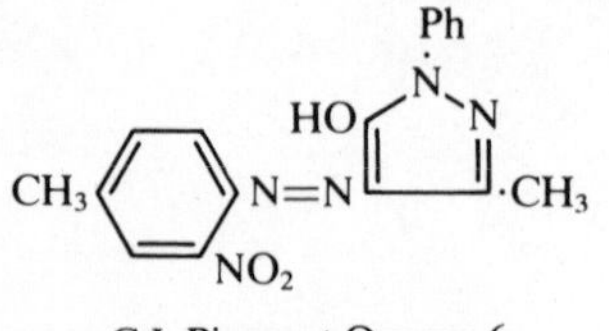

C.I. Pigment Orange 6   **Fig. 15.5**

C.I. Pigment Orange 5, 12075, 2,4-dinitroaniline → 2-naphthol, is a bright reddish-orange which, like others derived from 2-naphthol, is widely used for its brightness and strength; its other fastness properties, particularly solvent and vehicle 'bleed', are inferior:

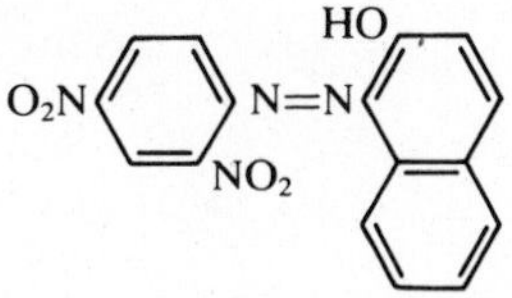

C.I. Pigment Orange 5

Fig. 15.6

The pigments derived from components of the Naphthol AS type show marked improvement in solvent and vehicle fastness as in C.I. Pigment Red 2, 12310, Permanent Red FRR (Hoechst), 2,5-dichloroaniline → 3-hydroxy-2-naphthanilide:

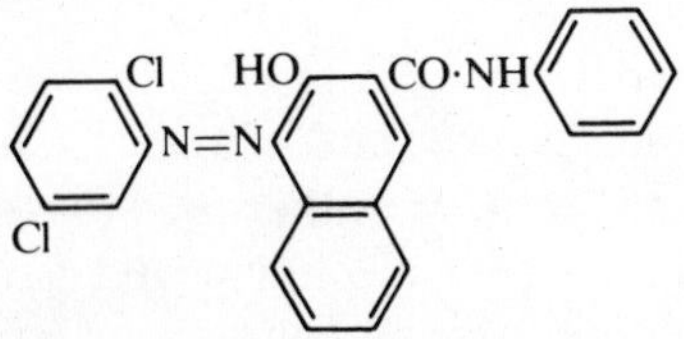

C.I. Pigment Red 2

Fig. 15.7

Disazo pigments

The important disazo pigments are widely used in the manufacture of printing inks and in the mass coloration of rubber. Typical examples are the benzidine yellows, noted for brilliance and high tinctorial strength.

C.I. Pigment Yellow 12, 21090, 3,3′dichlorobenzidine ⇉ acetoacetanilide (2 moles):

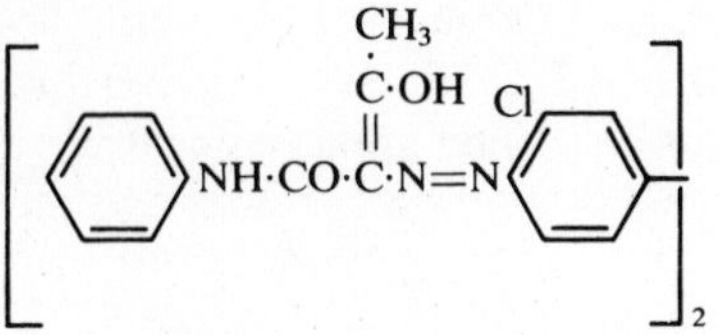

C.I. Pigment Yellow 12

Fig. 15.8

C.I. Pigment Orange 13, 21100, Permanent Orange G, uses a pyrazolone as coupling component:

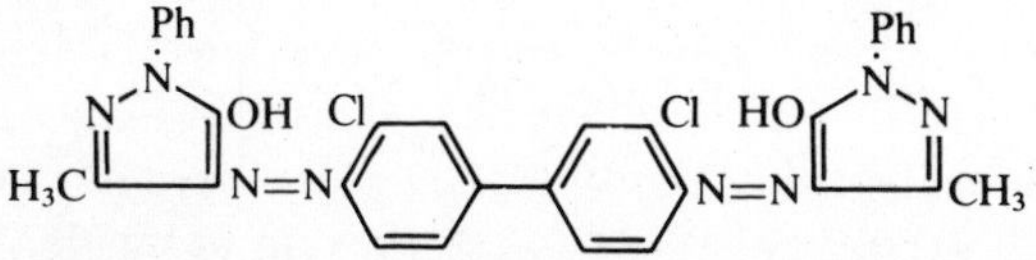

C.I. Pigment Orange 13

Fig. 15.9

C.I. Pigment Blue 26, 21185, Dianisidine Blue, is obtained from tetrazodianisidine and 3-hydroxynaphtho-*o*-anisidide:

C.I. Pigment Blue 36   **Fig. 15.10**

As noted earlier (p. 50), benzidine itself is a 'prohibited substance' under the Carcinogenic Substances Regulations Act 1967 and is no longer manufactured. Colorants derived from benzidine are now neither manufactured nor used. Certain derivatives e.g. 3,3'-dichlorobenzidine, tolidines and dianisidines are designated 'controlled substances' under the Act. Their manufacture, that of derived colorants and their use are permitted provided that well-defined safeguards are rigidly observed.

The nitro dyes are represented in the pigment field by the formaldehyde condensation product of 4-chloro-2-nitroaniline, C.I. Pigment Yellow 11, 10325 (see Chapter 2, p. 13).

The azine class provides Aniline Black or C.I. Pigment Black 1, 50440, obtained by the oxidation of aniline in the presence of a catalyst such as a copper or vanadium salt. This process is also carried out on the fibre (see Oxidation Bases, p. 174).

Certain vat dyes, e.g. Indanthrone, C.I. Vat Blue 4, and chlorinated derivatives, e.g. C.I. Pigment Blue 22, 69810, and C.I. Pigment Blue 21, 69835, have proved suitable for use as pigments, but find wide application as vat dyes (see page 134).

Modern high-grade pigments

In 1935 the first of the phthalocyanine pigments, Monastral Blue, was introduced by ICI following its discovery, independently, by de Diesbach and von der Weid at the University of Fribourg and by Dandridge, Drescher, and Thomas at the Grangemouth factory of Scottish Dyes Ltd., later Imperial Chemical Industries Ltd., Dyestuffs Division. The phthalocyanine pigments possess remarkably high all-round fastness properties, in particular towards light, heat, water, acids, alkalis, and are virtually insoluble in solvents and vehicles. They were found, by Linstead and co-workers to contain a chromophoric system called the tetrabenzoporphyrazino nucleus, a structure related to that of chlorophyll and also haemin, the red colouring matter of blood corpuscles.

C.I. Pigment Blue 15, 74160, Monastral Blue or copper phthalocyanine has the structure:

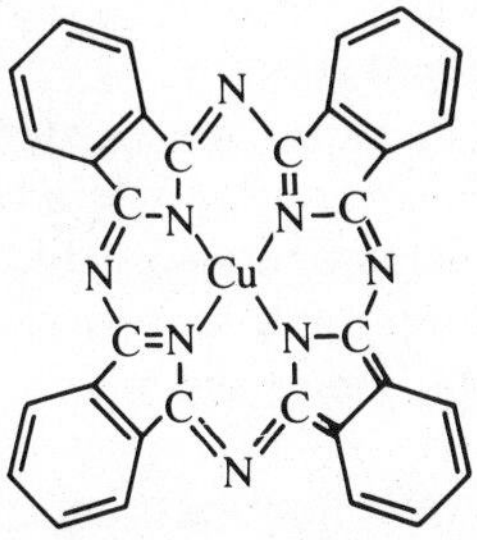

Fig. 15.11

Copper phthalocyanine, the most important and widely used of this class, is produced when, for instance, phthalonitrile, or a related compound such as o-cyanobenzamide or phthalamide, is heated with a cuprous salt. The famous urea process, the subject of a number of ICI patents and the result of pioneer researches by M. Wyler and R. L. M. Allen, consists in heating together urea, phthalic anhydride and cupric chloride. It was later found that various catalysts improve the yield and among these are boric acid, ammonium molybdate and ammonium phosphate. There is good evidence that a precursor, diiminoisoindoline (see Phthalogen Dyes p. 173), is formed. Copper phthalocyanine results from the condensation of four diiminoisoindoline molecules with final formation of a complex with a copper atom. According to Wolf, Degener and Petersen (R. L. M. Allen[17]) the penultimate stage is the formation of:

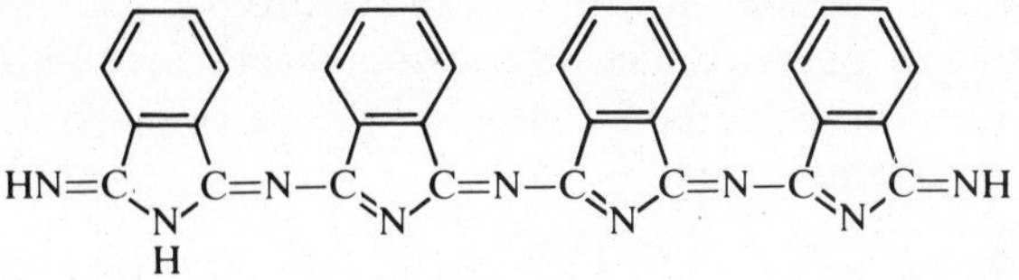

Fig. 15.12

Conditions of reaction and of after-treatment are all-important in obtaining the pigment in the right physical form. The chief phthalocyanine pigments are the α and β modifications of copper phthalocyanine itself, α being an intense blue, β slightly greener; also the greenish-blue metal-free phthalocyanine, the green polychloro copper phthalocyanine (up to 16 Cl atoms), and the most yellow of the green derivatives, polychloro-bromo-copper phthalocyanine.

Metal-free phthalocyanine may be prepared from sodium phthalocyanine by demetallization with a strong acid, or directly from phthalonitrile by heating, in an inert atmosphere, under pressure. It is a bright greenish-blue pigment.

Polychloro-copper phthalocyanine can be obtained by passing chlorine gas through a melt of copper phthalocyanine, aluminium chloride and sodium chloride at 200 °C. All sixteen hydrogen atoms of the four benzene rings present in the molecule can theoretically be substituted, but in practice 12–14 Cl atoms are introduced, a true green pigment resulting.

In view of the outstandingly beautiful blue and green hues of these pigments a great deal of research has been done to obtain derivatives which can be used as dyes (see Reactive Dyes, Chapter 13, Phthalogens, Chapter 11).

The blue and green phthalocyanine pigments, in setting a new standard in fastness properties, brilliance and colour strength, posed a problem to colour chemists in that outstanding yellows, reds and violets with comparable properties were not known. Intensive research by the major dye concerns has, after twenty years' work, produced a full palette of high-grade pigments.

Table 15.3   Modern high-grade pigments

Class	Colour range
Azo coupling	Yellow
Azo condensation	Yellow, orange, red
Derivatives of 4,5,6,7-tetrachloroisoindolin-1-one	Greenish-yellow, orange, red, brown
Anthraquinone	Yellow, orange, violet
Perinone, Perylene	Orange, red, violet
Quinacridone	Maroon, scarlet, red, magenta, violet
Dioxazine	Violet
Phthalocyanines	Blue, green

Azo pigments

It is convenient first to consider those mono and disazo pigments, based on classical lines, in which properties sufficiently outstanding to merit the description 'high-grade' have been achieved by the use of more complex diazo and coupling components. Examples are:

Nickel Azo Yellow (DuP):

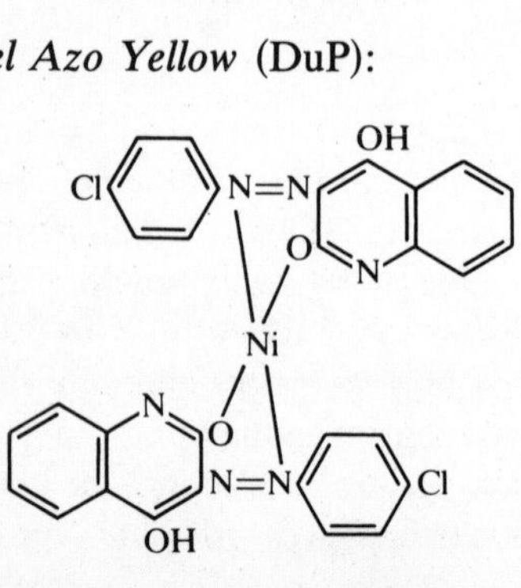

Fig. 15.13

which is the 1:2 nickel-dye complex obtained from the dye *p*-chloroaniline → 2,4-dihydroxyquinoline.

Benzidine Yellow Greenish (*Hoechst*) is obtained from 2,5,2',5'-tetrachlorobenzidine ⇌ *acetoacet-m*-xylidide (2 moles):

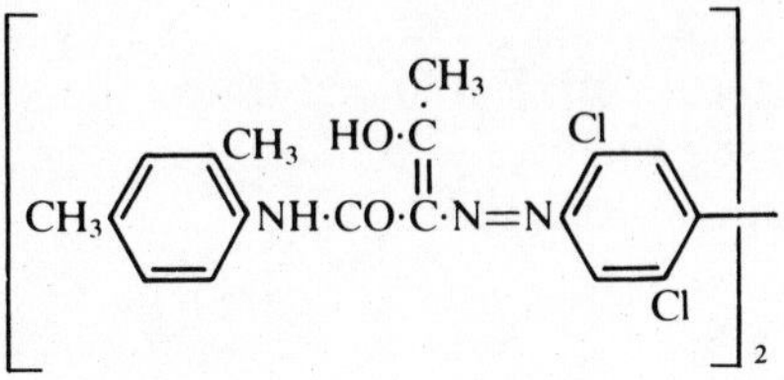

Fig. 15.14

Azomethine pigments

The metal complexes, particularly copper complexes, of certain 2,2'-dihydroxyazomethine dyes possess excellent light and heat fastness and are fast to cross-lacquering and migration. CIBA-GEIGY describe pigments having the structure:

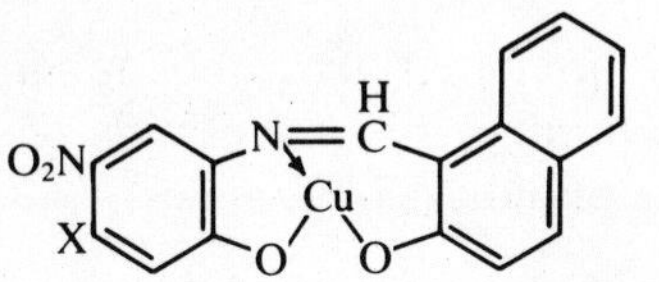

B.P. 1 261 590(X = H);   U.S.P. 3 700 709(X = Cl)

Fig. 15.15

The method of synthesis consists in condensing 2-hydroxy-4-nitroaminobenzene with 2-hydroxy-1-naphthaldehyde in dimethylformamide followed by conversion into the copper complex. In an analogous manner, BASF (B.P. 1 195 766) obtained a pigment from 1,2,4,5-tetraaminobenzene and 2-hydroxy-1-naphthaldehyde. The structure is:

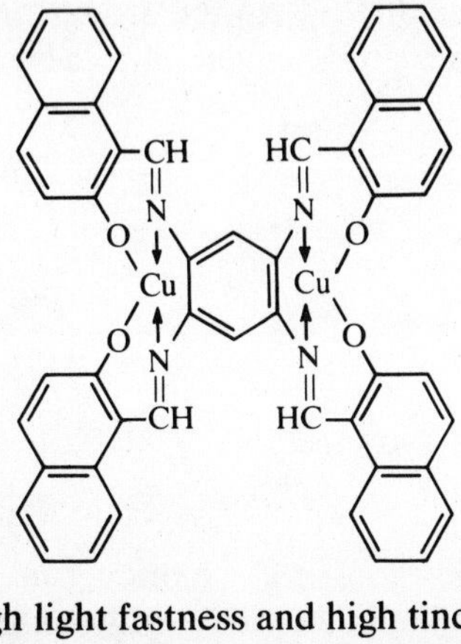

Fig. 15.16

and high light fastness and high tinctorial strength are claimed.

Azo condensation pigments

High molecular weight azo pigments cannot be synthesized by the classical method of diazotization and coupling in aqueous medium by reason of solubility difficulties, lack of reactivity, and so on. The problem has been solved in an ingenious manner by the work of CIBA in introducing the azo condensation pigments.

The following example (Gaertner[27]; Inman[29]) illustrates the difference between the classical coupling method and the more efficient azo condensation method. The desired pigment, Pigment Red 144:

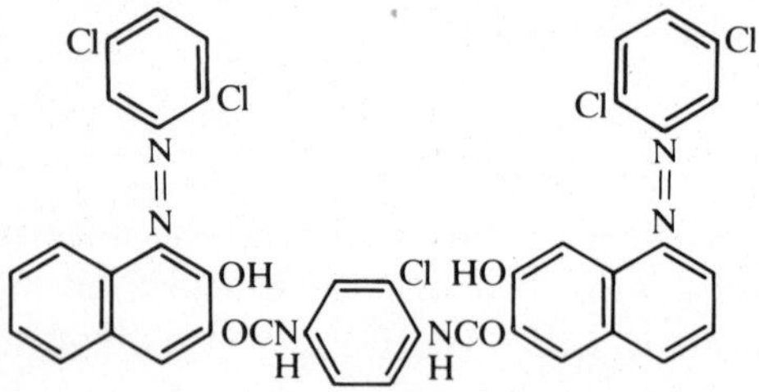

Fig. 15.17

would by the classical route be prepared by coupling diazotized 2,5-dichloroaniline (2 moles) with the product of condensation of 2-chloro-1,4-diaminobenzene and 2,3-hydroxynaphthoic acid (2 moles):

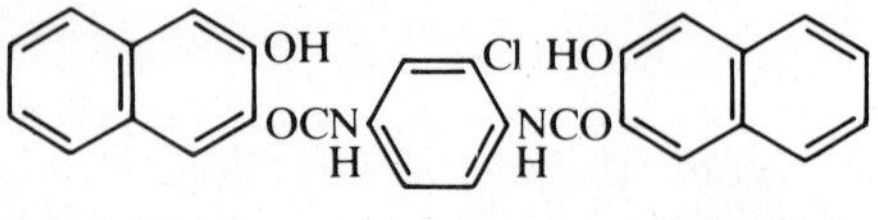

Fig. 15.18

The coupling of the diazonium salt (2 moles) with this product is a very difficult step indeed for not only is (15.18) very sparingly soluble in dilute aqueous alkali, the monoazo product is even less soluble so that the introduction of the second arylazo group is nowhere near quantitative. In the azo condensation method the 2,5-chloroaniline is diazotized and coupled with 2-hydroxy-3-naphthoic acid giving:

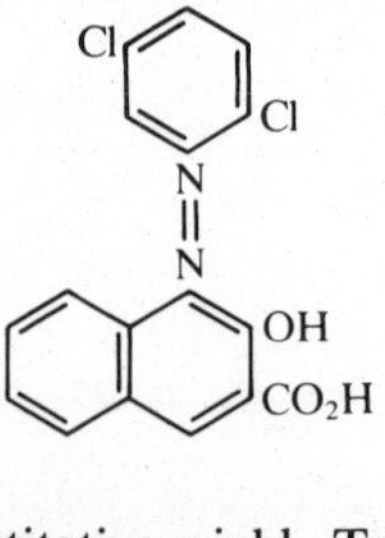

Fig. 15.19

in quantitative yield. Two moles of (15.19) as acid chloride can now be condensed with a mole of 2-chloro-1,4-diaminobenzene to give the disazo pigment (15.17) under vigorous reaction conditions, i.e. in a boiling solvent, in a yield of 95% theory.

In general it can be said that improved fastness is obtained by increasing the molecular size of the pigment. The presence of —CONH groups confer stronger hydrogen bonding (see also under Quinacridones, p. 225). A range of yellows, oranges, browns and reds are available which are of very good all round fastness, e.g. towards light, weathering, migration, bleeding, alkalis. They are used in the mass coloration of plastics such as polyvinyl chloride and also in the manufacture of high grade lacquers for automobile finishes.

Tetrachloro-iso-indolin-1-one pigments

In 1965 the former Geigy concern, now merged as CIBA-GEIGY AG, introduced a class of pigments embodying an entirely new chromophoric system. A typical example is:

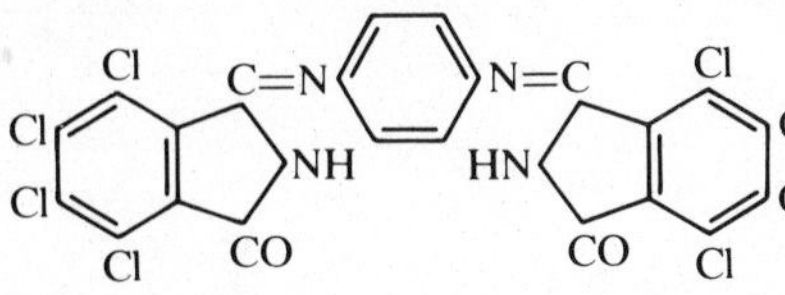

Fig. 15.20

which is a condensation product of the phthalimide derivative (Fig. 15.21) (2 moles) and p-phenylenediamine:

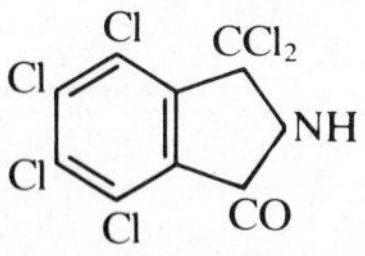

Fig. 15.21

It should be noted that the presence of all eight chlorine atoms in the pigment molecule is essential. their absence results in products unsatisfactory as pigments. By using other diamines, a full range of shades from greenish-yellow, orange, red, to brown, can be obtained, the fastness to light, heat, weathering and solvents being comparable with the phthalocyanines, quinacridones, dioxazines and perylenes.

High-grade anthraquinone pigments

A few of the textile vat dyes have outstanding properties as pigments e.g.
Indanthrone Blue C.I. Vat Blue 4, 69800.
Flavanthrone Yellow C.I. Vat Yellow 1, 70600.

and recent research efforts have been directed towards the synthesis of members of this class which will be specially suitable as pigments.

Examples from recent patent literature include B.P. 998 704 (BASF):

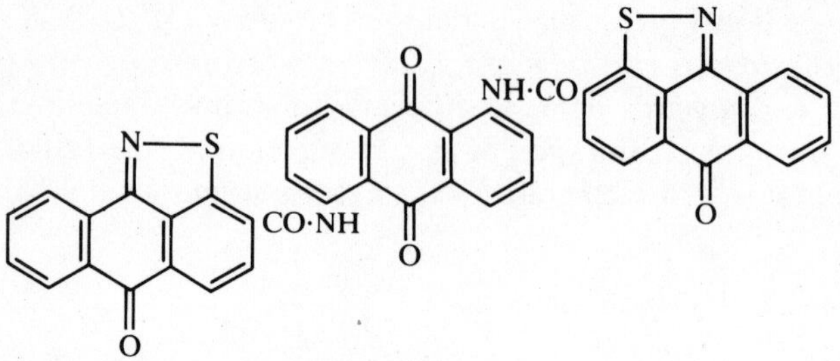

Fig. 15.22

(yellow-range, light fastness as pigment 7–8, but dyed on cotton 5–6), and B.P. 984 110 (CIBA):

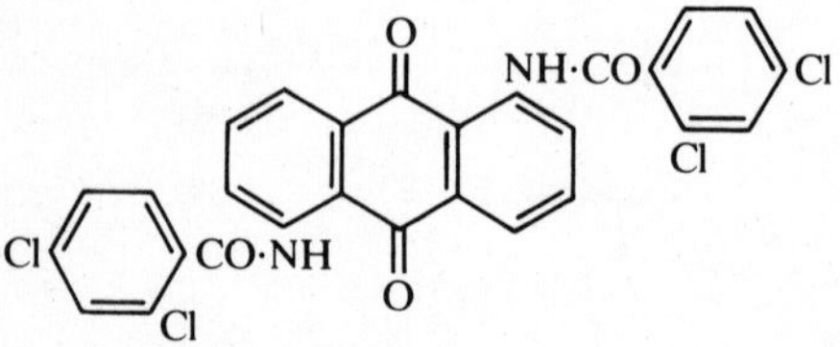

Fig. 15.23

Perinone and perylene pigments

Examples of perinone pigments are C.I. Vat Orange 7, 71105:

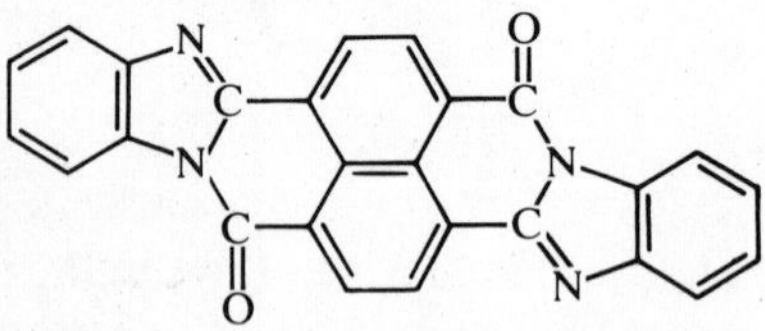

Fig. 15.24

and C.I. Vat Red 15, 71100:

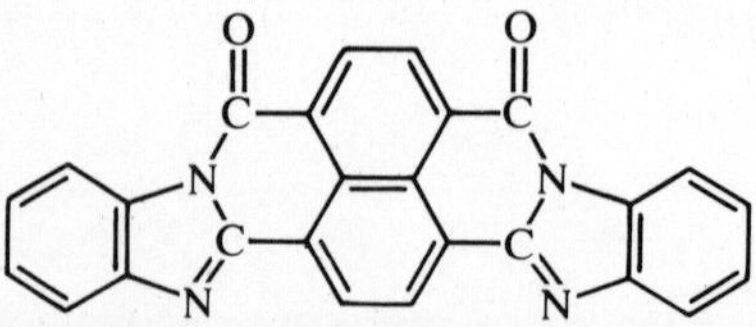

Fig. 15.25

Both are derived from naphthalene-1,4,5,8-tetracarboxylic acid and o-phenylenediamine. The orange is the more important, having superior fastness to light, heat and solvents; the red is inferior by reason of solvent bleed and migration.

The perylene pigments were developed by Hoechst and are di-imides of perylene-3,4,9,10-tetracarboxylic acid. The three best examples are:

Perylene Red,   R = MeO   C.I. Vat Red 29, 71140
Perylene Maroon,   R = Me—   C.I. Vat Red 23, 71130
Perylene Bordeaux, R = H

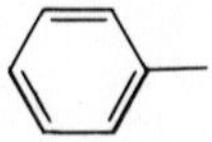

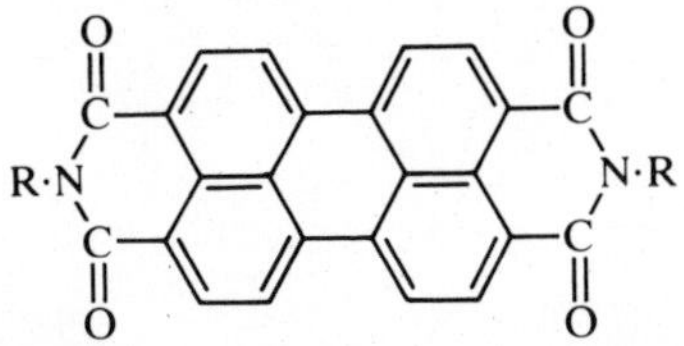

Fig. 15.26

They have light fastness ratings comparable with those of the phthalocyanines. Their excellent migration fastness makes them very suitable for the coloration of plastics. The high resistance to heat of C.I. Pigment Red 123 (R = p-substituted phenyl) makes it suitable for the melt-coloration of nylon (300 °C).

Quinacridone pigments

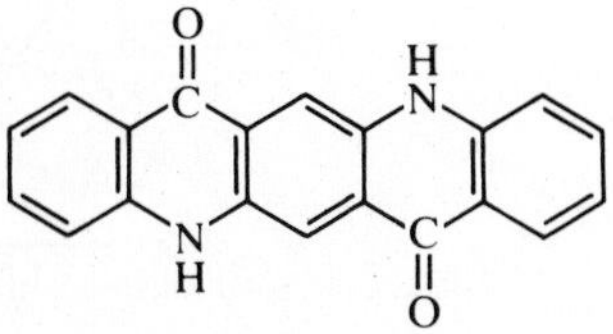

Quinacridone

Fig. 15.27

This class was introduced by du Pont in 1958. The substance quinacridone was first described in 1935 (Liebermann), but its value as a pigment was not realized until the chemists of du Pont had discovered special 'conditioning' processes whereby different crystalline modifications, varying also as to particle size, could be consistently produced. Thus three pigments were obtained:

Quinacridone Red (yellowish) γ modification, particle size $\leqslant 1\,\mu$
Quinacridone Red (bluish) γ modification, particle size $\geqslant 1\,\mu$
Quinacridone Violet β modification.

The high stability, resistance to heat and especially insolubility in solvents are at first sight surprising in such a relatively simple molecule. There is good evidence for supposing that quinacridone molecules are linked together in the crystal lattice by hydrogen bonding between NH and CO groups (Fig. 15.28), for if NH groups are methylated or, for example, replaced by S then the possibility of hydrogen bonding is removed and the resulting products show increased solubility in solvents.

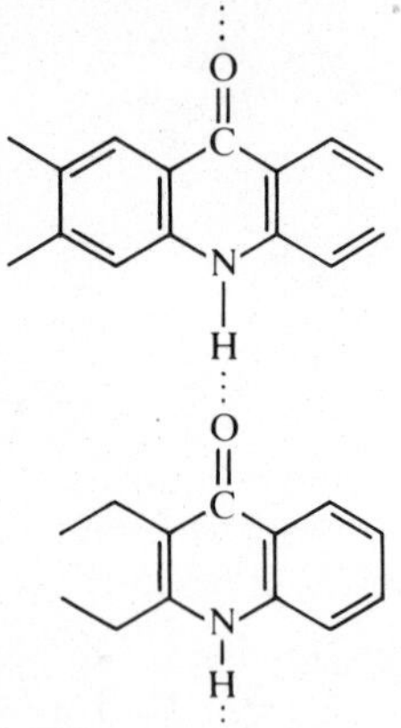

Fig. 15.28

The quinacridones may be synthesized from 2,5-dibromoterephthalic acid according to the following scheme:

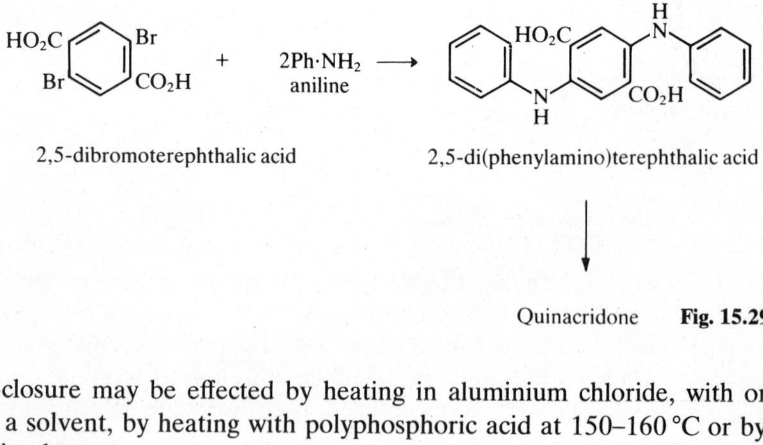

2,5-dibromoterephthalic acid

2,5-di(phenylamino)terephthalic acid

Quinacridone   Fig. 15.29

Ring-closure may be effected by heating in aluminium chloride, with or without a solvent, by heating with polyphosphoric acid at 150–160 °C or by heating in oleum.

Thioindigo pigments

The chemistry of the thioindigoid vat dyes used for textile dyeing and printing has already been discussed (Chapter 9). This chromophoric system has found application in the pigment field, especially where suitable substituents in the aromatic nuclei bring about an increase in resistance to solvent bleed and migration. The best example is the reddish-violet Thioindigo Bordeaux of light fastness comparable, even in light tints, with the phthalocyanine pigments:

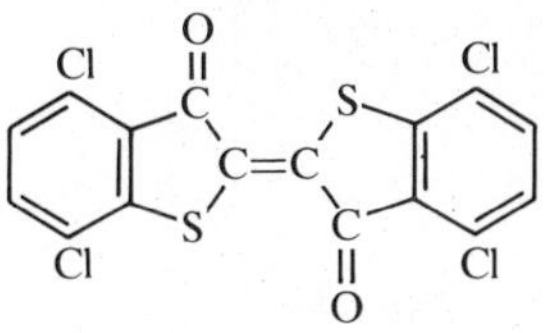

Thioindigo Bordeaux   **Fig. 15.30**

It is interesting to note that alteration in position of any of the four chlorine atoms, the removal of one atom to give a trichloro derivative and the addition of a fifth atom to give a pentachloro derivative, all induce solvent bleeding in the products.

Dioxazine pigments

In 1952 Hoechst introduced Carbazole Dioxazine Violet, an intermediate previously used in the production of a blue substantive cotton dye of high light fastness, having discovered special conditioning processes to transform it into a high-grade pigment:

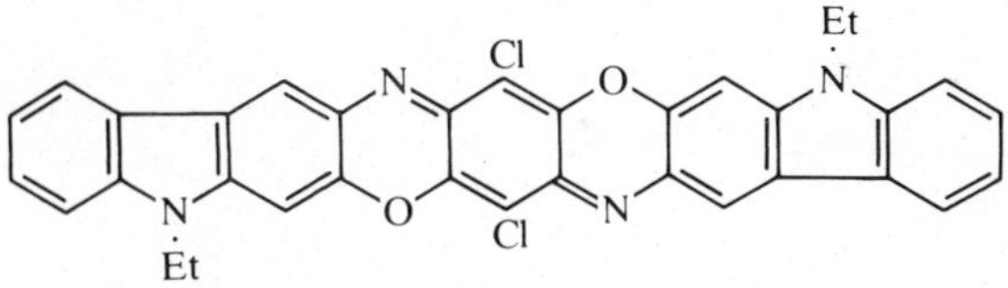

Carbazole Dioxazine Violet   **Fig. 15.31**

It is a beautiful violet pigment, of high tinctorial strength and of good light fastness. Its fastness to solvents and plasticizers is, however, somewhat low for an otherwise high-grade pigment. A recent patent, U.S.P. 3 814 726, by CGY claims that certain halogenated dibenzanthrone- and isodibenzanthrone-sulphonamides have excellent light and migration fastness and are useful for shading copper phthalocyanines. They have greatly improved resistance to flocculation compared with the dioxazines.

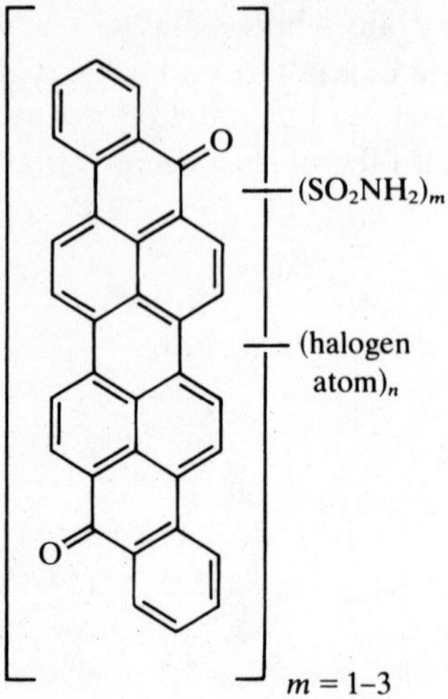

m = 1–3
n = 1–5

halogenodibenzanthronesulphonamide

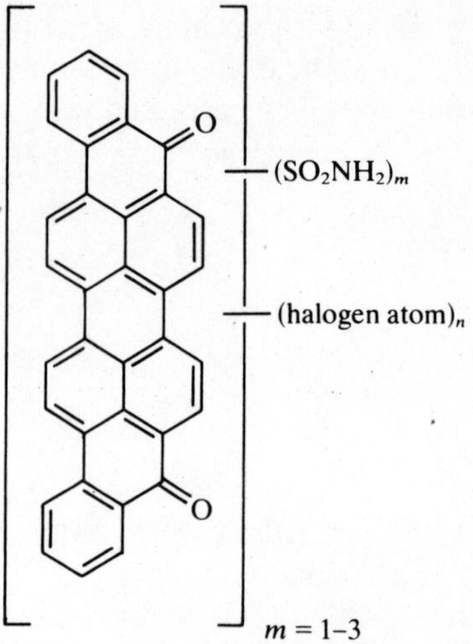

m = 1–3
n = 1–5

halogeno*iso*dibenzanthronesulphonamide

Fig. 15.32

16

The Manufacture of Intermediates, Dyes, and Pigments

General

One of the main problems in the organic chemical industry is how best to transfer processes worked out on the small scale in the apparatus of the laboratory, to the specialized plant items of large-scale manufacture. In the case of new products and untried routes to products, the new processes are tried out in small scale, 'semi-technical' plants specially built for the purpose in constructional materials the same as, or similar to, those to be employed on the large scale. Once the details have been worked out, tentative trials are made in larger plant with the aim of establishing a process to give a satisfactory product at the lowest possible cost.

Materials of construction and types of plant

Something of a revolution has been apparent in the technique of dye manufacture since the Second World War. Prior to this time the most common piece of plant was the wooden vat, in which all manner of aqueous processes could be carried out provided that the extremes of corrosive conditions were avoided. The vat was almost universal for the manufacture of azo dyes, transfer from one vat to another being done through lead, enamelled, or rubber-covered pipes by gravity or by centrifugal pump. The older type of azo manufacturing building was usually five or more storeys high, the first diazo solution being made on the uppermost floor, the coupling component and subsequent coupling stage on the next lower floor, the 'batch' descending from floor to floor until the product was filtered off, washed and dried on the ground floor. Vats were also used in the many 'drowning', 'quenching' or dilution operations that are important in nitrations, sulphonations, aluminium chloride melts, etc.

Over the last thirty years the techniques of rubber-lining and of tile-lining large closed metal vessels, capable of withstanding 1–2 atm air or nitrogen pressure for purposes of transfer of their contents, have so improved that this type of vessel has almost entirely superseded the wooden vat. It is now possible also to fabricate larger glass-lined steel or enamelled cast-iron vessels than formerly and so the trend towards larger capacity, highly versatile plant has become established practice. The use of pressure vessels of course makes pneumatic transfer easy and it is no longer necessary to construct tall, costly buildings for housing dye-making plant.

Again, in contrast to wooden plant, modern rubber- and tile-lined plant is comparatively easily cleaned out between the manufacture say of a blue or violet dye and the manufacture of a bright yellow dye, a procedure which would have been disastrous with wooden equipment since vats were almost impossible to clean out with the requisite degree of thoroughness. In consequence groups of equipment or 'units' tended to be kept solely for the manufacture of one product or at the most a small group of products where no problems of contamination arose. It was not uncommon in these circumstances for parts of a manufacturer's plant to stand idle for many months, incurring the same overhead costs as though it were producing saleable products. Modern design has also reduced wasteful unproductive working of this type in that vessels may be easily and speedily connected to other vessels by pipe-line systems making possible a very large number of combinations of plant. Flexibility and concentration of this kind are essential to the highly competitive dyestuffs industry in

Table 16.1 Chemical conditions and constructional materials

Conditions	Material of construction
Nitrations with mixed acid	Cast-iron, steel, stainless steel
Sulphonations	Cast-iron, steel, enamelled cast-iron, glass-lined steel
Béchamp reductions	Tile-lining on steel or cast-iron
Alkylations (alkaline)	Steel
Alkylations (acid)	Enamelled cast-iron or glass-lined steel
Reactions in reflexing solvents under acid or neutral conditions	Enamelled cast-iron or glass-lined steel. Reflux condenser and pipes in mild steel or glass
Potash or caustic soda fusions	Cast-steel
Chlorination using chlorine gas	Nickel, where iron would act as a carrier and must be excluded, otherwise cast-iron, steel, or stainless steel
Brominations	Enamelled cast-iron, glass-lined steel
$AlCl_3$ fusions	Enamelled cast-iron, glass-lined steel
Reactions in dilute aqueous acid or alkali (dilutions or 'quenchings', diazotization, coupling, etc.)	Rubber-lined or tile-lined on rubber-lined mild-steel vessels

its task of producing several thousand different dyes and related products every year.

The materials of construction available to the dye manufacturer are much more diverse than formerly. These include cast-iron itself or as support for enamel and vitreous coatings, useful for strongly acid conditions and in cases where iron rust would be deleterious, mild steel, cast steel (autoclaves), glass-lined steel, stainless steel, lead, copper, rubber lining, ceramic tiles on rubber lining, borosilicate glass and for special applications, despite the cost, the less common metals like nickel, titanium, zirconium and tantalum.

Lead and copper, formerly widely used in chemical plant manufacture, are now no longer used extensively.

Plastics and polymers are being introduced for the construction of piping, flange packings and seatings for valves; polytetrafluoroethylene is greatly favoured as a packing material on account of its remarkable resistance to chemical attack. It is however expensive and is normally used in thin sheets covering cheaper material such as rubber. Laminated fibre-glass is now being used for ducting, coverings for filters, vessels and so on, but, being bonded with an organic resin, is rapidly attacked by concentrated sulphuric acid. Cloths are now very little used on vacuum filters, porous tiles having largely superseded them. Cloths must of course be used for filter-presses and in addition to cotton and wool the newer fibres, polyester, polyamide and poly (vinyl chloride) are used extensively.

The technique of manufacture

In Fig. 16.1 the plant required for the manufacture of 4-amino-3-nitrotoluene, m-nitro-p-toluidine (see p. 37) and its conversion into C.I. Pigment Yellow 1, 11680 (p. 216) is given diagrammatically in the form of a flow sheet. The process starts from toluene, the first step being that of nitration. In modern plant the entry of mixed acid is controlled by a pneumatically-operated valve actuated by an instrument having a 'sensing-probe' or thermocouple in the reaction mixture. Entry of mixed acid is allowed between certain temperature limits and stops entirely above the upper limit. Flow is also arrested if for any reason the agitator stops. The working up of the nitrotoluenes has already been described on p. 36 and the Béchamp reduction stage on p. 47. Thereafter p-toluidine is converted into the N-acetyl compound, the product nitrated and the acetyl group hydrolysed to give the amine, which is then diazotized prior to coupling with acetoacetanilide. Special care is needed in the manufacture of dyes and pigments to prevent the entry of 'tramp' metal (nuts, bolts and other small metal objects) into the product since, in spite of precautions such as magnetic traps to prevent such entry into the grinding equipment, serious fires and explosions may be caused. In the case of pigments the entry of dirt or any kind of extraneous matter is particularly serious once the pigment has been formed as then there is no longer the opportunity of filtering-off insoluble matter from a solution of the product, as may be the case with dyes.

The manufacture of an intermediate of the naphthalene series, H acid (see Table 3.8, p. 71), is exemplified in Figs. 16.2 and 16.3. Here the starting material is naphthalene which is progressively sulphonated with oleum first at 40 °C, then at 60 °C, and finally at 150–155 °C to give naphthalene-1,3,6-trisulphonic acid. The sulphuric acid solution of this product is now transferred by air pressure to the 'nitrator' where nitration with mixed acid is carried out between 35 and 40 °C. During this and other nitrations a certain amount of nitrous fumes, red oxides of nitrogen, are evolved and manufacturers are bound by law to prevent their entry, and that of other noxious gases and vapours, into the atmosphere. The absorption of nitrous fumes is usually accomplished by means of a packed tower down which weak sodium carbonate is allowed to flow to drain. The nitration mixture containing the 8-nitro compound is now transferred by air, 'blown out' to a tile-lined drowning vessel where excess acid is neutralized by running in a suspension (slurry) of calcium carbonate in water; in large plants there may be provision for recovery of carbon dioxide. The neutral solution of the calcium salt of the 8-nitro sulphonic acid body containing suspended calcium sulphate is now filtered on stirred vacuum filters and the gypsum is washed to extract residual calcium salt, the washings being added to the main batch and the gypsum eventually discarded. The total filtrates now pass to the 'reducer' containing iron borings, hydrochloric acid and acetic acid, the temperature being kept at 90 °C. On completion of the reduction, which point is determined by analytical tests in the laboratory (see Control, p. 237) the agitator in the reducer is stopped. After a short settling period, the supernatant liquor is transferred through a dip pipe to the filter press, which retains iron and other insoluble matter, the filtrates passing to the isolation vessel. The addition of common salt precipitates the mixed calcium and sodium salts of Koch acid ('salting-out') and the product is filtered on vacuum filters; the filtrates are discarded. The product is dissolved in hot water and all the calcium present is precipitated as carbonate by the addition of sodium carbonate ('ashing out'). The solution of sodium salts is now freed from calcium carbonate by passing through a small filter press (screening) and the filtrates are allowed to flow into an evaporation vessel. The product is too soluble to permit isolation by 'salting-out' and the solution is reduced to small bulk by evaporation. Where the plant for the next stage is some distance away, the concentrated solution, which remains fluid in this case if kept hot, may be transported in specially heated mobile tanks. Fig. 16.3 shows the plant lay-out and flow of materials for the final stage, the conversion of Koch acid into H acid (see Table 3.9, p. 71). The requisite quantity of molten charge is drawn from a mobile tank and weighed into the 'melt-pan' or low pressure steel

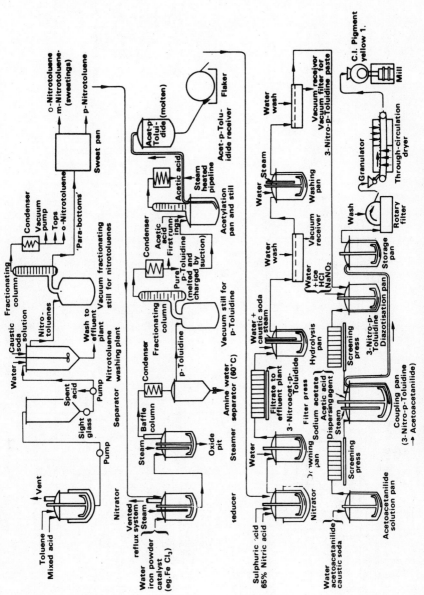

Fig. 16.1 Plant flow sheet: the manufacture of a monoazo pigment.

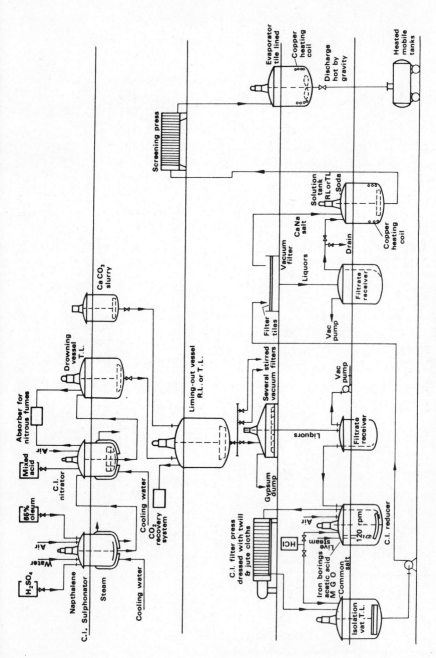

Fig. 16.2   Plant flow sheet: the manufacture of Koch acid from naphthalene.

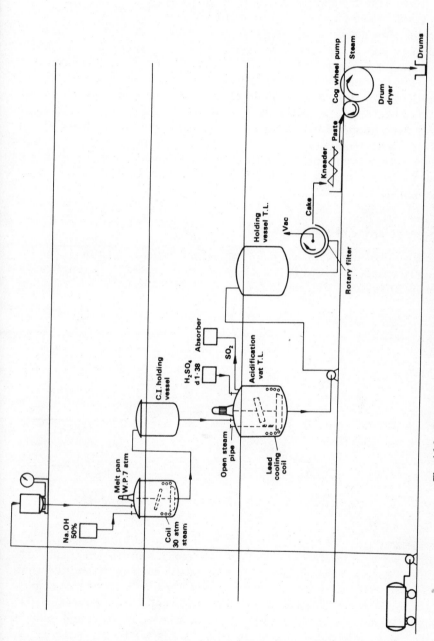

Fig. 16.3 Plant flow sheet: the manufacture of H acid from Koch acid.

autoclave. Caustic soda solution, containing 50% by weight of NaOH is added, the vessel closed and the reaction carried out at 178–182 °C, 5.5–6.5 atm pressure. In exchanging the sulphonic acid group in the *peri* position for a hydroxy group, sodium sulphite is formed. This becomes a source of sulphur dioxide when the reaction mixture is acidified and must be removed from the exit gases by counter-current absorption in weak aqueous alkali. The weakly acid 'slurry' of H acid is now pumped to a holding vessel, thus freeing the acidification vat for the next batch, and fed to a rotary filter from which moist product is continuously scraped off. After passing through a kneading machine to break down lumps, the product is dried by being fed on the surface of heated, rotating drums from which the product is scraped as a dry powder. After being sampled for analytical testing the product is stored in drums until required for dye-making.

The manufacture of a monoazo dye

Fig. 16.4 combines a plant flow sheet and process description for the manufacture of C.I. Acid Red 1, 18050, Kiton Fast Red G previously mentioned in Chapter 1, p. 4, and Chapter 5, p. 97. The process consists essentially

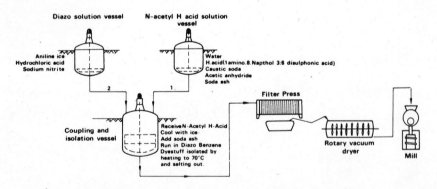

Fig. 16.4 Plant flow sheet: the manufacture of a monoazo dye.

in the acetylation of an alkaline solution of H acid with acetic anhydride at 50 °C, when complete *N*-acetylation and some *O*-acetylation occurs. The solution is made more alkaline by the addition of sodium carbonate, the whole heated to 95 °C, and kept at that temperature for 1 hr to ensure the complete hydrolysis of the *O*-acetyl group; the *N*-acetyl group is virtually unaffected by this treatment. The solution is now run down to the coupling and isolation vessel and ice is added until the temperature is within the range 0–5 °C. Meanwhile the requisite quantity of aniline is diazotized, in a separate vessel, in hydrochloric acid solution containing free ice by running in sodium nitrite solution. Both diazo and coupling components are tested in the laboratory by analytical procedures and adjustments made as necessary to ensure equimolecular proportions. The diazo solution is now run into the mechanically agitated coupling component. When coupling is complete, the dyestuff solution is heated to 70 °C and the dyestuff 'salted-out' by the addition of dry salt to give a final brine concentration of 20% weight/volume. The colour is now filtered in a press and air is blown through to remove as much mother liquid as possible. Successful filtration depends on the dyestuff having been precipitated in the right physical form, in this case the result of heating the dye liquor to 70 °C before salting. The exact conditions for the isolation of each dyestuff have to be determined by trial and error. Even so variations can occur at earlier stages resulting in a poor physical form, the filtration taking many hours or even days longer than it should. In consequence it may not be possible properly to free the dye-paste from mother liquor and if the latter contains dark, coloured impurities the shade of the finished dyestuff may be unacceptably dull or 'off-shade'. Again the retention of undue amounts of saline matter in the dye-paste may be undesirable since after drying the saline matter will still be present and will have the effect of diluting the dye, rendering it unsuitable for instance as a printing colour. In many cases, however, especially in textile applications, the concentrated, dry dyestuff is 'standardized' or 'cut' by being ground in a mill with a suitable diluent or 'cutting agent' such as dextrine, sodium sulphate, common salt, until a specific strength, acceptable to the dyer is attained. For a given dye there may be a number of different strengths or 'brands' required by various sections of the consuming industries.

Vat colours and also disperse dyes may be sold as aqueous pastes of various strengths which may or may not contain additives such as surface active agents. Solubilized vats, disperse dyes, reactive dyes and others may also be marketed as the granular, non-dusting powders resulting from certain spray-drying techniques, a method of drying particularly applicable to heat-sensitive materials.

The control of manufacture

Raw materials

The raw materials entering a dye-making factory are subjected to regular scrutiny as to quality. This principle applies not only to purchased intermediates but also to intermediates produced within the factory for conversion into dyes or other sales products. Well-equipped analytical laboratories are thus a necessity and in addition to the classical chemical methods of analysis involving acidimetry, alkalimetry and the determination of functional groups, physical properties such as specific gravity, refractive index, ultraviolet, visible and infrared absorption spectra and especially the separation techniques of gas–liquid, alumina column, paper and thin-layer chromatography are employed for purposes of identification and comparison.

Plant operation

In the modern plant full advantage must be taken of the substantial advances in instrument technology that have taken place over the past twenty years, if consistent, low-cost operating is to be realized. Reference has already been made to the control by instrument of the flow or rates of flow of mixed acid in nitrations, and of oleum in sulphonations according to the temperature of the reaction mixture or to whether or not the agitator is in motion. Such control may also be linked to other parameters such as pressure, pH value of reaction mixture, and is applied not only to the flow-rates of entering chemicals but also to those of services such as steam (through external jackets or internal coils), cooling water, circulating oil. Again it is often necessary, in certain processes, to subject a reaction mixture, contained in a vessel capable of being heated or cooled as required, to a cycle of temperature changes which, in the absence of control instruments, have to be carried out by hand operation of steam and cooling water valves. Such a cycle can be accurately reproduced by means of a cam-controller, in which a cam is cut from a disc of metal, the profile corresponding to the various temperatures desired. The cam is rotated by clockwork mechanism and in rotating actuates a control arm by moving it up and down (or keeping it steady where a set temperature is required, the cam at this stage being part of a circle). Such arm movements are transmitted, by electronic means, to mechanisms which actuate steam, water and other service valves as required. In this way very consistent operation can be obtained with resultant savings in man-hours and supervisory effort. With a few exceptions, dye and intermediate manufacture has been carried out in batches in contrast to the continuous and semi-continuous processes characteristic of other areas of chemical manufacture, where digital computer control is well established. However, there are strong indications that computer control is being actively developed by the major dye manufacturers and, in fact, a fully-automated, computer-controlled multiproduct azo plant has been in successful operation since 1972 at the Huddersfield works of ICI Organics Division.

Process control

The importance of chemical control during manufacture is obvious. The methods employed are mainly those of the analytical laboratory together with preparative tests in which aliquot samples are taken from the plant and either subjected to special tests, devised by the works chemist in charge of the manufacture, or worked up in laboratory apparatus by processes corresponding to those to be undergone by the main batch. These small-scale preparations and samples of the finished batch itself are submitted to the analyst or colourist for testing against specification or standard sample. Among the direct methods of assessing the quantity of dye present in a solution, the use of titanous chloride is important. Special apparatus, which can be swept out with carbon dioxide to remove atmospheric oxygen which would interfere if present during the determination, is used. The method depends on the ability of certain chromophoric systems, e.g. the triarylmethane system, to undergo reduction and hence decolorization by the action of titanous chloride. Another method, the determination of optical density, relies on absorption spectrometry, the intensity of absorption at a principal absorption peak being measured in comparison with a similar sample of known strength.

There are many qualitative or semi-quantitative tests used by the dye-works chemist in following the course of his manufactures. A time-honoured method is the use of filter paper, on to which small samples of the batch in progress may be spotted and the appearance of the edge of the spot or 'run-out' examined, or its behaviour noted towards reagents spotted alongside in such a way that the edges merge. This method, of great use in azo chemistry, can be used to confirm the presence or absence of diazo or coupling components as the case may be. Such methods have, in recent years, undergone considerable extension and refinement by the introduction of chromatographic techniques. Of these the latest development, that of thin-layer chromatography, is perhaps the most important and useful in dye chemistry. As the name of the method implies the adsorbent or stationary phase is spread as a thin layer on plates of glass or metal, a very small quantity of the material to be examined is placed, usually by means of a micro-pipette, as a spot at the lower edge of the plate. This edge is placed in a solvent or combination of solvents ('eluent') and the plate supported in a vertical plane. The ascending solvent carries the constituents of the spot upwards at varying rates and, if all the conditions are satisfactory, a good separation or resolution is effected. In principle the thin-layer method is no different from that of packed column or paper chromatography. It has a number of advantages however that are worth mentioning here.

(a) The method is simple—the most complicated part of the equipment is the spreading device which deposits a uniform layer of a suspension of the adsorbent in water or other medium: the plate is dried and is then ready for use.
(b) The method is rapid—separations can often be effected in $\frac{1}{2}$ hr or less compared with several hours with packed column and paper techniques.
(c) In general separations are sharper, i.e. the various zones are more widely spaced than with other methods.

The absorbents used include alumina, powdered cellulose, or silica gel, the latter being particularly useful by reason of its inertness. Not all the

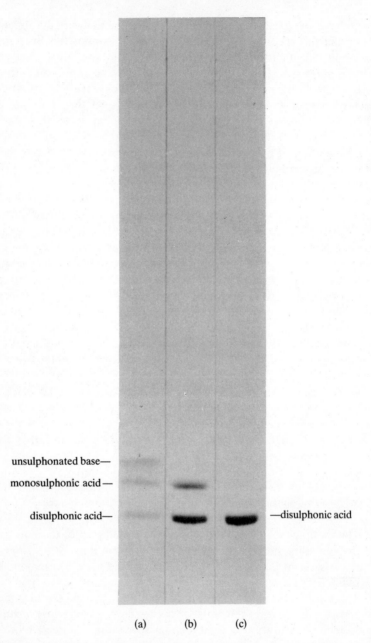

Fig. 16.5 The sulphonation of 1,4-*bis*(*p*-tolylamino)-anthraquinone in 4% oleum at 25 °C. Sample (a) was taken at an early stage, sample (b) at the half-way stage and sample (c) when the correct degree of sulphonation had been reached.

constituents of the material under examination are necessarily coloured and it is often possible to detect the presence of, for example, a leuco compound, by spraying the developed chromatogram with an oxidizing agent, or of a coupling component by spraying with diazotized p-nitroaniline solution. It is important to determine by trial and error the best solvent or combination of solvents for a given intermediate or dye class. Chromatography does not solve all the problems that arise in the manufacture of dyes and it is not uncommon for misleading results to arise from combinations of solvent and absorbent that are unsuitable for a given purpose, i.e. they effect only partial separations and some components remain undetected.

Fig. 16.5 illustrates the use of thin-layer chromatography in industrial practice. The case relates to the large-scale sulphonation of 1,4-bis(p-tolylamino) anthraquinone, C.I. Solvent Green, 3, 61565, by first dissolving the base in sulphuric acid (100%) and then adding at 20–30 °C in a steady stream with good agitation, that quantity of oleum (20% SO_3 by weight) needed for converting the base into the disulphonic acid which, as disodium salt is an acid wool dye giving level green shades. As soon as all the oleum has been added a sample (a) is taken of the 'sulphonation mass' followed by others (b), (c) etc., taken at prescribed intervals. For qualitative testing each sample is treated as follows: four drops are diluted with 5 ml distilled water and neutralized with 10% aqueous sodium carbonate solution. A small quantity is pipetted onto a glass plate (20×5 cm) bearing a thin layer of powdered silica-gel so as to form a narrow stripe, 2 cm long parallel to and about 3 cm from one of the 5 cm sides. The plate is now lowered, stripe downwards into a specially designed glass vessel in which the plate is held vertically, its lower end immersed to a depth of 1 cm in an eluent solvent mixture. A suitable solvent in the above case, has the composition (by volume): n-butyl alcohol (4), t-butyl alcohol (3), water (3). After about 10 minutes separation into zones is clearly discernible.

In the illustration, three zones are present in column (a); the unsulphonated base occupies the highest zone, the monosulphonic acid the middle zone and the disulphonated product the lowest zone. In column (b) there is no upper zone, indicating that unsulphonated base is no longer present. In column (c) the middle band indicating the presence of monosulphonic acid has disappeared. When this last stage is reached the main sulphonation mass is diluted by running it into a large volume of ice-water mixture, the disulphonic acid being precipitated as a dark green solid. If sulphonation is unduly prolonged beyond stage (c) the yield of final dye is reduced and its substantivity on wool rendered inferior. On the other hand incomplete sulphonation, by reason of the presence in the final dye of unsulphonated base and monosulphonic acid, causes undesirable staining of secondary cellulose acetate in the dyeing of wool/CA blends.

Dye testing

Although synthetic dyes and pigments may be regarded as organic chemicals possessing certain properties their ultimate role is to impart colour to some substrate or surface as the case may be. As such their ultimate evaluation and testing is the prerogative of the colourist. The colourist is a skilled dye or pigment technologist whose function is to test the products of the dye-maker under the same or closely similar conditions to those employed by the dyer, printer or other user. In this the colourist is guided by the recognized criteria and fastness tests described more fully in Chapter 2 in the case of dyes and in Chapter 15 as affecting pigments. The colour testing laboratory, usually described by the all-embracing term 'dyehouse', is not only a service to the manufacturing departments and the sales organization but also provides customer service, a strong tradition in the industry dating from the time of Perkin. It is not always understood that very rarely does a dyer or printer use a simple dye for a given purpose but mostly uses combinations of dyes to achieve the desired hue or fashion shade. In this the advice of the colourist is invariably sought by the dyer before work on an important contract or commission is begun. In many cases the colourist is called upon to match a 'pattern' submitted by the dyer who, more often than not, requires a particular shade dictated by current fashion. The pattern may be a dyeing on cotton, whereas the dyer may wish to match the same shade on a different substrate such as wool, acetate silk or nylon. Great skill is therefore required in arriving at a suitable combination of dyes to match the pattern satisfactorily. Not least among the colourist's difficulties is to hit upon a combination of dyes that are not only a match in daylight but also in artificial light (metameric match). In this, computer methods are currently being successfully developed by which mixtures of dyes can be selected having closely similar absorptive properties in the visible region to those of the pattern.

The Alkali Act, effluent treatment

In the United Kingdom most of the major dye and intermediates manufacturers have their factories in the north, i.e. Lancashire and Yorkshire and in the Scottish midlands between the Forth and Clyde. In the north of England, proximity to the major centres of the wool and cotton textile industries, to the Cheshire salt deposits and hence to supplies of chlorine and alkalis, to the heavy chemical and tar-distillation industries, were all factors which led to the establishment in that area of dye-making factories. The Alkali Act of 1863 had its origins in these surroundings. It came into effect in 1864 and required the absorption by manufacturers of 95% of the hydrochloric gas evolved from a stage of the Leblanc process, instead of being allowed to pass freely into the atmosphere. In order that the provisions of the Act might be enforced and to provide for the regular inspection of chemical factories, the Alkali Inspectorate was set up. The scope of the Inspectorate is not of course limited to the case of hydrochloric acid, and it has powers to forbid or restrict the entry into the atmosphere of all noxious and corrosive vapours, e.g. hydrogen sulphide, sulphur dioxide, sulphur trioxide, chlorine, bromine, 'oxides of nitrogen' and so on. Manufacturers nowadays, as a matter of course, install adequate absorption equipment as part of the manufacturing unit to deal with those processes from which noxious gases are evolved. Recovery of useful chemicals may result from such absorption, e.g. sodium sulphide solution from the absorption of hydrogen sulphide in caustic alkali arising from one process may be used elsewhere in the factory for the reduction of nitro compounds. Again where the evolved gas or vapour is reasonably free of contaminating substances the recovery of usable hydrochloric acid, bromine and so on can help to reduce the cost of the product concerned. Important examples are the recovery of bromine by oxidation of the hydrogen bromide evolved from the bromination of indigo and the recovery of hydrogen sulphide, as 35% aqueous sodium hydrosulphide, from the sulphurization of p-toluidine in Primuline base and dehydrothio-p-toluidine manufacture.

Dissolved waste substances in the considerable aqueous effluent produced by a dyestuffs factory are also subject to control. Local authorities, for example the Manchester Corporation Rivers Board, have powers to regulate the nature of such effluent and it is not permitted to discharge to drain liquors containing sulphide, cyanide, mineral acids, undue quantities of alkalis, suspended matter in quantities above a certain limit and so on. In consequence most dyestuffs factories have an effluent treatment plant, mostly for the neutralization of acid liquors with a cheap alkali such as lime or powdered limestone, so that the factory effluent may be safely disposed of by discharge to a river or municipal drain or sewer system.

The Factories Act and other industrial legislation

The hazards associated with the exposure of workers to certain chemical dusts and vapours have been recognized for many years and part of the Factories Act, The Chemical Works Regulations, controls the conditions under which the manufacture of the nitro and amino derivatives of benzene and its homologues is carried out. The skin and respiratory system are the most effective and dangerous routes by which workers can absorb noxious substances and it is an important aim of plant design to prevent or at any rate to minimize contact between chemical and operator. This is accomplished partly by the provision of adequate draughting to take away noxious dusts and vapours and also by devising enclosed plants operated by remote control and by using mechanical handling methods. Where dry powders are handled, or where even very low concentrations of gas or vapour are harmful, efficient breathing apparatus having an independent air supply has been developed and is in use.

Reference has already been made to the carcinogenic hazards associated with 1- and 2-naphthylamines, benzidine and related substances, and with the manufacturing processes for auramine, and magenta. In the UK the implementation by the manufacturers concerned of the Code of Practice of Scott and Williams has been highly effective. There has been no case of tumour in anyone who was first employed after the introduction of this Code which was later the subject of legislation, viz. The Carcinogenic Substances Regulations 1967. More recently 'The Health and Safety at Work, Etc. Act, 1974' which deals with this and many other aspects of health, safety and protection of workers has come into operation.

Bibliography

Reference works, Journals and Annual Reviews

1 S.D.C. and A.A.T.C.C.—*Colour Index*, Third Edition 1971.
2 *The American Dyestuffs Reporter.*
3 *The Dyer*
4 *Journal of the Society of Dyers and Colourists.*
5 *Journal of the Oil and Colour Chemists' Association.*
6 S.D.C. *Reviews of Progress in Coloration and Related Topics*, Volume 1 (1967–1969) and subsequent issues.
7 S.D.C. and T.I.—*Review of Textile Progress* (I–XVI).
8 S.C.I.—*Annual Reports on the Progress of Applied Chemistry.*

Textbooks of dye chemistry

9 H. E. FIERZ-DAVID, and L. BLANGEY, *Fundamental Processes of Dye Chemistry*, Interscience, 1949.
10 K. VENKATARAMAN, *The Chemistry of Synthetic Dyes*, Vols. I and II (1952) and Vol. III (1970) to Vol. VII (1974), Academic Press.
11 H. A. LUBS *et al.*, *The Chemistry of Synthetic Dyes and Pigments*, Reinhold, 1956.
12 N. DONALDSON, *The Chemistry and Technology of Naphthalene Compounds*, Edward Arnold, 1958.
13 *An Outline of the Chemistry and Technology of the Dyestuffs Industry*, Imperial Chemical Industries Limited, 1968.
14 A. SCHAEFFER, *Chemie der Farbstoffe und deren Anwendung*, Theodor Steinkopf, 1963.
15 H. R. SCHWEIZER, *Künstliche organische Farbstoffe und ihre Zwischenprodukte*, Springer-Verlag, 1964.
16 P. RYS and H. ZOLLINGER, *Leitfaden der Farbstoffchemie*, Verlag-Chemie, 1970.
17 R. L. M. ALLEN, *Colour Chemistry*, Nelson, 1971.

Special topics

Colour and constitution

18 E. COATES, Colour and Constitution. *J.S.D.C.* **83**, 91, 1967.
19 F. JONES, The Colour and Constitution of Organic Molecules, Chapter II, *Pigments* (Paterson *et al.*), Elsevier, 1967.
20 S. F. MASON, Colour and the Electronic States or Organic Molecules, Chapter IV, *The Chemistry of Synthetic Dyes*, Vol. III (ed. Venkataraman), Academic Press, 1970.

Disperse dyes

21 T. VICKERSTAFF and E. WATERS, The Dyeing of Cellulose Acetate Rayon with Dispersed Dyes, *J.S.D.C.* **58**, 116–125, 1942.
22 A. H. KNIGHT, Recent Trends in the Search for New Azo Dyes: II Dyes for Acetate Rayon and Nylon. *J.S.D.C.* **66**, 169, 1950.

23   C. MÜLLER, Recent Developments in the Chemistry of Disperse Dyes and their Inter-
     mediates. *American Dyestuff Reporter*, March 1970, 37–44.
24   J. M. STRALEY, Disperse Dyes, Chapter VIII, *The Chemistry of Synthetic Dyes*, Vol. III (ed.
     Venkataraman), Academic Press, 1970.
25   M. C. CLARK and J. D. HILDRETH, Review articles on disperse dyes in *Annual Reports on the
     Progress of Applied Chemistry*, Vol. 55 (1970), 56 (1971), 57 (1972) and 58 (1973), Society of
     Chemical Industry.
26   J. F. DAWSON, (a) Developments in Disperse Dyes, *Review of Progress in Colouration*, Vol. 3,
     S.D.C., 1972. (b) *Dyer*, **153**, 255–256, March 1975.

Pigments

27   H. GAERTNER, Modern Chemistry of Organic Pigments, *J. Oil and Colour Chemists'
     Association*, **46**, 13, 1963.
28   D. PATTERSON, *et al. Pigments: An Introduction to their Physical Chemistry*, Elsevier, 1967.
29   E. R. INMAN, (a) Organic Pigments, Lecture Series 1967, No. 1, R.I.C. (b) Modern Trends in
     Organic Pigments, *Review of Progress in Colouration*, Vol. 2, S.D.C., 1971.
30   W. CARR, *J. Oil and Colour Chemists' Association*, **50**, 1115, 1967.

Reactive dyes

31   C. V. STEAD, *Chemical Basis of the Technology of Reactive Dyes*, Colourage Annual, 1969.
32   W. F. BEECH, *Fibre-Reactive Dyes*, Logos Press, 1970.
33   R. R. DAVIES, Developments in Reactive Dyes, *Review of Progress in Colouration*, Vol. 3
     S.D.C. 1972.
34   P. RYS and H. ZOLLINGER, Reactive Dye-Fibre Systems, Chapter VII, *The Theory of
     Coloration of Textiles*, The Dyers Company Publications Trust, 1975.

Technology of dyeing

35   T. VICKERSTAFF, *The Physical Chemistry of Dyeing*, Oliver and Boyd, 1954.
36   S. R. COCKETT and K. A. HILTON, *The Dyeing of Cellulosic Fibres and Related Processes*
     Leonard Hill, 1961.
37   C. H. GILES, *A Laboratory Course in Dyeing*, Third Edition, S.D.C. Publication.
38   C. L. BIRD, *The Theory and Practice of Wool Dyeing*, Fourth Edition, S.D.C. Publication,
     1972.
39   ——, *Standard Methods for the Determination of the Colour Fastness of Textiles*, Third Edition,
     S.D.C. Publication,
40   ——, *The Theory of Coloration of Textiles*, The Dyers Company Publications Trust, 1975.
41   E. R. TROTMAN, *Dyeing and Chemical Technology of Textile Fibres*, Fifth Edition, Griffin,
     1975.

Miscellaneous

42   D. A. W. ADAMS, et al., *The Chemistry of Natural and Synthetic Colouring Matters*, Academic
     Press, 1962.
43   F. M. HAMER, *The Cyanine Dyes and Related Compounds*, Interscience, 1964.

Reaction mechanisms

44   R. O. C. NORMAN and R. TAYLOR, *Electrophilic Substitution in Benzenoid Compounds*
     Elsevier, 1965.
45   P. A. SYKES, (a) *Guidebook to Mechanism in Organic Chemistry*, Third Edition, Longman,
     1970. (b) *The Search for Organic Reaction Pathways*, Longman, 1972.

Toxic hazards in dye manufacture

46   T. S. SCOTT, *Carcinogenic and Chronic Toxic Hazards of Aromatic Amines*, Elsevier, 1962.

Historical

47   C. PAINE, *et al.*, *Perkin Centenary, London*—100 *years of Synthetic Dyestuffs*, Pergamon, 1958.
48   D. W. F. HARDIE and J. DAVIDSON PRATT, *A History of Modern British Chemical Industry*, Pergamon, 1966.

Commercial Name Index

(Dyes, Pigments, Azoic Components and Fluorescent Brightening Agents)

C.I. Reference Number Index

Name Index

General Index

264 GENERAL INDEX

J